FIFTY YEARS

IN THE

MAGIC CIRCLE;

BEING

AN ACCOUNT OF THE AUTHOR'S PROFESSIONAL LIFE; HIS WONDERFUL
TRICKS AND FEATS; WITH LAUGHABLE INCIDENTS, AND
ADVENTURES AS A MAGICIAN, NECROMANCER,
AND VENTRILOQUIST.

BY

SIGNOR BLITZ.

———

———

Illustrated with Numerous Engravings, and Portrait of the Author on Steel.

British Library Cataloguing-in-Publication Data
A catalogue record for this book is available from
the British Library

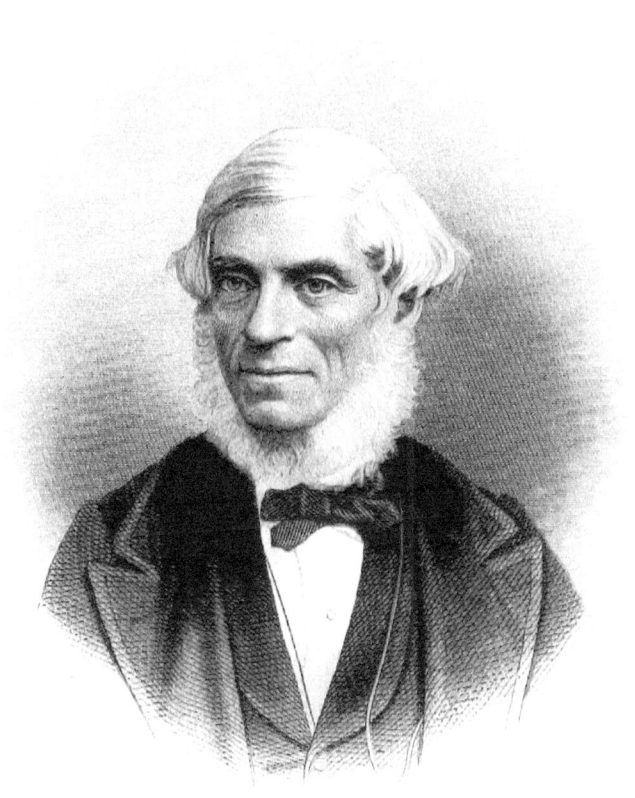

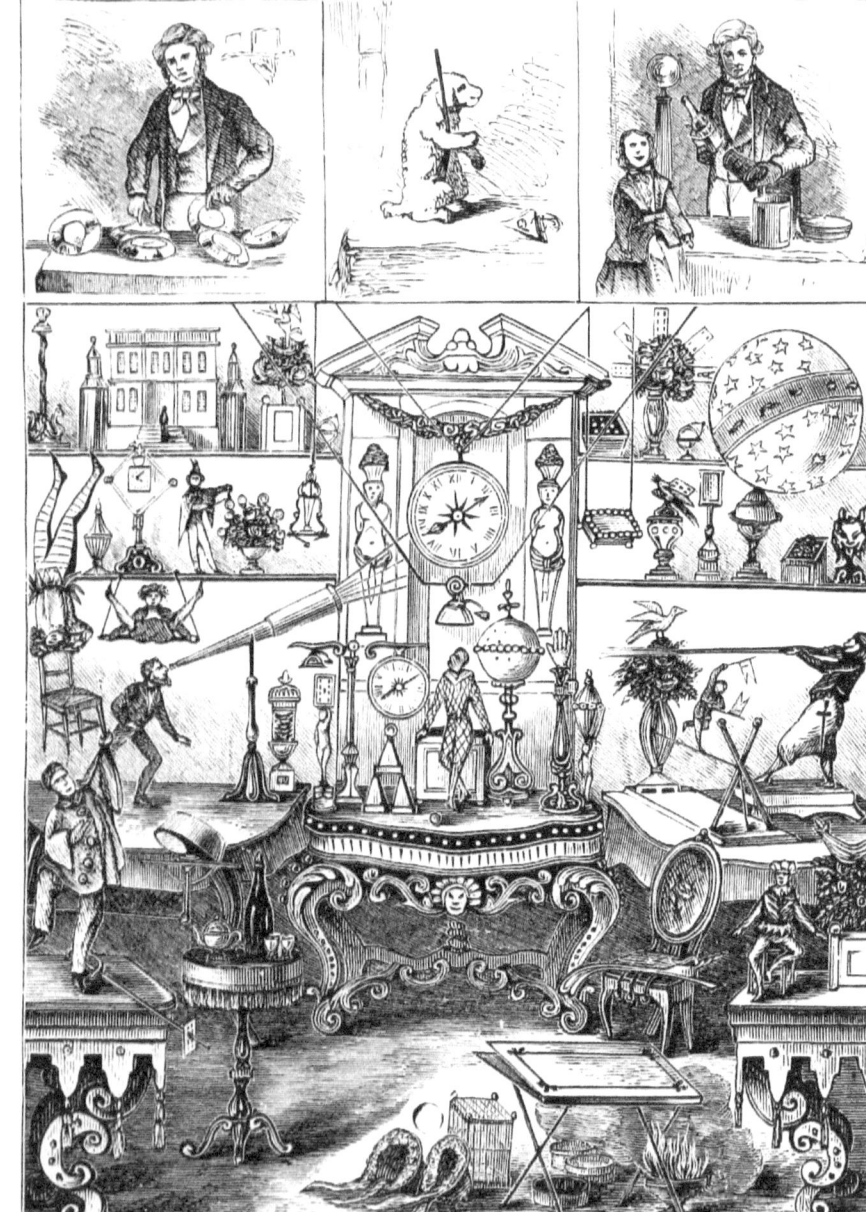

A Brief Introduction to
Magic Tricks

Magic is a performing art that entertains audiences by staging tricks, or creating illusions of a seemingly impossible, or supernatural nature – *utilising natural means*. These feats are called magic tricks, effects, or illusions. Some performers may also be referred to by names reflecting the type of magical effects they present, such as *prestidigitators* (sleight of hand), *conjurors* (purportedly invoking deities or spirits), *hypnotists* (involving individuals mental states), *mentalists* (demonstrating highly evolved mental abilities) or *escape artists* (the art of escaping from restraints or traps). The term 'magic' is etymologically derived from the Greek word *mageia*. Greeks and Persians had been at war for centuries and the Persian priests, called *magosh* in Persian, came to be known as *magoi* in Greek; a term which eventually referred to any foreign, unorthodox or illegitimate ritual practice.

Performances which modern observers would recognize as conjuring have probably been practiced throughout history. But for much of magic's history, magicians have been associated with the devil and the occult. During the nineteenth and twentieth centuries, many performers capitalised on this notion in their advertisements and shows. In the UK, this association dates back to Reginald Scott's *The Discoverie of Witchcraft*, published in 1584, in which he attempted to show that witches did not exist, by exposing how many (apparently miraculous) feats of magic were done. The book is often deemed the first textbook about conjuring, but all obtainable copies were burned on the accession of James I in 1603, and those remaining are now very rare. For many centuries, magic was performed either on the street as a type of entertainment for the common masses or at court, for nobility. During the early 1800s however, large-scale magic performances began making their way onto the theatre stage. Modern entertainment magic owes much to Jean Eugène Robert-Houdin (1805–1871), originally a clockmaker, who opened a magic theatre in Paris in the 1840s. His speciality was the construction of mechanical automata which appeared to move and act as if they were alive; a feat which wowed his audiences for many years.

The escapologist and magician, Harry Houdini took his stage name from Robert-Houdin and developed a range of stage magic tricks, many of them based on what became known after his death as 'escapology'. Houdini was genuinely skilled in techniques such as lock picking and escaping straitjackets, but also made full use of the range of conjuring techniques, including fake equipment and collusion with individuals in the audience. In the modern day, these forms of magic easily transferred from theatrical venues to television specials; a transition which has opened up myriad new opportunities for deceptions. It has also brought stage magic to vast audiences, as most television magicians perform before a live audience, who provide the remote viewer with a reassurance that the illusions are not obtained with post-production visual effects. Some modern illusionists believe that it is unethical to give a performance that claims to be anything other than a clever and skilful deception. Most of these performers therefore eschew the term 'magician' (which they view as making a claim to supernatural power) in favour of 'illusionist' and similar descriptions. On the other side of the coin, many performers say that magical acts, as a form of theatre, need no more of a disclaimer than any play or film; this viewpoint is reflected in the words of magician and mentalist Joseph Dunninger, who stated that 'for those who believe, no explanation is necessary; for those who do not believe, no explanation will suffice.'

Although there is also discussion among magicians about how a given effect should be categorised, they broadly fall into the following categories: 'Production' (where the magician produces something from nothing; a rabbit from a hat for example), 'Vanish' (where something disappears), 'Transformation' (where a silk handkerchief may change colour), 'Restoration' (where the magician will destroy an object, then restore it to its original state, 'Teleportation' (where a borrowed ring may be found inside a ball of wool, or a canary inside a light bulb), 'Levitation' (where the magician, or some person or object defies gravity), and 'Prediction' (where events are predicted under seemingly impossible and unexplainable circumstances).

TO

My American Friends and Patrons,

IN GRATEFUL REMEMBRANCE OF THEIR

FRIENDSHIP AND KINDNESS,

THIS VOLUME

IS

Affectionately Inscribed.

PREFACE.

In presenting my Autobiography, I am fully aware of the grave responsibility I assume, and equally so of the presumption of a person describing, in a measure, his own character;—yet it is essentially better to relate one's adventures himself, than to entrust them to the dictation of others. The reminiscences of my life may not be entitled to any special merit, beyond the amusement they may afford for the moment; yet, to pass away as others have done whose record would have been useful and interesting, we should be derelict in duty to ourselves and the public. Not that my life presents any particular traits above a busy career; yet, if of no special benefit to mankind, it will not be detrimental to the morals and impulses of those who may be pleased to peruse it.

It is an axiom that positions and fortunes are frequently the result of outward circumstances and incidents, and if the experience of every man was written, what a variety of books we should have for society!

My whole object has been to present facts,—to draw from truth, not fiction,—to present events as they occurred, rather than appeared,—to demonstrate the variety and peculiar phases of mankind; not only to smile at the follies and foibles that surround us, but to sympathize with the aggravations and misfortunes of poor humanity,—to create a laugh rather than a tear. Life is like a vast ocean: to many, it is calm and placid, with picturesque harbors; to others, a boisterous voyage, of great perils, and ofttimes shipwreck.. My own pilgrimage has been a felicitous one, for I have always yielded to those convictions on which our individual prosperity is based; yet, favored or afflicted, who can or should but feel happy?

The bright sun shines alike for the good and wicked. The gates of heaven are open to all who seek an entrance therein, or entertain hopes of the future.   .

Time brings forth something new daily; indeed, we have become so dependent upon novelty, that unless our anticipations are satisfied in this direction, we are all discontented and unhappy. This feeling has inculcated itself so tenaciously in our ordinary habits, that I almost doubt the propriety of appearing as an author, fearing the same sensitiveness may operate in regard to what I present to my readers.

We have not all the faculty of being great, or endurable, out of our just sphere; yet something, however little, may be contributed to gratify the most morose or fastidious, to cheer the distressed and desponding, to invoke charity and kindness, and infuse rational gayety around our homes, places of business, and general duties; in short, to induce us to feel and act better; above all, to know ourselves, and fulfil the mission we have to complete; for, indeed, there are a thousand duties to perform, which, however trifling they may appear, are not less momentous when combined, for they reveal their own truth, and create a moral brilliancy in the atmosphere of our daily associations, and repudiate the inconsistencies that mingle in the general formation of our habits.

During my fifty years before the public, it may be presumed that my experience and association with distinguished persons in the Old and New Worlds have been almost unlimited.

Their pleasantries and anecdotes, with brief sketches of their eccentricities, I have given, to the best of my recollection. During this long period I have never made a memorandum, therefore have written entirely from memory; consequently, there may be some slight inaccuracies in regard to dates and circumstances; if so, they will in no way invalidate the facts.

Before concluding these remarks, it will be a pleasure to express my grateful thanks to all my American friends, to assure them of my warm regard for their uniform kindness and indulgence to me in my professional capacity, and an appreciation of their esteem and attention in private life. I can only regret my inability to return a proportionate compensation, one at least adequate to what they are entitled to receive; but, however deficient I may be in this respect, I can congratulate them upon the growth of their beautiful country—the increase of the population from 14,000,000, at the time of my arrival in America, to the present estimate of 40,000,000, which is not only marvellous and unsurpassed in the history of nations, but enables us to anticipate the great destiny that awaits her future.

New States and Territories have been admitted into the

Union in rapid succession; their huge forests have disappeared, and countless towns and cities occupy their space. The whole surface of the land presents an industrious and progressive race. In every department of life a vitality prevails that proves the advantages which republican institutions bestow upon labor and capital,—the independence it provides for thought and action, and the opportunities for all classes to become wealthy, happy, and contented.

To Signor Blitz.

DEAR BLITZ! thou art the prince of fun,
  The very soul of wit and mirth,
And aged sire and youthful son
  Admit thy art and own thy worth.
The mother and the child alike,
  Are moved to merriment by thee;
And thus thou art a blessing sent
  To gladden dull humanity!

How many a pleasant hour has passed,
  Beneath the magic of thy wand!
How many a snow-white egg has grown,
  Before thy wondrous sleight of hand!
Thy pleasant smile—thy rapid speech—
  The tricks that made e'en cynics gay—
Thy never-failing fund of wit—
  Oh! can they ever pass away!

Time has but gently touched thee yet,
  And though thy locks are getting gray,
The eye is full of living light—
  The face is open as the day.
GOD bless thee, Blitz! and when at last,
  The sands of life are nearly done,
May angels watch around thy couch,
  To bear thee to th' ETERNAL ONE!

Truly Your Friend,
ROBERT MORRIS.

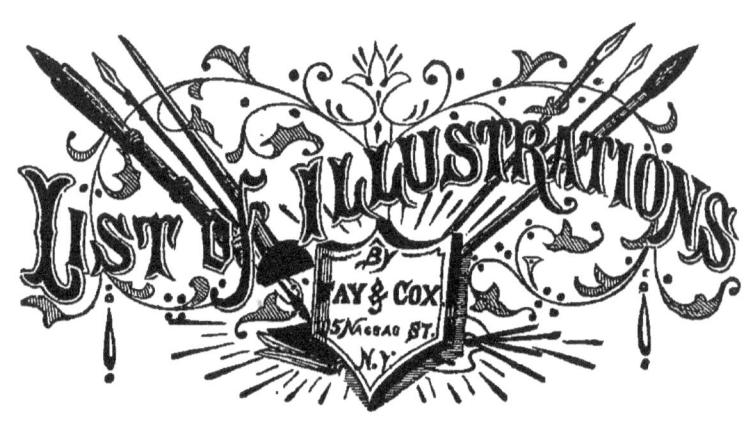

List of Illustrations

BY
FAY & COX
5 NASSAU ST.
N. Y.

ALSO NUMEROUS SMALL ENGRAVINGS.

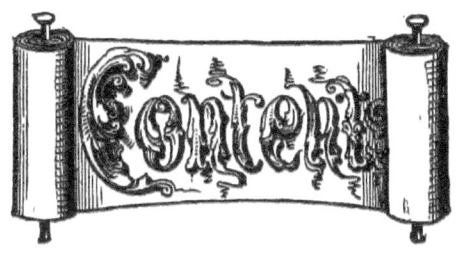

CHAPTER XX.

ON THE MISSISSIPPI RIVER.

CHAPTER XXI.

IN THE BRITISH PROVINCES.

CHAPTER XXII.

NOVA SCOTIA.

CHAPTER XXIII.

LAUGHABLE INCIDENTS.

CHAPTER XXIV.

AMUSING INCIDENTS.

CHAPTER I.

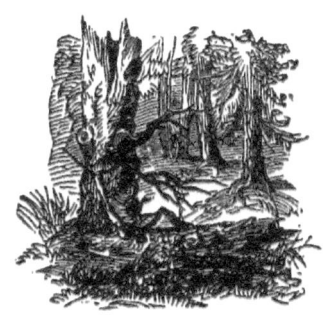 IFE certainly presents to us, as we move along, many strange and changeful scenes. At one time, all is light and golden sunshine around us; at another, the sky wears a sable hue, and the scene is changed to darkness and gloom; naught but sad looks meet our gaze wherever we turn, whilst sighing is the only music that falls upon the ear. And how oddly, too, is the world divided. The opinions and ways of its people are so diametrically opposed to each other, that for us to laugh and amuse ourselves, no matter how innocently, is with some a crime for which there is no forgiveness, while at another time the whole people among whom we are placed are holding *momus* carnival, and he who perchance wears a serious or saddened face, dampens their enjoyment, and by his presence casts a shadow over the hour's festivity.

"Life is filled with variety."

So says the song, and no one doubts its truth. It is a very old, and not at all remarkable observation, that, go the world through, "we shall find no two things alike." But the people who are always so very busy moving about, engaged in all sorts of plain and mysterious doings, and pursuing no particular object which is of any use, are the most remarkable studies we can find for an hour's contemplation. What do they all want? What are they seeking for? If asked the question, they reply: "To live, and live happily." But in the answer, how varied and diversified are the thoughts and ideas they have as to its nature, or how this particular object is best attained! One seeks for wealth, another for power and influence, and another for some sensual pleasure,—aye, for anything that they do not at present possess, supposing that its possession will bring happiness.

"Happiness! How idle the thought! There is none here," sighs the gloomy brother of the Church. "The world is too full of sin; it is a dream, a mere fantasy of the brain, in which mortals would forget how wretched they are."

Such witless sighing and croaking oddly contrast with the full, free bursts of glee which break forth from the merry troops of children we meet on every hand, or the loud and joyous songs of the bright birds, to whose pure notes the streams and winds join their full chorus.

It was a laugh which gave birth to Eden's first echo. and why not still let it live on?

Laugh, laugh, and be happy; *live* above the thought of wrong, and it will not exist in action. Make all around you reflect nature's purest, sweetest smiles, and your prison doors would soon need no bolts, superstition no bigots, or fanatics' railings against this poor, miscalled, misused world of ours. Live, and in living, live not for *self*, party or sect, but for all humanity around you, and we say that he who gives to us one hour's pure pleasure, is a far greater philanthropist than he who prates of charity and heaven, which can only be obtained,—so says his creed,—by passing through lives of sighing, fasting, and continued slavish fear of Him who would have us in all things free, living for the beautiful and good alone.

My Birth.

The 21st of June, 1810, was memorable for introducing into the busy world so humble an individual as myself. What hopes and expectations were awakened in the hearts of my parents, it is out of the question for me to imagine, yet it is no presumption for me to assert that such occasions generally give rise to the most sanguine expectations, and the natural inference is that my progress and lot were seriously and satisfactorily reflected upon, and fully engraven on their respective minds. Indeed, as I advanced in years, I became convinced they had truly entertained large anticipations and ideas respecting me, and, while I admit their cherished object, to a certain extent, was not realized, yet they lived to witness me, in a trifling respect, peculiarly noted.

I was born in a very delightful and pretty town on the sea-side, opposite a fortified coast, whose tall white cliffs were distinctly visible to the naked eye, and frequently, on a clear day, by the aid of a glass, the sentinel could be observed at his post.

My parents were respectable, my father being engaged in mercantile pursuits, and for that locality, well off in the world, living quietly, caring but little for the State or its doings. The town was celebrated for the convivial character of its inhabitants. The "Black Eagle," (the chief inn of the place) was the favorite and popular resort of old and young, for here peace and war were discussed, and the dealers in scandal and gossip found ready worshippers.

On all great occasions, when labor had to give place to song and dance, and wine was in demand, the landlord of

the "Black Eagle" was the most important personage in
the place, for the best wines had "mine host" in his cellar,
and the sweetest tempered little wife in the neighborhood.

It was here I frequently accompanied my father, and
mingled among the gay and happy throng, astonishing all
present with a few adroit tricks I had acquired unknown to
any person, from certain gypsies who occasionally visited
the place for traffic. Indeed, it was a question whether another such a boy as myself could be found in the whole empire. How I learned those apparent wonders, or who was
my teacher, soon became a matter of much discussion, and
there were not a few who, on such occasions, would shake
their heads in a most wise, but incomprehensible manner,
and point in that direction called downward, much to the
dismay of the greedy listeners; while others took most special care to keep at all times a respectful and proper distance
from me, for it surely was well for all Christian men not to
make too early an acquaintance with any of the peculiarly
favored ones of their most to be dreaded enemy.

Under such a state of things, it was not long of course
before all things in the village went wrong; the sheep were
lost, and the cattle would get into places where they were
never known to go before, and the fowls oftentimes were
discovered with eyes wide open at midnight, and during one
night in particular, not long before "St. Agnes' Eve," one
half the gentlemen's hens held a caucus, which continued for
two hours, and when the day dawned it probably never
looked upon so many pale and affrighted faces.

No work, of course, was done, for all the village felt that
there was something wrong which demanded attention, for
what might next occur none could foresee. The priest was
consulted, so was the burgher, but none could tell or account for the mysteries of the morning, save in one way,—
young Blitz must be at the bottom of it all, for he had

already confounded the wits of the wisest, and until he came among them, even the "oldest inhabitant" could tell of no such goings on, since his first memory of the town. What was to be done? As usual in such cases, none could tell, and after a day's deliberation as to the cause of these marvellous signs and appearances, all were just as wise as when they began. After this, the house of my parents became more famous than ever, and though there were some who persevered in having nothing to do with me, yet they might be seen standing a long way off, gazing at my person, and alleging that they saw most mysterious sights of beings passing in and out of the chimneys, through the windows, and of red and blue fires burning around the house at midnight, by which these beings were engaged in performing the most complicated dances to wild and unheard of music. But, by the many who had constant intercourse with the family, and saw no great or marvellous changes in them, these tales were not believed.

Gradually the excitement died away, and the good people, priests, burghers, women, and all, began to regard my performances with pleasure, and the peculiar tricks were accredited, not to the gentleman unnamable, but as they should have been at first, to my boyish genius.

So it is that the most unaccountable phenomena or performances, which we usually attribute to supernatural influences, by repetition or acquaintance with a few of nature's simplest laws, lose at once all their power for producing superstitious persecution, and we turn away from them, waiting most eagerly for other marvellous events or doings, so that again we may be able to show the folly and absurdity of human thoughts, in attributing everything which we in our poor simplicity cannot account for or comprehend, to the most ridiculous or worst of causes.

School Days.

My school days were limited in their duration, for at that period little or no attention was given to education, and but few comprehended or advocated the expanding influences produced from knowledge. If an individual could read and write, his superiority was admitted, however deficient in all other branches. My teacher was an old veteran soldier, who had the misfortune to lose a leg in one of those severe battles occasioned by the ambition of Napoleon. Of his intellectual qualifications I will say but little; his disposition was usually mild, and manners affable, but when excited by any turbulency on the part of his pupils, he would impetuously rush among them, flourishing a huge cane for the purpose of chastising them, which he rarely accomplished, as the boys invariably eluded his iron grasp and warlike blows, by secreting themselves behind and under the desks. At this moment I can photograph him in my mind's eye as he in his anger is distributing his blows upon the air, apparently fighting his former battles over again, with a more mischievous but less savage foe.

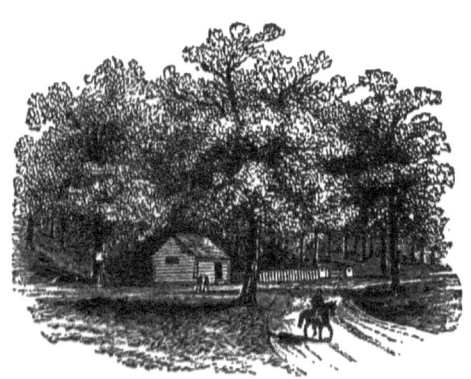

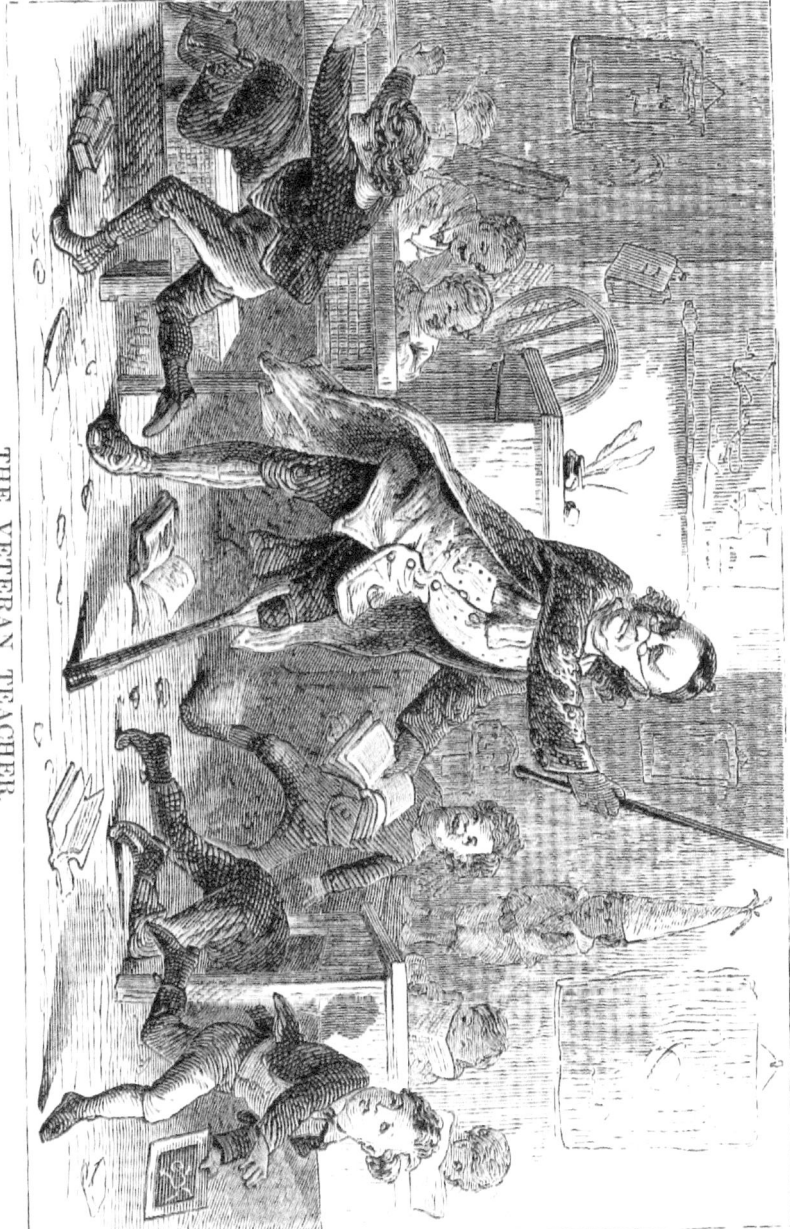

THE VETERAN TEACHER.

CHAPTER II.

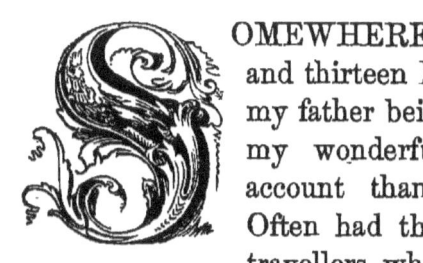OMEWHERE ˜between the age of twelve and thirteen I was removed from school, my father being strongly induced to turn my wonderful doings to some better account than they had hitherto been. Often had the suggestion been made by travellers who had visited the town, that if they possessed such a child, the first thing which they would do, would be to send him to the great cities, where his genius would be productive of something more substantial than the mere entertainment and praise of his townsmen, or a piece of gold occasionally from some generous stranger.

It was not long before these suggestions were acted upon, and after a great deal of time and discussion in preparation, I left my native village, in the month of September, 1823, in charge of a special attendant, provided for me by my father, who had given us full and explicit directions as to our mode of procedure. Through all my life I had never been beyond the shadow of my home. It was a sad time for me, and for my mother, for I was her dearest child; yet it was a hopeful one—and when I kissed the tears away from her pale cheek, I bade her be of cheerful heart. "Don't grieve, mother, for me; for will not our Father in heaven hear you when you ask of Him to remember and

2

protect your Antonio? Yes, yes, indeed he will; and I shall come home again in a little time, a great, rich man, mother. Don't fear for me. Good, good-by, mother; " and turning away from my home, with a pure heart full of golden hopes, often looking back to the green fields and hills, where my light feet but yesterday bounded so joyously to the wild free notes of my own mountain music, and in a half sighing, half laughing voice, still crying to the distant form, now almost unseen, "Home, home! I shall soon come back a great rich man, mother."

First Performance.

After a long journey we arrived at Hamburg, where I made my first appearance, and began my public career on the stage, at thirteen years of age. It was not long before all Hamburg had something to say of me,—and the first question with all was, not as to the state of trade, or the health of the people, but—"Have you seen that mysterious boy?" All were anxious to know from whence I came, who I was, and how I accomplished my wonderful performances.

From the common and middle classes of the Hamburgers, my fame soon reached the higher and more aristocratic class, and I soon became an object of attraction to the greatest. Parties and entertainments were given on my account, and my company was courted by all ranks with marked attention.

From Hamburg I went to Lubeck, from thence to Copenhagen, back to Potsdam, and so to all the principal cities of northern Europe, creating in each as much excitement and attention as in the first.

There are not a few, however, who always in such cases seem to feel that it is their bounden duty to place themselves in the way of the fortunate success of any one, no matter who he is, and do all they can to impede his progress. Unfortunately I found many of this class always in my way wherever I went.

THE CONCEITED DOCTOR.

At Lubeck I met with one, an old doctor, who annoyed me considerably, and was not at all disposed to yield his praises quite so liberally as the rest of his townsmen. He doubted everything, disputed every feat of mine, and often tendered his services to do the same things himself; and he even went so far out of his way as to charge me at one of my performances with being an impostor, in league with the devil. I replied—not at all provoked at such an interruption, for I was always ready then, as now, for a bit of fun— " Well, if I am an impostor, as you say, I do all my mischief where it can be seen and avoided. I keep nothing hidden, as you do, my dear Dr. Von Kelperstein."

" Hidden, sir? I hide nothing. *I* hide mischief? What do you mean, you—you child of the arch enemy?"

" Oh, nothing, Mynheer Doctor, only that you pretend to be such an honest and good man, when even at this moment, old as you are, you have half a dozen *love letters* in your pockets, which you mean to send to as many young ladies before to-morrow night!"

Now the immaculate doctor thought this rather too grave a charge, and so did the audience, for though he was an odd sort of a body, and few of his patients ever got out of his hands alive, yet he was always accounted a prudent man—a perfect Joseph in this respect; besides, he was a bachelor, and old enough to be grandfather to many of them.

Dr. Von Kelperstein write love letters! To *whom?* No! no!—that won't do—and hereupon I was demanded, both by the audience and the doctor, to make good my grave charge.

"Very well," I replied; "pray let any two gentlemen, with the doctor's permission, search his pockets, and if they do not find the letters, and perhaps still stronger evidence, then I am willing to abide your decision."

"Oh, certainly, certainly, let them—let all Lubeck put its hands in my pockets; pho! pho! I know that no such things can be found there. *Me* write love letters! Ha! ha! What an idea! Oh, you young villain!"

In accordance with my suggestion, the doctor's pockets were examined, when, to his amazement, and to the no small astonishment and delight of the audience, the half dozen letters were found upon his person, together with a night-cap of such a shape and material as ladies only wear. The letters were unsealed, but very nicely folded up; their beginnings were indited in the most rapturous strains that a poor soul could ever dream of. The doctor was confounded.

"There, doctor, did I not say true? Suppose we read them *all* through. Fie, fie, man! *you* talk of trickery, and do *such* things."

The poor man was too much out of his wits to answer, and left the hall in a state of mind never to him or *all Lubeck* to be forgotten, and Dr. Von Kelperstein's *love letters* were often the subject of many a merry laugh, while he took good care never to place himself in any situation which might tend to recall them to his memory.

RETURN HOME.

After travelling two years I returned to my home. My first campaign had been quite a successful one, and the money which was realized therefrom was sufficient for the comfortable maintenance of my parents and myself for some time to come. But I was to have a very far different meeting from the one which I had so hopefully talked of at parting, and so pleasantly anticipated as each month went by.

My beloved mother had scarce folded me in her arms, before she was taken down with a fatal disease, which terminated her existence in a few hours. My father became frantic at his loss, and for a time knew nothing of what was passing around him. Such was my first welcome home.

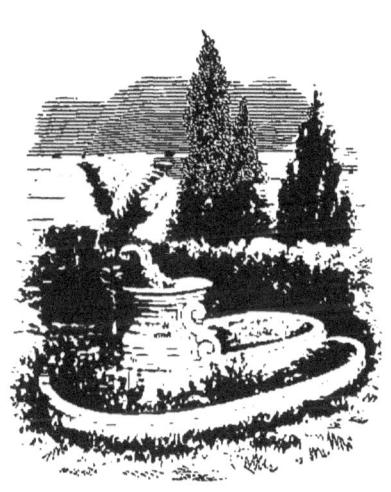

CHAPTER III.

BOUT six months after the loss of my mother, I again began to think of making another and more distant tour. My home had but little to charm or delight, for there was now no gentle voice of a mother to cheer and caress me; no mother's ear to listen to my tales of the many wonders which I had seen, or look with eyes of fond delight when I spread before her the many gifts which I had received, as tokens from friends wishing still to be remembered. My father could not at first bear the thought of such a thing as parting, but after many struggles, and my oft-repeated importunities, he at last consented, on the condition that I should return at the end of a year.

"Most assuredly, father, it shall be as you desire, but let me for awhile seek to forget in other places far away, if I can, my poor mother. Gabriel will again go with me; and now give me your blessing. With our Holy Father's care, you need not fear for your Antonio's absence, or for his return; but think of them both as past, and he beside you, never to leave you again, father; no, never."

A few days after this, my father blessed and parted with me, his boy, and I saw my home, father, and the green shadowed spot where my mother lay, for the last time, and then turned my thoughts and footsteps toward England, where I landed near the holiday times of Christmas, 1825.

My arrival in England was marked by no particular circumstance of note, for I came unheralded and unknown— a stranger to every face I met; but I was resolute, young as I was, and with a stout heart I commenced operations in earnest, assisted by my attendant, Gabriel.

First Appearance in England.

My first appearance before an English public took place, at Dover, in December. The room was very well filled by quite a respectable audience, who, whatever might have been their expectations as to what they were to see for their two shillings during the performance, at its close became so wonder struck, that many had very serious thoughts as to whose company they had been in; and there were not a small portion of this, my first English audience, who felt quite serious misgivings as to my being of mortal make.

Of course their astonishment soon found utterance, and not many days passed before the "young stranger" enjoyed a very wide reputation; and tales were told of my doings, and affirmed to by the churchwardens and beadles, which left but little need, on my part, of other assistance to notify the public, and my new friends in particular, of what they would see in honoring my performance by their attendance.

As I passed along the streets, I would be followed by crowds, all very anxious to get a look at me, and enjoy some of my peculiar favors, for I was, among the lower classes, believed to be capable of doing anything, and to enjoy my favor was not an item to be treated lightly.

Clerical Opposition.

I soon found myself in business, for, besides my stated performances, there were many who sought me out to gain favors for their own personal benefit, and I was requested to do all sorts of things. One poor old fellow offered me a few shillings to restore his sick child to health; another wished for a coat; another, a young lady, wished to know as to the truthfulness of an absent lover; while still others, on whom Sir Cupid as yet seemed to have had no special favors to bestow, anxious to solve all doubts, sought the all-talked-of magician to know whether love had anything in store for them.

Every event or circumstance which had occurred, was brought for solution, and there were not a few who possessed credulity enough to believe that I had the power to grant each and every favor, and to set all mysterious doings and doubtful matters right. From the smaller provincial towns, we made our way into the cities, and, after being in England some four or five months, I arrived at, and made my first bow in, the city of Exeter (where my reputation had preceded me), in the early part of 1826. When the good bishop heard that I had really come under his very nose, he was not at all pleased with the idea, and bethought himself how I was to be avoided. He knew of no better way than to preach, and prejudice the people against me. So, on my arrival, there was a general notice given for all good Christian men and women to avoid seeing, or in any way having anything to do with a mischievous lad, who, by his performances, was leading the heads and hearts of all the people astray.

Such an announcement, whatever might have been the idea of the reverend archbishop, did but little to allay the excitement, and the curiosity of all became from such a proceeding doubly aroused. I, on the other hand, felt, as the bishop seemed to regard me as a person of so much importance, that it was my duty, if possible, to maintain my position. Accordingly, I in return gave information that I would cause a watch to be transported from my exhibition room to the "Lady's Pulpit" in the cathedral on such an evening.

The evening came, and, notwithstanding the notice of the bishop, as many came to witness this astonishing feat as the place could hold.

At my request, persons were appointed on the part of the audience to watch me narrowly, while others were to visit the cathedral at the appointed signal, and procure the watch. Of course all my operations were most closely examined. The feat was to be performed by a pistol being loaded by any one of the persons appointed; the watch to be hung in a position where it could be seen by all; and when I fired at it, it should disappear, and then the others were to start immediately for the cathedral, where the watch should be found, as I promised, under a cushion lying upon the "Lady's Pulpit."

In fulfilment of this assertion, after the pistol was discharged, the committee started for the cathedral, and found the watch just as I had said it should be, in the very place named, under the cushion lying upon the pulpit of "Our Lady." It would be impossible to describe the excitement which this feat occasioned. All Exeter was in an uproar, and the bishop, together with all connected with him, became as much at a loss as to who this very singular being was, as the rest; but they were determined that his performances should not go on. They contended that it would not do for Christians to see such things, and every interest of the Church demanded that they should be put an end to at once, by an appeal to the ecclesiastical court. Before this body I was summoned to appear and give answer as to who I was, and by what agency or instrumentalities I was enabled to do such strange and mysterious performances.

Before the Council.

The scene presented at the sitting of the ecclesiastical council, before which I, Antonio Blitz, was summoned to appear, was rather a novel one. A bench of learned men, holding grave deliberations, listening to, and troubling their wise brains with, the fanciful tricks of a boy, and at one time half deciding upon a verdict that I should not be permitted to go at large, being a dangerous foe to the souls of all the good people of their several parishes. Wisdom must have taken a peculiar fancy for a residence, if she had any place beneath the wigs of such mortals.

In compliance with the summons, I made my appearance before the council, to answer to the call of the bishop, and hear the various charges preferred against me.

As far as I understood them, they certainly were of rather a funny character, and I could not possibly believe that the men who sat before me could really be in a serious mood.

But my doubts were soon put to an end, for the members were most gravely called to order, and the clerk proceeded to read a very lengthy written document, in which Antonio Blitz was charged as being an *idle, mischievous person*, deceiving honest people by base acts, and tempting them to look for riches, by giving themselves over to his master, —the arch-enemy of mankind. So read the clerk, and "Amen!" responded this whole bench of Solomons, while the beadle closed in by bringing down his staff with a most emphatic thump upon the floor.

To these charges I, Antonio Blitz, was called upon to reply. Whereupon I said, "that as the learned bishop and his friends seemed much to doubt my ability to do what I had done, without some other assistance than that of mortal kind, I begged leave to perform some few things before them, for surely the devil, whom they alleged as being my assistant, would not dare to make his appearance before such a *holy* body of men."

This proposal, among the more reasonable and curious, seemed very proper, and would, in *their* opinion, be a fair test of my *original* power to perform my peculiar tricks, and after some little hesitation it was acceded to.

An Experiment.

I went through several of my performances, and while doing them, the wigs were motionless upon the heads of the grave men, not a whisper disturbed me, and even the beadle's staff laid, as if struck with amazement, against his shoulder.

At last I called for a pistol, and commenced very deliberately the processs of loading. "What is he going to do now?" whispered the wise men one to another, and their attention became fixed, and their minds more excited than ever. After I had finished the loading, I observed that the feat which I was now about to perform had never been done by me before, but I doubted not of its success.

"What is it to be?" asked one of the black-robed judges.

"Simply this: I shall take a position somewhere about here," said I, placing myself immediately in front of the reverend bishop, and pointing the pistol directly toward him, "and when I fire, the bishop will disappear from the room, and you will find him sitting in his library, where I wish you all to go immediately after you hear the report, and see if I make not my assertion good."

"What! is he going to fire at his reverence? Horrible!" exclaimed the whole bench at a breath.

"Most certainly," I coolly replied. "It is only an *experiment.*"

"No, no, no, no! We are satisfied."

"Well, I cannot help it. I insist upon going through with the performance," and hereupon proceeded to take aim very deliberately, but the bishop, judges, clerk, court, beadle, and all, fled in utter confusion from the room, and though I was not permitted to carry out my experiment to its full extent by the discharge of the pistol, yet not one of the Reverend Bench were to be found again anywhere near me; and what became of them, or their charge of sorcery, I never knew, for I was not again molested, but very quietly took my leave the next day.

A Superstitious Magistrate.

From Exeter I proceeded through the southern and western counties of the kingdom, stopping at all the towns, but in many of them I was not permitted to perform, by an order generally originating with the curates of the parish. In Cornwall, there was no limit whatever given to the tales which were told concerning me, and here I was again arrested and brought before the magistrate of the borough, Colonel Tremain and openly charged with being engaged in the "Black Art." Now this colonel somewhat resembled, and reminded me of Shakespeare's early friend, Sir Thomas Lucy, and between him and myself there arose quite a discussion as to who was the conjuror.

"What mean you, sir, by bewitching the parish by your *black art* and conjuring?" asked the colonel in a *fierce* magisterial sort of a style.

"I am no *conjuror*, your worship," replied I, "nor do I have anything to do with the black art."

"Silence, sir, fellow, *I* know that you are a conjuror; for since you have been in this parish, there has not been a single complaint made by a wife against her husband, or a family disturbance of any kind. Sirrah! this was not so once—for I had always as much as I could do in these matters, and there has not a day passed that I did not send either husband or the wife to the tread-mill; sirrah, *I* say that *you are* a conjuror. *I*, say so, youngster, *I*, Richard Tremaîne, justîce, and chaîrman of the poor—house comm-îssîoner and colonel of Hîs Majesty's mîlîtîa în the county of Cornwall,—*I*, sir—and *you*, had better think, too, who I am."

"I do, your worship, and I say, with all due deference to your worshipful greatness, that unless you were a greater—"
"What! ha! a greater what?"
"*Conjuror* than myself, you could not so readily detect me." This reply put the colonel into a tremendous passion, and there is no knowing what he might have done, had not a son of his, returned just at the moment, who had heard of, and seen me go through with my performances.

He very soon set the matter right, and that same evening I was a guest of the colonel's, who, with the curate, soon believed me to be one of the most remarkable men alive, if I was not indeed a conjuror.

The poor Cornish miners looked upon me as a being not all of human make, and often did they solicit me for some personal favor.

Their condition was indeed miserable in the extreme, living two thirds of their short lives beneath the earth, scarce seeing the light of day. They were poor, poor indeed; and when I saw how degraded and abject they were, I often wished that the power attributed to me was mine; but my pity, and a few shillings, was all my art could give in answer to their importunities.

FIRST VISIT TO LONDON.

From the provincial towns, I turned and made my way to London. I had now been performing in England above

two years, yet I had never visited this, the great metropolis
of the world.

I arrived in London during the Lent season of 1828,
and commenced an engagement at the Coburg Theatre,
where my performances met with astonishing success, filling
the house nightly with surprised and delighted audiences.
•But even here there were many to be found with the same
feelings of credulity, as ignorant respecting my character,
and profession, and performances, as were those in the most
remote and benighted districts.

A Nervous Landlady.

Even in this metropolis (London) there were many who
regarded me with feelings akin to awe, and spoke of me as
one to be avoided.

My hostess partook of this feeling to such an extent, that
she deemed my presence unsafe to her bodily and spiritual
peace, and one morning politely told me that she preferred
that I would find lodgings elsewhere.

"Why, my good lady, what have *I* done?"

"Nothing, sir; you seem to be a very quiet little gentleman, but how do you live?"

"How do *I* live? Why, honestly I hope."

"What, with all them curious looking things in your
rooms? No sir, you are a —— I don't know what you are;
only please do go away, sir. I don't want your money, for
it would not stay with me, and I am a poor woman, and
let my rooms that I may live. Do go away, sir, do; and,
then, let me give you this, and perhaps you will not be
tempted again."

The gift proffered by the simple-hearted woman was a
Bible, in which, by some means unknown, save only to me,
there was found upon opening it, a five pound note. This

of course I returned to the good woman, whe was perfectly lost as to the cause of its being there.

After some further conversation, her fears and misgivings as to the character of her lodger gave way a little, and she permitted me to remain, and I think never had cause to repent her decision.

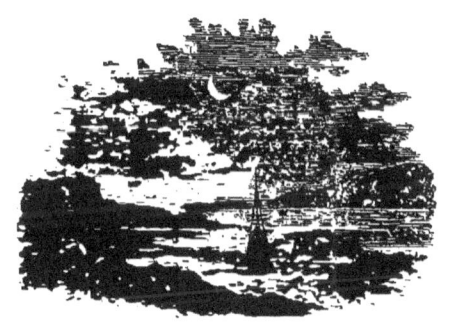

CHAPTER IV.

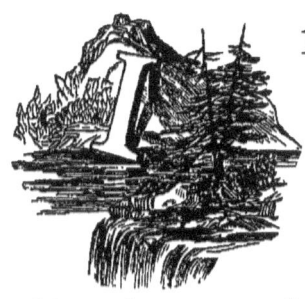 N the commencement of these sketches I had a little to say, by way of introduction, about a being making himself as happy as he well could, while acting his hour of life, and that it was a positive duty for every one both to seek for, and yield to others, as much pleasure as possible. There is no need whatever, because we laugh or make others laugh, that we should do wrong to effect it.

Smiles are the light of angels' faces, and I can see no particular harm in their being reflected from mortals. No, no! smile, laugh and be happy, say I; and the truthfulness of my theory I will maintain, against anything of flesh that's human. But, beside affording such benefits, amusements of any kind often bring with them important reflections and results. Even my performances, though for the most part only intended to amuse, and looked upon with thoughts only for the moment, yet through them it is no hard matter to account for the thousands of those mysterious beings who lived in the earlier history of the world, and have come down to us as magicians, philosophers, and divinities, and to trace the causes of their marvellous doings. The whole list of Greek and Roman divinities, who are said to have done such very famous things, were no doubt performers of the same order to which I belong, and so also were the thousand saints of the middle centuries, who now occupy such prominent places in the ecclesiastical history of some of the nations' creeds.

Both science and art have been often indebted to such performances for many valuable discoveries, and the reformer and moralist need not to turn away from them with a sneer, for were they better acquainted with these things than they unfortunately happen to be, they would find that no small assistance might be gained thereby in carrying out their operations much more successfully than they now do.

The finished gamester possesses many a trick, which all look upon with a smile to see a magician execute, but to which the gambler's partner owes his ruin.

LOST, BUT SAVED.

In connection with this, I have a little incident to relate in support of its truth, in which I was a timely participator. The landlady with whom I resided, and who was so much inclined to turn me from her doors, had a son, a young man, who, as far as appearances went, was one of whom his mother might well be proud. She was proud of him, for scarce a day passed without my having something to hear from her in his praise. In the fond parent's heart "her Harry" was the only deity of her earthly worship. He held a good situation as clerk, and was indeed a young man of good promise, and in whom his employers placed great trust and confidence. I frequently met and conversed with him, but always noticed that he appeared to be ill at ease and abstracted, seeming to forget himself, and wearing at times a most saddened face. The mother saw it, too ; but whenever she spoke of it he would turn her off by saying that it was nothing ; only the fatigue of his day's work ; or that he was not well ; or had to sit up too late, for he was

oftentimes not at home until near morning ; this he accounted for by saying that he was obliged to remain at the store,
or some such thing—and so it passed on ; the old lady
talking anxiously about Harry, while he grew more and
more abstracted and gloomy.

I, of course, did not feel exactly at liberty to question him,
still, I knew that *something* was wrong—but what, I must
wait to see, and I had not long to remain in suspense, for,
on going home one night from a party, where I had been
until a late hour, I found, on arriving at the door, the young
man pacing up and down the street in the greatest distress
of mind conceivable.

"Why, Harry! what is the matter?" I asked, not a little
alarmed at this sudden scene. "What are you doing
here?"

"I am a lost man, ruined, eternally ruined, and my
poor mother—"

"Ruined, lost, what do you mean?"

"I—I have lost everything—my salary, my mother's
little jewels which my father gave her—and to complete my
guilt, I have r–r–obbed my employers."

"You! you! robbed your mother, and your masters!
When, and for what purpose?"

"Yes, I have done it—and not an hour since I staked
the last crown of my thievings on the card table at ———.
I—I am damned forever," he cried wildly, throwing himself upon the doorstep, in an agony of grief.

Here was a scene indeed; a young man, before whom,
but a few months since, there were the happiest prospects
of an honorable life—a mother's only hope, and the esteemed
confidant of an honorable mercantile house, lying abjectly
upon the earth with every darling hope in ruin. Here, then,
was the cause of his silence, his moodiness, and his late
hours.

I saw it at a glance, and as quickly did I resolve to save him if possible. After some little entreaty I persuaded the young man to leave the place where he was and go with me to some more secluded locality. On my way I learned the whole story. It was a simple one, and just such as happens every day.

The young man, by the invitation of a friend, had been induced to visit ———, to see the place; next, to take a game or so for the pleasure of the thing; soon, to make it more interesting, small sums were staked, and lost of course; next, to win them back, debts were incurred, which if not paid, would lead to exposure. Poor Harry! he saw his position, but how could he return. His salary was small, and only came on quarter-days.

The *friend* suggested *borrowing, without asking a loan* —for he could replace it in a few days, and no one would be the wiser, for luck would turn. It was as ever, the old story over again—and he fell into the snare, first by robbing his mother, then, on this day, he had taken fifteen pounds from his employers.

After listening to his tale, I knew at once how the young man had been duped, and proposed that he should go with me to ———, "where," said I, "though I never gamble, yet I hope to teach you a lesson that shall cause you never to place your foot within this, or any similar place again. Come, it is now near morning, and if you wish to save yourself, do as I direct, and perhaps it can yet be done."

My companion led the way to the saloon, where I was to be introduced as a special friend. All, of course, were happy to see me, and with the young man near, I sat down at one of the card-tables and commenced to play. For a time I lost, but soon the game began to assume a more favorable turn, and after an hour's play, I arose from the table and left the place with above a hundred and fifty pounds in my pocket.

After I had gained the street, and was a considerable way from the house, where my visit had not been a very agreeable one to some who wished me to remain longer, I turned and said, "There, Harry, you see what I have done. This fortune, as you gamblers call it, is a *cheat,* and the money which I have taken from those scoundrels who robbed you, was done in accordance with *their own* princi-ples. *Here* are the cards I played with," and beneath the light of a street lamp I showed him a pack of cards, so arranged that I could always hold the game in my hands. Besides, I designated marks by which I could tell the character of every card in the hands of my opponents. "There," said I, "in those and similar ways, lie the art of gambling. You have been duped, but I know that you will not be so again."

"I see it all—but now it is too late!" exclaimed the poor fellow. "Now I see my disgrace."

"Not yet; promise me but one thing and you shall be saved."

"What is it? I will do—ay, *be* anything, only for my poor mother's sake."

"Give me your word of honor then, that you will never again touch card or dice box, and here is the money which I have won. Take it; pay back the sum which you have taken from your employers—make what *honest* and *true* account you can to your mother, and remember as long as you live, the night of the 10th of March, 1829."

The young man promised—and I never had occasion to doubt but that he kept his word.

CHAPTER V.

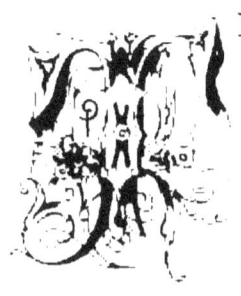 HE ladies, many of them, felt a great interest in my performances, and often, while in London, I was visited by numbers who were extremely anxious to know what was to be their future destiny; and as I could do so many very unaccountable things, they supposed that I also possessed the power of reading coming events. In this they were mistaken, and my applicants were obliged to leave me, in as much uncertainty as to what the future was to be to them, as when they came.

Others requested a private interview, to inquire concerning the past; of property stolen; of absent relatives, where they were, whether dead or alive; these, and similar inquiries, were made to me daily, supposing I was able to give the desired information.

In some of these interviews, although I could not feel myself at liberty to impose upon the credulity of my visitors, by pretending to know of things past, or reveal the mysteries of the hidden future, by nods, winks, and half intelligible sentences, yet I preserved more than one from ruin, in the expositions which I made of the arts pursued by those cheating tricksters, who unblushingly assert that they can read the destiny of every one, who will place within their grasp a guinea or a dollar.

It is a very unfortunate thing that there are so many who are inclined to be duped in this way, and ofttimes has the fortune-teller's tale had so much influence as to cause fears, doubts, and even misery, all of which had their origin from the revelation of *something* which was to come upon the head of the simple questioner.

THE BROKEN-HEARTED MAIDEN.

A young girl with her mother, or "two ladies," as they were announced by the boy-of-all-work, called upon me one morning at my residence, who, after making a good many excuses, and expressions of hope, that I would not regard it as an intrusion, went on to say—the elder lady I mean, for the younger remained perfectly passive, and, with the exception of an occasional sob, it would have been quite a difficult matter to have determined whether there was indeed anything animate or not, beneath that dark bonnet and veil, which stood beside its talking companion—"We have ventured to call upon you, sir," commenced the mother, for so she was to her companion—"we have ventured to—to call upon you, sir—"

"Yes, madam, you have called upon me," said I, anxious to relieve the poor lady from her embarrassment, and half guessing at the object of her visit. "You wish me, madam, to tell one or both of your for—"

"No, sir, no, no, sir, not that—for the *past* we know, and the *future* is as well known, we fear," exclaimed the lady hastily, while the agitation and sobbing became much more evident beneath the bonnet and veil. "No, sir, my daughter Marion only wishes to be more certain that *this* is indeed true." Here the lady took from her dress a paper which appeared to have been much handled, for it was worn, and stained in many places, and several of the characters upon it were almost illegible. "This, sir," said she, "is her fortune, told, and written out for her, the night before James left for the Indies, nearly three years since, and God knows how true the words written there have been thus far—for see, see, sir, what it says," pushing the paper into my hands.

While she had been speaking, the daughter, no longer able to conceal her anxiety, had thrown her veil aside, and now with her mother stood watching me in a most earnest, and anxious manner. There were tears upon her cheek, and hope had but little to do in giving expression to her eyes. The poor girl was indeed a sad picture to look upon, and when I saw how intently I was watched by her, I scarce knew how to act, or what to answer. It was no hard matter to read the whole story of their grief, and trace its origin to the paper I held in my hand, upon which the poor girl's fortune was written ; and, indeed, believing, as she appeared to, in its truthfulness, she had some reason for looking sad, for there was hardly an ill in the whole catalogue of woes, that she was not condemned to suffer—and was to die at last of a broken heart.

Some three years previous, her lover, in a playful mood, just previous to his departure for the Indies, where he was to go with his regiment, proposed that Marion and himself should have their fortunes told. So, in accordance with the suggestion, they sought the sybil's haunt, who, with much parade, told an indescribable quantity of stuff, which was anything but intelligible, and ended with giving them each a paper, which was not on any account whatever to be opened for a month after its delivery.

The morning after, James and Marion parted, each wondering what the strange paper could contain, and what would be its revelations, each promising to open and read their future destinies on the same day and hour. Foolish! many will say, and there is no doubt but all such things do betray a great deal of simplicity, yet the *greatest* are not free from committing like follies. On the appointed day poor Marion, who had scarcely slept a night since her lover's departure, took the paper from its place of concealment, broke the seal, read it, and had been unhappy and miserable ever since.

It was sufficient that it served to make the poor simple girl as miserable as she could well be, and would indeed fulfil at least one part of the prediction, which was, that she should die, as I have before said, of a broken heart.

I looked over the paper, and then fully understood the object of my visitors, and the cause of their apparent misery. I was called upon by them to give my opinion respecting the contents of that paper.

"Do you believe what is here written?" I asked, after hesitating for a while what to do.

"Yes—yes, sir," sighed the young girl, "for I could not help it, and I have not heard from James for two long years. Is it not true? Oh, do, dear sir, say it is *not* true—only say so—and here I will give you all I have in the world. Only tell me whether I shall see him again."

She could say no more, and in her endeavors to reach her purse to me, fell fainting in her mother's arms. When she was restored to consciousness the paper was nowhere to be found, but I told her that it was false, false in every particular, for the *future* was known to no one.

"Have you no reason?" I asked. "Think for a moment, if you can, who knows the work of the next hour, or what it will bring forth? Cheer up, cheer up! *I* tell you that paper is false, and see if *I* do not tell truly."

It would be almost impossible to describe the change in the faces of my two visitors. Where, but a moment before, there was to be seen only the deepest of hopeless grief, now were smiles; and the eyes of the poor girl sparkled with joy and hope, and they left me, full of expressions of gratitude, after promising that at the end of a few days they would call upon me again. Within a week they came, and *James was with them.* He had returned but the day before, and was now a young and promising officer in the service of the East India Company.

Disgusted with Managers.

I remained in London from eight to ten months, during which time I had been very successful, so far as making myself popular was concerned, although pecuniarily I realized but very little in comparison to what one would naturally expect from seeing the immense numbers who flocked to witness my performances. It was my misfortune to fall into the hands of bad managers, who, for the purpose of monopolizing me entirely to themselves, would make me very liberal offers, but ever failed to perform their engagements; consequently, I found, at the end of eight months, that I was very far from realizing my opening expectations, and resolved at once to have nothing more to do with managers of any kind, but in future to act upon my own responsibility. In 1829, having left London, I was again performing in the provincial towns, creating as much excitement and interest as ever. One week found me at Bath, next at Bristol, then away to Liverpool, where, after a very successful and profitable stay of two weeks, I started for Exeter, where I now ventured again to go, having little fear that its venerated bishop would, after our last meeting, trouble himself much about me.

Jack Ketch, the Hangman.

I left Liverpool for Bristol, very early in the morning, about two hours before day; and, on getting into the coach, though I could see scarcely at all, yet I soon satisfied myself

3

that, with the exception of one passenger, I had the inside all to myself, and of course, under the circumstances, I concluded to occupy as much of the coach as possible, and make myself as agreeable as the case would admit.

But there was one thing I would have preferred, and that was to have had my fellow-passenger a lady. But no; there was the hat, the coat—black, and of formal cut—and the whiskers! My companion was, like myself, of the masculine gender.

"Cold morning," said I.

"Yes, very," said the hat and whiskers.

Here we stopped for a time to speculate upon the probable character of each other, as the coach flew on at a rapid rate, to the occasional enlivening music of the guardsman's bugle and the sharp crack of the coachman's lash.

Gradually the day began to dawn, and offered us a little light upon the subject.

What might have been the speculations of my companion concerning me I was not permitted to know, but I found him to be quite a clever-looking kind of a personage, very well and carefully dressed, and for some time I was in doubt as to his not being a dissenting clergyman of some order or other. He talked very well, too, and appeared quite conversant with many of the leading questions of the day, upon which, during our ride, we had several discussions, agreeing on all matters save two—namely, the subjects of *suspension* and capital punishment. There we differed, and I found myself earnestly opposed by the gentleman on the opposite seat, who became at times quite excited. Said he:

"Do away with capital punishment! Oh, no, sir; never, never! I shall go against such a thing, most assuredly, sir, most assuredly. Why, sir, it is our salvation—the country's safety; and, sir, if *I* had my way, *I* would *hang* twice as many; and I think, sir, that we should live all the better for it; I know that *I* should."

·I found it was of no use in talking upon that point; for, say what I would in opposition to capital punishment, he only became more vehement in favor of "*suspension*"—it was the only way to bring people to their senses. I then spoke of the execution which was to take place the next day in Bristol, and asked my travelling companion if he intended to be present.

" Yes, sir, *I* shall most certainly be there."

So we rode on, varying the time in all ways to make the dulness and monotony of a long ride upon a dull, dark day, as agreeable as possible.

On arriving at the place of destination, I found a great number of people assembled around the hotel where I was to stop, and supposed that they had heard of *my* coming, and were there to get a first look *at me*, a circumstance which, as I stepped from the coach, excited my vanity considerably. But I soon found my mistake, and discovered that it was not *my* arrival that was the occasion of all this excitement, but that of the *famous* and *world-known* " Jack Ketch," who immediately followed me out of the coach, and had been all the way down my travelling acquaintance, sent for by the sheriff to act his part at the coming execution ! Quite an agreeable idea, certainly, to ride the whole day alone with the veritable " Jack Ketch " himself, the hangman of England.

No wonder the gentleman was not at all in favor of the abolition of capital punishment. What became of him I knew not, for almost before his feet touched the ground he disappeared, but appeared again, so I heard, upon the scaffold the next morning, and attended to his duties in his usually correct and business-like manner.

I think this a very good lesson to all public men, and advise them to remember that a hangman has as. much power to attract a crowd, as the most learned or talented.

CHAPTER VI.

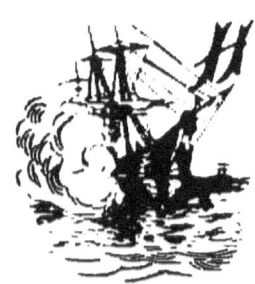

AVING previously arranged to visit Ireland at this period, I sincerely regretted the necessity of separating myself from those who had not only bestowed on me their public patronage, but manifested toward me the warmest friendship, and even given me a social welcome. Their liberal institutions, just laws, and highly cultivated country, strongly impressed my feelings, and with a sorrowful emotion, I left them.

Immediately after reaching Dublin, I commenced my entertainments, remaining nearly six months, amusing the citizens in public and private, and as few persons of my profession had ever visited that city, the impression I produced on the minds of many was extraordinary. Numbers consulted me respecting diseases and complaints, seeking advice and medicine, supposing I possessed the power to relieve pain, and suffering, and all the ills life is subject to.

When I justly remonstrated with these people, assuring them of my want of knowledge and inability to render them the necessary relief, their sad expression of countenance and disappointment frequently gave way to tears. Such scenes were frequent as they were lamentable and trying.

During my sojourn here, I gave two exhibitions at Dub-

A SPRIG OF NOBILITY.

lin Castle, in the presence of His Excellency the Marquis
of Anglesea—the Lord Lieutenant of Ireland—an old Wat-
erloo officer of distinguished fame and courage, and a pleasant and refined gentleman. At each representation, the
hall was crowded with invited guests of dukes, lords, and
ladies. A little incident occurred on one of these occasions
which afforded at the time much amusement.

An Aristocratic Cabbage.

A young gentleman about the age of twenty-five years,
in military dress, and connected with the nobility, was unusually talkative and officious, entreating me to perform the
most impossible things imaginable, and notwithstanding my
repeated assurance that they could not be accomplished, he
continued his importunities, greatly to the annoyance of the
company and myself. A short time previous to the close
of my entertainment it was necessary for me to procure
assistance for a particular feat. I had no sooner made the
request than the loquacious individual hurriedly arose and
presented himself. At the conclusion, he made a few steps
toward leaving, when he suddenly paused, and removed
from the button-hole of his coat a beautiful rose, of bright
crimson, and holding it up, desired to know if I could, by
means of my art, transform it into one of a larger size.
"Certainly," I replied, taking it in my hand and covering it
with a white linen handkerchief. I requested him to blow
upon it, and at the same moment remove the covering. He
did so, with great rapidity, when, to his utter astonishment,
and the general amusement of all present, there appeared a
huge cabbage! One can well imagine the chagrin of my
assistant, his fallen looks, and the merry and exciting laughter that followed.

Thirty years ago, even the educated and wealthy had not
wholly renounced the superstitious ideas associated with all

degrees of art and science. The mind of man had not the penetrating powers of the present day in accounting for peculiar causes and effects, and the influences resulting from circumstances. The time had not arrived for separating genius and credulity, in which the marvellous stories of witchcraft and ghosts had their bases of existence; early education favorable to this belief was common. But how fortunate is mankind, that as each generation advances, so intelligence increases, and proves the supposed mysteries of the past to be either the demonstrations of truth, or the romance of thought; and while many may dispute the laws which govern the senses, or the impressive character of the mind, none will deny that our natures are fanciful, and that we are inclined to embrace the false and imaginary.

Returning to matters of more interest to the reader, I will state that Dublin was the first city wherein I practically illustrated the art of ventriloquism.

For more than two years I had devoted all my leisure time and attention to its acquirement. I admired it greatly, for the amusing and singular effect it never failed to produce. This fondness for the art materially contributed to my improvement. It had never been my good fortune to hear but one ventriloquist, a gentleman in private life, who would occasionally entertain his friends. From him I gained my knowledge.

The Frightened Doctor.

Dr. Crampton, at this time, was one of the most eminent surgeons in the metropolis, celebrated for his great skill and medical attainments. His practice was extensive and remunerative. Attracted by my feats, we became personally intimate, and on one occasion he invited me to accompany him to the hospital to witness a dissection. The idea of being present at such an operation was repugnant in the extreme, but after a moment's reflection, I assented, resolving, if possible, to alarm the disciples of Esculapius. We entered the doctor's carriage, and, in a little time, arrived at the college, where directly I found myself in a moderate-sized apartment, with a long, narrow table in the centre. On the floor, in one corner, I perceived the bodies of two males and one female. The view was dreadful, and I could scarcely refrain from giving vent to my feelings of indignation; for, perhaps, these very subjects had been ruthlessly removed from their graves, and their living friends would have revolted at their becoming subjects, even to medical science. Every look I bent upon the bodies produced the strongest reasoning in opposition to such unfeeling indifference toward the dead.

What a theme was before me for philosophizing: those inanimate bodies may have been in their lifetime physically and intellectually great; their presence the charm of an affectionate household. While in this reflective mood, a body was removed from the floor and placed in position for being dissected.

Dr. Crampton had taken his knife in hand, and was about to make an incision, when a supplicating voice, apparently proceeding from the subject, exclaimed, "Oh, doctor, doctor, do not injure me! pray have pity, for I was once mortal!" "So were we, doctor!" muttered the two in the corner. At these sounds from the supposed dead, a perfect storm of excitement commenced, which it is totally impossible to describe. Many seized their hats and rushed to the door; others declared they had become the jest of concealed persons in the closet, beneath the floor, or on the roof. A hasty examination was made of every spot, but without success. After order had been slightly restored, the whole group of surgeons and students formed a circle around the table, and with the most earnest anxiety watched the body.

Dr. Crampton had no sooner lifted the knife—which in his surprise he had let fall—when another voice broke forth: "It is cruel to mutilate the remains of what was once a lovely woman."

Every eye was turned to the spot from whence these sounds issued, when the subject on the table cried out, "It is an outrage to thus abuse a woman!" At this juncture a general rush was made toward the door, in which I participated. Each and all expressed their belief that the devil had appeared to prevent the employment of the knife and its revelations.

When I descended to the street, I perceived Dr. Crampton walking rapidly toward his carriage. I followed, and as he was about taking his seat, I imitated the voices in the dissecting room; he instantly closed the door with much force, while I stood laughing before him, asking how he had appreciated my *first* attempt at ventriloquism. The doctor appeared amazed, and replied that I had successfully deceived him and the faculty. We separated under the promise that the affair should be kept a profound secret, in order that himself and students might not be subjected to the ridicule of the public. Forty years and more having now passed, and Dr. Crampton long since ceased to be numbered among the living, I can honorably assume the liberty of giving publicity to the incident.

This trial of my powers as a ventriloquist was satisfactory to myself, and convinced me that I had arrived at sufficient perfection to make the art a prominent feature in my exhibitions, which I have ever since done, creating a lively interest therein and begetting countless incidents of the most ludicrous and extravagant character possible.

CHAPTER VII.

DUBLIN was at this period a fine city, with a large and increasing population. It was famed for its institutions and public buildings. The citizens were liberal, kind, and hospitable, and by far more intelligent than otherwise. The extremes of wealth and poverty were more significantly visible than either in England, Scotland, or Wales; yet I had never seen people so gloriously fertile in inventive happiness.

To me they appeared practically buoyant and attached to the character for which they are so renowned; and as the peculiarities of a nation are disclosed by their habits, so the Irish are faithfully recognized in all parts of the world.

DANIEL O'CONNELL.

While I remained in Dublin I became acquainted with Daniel O'Connell. He was a man of warm impulses, devoted to his family, and indisputably a patriot and an ardent lover of his country.

Occasionally he attended my entertainments, frequently speaking at the close of the refreshing relief he realized in his mind. His influence with his fellow-countrymen was surpassingly great, he was the victim of much vituperation and enmity, and frequently observed that he considered himself the best abused man in the country. In his political principles, he was broad and expansive, a firm advocate

3*

of all appertaining to civil and religious liberty. This gained him the bitter hostility of his opponents, and resulted in the most zealous employment of his time and abilities in behalf of Ireland. In return for the sacrifice of a valuable profession, he was rewarded with an annual tribute, by the inhabitants of his native land and other admirers. He asserted "the government could make no act of Parliament which he could not drive a coach-and-four over." He was frequently prosecuted, and I believe but once convicted and imprisoned. When a friend at that time remarked to him, that he regretted that he did not run "his coach" in defiance of the law, O'Connell replied, "Ah! this is but a casual upset."

Ireland never had a truer advocate of her rights, or the oppressed a firmer friend. To his efforts are due Catholic Emancipation, and the removal of those laws seemingly obnoxious to his country. As time advances, O'Connell will become more admired, and better appreciated as a patriot and benefactor to his race.

Lady Morgan, the authoress, was also a frequent visitor at my morning *soirées*, as were all the resident persons of rank, and those temporarily in the city.

Irish Wit.

During the season, a band of Russian horn-players appeared at the Theatre Royal. Their style of music was original and novel; each instrument played one note only, *all* harmonizing correctly and producing the sweetest tones, much resembling those of an organ. The horns were of various sizes, from one foot to thirty, and the latter were supported on trestles. The company numbered nearly forty persons, who were said to be the slaves of a prince, who had given them permission to leave their country for two years.

They had visited Italy, Germany, France, and England, with much success. At one of their concerts the house was densely crowded, and the band had for some time delighted the audience, when suddenly a person seated in the gallery, in a full Hibernian voice, cried out, "Plaze, play up the Cholera Morbus." Immediately the whole audience in the gallery made the same demand, when the uproar became general, so that ultimately Mr. Calcraft, the manager, found it necessary to make his appearance. After learning their wishes he communicated with the leader, in French, who stated they were not acquainted with the air. On Mr. Calcraft's repeating this to the audience, the Hibernian in the gallery exclaimed, "Be faith and sure, Mr. Manager, is it not a Russian air,—for did not the cholera come from Russia in a ship laden with hemp?" At this explanation, a general clapping of hands and laughter took place which lasted several moments, much to the surprise of the Russians, who were of course unable to appreciate the musical capacity and ready wit of a fun-loving Irishman.

The band shortly afterward sailed for the United States, where they succeeded admirably, but an unfortunate disagreement among themselves caused a complete separation.

After the conclusion of my entertainments in this city, I proceeded to Drogheda, Dundalk, Armagh, Newry, and Belfast, astonishing all classes and ages, so that my success and prosperity exceeded my anticipations. The poor and ignorant gazed on me with fear and suspicion, doubting my identity with the human race, and nothing could prevail on them to believe my associations on earth were of an honorable character, and worthy of the countenance of a religious or thoughtful people, so positively certain were they that I must be the Prince of Darkness himself, or his agent. The last named city was already a place of great trade and importance, and much of its population originally emigrated from Scotland. Their habits, feelings, and interests were mercantile and progressive, industrious and economical, beyond measure.

During the continuance of my exhibition here I received the flattering attention of the wealthy, and the respect of the worthy poor.

The Marchioness of Donegal, who resided in the immediate neighborhood, gave me the use of her favorite assembly room, besides contributing her especial patronage.

I continued my journey, passing through Coleraine, and visiting Ireland's greatest curiosity, the *Giant's Causeway*, which is romantic and wonderful. I opened at Londonderry, a city celebrated in history for its siege and famous defence, the suffering and horrors of old and young, and the events necessarily associated therewith, and notwithstanding none were then living who participated in the struggle, every variety of reminiscence was related with as much accuracy as though it had but recently transpired. So vividly was all appertaining to its character portrayed by the inhabitants, that I doubt if an individual could be found ignorant of the facts. The city was prettily built, walled, and ancient in its appearance; noted for its estates of beauty, surrounded by wealth belonging to the nobility and persons of distinction.

THE TALKING CODFISH.

Passing one morning through the market, I came to a fish-stand and inquired the price of herrings.

"Four-pence a dozen, yer honor; how many will you take?"

"Are they fresh?" I inquired.

"Faith they are," replied the man; "they were in the sea before the sun rose this morning."

"That is not true," came angrily from a large cod on the stand,

"Be Saint Patrick, who are ye that dare dispute me to the jintleman?" cried the fisherman, in loud and excited tones.

"It is me, Barney!" said the fish. "You know we have all been in this stall for nearly a week; so speak the truth, you old sinner!"

Barney now clenched his fist, drew himself up into position, and, looking at the object of his wrath with great anger, was about to strike, when the fish exclaimed—

"Don't kill me, Barney, I am a mermaid!"

"And sure, what is a mermaid?" said Barney. "Speak out, or I'll stop your false tongue forever!"

"Why, Barney," said the fish, "I am the mother of all the fish that swim!"

"And sure, if it is a woman ye are," replied Barney, "the devil a bit will I forget mesilf."

By this time many persons had collected around the stall, and while Barney was recounting the story, with his eyes half out of his head, I quietly walked away; but one of the number recognizing me, shouted, "It was the ventriloquist, Barney. There he goes!" when a laughing chorus followed me in my departure.

I proceeded on my travels again, exhibiting at Strabane, Omagh, Ballina, Castlebar, Tuam, Galway, Gort, Ennis, and Limerick. In all these towns I was an object of mirth to many, and fear to others. The religious would at times cross themselves, apprehensive lest I might bewitch, or play some unholy prank upon them, and while I admit such anticipations on their part, it is pleasant to relate that no insult or unkindness was offered me.

The Dishonest Servant.

Limerick (the new part of the city) was handsomely laid out and well regulated, containing a lively community.

The proprietor of the hall I exhibited in was also the land-lord of the hotel. His family was composed of several members, who looked upon me with unmingled awe, for in their own minds they were confident I was in league with Beelzebub, for how was it possible that a man of flesh and blood could perform feats so miraculous and incomprehensible. While there, one of the ladies had a quantity of jewelry and money stolen from a bureau in her sleeping-room. She made me acquainted with the theft, and regarded the discovery a matter of certainty in my hands. What action I should take to recover the same, required consideration, for to some extent my reputation was liable to lose its prestige, which I was desirous of avoiding.

I personally examined the location of the room and stairs, and dwelt upon the character and circumstances of those who had continual access to all parts of the house, reflected upon their taste, and love of dress, gayety, liberal habits, and antecedents. A few days enabled me to form a probable opinion as to the culprit, yet, to proclaim this without the most positive proof, would have subjected me to great difficulties. I concluded, therefore, to make no special charge in regard to any particular person, but to request the lady to appear, with all the members of the family, in the hall. At the appointed time, the whole party had assembled. I then remarked that it was well known to all present that an amount of money and jewelry had been stolen, and that I was solicited to discover the person who had committed the act, and although it was exceedingly unpleasant for me to be employed in an affair so serious, and which must produce shame and disgrace, yet I considered it my duty for the honor and interest of each, to reveal the truth. I had, therefore, investigated the matter, and consulted with the Oracle of Fate and the spirit of our individuality, and had thus been able to detect the guilty one, who was then in our presence. At this statement a sudden sensation prevailed. Every countenance sparkled with amazement, accompanied by a restless anxiety to know who was the accused. .But as it was not in my power to gratify their wishes, I requested their indulgence in refusing for the moment to expose the individual, for I was fully convinced the property taken would be as mysteriously returned, which will avoid exposure, pain, and imprisonment, and perhaps, be the happy means of producing a repentant heart, and honest actions in future. But, should I be disappointed in my prediction, then there would be no alternative but to give publicity to the name of the offender. At the conclusion, my listeners dispersed, astonished greatly by the information imparted. That evening I attended a party, to which I had been invited, and did not arrive at the hotel till a very late hour, and when ascending the stairs to my bedroom, I was startled by the sudden apparition of a female before me, who, with despairing look and pitiful countenance, placed her forefinger to her lips, and extending her hand, offered me a package. For a moment the surprise produced a sensation approaching timidity. Re covering my self-possession, I recognized one of the servants engaged as chambermaid, who had listened to my observations at the meeting. In mournful and trembling tones, scarce above a whisper, she uttered, "Oh, sir! here is the stolen property. It contains all; I am a wretch, but for the peace of my aged parents do not expose me. It is the only offence of my life; promise to grant my request, and I will always pray for you;" at the same instant kneeling, and with uplifted hands, declared before the All-Seeing Eye, that she never would commit a dishonest act again.

Rising, she continued her petition for my silence, feeling assured I could read every heart.

From her shaking hand I received the parcel, and promised to keep the matter a secret, which I had no sooner declared, than she breathlessly disappeared.

For a second I remained motionless with astonishment. Recovering myself, I hastened to my room, but the graphic events I have related so occupied my mind that all sleep had vanished for the night. In the morning I had an interview with the lady, and handed her the package, which, on opening, she found to contain all the valuables stolen, and while she thanked me many times for procuring the same, earnestly entreated me to explain the proceedings, and name the thief. This request it was not possible for me to comply with. I referred her to my remarks at the meeting, when I had stated that if the articles were returned no exposure would be made, and as the object was accomplished, no further explanation could be given. The transaction remained a mystery to all, and increased my fame.

About this time the citizens were greatly alarmed by the appearance of cholera, as several cases had been reported, some of a fatal character. Unfortunately I was also attacked with the disease, although my medical attendant—a gentleman of the most excellent capabilities—ingeniously endeavored to persuade me, from prudential motives, to the contrary; but with grateful thanks to Providence, under the faithful care devoted to me by my friend Gabriel, and kind nursing, I rapidly recovered, and without delay took my departure, exhibiting at Tipperary, Thurles, Cashel, and Clonmel.

THE FRIGHTENED TAX-COLLECTOR.

At an exhibition in the first-named town, I discovered that some one of the audience had taken away one of my pets, a white rabbit, valuable for its sagacity and surprising knowledge.

On inquiry, I was informed that a Mr. Ryan, a tithe proctor—an office greatly despised—and a most unpopular man, was seen leaving the hall with it in his possession. I proceeded to his residence, found him at home, and mentioned the object of my visit. He indignantly denied all knowledge of it, and was anxious for the name of my informant. At this moment I perceived the rabbit running on the floor, in a back room, and on my directing his attention to the fact, he firmly declared I was mistaken, as the rabbit I saw had been purchased by him several months previous. The angry discussion between us was suddenly interrupted by the rabbit jumping toward us, shaking his ears, and, in a gruff tone, saying, "Ryan, you are a scamp, and the Lord have mercy on your soul!"

"Who dares call me a scamp?" screamed Ryan, in a towering passion.

"I do," the rabbit answered. "You never paid a ha'penny for me, Ryan. Did you not bring me here last night from the hall? And you are so mean that I am starving for food, and dying of thirst. Oh, beware, Ryan! the devil is after ye!"

"What!" he retorted; "are you the invisible demon? Take that," giving a furious kick, which luckily did not reach the rabbit, which instantly replied with solemnity: "Ryan, to-night I will call all my imps from below, and take you to the deepest region of fire." Here Ryan betrayed fear and agitation, and insisted on my taking the rabbit, who was undoubtedly a bewitched animal. I eagerly acceded to his wishes, but was obliged to remove it from the floor myself, so convinced was Ryan as to its being a representative from the abode of darkness. In a few hours every man, woman, and child were rejoicing at the fright of Ryan, at the same time regretting that I had not indicted him in the Criminal Court for his shameful conduct.

I again pursued my travels, appearing at Wexford, Carlow, New Ross, Ennis, Athy, and Kilkenny, meeting with pecuniary reward and the applause of thousands.

Kilkenny at the time was under martial law, and, notwithstanding I often became forgetful of the restraint upon my personal liberty, I encountered no embarrassments, but, on the contrary, realized many pleasing incidents, one of which I will relate in the following chapter.

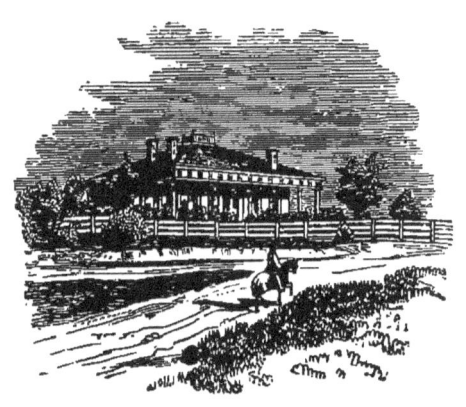

CHAPTER VIII.

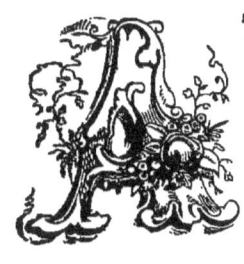T the close of an entertainment, between the hours of ten and eleven, I walked to "The Bridge," a charming spot, where I seated myself to admire—after the fatigue of the evening—the trees, as they, in their lovely foliage, gracefully drooped over the placid water, and the millions of sparkling stars that illuminated the heavens. While contemplating the sublimity and grandeur of the scene, I was disturbed by the approach of a number of soldiers, accompanied by a sergeant, who accosted me in the Scotch accent, and inquired my residence and object in being absent from home at such a late hour. I gave him my address and occupation, which appeared satisfactory, although he informed me it would be necessary to escort me to my hotel. I endeavored to be excused, but without success. Then I resorted to stratagem, by stating my willingness to accompany him as soon as my friends under the bridge had finished their bathing. At this announcement he inclined his head over the railing, and in the broadest accent, shouted, "Halloo! gentlemen."

"You are mistaken, sir," was the answer, in a woman's voice.

The sergeant's astonishment, and that of his men, appeared great indeed, on learning that the bathers were of the gentler sex. Then assuming a softer tone, he entreated, "Be ye good wives or daughters, hurry out, for it is na right to be from your house at midnight; come, and I will see ye safe home."

"No, you will not; we are learning to swim, and intend remaining until the break of day," was the response.

Here the sergeant evinced the deepest concern, and observed, "You are violating the laws of His Majesty's Government."

"We do not care a straw for the king or his laws," the voice from beneath the bridge replied.

"If that is the case," responded the sergeant, "I shall order the guard to arrest you."

The parties below now commenced laughing heartily, and said it was a rich joke for a dozen men to attack them in the river.

The sergeant displayed much excitement, and threatened that, unless the ladies obeyed, his men would immediately execute orders.

"You had better not, for we will drown every one of them," replied the bathers.

The sergeant now ordered his men to stack arms, after which he distributed them at different points of the bridge, when for a moment he paused, and again asked the supposed bathers if they intended to submit.

"No," they defiantly replied.

"Then over the bridge, boys, but dinna behave rude."

Splash! dash! went the men, drenching themselves from head to foot. A moment was sufficient to convince them that there was no human creature visible—and they communicated the fact to the sergeant, awaiting further instructions.

"That's na possible," he cried, in loud tones; "ye must all be blind; dinna ye hear the converse with the twa persons?"

"True," the men answered, as they stood shivering with cold, "but they have made their escape."

"Na, na, it canna be sae; look well, with your e'es *open*."

"It is no use, sergeant," the men angrily exclaimed, with chattering teeth.

"Well, then, come up, and I'll gang down mesel."

The men, well pleased to vacate their unpleasant situation, commenced climbing the abutments, and had nearly reached the surface of the bridge, when they were interrupted by loud calls for help from the supposed females, who cried out distressingly, "We are sinking—help! help!"

"Hark! dinna ye hear the twa? Down once more, my lads, and capture them," commanded the sergeant, in truly martial style.

"Yes, yes; come quickly, and save us!" came despondently from the water.

The men a second time reluctantly plunged into the river, and with great care searched for the troublesome bathers, but failing in their efforts, became weary and discontented, declaring most emphatically that they were the dupes of invisible beings.

"It is na sae," cried the sergeant. "Mount the bridge, and I'll see for mesel."

The poor fellows soon reached the top, when their commander gave orders to keep strict guard while he satisfied his own mind. At the same moment he threw himself on the outside of the bridge, and descended to the water, where he cautiously peered about, calling on those he imagined were *somewhere* secreted, to surrender; repeating his demand in vain, he gave utterance to language more forcible than elegant. Again, and again, he wandered back and forth, around and about, to find his would-be prisoners, but only to add the more to his mortification. Finding his *personal* exertions equally unsuccessful as the combined efforts of his men, he turned to the bridge for the purpose of joining the guard, when a hasty cry reached his ear:

"Sergeant, are you a Christian, to desert us in our danger? We entreat you to use despatch, and rescue us from death! We are on the opposite side of the bridge."

"You are mistaken. I am not the heathen you suppose, but a good Presbyterian."

Flattering himself he had now succeeded in his object, he moved in the direction advised, when, to his great indignation, no one awaited him.

"Well," he exclaimed, "ye are like the lightning that flashes in the eye, and dinna, dinna remain. Are ye some weird sisters of the spirit world, whose consciences the de'il has tortured, and sent forth with witchcraft powers, to plague and dupe humanity? A better game of hide-and-seek I never played. But whether of heaven or earth, ye canna be gude folks; and so, as it is of no use for a man to waste his philosophy on unseen bodies, I'll gang back."

Obtaining his hold upon the bridge, with little difficulty he stood before his companions, whose doubts of ever beholding him were visible on every countenance.

"Well, men of Company D, the de'il has given us a wild-goose chase, and it is of no use endeavoring to solve the mystery. John Knox, of pious memory, could na unravel the adventure of this night."

During the delivery of this speech I moved to the end of the bridge, where I concealed myself, remaining motionless until I heard the words given, "Shoulder arms! Right about face! March!" In a few moments I followed their footsteps, arrived at the hotel, and laughingly related the pastime I had been engaged in. All were interested and amused at the occurrence, and did not fail, the following morning, to give publicity to the exploit of the sergeant and his guard.

I resumed my travels, and entertained the citizens of Waterford, Tranmore, and Dunmore. The latter places were delightfully situated on the sea-shore, and attracted numerous visitors for the benefit of salt-water bathing.

For several weeks I resided in this pleasant neighborhood, released from all care and professional fatigue, corresponding with my father, and giving him a general statement of my course and circumstances. My love for, and duty toward, him were always prominently before me, and nothing could induce me to forget myself as a son, by occasioning for a moment the least pain to his feelings. My mother's image, her fond affection, and the happiness with which they lived together, devoted me the more intensely to him, for I knew of no act by which I could exhibit the expression of my heart for her memory than by an unwavering attachment to my father.

In every instance the good offices and advice of my friend Gabriel were generously given, to promote and continue this filial fondness and obedience. After an agreeable sojourn at this romantic spot, I appeared at Roscrea, Doneraile, Lismore, Cappoquin, Cork Cove, Middleton, Fermoy, Kinsale, Youghal, Bandon, and Mallow. The city of Cork, second in population to that of Dublin, was notable for its spirit and unbounded hospitality—lovers of amusement, and generous to strangers. My success was a perfect triumph, and every exhibition I gave, added the more to increase public attention and excite the imagination. Rich, poor, old and young, became attracted to my performances; and while great numbers patronized and encouraged me with applause and a liberality unprecedented, a large portion seriously considered whether the laws permitted such demonstrations to be tolerated, which they considered far exceeding the magical transformations attributed to the powers of Roger Bacon, Dr. Faustus, and other renowned magicians who flourished in the dark ages. Private meetings were held by the superstitious and ignorant, to discuss this question and recommend the authorities to interfere, and forbid the countenancing my practices in demonology and witchery of the voice. To aggravate in a greater degree the fears and suspicions of the timid, strange stories were invented and circulated by merry wags, whose practical jokes were eagerly listened to by the lovers of marvel—such as, owls were seen flying at midday over the building I occupied; cats and mice gambolled together in my presence; cows and horses would kneel as I passed them; and rats and mice were seen feeding from my hand.

It was declared that all the church bells tolled at a certain hour during the night, and that I never failed to attend a consultation of evil spirits in the surrounding churchyards in the gray dawn of morn; that every dog growled as his master's children cried in their sleep; birds sang that had never warbled before; in fact, all were bewitched, while countless voices attended my daily walks. These, and every variety of fabulous tales, were the theme of conversation, so that I had frequently to contend with ardent and determined believers in these reports. No denial or assurance on my part would convince them I was not associated, or in some manner implicated, with the demon of unrighteousness.

That minds so feeble should exist in the nineteenth century, compared unfavorably not only with the progress of the times, but indisputably proved that that basis of credulity which marked their ancestral faith in the supernatural powers of man, has yet a lingering element in the characters of their descendants.

Taking into consideration that this existed at a period when revolutionary movements, on land and water, were producing wonderful benefits to commerce and industry, annihilating space and time, with the great achievements which civilization was developing in all parts of the world, we perceive how little the intellectual man had correspondingly advanced.

Happily, at this time, a new era had commenced to reveal its benign and commanding influences. Energetic attention to educational wants, commenced in earnest—schools, and the publication of periodicals in every department of science and knowledge, calculated to enlighten the mind, and explain and make clear certain phenomena of life, were established and prosperously progressing. If we attempt a comparison of the improvements in social and rational views, which have predominated since these opportunities have been afforded, we undoubtedly discover a removal of those ideas which gave a degenerating feature to the belief and habits of the people.

After giving exhibitions at a few other places, I completed my tour; and, without commenting upon its institutions or political struggles, will simply add, that I bade adieu to Ireland, and re-crossed the Channel to England, carrying with me a grateful appreciation of their kindness, and a lasting recollection of their lovely land.

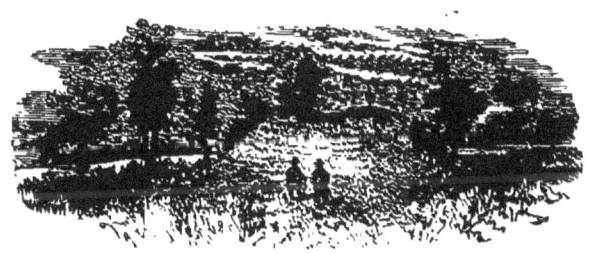

4

CHAPTER IX.

ISHING to visit Scotland—a land interesting in its historical associations, and celebrated as the birthplace of Sir Walter Scott and Robert Burns—I passed over into Dumfries, a town of some important. Neat and compactly built, though irregular, it is picturesquely charming to the eye. Situated on the river Nith, across which it communicates with its suburb Chaswelton, it is regarded as the provincial capital of South Scotland.

The surrounding country was cultivated to perfection. The extensive farms, and immensity of their productions, appeared almost incredible.

My audiences were peculiarly characterized for their observing manners. The surprise I originated was manifested in the strange and apprehensive looks of all present, for they regarded me with suspicion, and doubted my real dealings with the natural world.

During my sojourn the coronation of King William the Fourth took place. The event was celebrated with much enthusiasm, which evinced attachment to the English throne.

The amusements provided for the day were numerous, and of a varied character, an interesting feature of which was the various trades of the place walking in procession to an appointed spot according to the custom of the time, to contend at target-shooting, for the possession of a silver gun presented as a prize, and to be won and retained by the trade represented by the best marksman, and held by them until the next assembly, when another trial takes place. This had become a local custom, and was prized as a memento of interest by the *bourgeois*. In the evening there was a large assemblage at the Trades' Hall, where addresses were made appropriate to the occasion. The king's health was drank in a hundred or more gallons of punch, and almost every house was illuminated, and the streets lit up by bonfires.

A second pleasing incident was the return of Colonel Burns, who was the eldest son of the immortal poet, after an absence of twenty-five years in India. He arrived home on a visit to his mother, and the second morning after his return I had the pleasure of receiving an invitation to meet him at the residence of Mr. McDermot, the talented proprietor of the Dumfries *Courier*.

The party was a social and convivial one, and deeply interesting by reason of the many anecdotes related, and which were connected with the great bard's memory. Colonel Burns was a modest and unpresuming man, short in stature, with an inclination to corpulency, between forty and fifty years of age, and I judged near-sighted, from the necessity of wearing glasses. During the evening I enjoyed the pleasure of hearing him sing one of his father's celebrated songs, which he executed with excellent taste and sweetness. Previous to my departure I called upon the widow of the poet, who resided in a secluded street, and humble house. There was an air of comfort, without any approach to ostentation. She received me kindly, and freely replied to all my inquiries relative to her husband, mentioning many little circumstances connected with his habits and peculiarities. Her conversational powers were not brilliant, neither was there the beauty and romance that had once attracted the poet.

Dumfries contains many objects of immense interest, particularly the monument erected to the memory of Burns, a beautiful piece of sculpture, in which the poet is represented at full length, with his hands grasping the plough, and an angel crowning him with a wreath.

Terminating my engagement at Dumfries, my next visit was to Glasgow, a city of great importance, abounding with wealth, enterprise, and largely engaged in mercantile pursuits. Much life and animation prevailed, and probably no place in the kingdom possessed so many natural and varied advantages.

Improvements were progressing of extraordinary magnitude, denoting remarkable prophetic knowledge of the future, in the erection of manufacturing establishments, and increasing the facilities for navigation, besides extensively extending and beautifying the public streets and private residences.

My entertainments were given at a hall in the Arcade, at that time a popular place of resort. Of the thousands who came to see me, hundreds returned home with the full conviction that I was either the d——l himself or closely allied to his satanic majesty. The whole population became greatly excited, some appearing friendly, while others, incompetent to distinguish between the supernatural and the real, characterized me as deserving the fate of the witches and wizards of old, whose temerity was rewarded on the scaffold or by the faggot. Although enjoying the advantages of education, the Scotch people were, nevertheless, peculiarly superstitious, and have ever been the most ready converts to the improbabilities prevailing in all ages, and the numerous stories, revived in regard to the freaks and incantations of the spirits and magicians of their own country was amusing, and extensively aided in giving me a marked position in their minds. My success continued undiminished for months; crowds were frequently unable to gain admission to my exhibitions, and I was a mystery beyond comprehension.

In order to continue the interest I had created, I never failed to produce sensation and wonder by the exercise of my ventriloquial powers.

THE SPIRIT OF THE MILL.

One afternoon I accompanied a party of gentlemen to inspect a new cotton-mill. They were all pleased and not less astonished at the wonderful attainments which skill and ingenuity had produced. While occupied in examining the engine, a voice suddenly exclaimed—

"Stop the machinery!"

At once all eyes were directed to the spot, and the engine immediately ceased its revolutions.

"Who are ye?" cried the engineer, stooping down, shocked at the idea of being obliged to stop during the presence of visitors.

"I am between the shafts, and almost crushed to death," called out the sufferer.

"Well," responded the engineer, "come out, gude man."

"I wish I could. Lend a helping hand."

"But I cannot see you," crossly answered the engineer. "Where and who the de'il are ye?"

"Why, mon, I am Jamie Douglass, and ye dinna care where to find me."

"If I cannot, you will be crushed," retorted the vexed and anxious man.

"Ha! ha! ye must not do that, for it would be murder."

"Indeed it would," shouted a gruff voice.

At this the whole company became alarmed, anxiously looking around to discover the object in danger, when Jamie said—

"Do you think the *Spirit of the Mill* has a body like yourselves?"

"Spirit, good or bad," declared the engineer, in a passionate voice, "here goes the works."

Immediately thereafter, a terrific shriek appalled the bystanders, but at this moment a gentleman present, recollecting my profession, cried out—

"Go on, engineer," pointing to me, "there is the Spirit of the Mill—Signor Blitz, the ventriloquist!"

Much humor followed this disclosure, in which the engineer heartily joined.

The Babe in the Violin Case.

During my exhibitions, Paganini, the celebrated violinist, gave several concerts in Glasgow. His superiority over all previous professors of this instrument, and the many romantic stories connected with his life, secured for him great fame. His genius consisted in performing on a single string varied airs, displaying great brilliancy of execution, and producing the sweetest tones conceivable.

It was said he had been a long time imprisoned in Italy, his native land, on account of his political principles, during which time he had fully developed his talents and made himself master of the instrument.

He was tall and awkward-looking, cadaverous in feature, ungainly in form, with long black hair, said to be very wealthy, and characterized as extremely penurious. No instance was ever known of his contributing a penny to the distressed, or to a benevolent institution. One morning I called and found him quietly seated in his room alone. After conversing with him a short time, I noticed his violin-case lying upon the table, when suddenly the cry of a child issued from therein.

"Who is that?" said Paganini, quietly looking around.

"It is me, with the babe," answered a womanly voice.

"My Got! what is this?" inquired the astonished violinist.

"You well know," plaintively answered the woman—at the same time the infant again commenced crying.

"Me know you are a bad woman," vehemently declared the excited man.

"And did you not make me so, you old Italian fiddler."

After this there was apparently a commotion in the box, when Paganini became alarmed, and was about to leave the room, when I unmasked myself, and explained that he had been a victim to the vagaries of ventriloquism; which, on learning, delighted him prodigiously, and grasping me by the hand, exclaimed, "Bravo, signor!—bravo!"

That the destinies of men are unfathomable is an unquestionable truth, and no human agency can reach the operating influences which control our actions. The purposes of the mind to-day are changed and governed by the events of to-morrow. We perceive the shadow without the power to realize the substance, proving all life to be responsible to the benign rule of an All-Wise and Supreme Being, rather than to our own wisdom.

Marriage.

In closing this account of my merry doings in Glasgow, I must not omit to describe an adventure of a personal character—one memorable to me above all others—which no time can efface, and memory will ever fondly cherish.

Walking one afternoon in company with Gabriel, we met three ladies, and as we passed them, I observed to him that *the centre lady would be my wife*. All three were entire strangers to us. Can it be considered an accidental circumstance, a decree of fate, or attributable to the magical influences of my art, when I assert that within a few weeks I was united by marriage to the lady in question? To describe the beauty of her person, the accomplishments of her mind, or the affection of her heart, would be impossible. For nearly thirty years we lived affectionately and happily together, and were blessed with a large family of children, who were her special care, until the wise Creator removed her to a home in heaven.

My marriage was the great event of the day, for at every fireside and in every home the matter was discussed and opinions freely expressed. I was accused by many of having secured her affections by witchcraft, and was also declaimed against as a sorcerer, and guilty of exercising mystic powers.

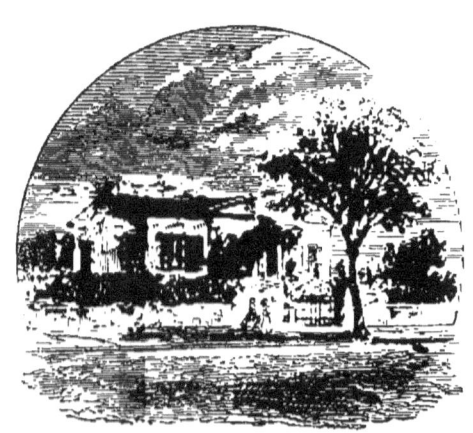

CHAPTER X.

ERY brief was my retirement, and having again resumed business, I arrived at Edinburg, the capital of Scotland. It would occupy a large amount of space to describe the many objects of attraction, both local and national, with which this city abounds. The never-failing interest appertaining to her kings, queens, and nobility, their history, love of country, and heroism, deeply impressed my mind with a sympathy for the people.

There is no nation whose past history contains so much to charm and admire, and where the peculiar traditions of their ancestors are so fully developed.

The city presents innumerable monuments of Scottish events—every footstep is hallowed with precious memorials of the past.

The contrast existing between the buildings of the old and the new town was surprising. The antiquity of the former, compared with the beauty of the latter, illustrated the progress of the age.

Probably there is not a city in the world where the inhabitants are so cultivated, and have reached so high a standard in literature and science, or where elegance and refinement are such prominent features in the courtesies of life.

4*

I commenced my exhibitions at the Assembly Rooms, the audiences being composed of the nobility, professional men, learned divines, and citizens of less distinguished but respectable and intellectual character. The applause I received, and the general interest I produced, increased wonderfully. Soon I became the magnet of attraction, and the dread of the superstitious; for while there were some who patronized and appreciated my dexterity, there were many others who credited me with every species of necromancy, and alleged that my feats were evidences of a wizard's skill, and legions of spirits were at my command, to stalk the earth with hideous forms, and tantalize poor humanity with their malicious freaks and incantations. These, and similar inventions of the most ridiculous nature, were promulgated and believed by a large class. Scotland ranks far above all other countries in the magnitude of her legendary traditions. Every mountain-dale, town, and district are, in more or less degree, distinguished for some remarkable or wonderful event, and her people have always been interested in the associations connected with the spectral and supernatural. It may be truly said their faith in demonology was great. For weeks the hall continued crowded, and the constant change of entertainment I produced, assured those whose minds were impressed with the potency of my art, that I was unquestionably a wandering *genii*.

THE BOTTLED JANITOR.

The janitor of the room greatly annoyed me by his disagreeable character, and, on every occasion possible, inconvenienced me by disturbing my apparatus and disarranging it to the utmost degree. He seemed to be governed by the idea that I was an operator in the "black art," and possessed the power of calling evil spirits to my assistance, and was fully in league with the devil. One day, being unusually provoked at his interference, I requested him to refrain in future from disarranging my machinery, otherwise I should be under the necessity of bewitching him, at which he appeared terrified.

Perceiving the effect I had produced, I was determined to make it successful. I hastily seized an empty porter bottle, and elevating it, threatened to place him inside, and cork him up. I had no sooner declared my intention than he made a rapid retreat to the door, and ran with speed to the agent of the building, and with a troubled look, and frightened manner, stated that I intended to bottle him up. The agent—a worthy, amiable gentleman, and something of a wag—was well acquainted with his propensities, and being anxious to aid me in my efforts to prevent his interfering with my apparatus, replied:

"Well, man, if the signor said so, he will most certainly do it."

This so alarmed the janitor, that he hurried away, and no persuasion could induce him to attend the room during the remainder of my stay.

Several laughable events of a like character took place whilst I remained here, among which was the following:

THE TALKING HORSE.

One morning I accompanied a friend to a livery stable, for the purpose of purchasing a horse. After examining several, he inquired the price of one he concluded would suit.

"Twenty-five pounds," answered the owner.

"Too much," said the gentleman.

"No, he is a bargain—only nine years old," replied the stable-keeper.

"Don't cheat the gentleman, Davison," seemingly spoke the horse, in a sonorous tone, at the same instant shaking his mane.

The man looked around, supposing a fourth person was present. Perceiving his mistake, he commenced praising the animal in glowing terms, when he was again interrupted, seemingly by the horse saying—

"You have uttered more lies than I have eaten oats for a week."

"Who dares contradict my word?" cried the proprietor, in an excited manner, again turning his head to ascertain who was speaking.

"It is me," said the horse; "and you well know I am twenty years old, and blind of an eye."

Here the man became enraged, and was about to act brutally toward the beast, when I decided to interfere and unfold the deception. The announcement puzzled him beyond belief, and he laughed so heartily that it was many minutes before he could calm himself. My friend secured the animal, who was ever after celebrated as the talking horse.

After visiting many other places of note and interest, I desired to return to my native land, and pass a few days with my father.

I hastened to England, and having pleasantly settled my family in Manchester, in company with Gabriel I started for the village of my birth, where we arrived safely.

The surprise and pleasure that all experienced after an absence of nine years, the imagination of the reader can readily estimate.

During the few weeks I remained, I occupied myself in visiting every spot dear to memory. Time had made its changes. The mountains, hills, and rivulets were there, it is true; but the former appeared less high and the latter less deep and inviting. Old people had become *more* aged, the young grown to manhood, and many of both sexes had passed away; and, above all, the form of my dear mother was absent, which rendered the scene more

melancholy to my feelings; yet, for the sake of my surviv-
ing parent, I exhibited a cheerfulness I did not feel. The
day at last arrived for taking leave, perhaps forever, of my
father. Every arrangement for his future comfort was made,
and I took my departure. Words cannot express the character or grief of the separation—the heart only knows its
own bitterness. I reached Manchester alone—for Gabriel
remained to settle some personal matters—and found my
family anxiously awaiting me.

MANCHESTER.

In a few days I appeared before the "Cotton Kings."
As in all other places, I was received as one of the wonders
of the age; and, as my name and fame in necromancy had
preceded me, the curiosity of the people was awakened, and
in the family circle, as well as in public, my tricks and
performances were the absorbing topic. The people were
so amazed and delighted, that I was astonished at my
success.

A CLERGYMAN IN TROUBLE.

One morning a clergyman called upon me. After seat-
ing himself, he proceeded to communicate the object of his
visit by addressing me in the following manner:

"Signor Blitz, I am a minister of the Gospel in this
city, and I have solicited this interview to remonstrate with
you upon the impropriety and error of your ways. You are
leading thousands of poor sinners to Satan."

My reply was not violent, neither did I betray anger;
but, in a quiet tone, I requested him to explain more ex-
plicitly the nature and character of my evil doings.

He answered: "You are a necromancer—at war with
religion and morality; your feats are destructive and antag-
onistic to righteousness."

I inquired by what means I could support myself and family, in case I abandoned my profession, as I was totally unacquainted with any other pursuit. He slowly arose, and directing his hand toward my apparatus, which was distributed on several tables, replied in an animated tone,—

"Throw away that trumpery, Signor Blitz, and turn from wickedness to righteousness, for blessed are the good."

I answered that he was mistaken in regard to the sinful tendency of my art; that I was no evil spirit in form or principle; and, furthermore, my exhibitions were of a nature calculated to remove the long-prevailing impressions attached to the history of magic, by demonstrating to the mind that the rapidity of the hand, and the mechanical inventions of the nineteenth century, were more wonderful in effect than the mysteries of the ancient magicians; but, apart from this explanation, I would cheerfully listen to any advice he had to offer.

"Preach the Gospel, Signor Blitz, and live for heaven," said he.

Perceiving it was out of the question to convince him of the morality and propriety of my vocation, I determined to change my tactics, and exercise my craft by punishing the reverend gentleman for his unwarrantable assurance. Under the pretence, therefore, of regulating some machinery, I lifted a silver snuff-box containing rappee, which I, unperceived, slipped into the pocket of his coat. After a little time I requested him to excuse my terminating the discussion, as I expected some gentlemen by appointment, and I had some preparations to make before they arrived. He turned to take his leave, requesting to meet me the next day at eleven o'clock. No sooner had he reached the door, than I recalled him, and demanded the immediate return of my silver box.

STOP THIEF! STOP THIEF!

"I do not understand you, sir. I have no box," he replied.

"I understand *you* perfectly well, sir. You came here under the plea of preaching the Gospel, and stole my snuff-box."

He earnestly declared that I accused him falsely, for, on the sacred honor of a clergyman, he had no silver box, and, moreover, he never took snuff.

I said "such might be the case, but it was evident he had taken a snuff from my box, and by searching his coat I should learn the truth of my charge."

He immediately placed his hand in his pocket, and, discovering the box, his ruddy countenance assumed a pale hue, and every feature was convulsed and agitated; the very hair of his head appeared to leap with fear as he exclaimed—

"It is incomprehensible!"

I reminded him that as the box was surely found in his possession, it was my duty to deliver him in charge of an officer, to be committed for theft. He now became quite excited, and withdrew toward the door, still persisting in his honesty. I followed him, and, notwithstanding there were more than a dozen steps to descend, he made two jumps and landed on the first floor, during which I cried, "Stop thief!" to the utmost capacity of my lungs.

Many of my readers may construe the treatment I prescribed as unnecessarily severe; but, on reflection, this will appear less harsh, and infinitely more judicious, than insulting him by loud and angry words or more vigorous treatment. It is sufficient to say that the reverend gentleman did not present himself on the following day at the time appointed.

Manchester was, at this period, a very large commercial and manufacturing town, and every person seemed to be engaged in some mercantile or mechanical pursuit. As in all large cities, there were many very rich persons, and a much larger number of persons miserably poor and distressed. Several of these cases of poverty and suffering came under my personal observation, one of which, wherein I was deeply interested, I will relate:

How a Poll-Parrot Paid the Rent.

One day my attention was directed to a shop of rather humble appearance, from the circumstance of seeing the owner of it always sitting at his work, and a group of pretty, happy children playing about the floor, who, from the dark color of their dresses, were evidently motherless. I discovered from the sign over the door that the poor trades-man was named John Penny, and that he exercised the art and craft of boot and shoe making. He was tall and thin, with a rude visage, and long hair, combed straight down his cheeks; his countenance was thoughtful, not to say seri-ous, but there was an air of meek resignation about him very touching; and having a wife and family of my own, I gazed on the thoughtless children, and could not help thinking of my "ain Mary, and the wee bit bairns I left at hame." I found it impossible to resist giving poor Penny a turn, and to improve my "understandings" at the same time, by ordering a pair of boots. The humble tradesman, who was, as usual, at his work, gratefully acknowledged the order, but in answer to the very natural question—when I could have the boots, replied, with a deep sigh, that he did not exactly know; the order would be executed as soon as possible. From my knowledge of the world, I thought perhaps the poor fellow had not the means to purchase the materials, as there was a sad blank air of poverty about the shop.

"I will leave you half a sovereign as a deposit, only have them done as soon as possible," said I.

To my surprise John Penny refused to take my advance. "It will be time to pay when you get the boots," said he, significantly.

I was perplexed, and looked earnestly at the son of St. Crispin, whose countenance was more thoughtful, and his look more sorrowful than ordinarily.

"Don't think me impertinent," I said, "but is anything the matter; you seem unhappy."

"No, nothing in particular."

"Nay, nay, I'm convinced there is," I replied, my sympathy beginning to be much awakened; "come, tell me what it is."

"Well, sir, you are pressing," returned Penny, sighing deeply; "I will confess there is—my rent. I was one of the congregation of the Rev. Mr. Tramp, the minister of our local chapel. I am some back in my rent."

"You don't mean you were one of the Millerites?" I remarked, scarcely able to conceal a smile.

"I confess that I was," replied Penny. "I stood high in favor with that singularly pious man. All his congregation dealt with me for boots and shoes; I thought I had received a special call to furnish the jumpers with uppers and soles; but, alas! one fine morning the holy man was *translated* (so his followers called it), for he was nowhere to be found. This sad defalcation caused me to go back, and I could not meet my payments."

"Why, how much do you owe?" I inquired.

"I am now nearly three quarters in arrears; it will soon be upward of thirty pounds."

"Who is your landlord?"

"Why, Squire Summer."

"What, of the Legion Mills?"

"Yes."

"Why, he is one of the cotton lords, and very wealthy;

now, if I was to become your surety, would he give you time?"

"He has been very patient; I cannot complain of him; but he is a man of business—a man of money. Never having known want himself, he cannot conceive it to spring from any cause than improvidence, and therefore has little sympathy for me. The last time he was here he said he should call once more, and then, if the money was not forthcoming, the law must take its course. I expected him yesterday, and—"

"Eh, mercy, man! what's the matter with you?" I said. "You tremble."

"Yes, I see he is coming; he has that fellow Broadman, the broker, with him."

I looked out and saw, indeed, the squire, his footman, and a very shabby, suspicious-looking man, apparently an employee of the broker. I had scarcely time to cast a rapid glance around the scantily-furnished shop, and call my thoughts together, ere the party were at the door, and had entered.

"Let them come," cried Penny, with an air of despairing resignation. "I have struggled, Heaven knows, as long as I was able, and can do no more."

"Well, Mr. Penny," observed the squire, leisurely advancing to the counter, "you know of course the cause of my visit?"

Here a huge, staring poll-parrot, sitting in its cage, which formed one of the few articles of furniture in the shop, began to whistle "Call again to-morrow!" to the astonishment of all present, excepting myself, which she followed by, "I know a bank." The squire, however, resumed:

"You are of course provided, Mr. Penny?"

"Alas! no, sir," said the poor tradesman; "it is useless to deceive you any further. I cannot pay you at this moment, nor do I know how soon I can; take my little property; let it pay so far as it will; I will do the best I can. Providence will not forsake me."

"What's the time?" interrupted the parrot; "polly wants her breakfast."

The children, who had by this time stolen silently in, anxious to know what was going on, were as much surprised as their father at polly's sudden loquacity; their little round eyes dilated with wonder and twinkled with delight; but the awful presence of the great man somewhat repressed them.

" Well," continued the prudent man of cotton, after a short pause, "if that's the case, I may as well have the things as anybody else. John Broadman, you will do what is necessary."

"Polly! polly! polly!" here exclaimed poll.

" That's a fine bird," remarked the squire, his attention being attracted to it.

"I must leave a man in possession," said the broker; "but before I go, I may as well make out the inventory, for I suppose there is no chance of matters being settled without a sale, Mr. Penny?"

" None whatever."

" Then I'll proceed to my work at once. Item one, Dutch clock."

"What's o'clock? what's o'clock? Polly wants her breakfast," said the bird.

Poor Penny looked stupefied; the children, who had been regarding the scene, as I have said, half with curiosity, and half with fear, could not help clapping their hands at poll's way of talking; but a look from their father restrained them. Broadman continued:

" One high desk and counter; one chair; one shoemaker's bench and tools; three chairs; two tin candlesticks; six boot-trees—"

"Woodman, spare that tree," sang polly.

"Clever bird, that," said the squire. "You put the parrot down, I suppose, Mr. Broadman?"

"Oh, no, we never mention her," sang the parrot, twisting her head very knowingly.

"Answers quite like a Christian, and seems to understand everything," said the squire.

"What's o'clock?" cried Poll.

"Wonderful, upon my honor," ejaculated the squire. "Now I think of it," said he, "my daughter Cecilia has been worrying my life out the last six months to get her such a bird as this; one that can talk, sing, and whistle. I'll tell you what I'll do, Penny: I don't want to be hard upon you; let me have the parrot, and give me a note of hand for ten pounds balance, and I'll withdraw the distress, and give a receipt for fifteen pounds."

"Don't you wish you may get it," saucily chattered poll, as if she understood what the landlord was talking about.

"Such a bird as that is worth more money," I observed. "I'll give that much myself."

"Whistle and I'll come to thee, my lad," whistled poll.

"Wonderful!" said the squire. "I must have that bird; I'll take it as payment for the rent in full. Penny, will that suit you?"

Poor Penny seemed thunderstruck; he hesitated as if he had some compunction. The squire observed it, and quickly said:

"That's not enough? Well, then, I'll make it twenty pounds. Here's a receipt for the rent, and there's five sovereigns—will that do for you? Broadman, withdraw your man."

"You don't lodge here, Mr. Ferguson, with your ninepence," added polly.

The squire was delighted; I thought the arrangement honorable to all parties, and poor Penny, apparently unwilling, delivered the bird to the squire.

"Good-by, poll," cried all the children.

"Good-by! 'My native land, good night!'" sang poll, appearing very grave, and turning her head first on one side and then on the other, placing herself in her swing and violently rocking backward and forward, seeming to give the signal for her departure.

As soon as the shop was fairly clear of the squire's party, Penny turned to me, and with an air of perplexity, begged I would look in the following morning, when he would have some skins from which I could choose the leather for my boots, for, just at that moment, he felt quite bewildered.

Highly delighted that John Penny had got so well through his difficulties, I did not intrude, but considerately took my leave. I was, however, a punctual visitor at John's the following morning, and found the honest cordwainer had laid out the five pounds he received over and above his rent the preceding afternoon to the very best advantage. He had stocked his shop with a good supply of leather and other articles necessary for his trade, and now only wanted customers.

While I was selecting the material for my boots, the squire suddenly made his appearance, followed by his footman, bearing poll.

"Well, Mr. Penny," said the great cotton lord, "we have brought back your parrot, and it is very extraordinary that it has never spoken a single word since I took it away, —never sung a single song, nor whistled a single tune; it has done nothing but squeak, squeak, and scream, till my head has been ready to burst; in fact, without any wish to offend you, she is a perfect nuisance. Return me the five pounds I paid you, and I'll forfeit the rent."

"I am sorry to say," said the conscientious John Penny, "that I have laid out the five pounds; but, however, as the bird don't suit you, if you will take my note of hand for the five pounds—"

"Why, stay! stay!" I said. "Parrots very seldom talk in a strange place at first. Put poll in her usual place, and then see."

The cage was accordingly restored to its former place, when, to the utter astonishment of all present, poll immediately began to sing—"Home, sweet home; be it ever so humble, there is no place like home."

"Well, I declare!" said the squire, lifting up his hands, "this is wonderful; but I've heard of such things before. What a sensible, intelligent creature she is! I must give her another trial. Take her back, John."

"I'll gang nae mair to yon town," whistled poll; but, however, to no effect, for she was borne off, crying, "What's o'clock? what's o'clock?"

"You appear to be surprised at my amazement, sir," said honest John Penny, when the party was out of sight, "but will not be so long, when I tell you that until yesterday, I never heard that bird utter a single syllable. As Mr. Sumner has said, she had never done anything but squeal and scream, disturbing the whole neighborhood; but they got used to it at last, although they threatened at first to break my windows and wring her neck. It was a long time before I could get to like it myself; but use reconciles us to anything, and I think now I shall miss her, disagreeable as she was."

I called again the next morning, and while there, who should appear but Squire Sumner, accompanied, as on the previous day, by his man, with poll.

"Bless me, sir!" said Penny; "is it you?"

"Yes, Mr. Penny, I have come again," returned the

squire, "with this diabolical bird, for not a moment's peace have we had."

"What! do you find her too talkative, sir?" inquired the shoemaker, with great simplicity.

"Talk too much! Why, the obstinate brute—confound her—she has never talked at all! Put her in her old place again, John."

"Don't I look spruce on my noddy?" whistled poll.

"You have found your tongue, have you?" said the squire; "but I am not to be done a third time. Keep your bird, Mr. Penny; I wish you joy of her."

"But I have spent the money you gave me for her," said honest John, "and I don't know when I shall be able to pay it back again."

"Oh! never mind the money; only release me from such a torment as this, and I'll put up with the loss the best way I can."

Poor John was somewhat reluctantly prevailed upon to take back the bird, and as soon as the squire had departed, and was fairly out of hearing, said, "It's an ill wind that blows nobody any good. Had I not been seized for my rent, my parrot *might never have spoken.*"

I could not refrain from having a good laugh, as I disclosed the secret to Penny, and explained to him how I, as a ventriloquist, had talked and whistled instead of the bird, and, as it appeared, to a very good purpose.

"I see it all," said John. "May God bless you!"

AN AERIAL VOYAGE.

My nature from childhood had always sympathized with the spirit of adventure, and love of romantic truth. The history of travellers, on sea or land, deeply interested me, especially if connected with peril and dangers. I had long wished to ascend the heavenly dome and behold its magnitude, unknown or invisible to the natural world, and wander in the midst of its ethereal beauties.

The opportunity of gratifying my desire presented itself, when exhibiting at Kidderminster, a town in Worcestershire, noted for its great carpet factories. Here, in company with Mr. Green, the celebrated aeronaut, and a companion, I took an aerial voyage.

It was the closing day of summer, at the hour of four, P.M., accompanied by the cheers of a vast concourse of people, that we ascended toward the broad canopy of that infinite and unknown space, so incomprehensible to the understanding. The sun, though declining toward its western home, was resplendent with beauty and glory, its rays illuminating the whole horizon with golden tints of soft and mellow light. The view, far and near, was a natural and beautiful picture. The mountains and rivers, the villages and towns, the green fields, the streams in their winding course, all gave a rich harmony to the scene, and indelibly impressed the mind with the mightiness of the Great Omnipotent. I have not the descriptive powers to portray in a graphic manner the panoramic view. My feelings were varied, mingled with awe and solemnity, especially as we receded from earth and its familiar objects, and beheld their pigmy aspect.

As the balloon gracefully floated away into spheres unknown, this prospect, so lovely and sublime, ultimately faded into obscurity. With what impulsive thoughts and inspirations I gazed on the fleecy clouds, as we pierced their ethereal vapor, under the pilotage of Mr. Green, whose pleasant and communicative disposition aided much to relieve apprehension and strengthen our confidence as the frail bark rose majestically and buoyantly through masses of mist, and the most variable elements and temperature, creating imaginary presentments of the most unavoidable and gravest sensations. Upward and onward we continued our journey, directing our course to all points of the compass, occasionally ascending through clouds so dense, we were imperceptible to each other, passing with rapidity from thick and gloomy atmospheres to those of pure, transparent light.

After an hour of unbroken and sightless travel, we commenced our return to "mother earth," the first glimpse of which gladdened me exceedingly, and the nearer we approached, the more magnificent the landscape appeared.

The sun had considerably fallen, spreading his broad beams of amber brightness over tree-tops and hill-sides, and the rivers and brooks were especially lovely in their reflections. We ultimately landed in a fruit orchard, the proprietor of which was a gentleman farmer, and, as a singular incident, was celebrating the fifteenth anniversary of his wedding-day. A large party was assembled, and at the time of our sudden descent, were in the midst of their mundane pleasures, drinking the choicest wine to the health of their host and hostess. We were congratulated on the safe ending of our perilous journey, and welcomed with great hospitality. After a pleasant interview with the gentleman and his guests, during which we were regaled with delicious refreshments, we returned, in a carriage drawn by four horses, to Kidderminster, a distance of twelve miles, which place we reached after an hour of rapid driving. When we had paraded through crowded streets, we alighted at the town hall, where I was welcomed by a large audience, before whom I gave my usual entertainment, with a description of our aerial voyage.

I MEET A FRIEND.

Some years subsequent to this event, I was performing in the city of Worcester, the capital of the county, and one day was invited to dine with the governor of the prison,

5

who was a person of position and large income. When I entered the jail, and was passing to the family apartments, I was suddenly accosted by a voice from behind an iron grating, calling me by name.

"Ah! Signor Blitz! how are you; do you not remember me?"

"No," I replied, "I have not the pleasure of recollecting your countenance."

"Why, Signor, when we met before, it was under more agreeable circumstances."

"Ah, sir, pray where was that? What is your name?"

"You landed in a balloon, Signor, in my orchard, while I was celebrating the return of my wedding-day. I was a rich man at that time, but reverses of fortune have brought me here."

"It pains me to hear it. How did it occur, sir?"

"By indorsing for friends. I lost all I possessed, and am now here, an insolvent debtor."

This little episode destroyed the pleasure of my visit, as well as my appetite for dinner, for it recalled to mind the former affluence of this gentleman, and led me to reflect upon the mutability of all things in life.

Another incident, singular in its character, connected with the balloon, which may amuse my readers, I will relate:

Personal Jokes.

I dined at the house of Mr. Cartwright, at Stoke, in Staffordshire, where I met several distinguished gentlemen. After dinner I was solicited to exhibit some specimens of my art. One of the company, the Rev. Mr. Vale, of the Episcopal Church in that neighborhood, seemed very much amused, and inquired to what locality I expected to be assigned in the next world.

"To heaven," I responded.

"Oh! no, I fear not, after witnessing your *magic* power."

I again asserted that I felt convinced I should finally reach that spot, as I had already travelled farther in that direction than any gentleman present probably ever would. The whole party here exclaimed—

"No, Signor; oh! no, Signor!"

"Yes," I replied, "it is so, I am very sure; for I have been in a balloon for miles above the earth."

"So has Mr. Vale!" they all proclaimed, with much merriment.

"Is that so?" I asked, addressing Mr. Vale.

"Perfectly true, Signor; and when I crossed the river Severn, I could see myself reflected as in a mirror, so powerful was the sun!"

"Oh! that is nothing, Mr. Vale, to my experience, for we approached so near the sun, *that it scorched my hair!*"

This relation of mine produced roars of laughter, and entitled me to the honor of having reached nearest the all-desired haven. Mr. Vale was a highly cultivated gentleman, of great learning and force of character, and has since become a distinguished light of the Church. His parishioners, at the time he made his excursion in the balloon, contributed the necessary means to pay the expenses, and the following Sunday he delivered a beautiful and scientific discourse upon the heavenly bodies, and their inseparable identity with the wisdom and power of God.

CHAPTER XI.

HAT liberality, as a general rule, produces its legitimate effects and influences, cannot be questioned. The greater number of good actions we perform, and the more we sympathize with the sorrows, trials, and afflictions of our fellow-men, the more enlarged will be our happiness and reward. Kindness is a balm, and at times it is infinitely more precious than gold.

These observations have been provoked by the following incidents, which, though they may not interest my readers, will yet enable them to distinguish good sense and wisdom from the pharisaical disciplinarian.

My eldest son was born in Newcastle-upon-Tyne, and shortly after was christened in St. Andrew's Church, of that city, which was kindly opened for that purpose. At the conclusion of the ceremony, I repaired to the vestry to register the event, at the conclusion of which I shook hands with the rector, at the same time passing him an English sovereign.

"What's this, Signor?" he inquired, as he unrolled the paper containing it. "Here, take back your gold, Signor, and send me half a dozen tickets."

This liberal pastor made a deep impression upon my

mind, and he evidently would have made me a better man, from his unprejudiced construction and patronage of my professional life.

The Opposite Picture.

My second son's birth took place at Exeter, and he was christened at St. Sidwell's Church.

The officiating clergyman was of a different disposition from the former, less tolerant, more bigoted and dictatorial. He descanted upon the generosity of the age in permitting the child of a *necromancer* to be received into the sanctuary of God; that in times past the dogmas of the Church did not acquiesce in the spirit, but viewed with doubtful character the presence of all those whose professional antecedents were considered at variance with religion and morals, and for some time continued in this strain; notwithstanding which he did not refuse the customary fee, preferring the *magician's gold* to his tickets !

Individual Oddities.

The oddities of the human race are proverbial. The whole world is noted for them. In every path of life and society they are visible. The good and bad, old and young, rich and poor, *all* betray a singularity of thought and action, or some equivalent to its claim, which attracts attention; but this aptitude not unfrequently develops a sordid caprice, an omen of a faulty spirit, ever prepared to declaim upon individuality and its eccentricities; truly forgetting how prominently their own oddities are exhibited to those whom *they* specify as "peculiar."

Society is comprised of odd people, in dress, movements, appearances, amusements, and the generalities which give notability; and I know of none more so than the following:

A Wig Regiment.

During my perambulations, I met, on several occasions, the 4th Irish Dragoons. The officers were gentlemen of independent means, and much given to pleasure and diversion.

There was a social freedom in their general deportment, unusual and remarkable for their position, which procured in return respect and popularity. Several of them were admirable amateur magicians, extravagantly devoted to the art, their proficiency never failing to produce enjoyment and effect, and as I had frequently been their instructor, my personal relations with them were of a most cordial nature, not subject to any special rule of etiquette, so usual in the English army.

The colonel who commanded was a Scotchman, a strict disciplinarian in all military matters, a constructionist in the extreme; but when not occupied with military duties, was greatly disposed to mirth in all its varieties. His nature betrayed all the kindred characteristics of his nation, being intelligent, of good judgment, and with a courteous demeanor. From my first acquaintance with the officers, the peculiarities of their hair amazed me not a little. To-day, one had a beautiful brown hair, another was remarkable for its blackness, a third, for its lighter shade; but on the following day the colors of each head would be so metamorphosed that I could scarcely satisfy myself respecting the identity of the persons. I reasoned whether it was on my part a fantasy—an imaginary speculation—or one of those optical illusions the eye is susceptible of. Day after day these phenomena continued: he of the black head yesterdry, was brown to-day; and the one of the brown, became black, while the lighter shade had also changed. All my endeavors to discover by what skill or process they accomplished the novelty of their appearance were fruitless. There were no visible indications that these displays were false, neither was the chameleon mystery confined to any given number, for every officer connected with the regiment enjoyed the wonderful facility of transforming the hair of his head at option. The whole circumstance was an enigma, the solution of which would never, perhaps, have been explained, but for the following incident:

A party was given in the mess-room at the barracks. The company was limited in number, but a memorable one for its admirable humor, spirit, and cultivated conversation; each contributing to its hilarity, which, of course, I participated in.

I gave numerous illustrations in magic and ventriloquism, and the colonel expressed a desire that the officers would unite and astonish me with a particular feat, original, and known only to themselves. There was a ready, and almost studied acquiescence to the invitation.

They all arose and bowed. I was requested to turn my head, and, at a given signal, face the assembly again; I did so, and beheld the most grotesque sight I ever witnessed. Imagine the droll appearance of twenty gentlemen attired in military dress, of various years and proportions, with heads perfectly—bald! without a vestige or evidence of their ever having been graced with that ornamental appendage—hair. I more than laughed: I was convulsed. It was a comical combination—a barbarous picture of invention, one that I never had encountered before!

I gazed upon the whimsical and extraordinary scene, until my risabilities were provoked beyond control.

I was again desired to turn from them, and then renew my observation, when lo! they were again decorated with handsome heads of hair, which, while it amused and astonished me, revealed the great secret that had so much perplexed my imagination in regard to the colors of these remarkable heads!

" Is not this equal to any of *your* wizard tricks, Signor? " inquired the colonel.

" Yes, sir, quite so ; completely ahead of me."

The affair was a rich and excitable exhibition of oddity on the part of the officers, the object of which being a mere notional freak, for the love of variety and creating a sensation, had induced them to the Vandalism of having their heads shaved, in order to appear as they best wished, adorned in different manufactured hair ; and ever after I never failed, when relating the anecdote, to term her Majesty's 4th Dragoons the " Wig Regiment "—an appellation they were so meritoriously entitled to.

PICTURE OF A RICH MAN.

At Newcastle, in the potteries, I received a special invitation from the Marchioness of Stafford, to give a private entertainment at Trentham Hall, a favorite country residence of this distinguished family, where a numerous and fashionable party of nobility were visiting.

The wealth of the Marquis was almost fabulous ; in every part of England and the British dominions, or wherever an Englishman was known to reside, his immense riches were recognized and commented upon. I had frequently listened to the stories that were circulated in regard to his more than princely fortune with surprise ; and who would not, on learning that one single man was in receipt of six thousand dollars per day, or nearly four dollars and seventeen cents a minute, without any contingency.

My accepting the engagement had a twofold object—an ambition to appear in the presence of society so noble, and a peculiar curiosity to behold (at that time) the richest man in the world. Being but a youth, my faculties were greatly exercised in regard to worldly possessions. I concluded, in my unsophisticated opinion, that these very fortunate inheritors of untold means must be happiness personified, and were totally exempt from sickness or grief; that pain, sorrow, and affliction were unknown, and that the drapery of mourning never entered their homes.

In accordance with previous arrangements, I proceeded to the mansion in advance of the hour, and was received by the marchioness with much grace and affability. The exhibition took place in the grand entrance-hall, which was very spacious. A number of large screens were drawn through the centre, to within a short distance of my table. On one side were seated the lords and ladies; on the opposite, the domestics of the establishment; so that, while neither party could be observed by the other, they all had ample opportunity of witnessing my performances.

When the nobility made their appearance, a more brilliant company of elegance and beauty never met my eyes. Their dignified bearing, with the gorgeous dresses and sparkling jewels, produced the most pleasing effect. But my attention was especially directed to the marquis, a plain, quiet-looking gentleman of seventy years or more; small in stature, with a constitution so broken and feeble, that he was quite unable either to take a seat at the commencement, or leave it at the close, without assistance. He smiled gently, while all others laughed heartily; he appeared surprised, the rest bewildered; they looked cheerful and happy, he calm and reflective. Having concluded, I received marked approbation and congratulations from all; but my vanity, and the strange impressions arising from his presence, induced me to inquire of the Marquis if I had afforded him any amusement. He replied in a soft tone that he had enjoyed the wonders I produced very much. "They were inexplicable, and very mysterious." For several minutes

I was absorbed in thought, and with difficulty I could realize the person before me to be the great millionaire, who was so bent and helpless that, notwithstanding his vast estates, he could not command or resist the current course of Nature's laws; that neither his gold nor silver could prolong his life a single day or moment; but, like the poor and humble, must yield his spirit to the invisible Conqueror of man. These, and a thousand other thoughts, rapidly occupied my mind, and so completely changed my previous views as to the importance and true appreciation of money, that I could not help comparing my own favored condition with the important personage before me. If I had not his titles and immense wealth, yet was I blessed with health, and youth; with a buoyancy and hope of long life, and with talents and energy to provide for the immediate necessities of my loved ones; for God in His goodness had considered me deserving of those gifts, and I trusted my return would merit His acceptance; for he who seeks Him in sunshine, will never fail to receive His love and care in the hour of darkness.

After partaking of refreshments, and having enjoyed a pleasant conversation with most of the company, I left.

Among those present were the Duke of Wellington; Earl and Countess of Gower; Earl and Countess of Wilton; Lord Sandon, and many of the resident gentry.

The following morning I received a handsome enclosure, with the annexed letter:

"TRENTHAM, August 10, 1831.

"I very willingly express the satisfaction the performance of Signor Blitz has given to the party who witnessed here his superior dexterity and surprising ingenuity this evening. His talent was agreed to excel any similar instance witnessed by those present.   "STAFFORD."

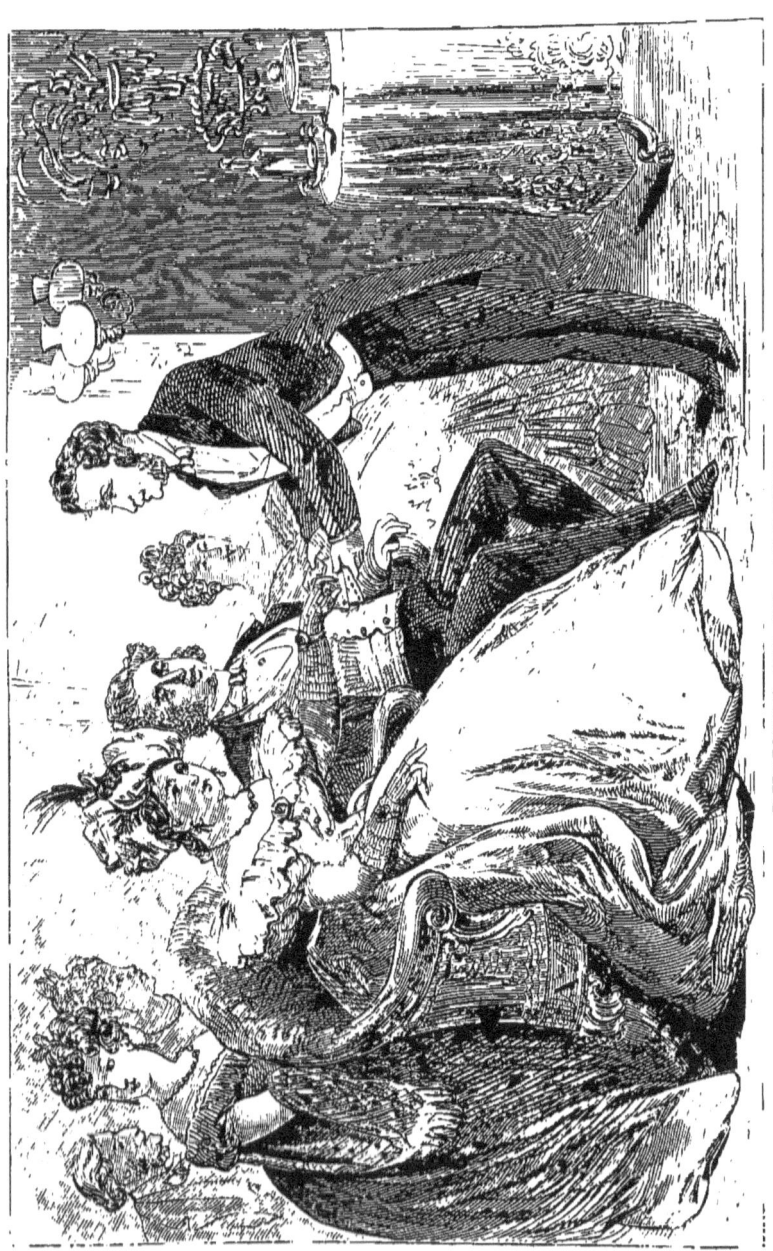

DUCHESS OF ST. ALBANS.

During my performances in Cheltenham, I was invited by the Duchess of St. Albans to give a private exhibition at her residence.

This lady was formerly "Miss Mellon," an actress of celebrity and merit, who afterward became the wife of Mr. Coutts, the eminent London banker, and subsequently married the Duke of St. Albans. This union, it was said, was eagerly courted on both sides—the one for title, the other for money.

The company on this occasion comprised dukes, lords, and ladies. My feats gave an agreeable satisfaction, and provoked much merriment. One produced an astonishing effect. I requested her Grace to draw a card from a pack, and, after destroying it, to retain *one* piece, which she complied with. The card she selected was, accidentally, a king. The remaining pieces were placed in a box, when, to the surprise of every one, it appeared *completely* repaired, with the exception of the piece in the possession of the duchess, *which was the head*, and on being compared with the card, corresponded correctly.

Her Grace manifested her surprise by exclaiming to the Duke of Gloucester, who sat by her side, "How singular, your Royal Highness, that I should behead a king!"

The duke looked grave, and asked "if it was ominous?"

"Hope not," she quickly replied.

This circumstance created the deepest feeling. Every countenance betokened intensity of thought, and all eyes looked prophetic. These feelings were influenced by the events then transpiring. Charles the Tenth of France had but recently abdicated his throne; Belgium had seceded from Holland; in fact, the whole of Europe was in a state of revolution and alarm. Even in England, political discontent and incendiary fires prevailed from one end of the country to the other. Her Grace was a large, majestic-looking lady, dressed in rich black velvet, with a stomacher, and an immense necklace and earrings of diamonds; also, buttons of the same adorned her dress from throat to hem. She wore a turban, which was literally covered with brilliants. Her hands sparkled with like gems, and her whole person was such a blaze of light, that it was painful to the eye! She was affable and courteous in her manner toward me, and her general character liberal and kind.

I received the following letter, enclosing a valuable souvenir from the duchess:

"Suffolk Lawn, Cheltenham,
"September 2, 1833.

"Signor Blitz has this evening performed his numerous and very ingenious tricks of legerdemain before the Duke and Duchess of St. Albans, and a numerous circle of friends, and afforded them much amusement and astonishment.

"St. Albans."

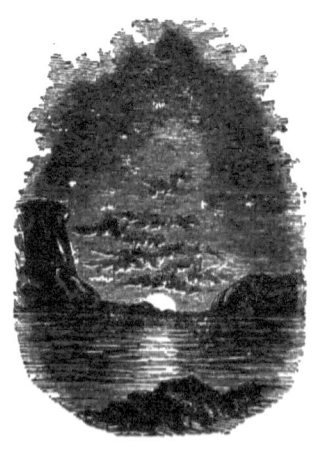

CHAPTER XII.

 Y farewell *soirées* were given at Liverpool, a large commercial city, and the principal seaport of Great Britain. The natural advantages of the city were many, which, combined with the liberal spirit of the citizens, caused its rapid improvement.

My exhibitions were successful, and engrossed general attention; but while all admired the adroitness I displayed, there were not a few who favored my being arrested for arts of sorcery and unnatural feats. There was no limit to the discussion as to my origin, and the actual character I assumed, and by reason of the interest I had created, my success was very satisfactory, and I continued for a long period to enjoy the fruits of a brilliant engagement.

For many months I had entertained the idea of proceeding to the United States; and as many Americans were constantly arriving at this port, I had frequent opportunities of conversing with them upon the subject, and in every instance received the most flattering inducements to visit their democratic and growing country. I consulted my wife, who approved of the enterprise, and induced me to make all preparations for that purpose.

I wrote to Gabriel, urging him to join me in the undertaking, and to my father I addressed an affectionate farewell,

Gabriel replied that it was impossible for him to accompany me so great a distance. His health and business affairs compelled him reluctantly to decline. My father betrayed great sorrow.

All arrangements having been completed, I engaged passage for myself, wife, two children, and two servants, on the packet ship "Columbus," of the old Black Ball line, commanded by Captain N. Cobb. On the first day of August, 1834, we left the dock at Liverpool, a large number of my friends being present to give me a cheering adieu, and wishes for the full realization of my hopes.

The passengers numbered between forty and fifty, and among the most prominent were a Catholic bishop of Mexico, on his return from Rome; Dr. Codman, a Congregational clergyman of Dorchester, Mass., and a Mississippi major.

The prelate was tall and thin, quiet in his movements, and modest in appearance; while the doctor was a fine, robust man.

On one occasion the bishop invited Dr. Codman, myself, and a few others into his stateroom, to examine his Pontifical robes, which were very rich and elegant. The doctor admired them very much, and jocosely asked how we thought *he* would appear in them. Having gained the consent of the bishop, we urged the doctor to put them on, which request he good naturedly complied with, and walked around in his peculiarly majestic style, much to our and his own amusement. He was truly a model in appearance for a pope. The only regret connected with the circumstance was, that the amiable doctor's congregation in Dorchester could not have the pleasure of seeing him so attired.

PORTRAIT OF A MISSISSIPPI MAJOR.

The major was a well-proportioned man, with an unprepossessing countenance, original in his actions, unamiable and unhappy in his temperament. He was uncouth, frightfully blasphemous, addicted to strong drinks, carried a huge bowie-knife, and disliked all mankind—which feeling was fully reciprocated by all.

He left New York, and after a three weeks' residence in Europe, returned in the same ship. He had been the proprietor of a plantation, with a large number of slaves, which he sold for bills of exchange on England. These he converted into gold, and had the full amount in his stateroom, packed in two large wooden boxes. He gave me the following account of his travels:

After his arrival in Liverpool, where he remained but one day, he proceeded to London, which place he reached at night. The following morning he engaged a carriage, in which he rode the whole day, looking at the public buildings, without entering the interior of any one! Concluding he had seen all the objects and sights worthy of notice, he left, the same night, for Edinburg, where he seated himself in one of the principal hotels, with his feet extended through an open window, and employed a Scotch bag-piper to play Yankee Doodle and the Star Spangled Banner for many hours, much to the annoyance of the people. One day satisfied his restless spirit, and he left Scotland for Liverpool, procured his gold, and, with the captain's permission, guarded it in person on board the ship, which he was fully able to do.

The importance he attached to his foreign visit was amusing, and ludicrous in the extreme. In his opinion, he had acquired an intimate knowledge of England, her institutions and people, toward whom his hostility was bitter, declaring he would prefer being a slave in Mississippi, than a freeman in the Old Country.

Previous to my visiting this country, many of my friends and relatives endeavored to dissuade me from leaving Europe, representing that America was wild and uncultivated, the society very indifferent, while outrages upon person and property were unlimited: but such arguments did not stop me.

Arrival in New York.

We arrived off Staten Island in the early part of September. The day was beautiful in the extreme, and Nature must have been sensible of the importance—to me—of the occasion, for she appeared decorated in all her varieties. The summer had passed, and the lovely autumn was everywhere putting forth the beauties of its season. Each object the eye gazed upon seemed animated, and uttered a welcome to the stranger; majestic trees courtesied to the soft and balmy wind, while the chanting of distant birds, mingling with the farewell and return songs of the sailors, as the various ships passed out and in, gave life and animation to the occasion.

The number of fine residences erected in elevated positions, surrounded by willows, weeping forth thanks to the Creator of heaven and earth, was a sublime view.

New York was at this time a city of great magnitude, and rapidly increasing. The eye could not fail to perceive her unsurpassed geographical advantages, or the mind wonder at the destiny which awaited her. The hurried footsteps of the people, their spirited manner of dealing, and general urbanity to strangers, aided greatly in distinguishing the marked traits between the inhabitants of the Old and New World. To me, the paramount object of life appeared to be *speed in conversation and action.* At meal or bedtime, the same characteristic prevailed, and in a brief period I myself became from an European walk Americanized to the *racing proclivities* so popular, and I may observe, necessary for success in this nation. The business capacities of all classes, the *sang-froid* with which they applied themselves to circumstances, strikingly surprised me, as likewise did their perpetual industry.

The constant arrival of shipping from all parts of the world, the countless number of drays and carts in constant motion, laden with home and foreign productions, and the crowded "Broadway," made a lasting impression.

"Young America" at this day was less matured, or at least he had not the giant semblance of the present, yet daily betrayed the element was progressing. The following event, I feel assured, will add much to confirm this view:

"Young America."

One evening I was standing at the corner of a street, smoking, when a youth approached me, holding a huge black cigar in his hand, and requested a light, which I refused, expressing my astonishment, and pleasantly advising him to discontinue the use of tobacco, for it was injurious to one so young, and would ultimately affect his health.

He replied "that it would not, for he was now *nine years old*, and had smoked two and three cigars a day for two years."

I inquired the price he paid for them, and who supplied him with the money.

He answered, "My father allows me twenty-five cents a week, and I pay one cent each. Try one," said he, removing his cap from his head, and taking out three.

"No, thank you, boy, your generosity and extravagance exceed your morals."

"Oh, it is time enough to leave off, sir, when older people do," he quickly retorted.

At this moment a gentleman passed us smoking. The boy immediately turned toward him and solicited that which I had denied. His request was granted, and he pompously

walked away, clouds of smoke issuing from his lips sufficient
to astonish a veteran in the art.

The hall accommodations in New York were inconvenient, for the only one of any magnitude I could obtain was
Masonic Hall, on Broadway, opposite the hospital. At this
place I made my *début* before an American audience. The
public places of amusement then open to the citizens, were
the Park and Bowery Theatres, and Niblo's Garden. Notwithstanding the novelty of my entertainments had been
anticipated in a measure by Monsieur Adrien, a very talented and ingenious Frenchman, I experienced the most
unbounded success and flattering countenance from the inhabitants at large; but, while I was patronized for my ability
to please and astonish, there was, with a very slight exception,
a total absence of an approach to the superstitious character
which had constantly marked my progress through the
"Old Country."

For weeks and months I continued the recipient of
crowded houses. The practical magician was but little understood. The great improvements in mechanical inventions, the elaborate perfection and effect with which feats
were presented to the audiences, produced much sensation,
and established the superiority of the modern performers,
so that in a brief time professors of magic arose in abundance. Adriens and Blitzes were represented in all parts
of the country. This circumstance is to be explained from
the supposition that the business was profitable, and capable
of being successfully pursued. Frequently my identity
has been disputed when I have visited the different towns
and cities professionally. In later years this has proved an
incalculable annoyance, there being not less than thirteen
people travelling the country using my name and profession,
circulating a verbatim copy of my handbill and advertise-
ment—not only assuming to be the *original* Blitz, but in

many instances claiming to be a son or nephew. I have been in constant receipt of bills of their contracting, for, not content with taking my name, they have not even honor enough to pay their debts. The thirteen now travelling in the United States exhibit under the following, and other names:

> Signor Blitz.
> Signor Blitz, Jr.
> Signor Blitz, The Original.
> Signor Blitz's Son.
> Signor Blitz's Nephew.
> Signor Blitz, The Great.
> Signor Blitz, The Wonderful.
> Signor Blitz, The Unrivalled.
> Signor Blitz, The Mysterious.
> Signor Blitz, By Purchase.
> Signor Blitz, The Great Original.

The greatest annoyance attending the movements of these impostors was, and is yet, the constant flood of writs, judgments, and bills served upon me for payment, or to enforce payment of claims these men had contracted and neglected to settle. Such demands have proved sorely grievous, from the fact that I have ever adopted the rule of promptly discharging all my professional indebtedness.

The peculiarities of these debts, and the letters addressed to me, betray a wonderful faculty for obtaining credit, and a not less singular determination to make me responsible for their liquidation. I will give a few specimens of their demands:

"NEW YORK, April 10, 1860.

"SIGNOR BLITZ—*Sir:* I am requested to enter suit against you for bill of groceries, amounting to ($84.68) eighty-four dollars and sixty-eight cents.   Said bill purchased of J. Downing, of this city.

"O. Brown, Attorney."

"New York, September 5, 1861.

"Signor Blitz—The enclosed bill of ($206.50) two hundred six dollars and fifty cents is for furnishing goods, obtained of G. Smith. If not attended to immediately, I shall enter suit for the same.

"William Baker."

"New York, April 25, 1863.

"Signor Blitz—*Dear Sir:* I am desired by my client to proceed against you for $211.16, for Brussels carpets furnished at your house, which you have previously received a bill of.   Yours respectfully,

"J. Wilton."

When I last exhibited in New York, in 1868, I was waited upon by an officer of the gas company for an unpaid bill of $100.   This was the more singular, as such corporations are not proverbial for trusting.   One evening, at the close of my performance, I was served with a writ for two notes of $300 each, given for rent of dwelling-house, on which judgment had been obtained.   The poor landlord lost his money; for of course I did not pay it.   There were many others of a similar purport constantly presented me for payment.

These letters are but a few of the hundreds that are in my possession, which came, and are still coming, from different cities and States—New York particularly.   Some of the writers of the legal ones are exceedingly persistent in their supposed claims, convinced beyond all doubt that I was "The" Blitz they wanted; and in several instances they required my photograph, after sending which, I heard nothing further from them. So, with halls, printing offices, and stores, I have been inundated with bills, and not unfrequently, in places where I have visited for the first time, I have been denied my own personality, and termed "Bogus," in consequence of statements made to that effect by *misrepresentatives*. For all this annoyance, I have no appeal but by a legal injunction, and, before it could be completed, the band of Blitzes are enabled to remove to distant parts, out of the jurisdiction of the court; and even if they could be convicted, they are so entirely destitute of pecuniary substance, that damages could never be recovered. But that is of the least importance, the question at issue being, whether men can with impunity defame and bring odium upon the name and character of whom they please. This is the difficulty to solve, for, while it is in fact obtaining money under false pretences, it is unfortunate for me that the law is not less intricate in its protecting powers, rather than that it should favor evil-doers.

The following is one of the many instances of the too ready adaptation of American character, for it illustrates their versatility and ability for change: ·

A MAN IN SEARCH OF BUSINESS.

I was acquainted with a person in New York City, who was the proprietor of a shoe-store, which, a few months after, he exchanged for a grocery establishment; but finding the duties laborious, and the profits small, in a little time he sold out and opened a bookstore, a close attention to which satisfied him that he was unacquainted with the general literature of the day, consequently he would be unsuccessful, and in the short space of five weeks he sold out the stock and lease of the premises, and in fourteen days after, associated himself as partner in a dry-goods house. Experience soon convinced him that the income was inadequate for the support of two families, so, without delay, he disposed of his interest, and became proprietor of a furniture warehouse. This was a branch of trade that did not give the necessary employment to one of an active temperament, and with great despatch he closed the same, and opened an exchange or broker's office,—a business requiring more mental knowledge than labor, and which had become exceedingly lucrative. He continued in this business for many years, retiring with a large fortune. That man, after a long search, found his proper vocation, and was certainly rewarded for his energy and perseverance.

An Aspiring Waiter.

A yet more striking instance of American persistence will be developed by an amusing anecdote, related to me by the proprietor of one of the principal hotels in Boston:

During one of those unbroken winters peculiar to the New England climate, when ice forms early in the season, and snow clothes the whole surface of the earth, leaving no green spot for the eye to gaze upon, a young man, twenty-four years of age, applied to the landlord for the situation of waiter, stating that wages were less an object to him than a permanent home during the severity of the season; sufficient money for necessary clothing would be all he should require. Arrangements were agreed upon, and he was to receive a compensation of eight dollars per month, with board and washing. At the expiration of the first month, when the landlord paid him the above sum, he expressed a wish to converse with him in private, on special business; and, entering an adjoining room, the following conversation took place:

Waiter. "Mr. ——, have you any desire to sell out? if so, can we make terms?"

Landlord. "Why? have you been commissioned by any person?"

"Oh, no; only I think, from the little time I have been in the house, I could succeed very well as landlord. I like the location, and believe I can save money here."

"Have you friends who will assist you in the purchase? The rent is four thousand dollars yearly, and my furniture, wines, and goodwill I estimate at fourteen thousand."

"No, I have neither friends or money, save this,"—producing the eight dollars—"but give me time, the same way I presume you commenced. So, if you are disposed to leave, I should like to enter upon the business with the least possible delay."

It is not necessary to state the refusal of the landlord, or the improbability of his quitting the establishment under such prospects. The following day, the young aspirant left the house, and in eighteen months from the date of this conversation, was keeping one of the most extensive and fashionable hotels in the Western States, from which he has realized wealth and popularity.

THE AMBITIOUS OFFICE SEEKER.

As an evidence of their readiness on all occasions to assume important situations, I will relate a proceeding which occurred during Mr. Van Buren's administration of national affairs:

At the meeting of Congress, a statement appeared in the newspapers of the day, that a disposition prevailed at Washington to elect a new postmaster to the House, the income of the office amounting, I believe, to some fifteen hundred dollars per annum, and the applicants for the place were numerous. One of them resided in a remote part of the State of Michigan, and immediately on learning the intention of Congress, left his home, walking over one hundred miles previous to taking any conveyance, and in eight days arrived at Washington. He lost no time in calling upon the member representing his district, introduced himself, and explained the object of his visit.

The honorable representative received him courteously, but regretted he had not written to him upon the subject previous to undertaking so great a journey, as there was a doubt as to the probability of his succeeding, on account of the number of candidates, particularly as two of them were very strongly supported by their respective parties; however, he would devote all his interest in his behalf. After a few days, the House went into an election for postmaster, and the person from Michigan was unsuccessful. The House now proceeded to elect a chaplain. The Michigan traveller, without the least hesitation, became a competitor with several reverend gentlemen. In this case he was equally unsuccessful. The House now prepared to elect a messenger. Nothing daunted by his former failures, he offered himself as a candidate, and was duly elected and confirmed as such. That his capacity for either of the departments was ample, I do not doubt; and had he been elected to either of the offices, would have been appreciated by the members.

The Hon. Judge Colquet, a senator in Congress from Georgia, a few years since, acted at the same time as General of the Militia, Judge of the Circuit Court, Senator in the State Legislature, and Clergyman in the Methodist Episcopal Church. In each of these departments he acquitted himself with dignity, to the satisfaction of himself and fellow citizens.

I will conclude my reference to the versatility of Americans, by calling attention to a busy fellow in Michigan, who kept a distillery, which manufactured a hundred barrels of whiskey per week, an extensive flouring mill which ground ten thousand bushels of grain each year, raised Berkshire pigs and Durham cattle, built extensive barns and outbuildings, traded in horses and cattle when a good bargain offered, besides attending to land surveying, and taking care of a wife and six children !

From these few cases of personal observation, my readers may form some idea of American enterprise, yet these are but trifling undertakings compared with those which their general character daily displays. In the most stupendous works, apparent obstructions and impediments are conquered, and overcome by the force of a spirited ambition, and by the energy and perseverance of the actors.. The wide-spread oceans, and the hundreds of rivers and lakes of the country, are all burdened with American produce, controlled by a sagacity of thought that removes the difficulties which operate on commercial affairs. In the light of day or shade of night, Americans are prepared for trade; and it matters but little whether it relates to a pound of butter, to a Government bond, or a gold mine,—they are always ready for trade and barter.

I once heard a native of Connecticut observe, that if it were possible to remove the Falls of Niagara, a joint stock company could be formed in a day, to remove and exhibit them throughout the country.

6

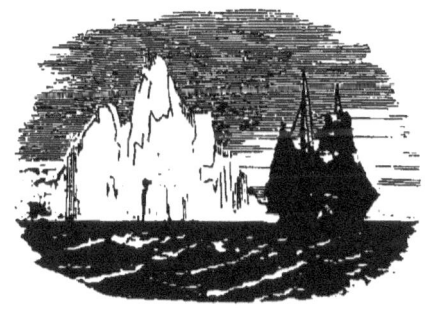

CHAPTER XIII.

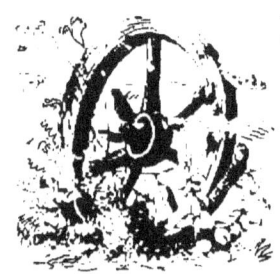

NLY a few weeks had expired after my arrival. in New York, before I accepted an offer made me. by Mr. William Niblo to appear at Niblo's Garden, at that time the most promi- nent and popular place of amusement in the city. The attractions were of a various character—such as to meet the taste of all lovers and patrons of exhibitions.

On popular occasions, a number of side entertainments were given in convenient locations, erected for this special purpose.

The musical department was confined to the principal hall, and was exceedingly good, comprising Mr. Watson, composer and director; Mrs. Watson, eminent as a ballad singer; Miss Watson, equally sweet as a vocalist—a *protégée* of the celebrated Paganini; Mr. Howard, remarkably touch- ing in his rendering of "Black-eyed Susan," "All's Well," "Minute Gun at Sea," "Oft in the Stilly Night," and other old favorite English melodies; Mr. Dempster was not less enchanting in his delineation of Scotch songs; Signor Faboy, with a splendid tenor voice; Mr. Norton, perfect master of the cornet; Signor Gambati, with immense power on the bugle and cornet; Mr. James Kendall; J. A. Kyle, and many others equally distinguished for their special merits. A better *mélange* of artists was probably never combined in one concert-room. For months these gifted performers nightly crowded the immense saloon with delighted audiences. My performances were given in conjunction with these gentlemen, upon the same platform, either before or after the concerts, as the nature of my feats might warrant.

The interviews at the rehearsals were at times rich and amusing, from the spicy debates that would occur between Norton and Howard. Both these gentlemen were natives of England, with strong prejudices and attachments. Howard had long suffered from inflammatory rheumatism, which ultimately resulted in disease of the spine, and he was obliged to support his slender and delicate frame upon crutches. His affliction produced a quick and nervous disposition. Norton was a fine, powerful-looking man, in the vigor of health and life, an inveterate joker, pompous in the extreme, and fond of connecting himself with the lords and nobles of England, alleging his intimacy and companionship with this and that illustrious personage; but of all the many laughable exchanges that occurred between them, none exceeded the following: One morning, there being a full attendance in the green-room, Norton drew up his gigantic frame, with this remark,—

"Howard, when I dined with the Prince of Wales— afterward George the Fourth—and William the Fourth — "

" *Who* did you say you dined with ? " nervously inquired Howard.

"Why, the Prince of Wales, and King William of England."

" You did! Why the d—l don't you speak the truth, Norton, and say *you blew the trumpet* while they dined! "

The mirth this occasioned may be well imagined. The

rebuke of Howard was a great annoyance to Norton, but it served for a long time to render him more moderate in asserting who were his friends and equals.

Howard was always ready at repartee. His reply to Signor Caselani fully proves this. Howard had been frequently provoked by the powerful tones this gentleman would produce from his instrument, so that at times his voice was inaudible. On the occasion of his benefit, Howard requested Caselani, as a favor, to play pianissimo. This the professor promised, and faithfully he kept his word, for, in every instance when Howard was singing, he never produced a note, but placed the bow between the strings, and leaned back in triumph. At the close of the concert he ran up to Howard and inquired if he had played soft enough.

"Yes, yes," he exclaimed. "If you will only do the same at all times, you will please me, and delight the company."

The trial of skill between Mr. Norton and Signor Gambati, on the trombone, for a silver goblet, presented by the manager, were splendid efforts of great artists. These gentlemen appeared in almost every city as rivals on this instrument, and deeply interested the admirers of sterling music in their admirable claims for superiority and mastership. Besides this array of musical talent, Signor Antonio, the pioneer on the flying trapeze, was one of the features, and many no doubt remember his grave but winning smile.

A Disturbed Dinner.

During my entertainments in New York, I frequently dined with Messrs. Price and Hamblin, managers of the Park and Bowery Theatres. Mr. Hamblin was a lively and convivial companion, told a humorous story, loved a good dinner, and enjoyed a glass of wine, and was never happier than when he had succeeded in urging me to play some prank on the waiters.

One day at dinner a roast pig was placed before him to carve. Hamblin, with knife and fork in hand, proceeded to do so, but at this moment the pig began to squeal and grunt terrifically. Hamblin and Price started from their chairs, and the waiter, who was standing on the right of the former, ran out of the room in his fright, dropping the plate he held.

"In the name of Heaven, what does, what *does* this mean!" exclaimed Hamblin, at the same time ringing the bell with energy.

In a few moments the proprietor appeared, and was requested to explain the singular affair. I could no longer retain the joke, but exposed the secret of my being the noisy pig, by squealing and grunting as before. At this, Hamblin and Price laughed immoderately, and gave me credit for so perfectly deceiving them, and ever after dubbed me the "King of Pigs." We returned to the table, and, notwithstanding our dinner was cold, passed a pleasant hour; but on no account could the waiter be induced to attend upon us.

Ex-President Van Buren.

At the Washington Hotel, which was situated at the corner of Broadway and Chambers street, the spot on which Mr. Stewart's dry-goods store is now erected, I had a pleasant interview with Ex-President Martin Van Buren, who was well known at that time in the political world as the "Little Magician." I was introduced by Captain Cobb as Signor Blitz, the "Great Magician." Shaking me cordially by the hand, he said,—

"Oh! Signor Blitz, I am happy to be acquainted with so distinguished a brother professor."

"Thank you, sir, for the honor, but *you* are the greatest, for no one in the profession has arrived at the pinnacle of such fame, or so successfully deceived the public," I laughingly remarked, in which laugh he heartily joined.

"I have frequently seen our names coupled," said Mr. Van Buren, "as wielding the magic wand, but I cheerfully resign to you the superiority; for you, Signor, please and delight all ages and sexes, while my jugglery is for political purposes."

After a social chat of a general character, we separated, Mr. Van Buren wishing me success, at the same time remarking that, as *he* had retired, *I* could no longer look upon him as a competitor in the art of deception.

Once after this, he visited my entertainments at the Society Library, on Broadway.

THE MARKETMAN OUTWITTED.

I was frequently in the habit of visiting the different markets in New York, contributing surprise to the venders, and adding notoriety to my name. Sometimes the dead turkeys, chickens, and geese that were exposed for sale, would express their indignation when represented to customers as being young and tender, by gobbling and cackling, declaring the falsity of the assertion, and in many instances the purchasers refused a good meal, and the owners lost a sale. One day, in the Washington Market, I observed a Quaker lady looking at a pair of chickens she was holding in her hand. I was soon by her side, inquiring the price of them.

"Seventy cents, sir," she replied; "but I think sixty sufficient—they are not large."

The chickens now declared, in a mournful strain, that they died for want of food and water. The Quakeress dropped them with consternation.

"These feathered imps—I would not eat them were they ever so sweet and fresh!"

"Why, madam!" spoke the man, whose face reddened at what the chickens seemed to utter; "do you suppose they are alive and can talk?"

"Did thee not hear with thine own ears?"

"Certainly we can speak! so you need not presume to pass us off for spring chickens, when we are tough with age."

At this the Quakeress shook her head and hurried away, while the confused marketman gazed upon the poultry with mingled anger and vindictiveness. Just then a passer-by saluted me as "Signor Blitz." This discovery caused the poultry dealer to utter in loud and excited tones, "Sold, by thunder!"

WONDERFUL MONEY-BAG.

One of the most amusing pleasantries in astonishing the mind, and almost of a nature to question with suspicious apprehension the secret power of a magician, may be found in the following:

I kept an account at the Leather Manufacturers' Bank, in New York. One day I deposited silver amounting to over one hundred dollars, which was contained in a stout linen bag, with my name printed upon the outside. The receiving teller gave me credit for the amount, and desired me to leave the bag, which he promised to return me when I called again, as it was near the hour of closing. In the course of a few days, I had occasion to transact business at the bank, and inquired for my bag, but it could not be found. The teller regretted the circumstance, and handed me as a substitute one of immense size, painted white, commonly used in the transmission of specie, and capable of holding one thousand dollars, saying, "Signor, you can take this and use it as an egg bag; perhaps you will supply a

few from it now." All the clerks and persons present
united in his request, feeling assured they had the advantage of me, by my being unprepared. Singular as it may
seem, I had an egg in my pocket, having just come from
the Fulton Market, where I had been, in company with a
friend, astonishing a countryman by swallowing a few dozen
of his eggs.

I remarked to the gentlemen, in reply to their wishes,
that if they had asked this in my exhibition-hall, I could
have gratified them; but as this was unexpected on my
part, I was not prepared for the occasion. This produced
great merriment at my expense, but it did not continue
long, for during the conversation I had removed, unob-
served, the egg from my pocket to the bag, and at the same
time I remarked with some spirit, that as they doubted my
capacity to produce them, I would prove that at *all* times
eggs were at my command.

"Ah! we don't believe that, Signor; we have caught
you this time!" one of them said; whereupon I placed my
hand in the bag and brought forth an egg, the appearance
of which caused a sudden reaction, for the looks of every
one portrayed the utmost amazement, which was not les-
sened when I continued the deception until one dozen were
consecutively taken from the bag. I wish it was in my
power to photograph to my readers the countenances of all
present, thus proving how much I had enhanced my character as a magician. For years afterward I was always greeted
upon entering the bank with smiles of welcome, but never
again solicited to exercise my art, although they frequently
referred to the marvellous bag.

THE ADVANTAGES OF BEING A VENTRILOQUIST.

During the erection of the Croton Water Works in New
York, I resided with my family at the corner of Fifty-third

street, on the Bloomingdale road. There were probably not less than two thousand laborers employed upon these works, who were chiefly of the Irish population; and the depredations and annoyances that were committed, without regard to person or position, were intolerable. No one could escape from their ruffian and lawless hands. Every orchard was pilfered, hen-roosts robbed, cows milked and driven away with impunity, and either sold or slaughtered; wood and fuel taken at pleasure; every dog was killed as an enemy; pigs were especially an object of their affection; indeed, everything available was removed; at night or by day these scenes took place. For all these annoyances the residents had no redress, political influence being subservient to the atrocious acts of the marauders. Pedestrians and persons in carriages were frequently stopped and plundered. The civil power was of little avail against this set of desperadoes. The only protection was to avoid encountering them, but this at times was impossible. I had occasion, one night, at the close of my performance, to walk home, and just before arriving at the corner of Forty-second street (the great depot and settlement for cabins and the families of the workmen,—a spot noted and dreaded for its drunken brawls, fights, and consequent attacks on passers-by), I was startled by a signal whistle, evidently given to denote that some one was approaching, and, as I walked on, signals were given to and from different parties. I experienced considerable fear, but in a moment a thought struck me: my ventriloquial powers could be brought effectually into operation, especially as it was a dark and gloomy night, and numbers were not distinguishable. I took the centre of the road, and hurriedly moved on, meantime commencing a conversation with imaginary people, calling, by different names, the responses being natural and in tones of voice entirely different, some laughing, singing, and shouting, accompa-

6*

nied by the barking of two dogs. This ruse, on my part, was a complete success. Probably I thereby saved my life, unquestionably my property, for I distinctly heard the scamps express their doubts as to the policy of the attempt, as the party was evidently too large for them; and thus I reached home in safety. My readers can easily perceive the value of being a ventriloquist, and I reflect with satisfaction on my possessing this amusing and useful art, for on this special occasion it was a matter of deep congratulation, as, shortly after my fortunate escape, several pedestrians were brutally beaten and robbed at or near this place.

The Astonished Medical Examiner.

Ventriloquism has also frequently afforded me opportunities to astonish and please those with whom I have had business transactions, as a simple illustration of which I will relate a scene that occurred in an insurance office.

Having resolved to effect an insurance on my life, I called at the office of the Mutual Life Insurance Company, of New York, for that purpose, where I held a pleasant interview with Dr. Post, recently deceased, but who then, and to the time of his death, was the gentlemanly examining physician. He inquired particularly in regard to my health and habits of life, and was especially inquisitive respecting my powers of ventriloquism, the exercise of which he concluded must be very injurious to the throat and lungs, and considered it necessary that I should undergo a strict examination. I assured him that I would with pleasure at once remove his doubts on that point, and instantaneously lifting a large cloth spread over a round table, held a conversation with several imaginary voices, so deep and powerful that the doctor started back with astonishment, and immediately signed my application, declaring further consultation needless. This little episode left an agreeable recollection, so that whenever I met the doctor we never failed to recall the circumstance, and enjoy a hearty laugh. Twenty-five years have now passed, and my lungs, notwithstanding laborious taxation, yet remain unimpaired, and the company, I believe, value my policy of insurance as one of their best.

AN INSANE WOMAN.

A very curious and entertaining affair was occasioned by my visiting the Insane Asylum at Bloomingdale, in company with a Mr. Bennett. When we arrived, the only person visible was a female patient, seated on a grass-plot, with her countenance wrapt in melancholy thought. On my wishing her good morning, she directed her face toward me, and with a vacant stare and demented look, exclaimed,—

"Ah, is that you, Old Scratch?"

At this courteous salutation Mr. Bennett could not resist the expression of "good" and instantaneously produced the following:

> "Surely the woman is not mad,
>   When calling Signor Blitz 'Old Scratch;'
> A better name could not be had,
>   Or one his looks so well do match."

These impromptu lines exacted from me a loud and appreciative laugh. Mr. Bennett was an Englishman, and well known in New York for his peculiar devotion to the game of cricket; indeed, he was such an enthusiastic lover of the art, that he was in the habit of sleeping with the bats, balls, and wickets beneath his pillow, and during the night, would rise and practise by himself. Whatever part of the country business might require his presence, these articles were always his travelling companions, enclosed in a leather case, giving constant speculation as to its contents. When at a place where none were to be found who understood the game, he was known to engage persons with one eye, leg, or arm, paying them by the hour for the purpose of this practice, such being his passion for cricket. A gentleman once complimented him for his great proficiency, and thought he studied by the Rule of Three.

"Oh, no," replied Mr. Bennett, "it is by *Practice.*"

Mr. Bennett was formerly lessee of Peale's Museum, which he conducted with much spirit, providing liberally for the public and the performers; and for some years previous to his death was in the employ of Mr. P. T. Barnum, who not only admired him for his honest principles, but compensated him handsomely, asserting that he considered him the most upright man he had ever known.

Mr. Bennett was gifted with a heart of great kindness, and respected for his spotless integrity. During twenty-five years' association with a large circle of friends, he was never known to have uttered a single falsehood; and once, when solicited to do so by his employer, which would have resulted in a pecuniary benefit to himself, answered, with true Roman dignity,—

"No, sir! You know I never speak an untruth for myself, and how could you expect me to do it for you?"

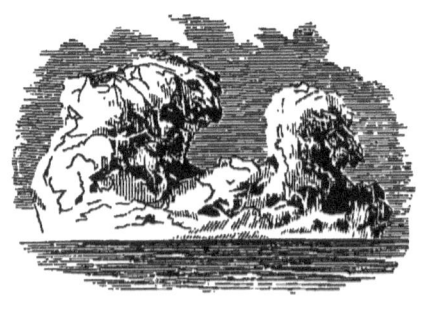

CHAPTER XIV.

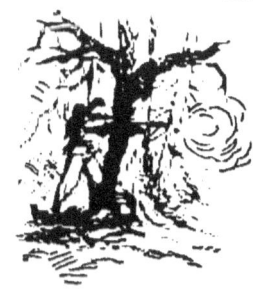

HE late Dr. Valentine, well known as the delineator of Yankee character and American life, was not less eccentric himself than were the peculiar people he represented.

Probably no professor in the mimic art contributed so much pleasure, and created so much mirth, or possessed so fertile a faculty to give enjoyment; yet, strange as it may appear, no man was so miserable and unhappy as himself. Afflicted with a nervous, irritable temperament, the delight he afforded to others was a pain to his own nature; and on many occasions I have heard him declare that he never remembered experiencing three consecutive hours of peace and contentment. Educated as a physician, his erratic disposition inclined him to studies more varied and congenial, and of a popular nature. Electricity, phrenology, and agricultural chemistry deeply interested his mind, and he at times advocated their principles with an earnest eloquence that attracted public attention. In addition to these branches, he was the inventor and suggester of many useful and important improvements, which, from his apathy to action, were in all instances appropriated by others.

The doctor was a practical and untiring developer of the

science and truth of agricultural chemistry. Numerous are the times I have listened to him, as he discoursed to his attentive hearers of the beauties and remarkable results of this necessary treatment in farming. Many would laugh and ridicule the facts he advanced; but then, with excited vehemence, he would drag forth from his pocket the mysteries of Liebig and Johnson on agricultural chemistry as a proof of his statements, and present the same to the doubting ones, with the words, "There, read this, gentlemen, and become convinced." The doctor was always prepared for an emergency, and carried about his person a volume by each of the above distinguished authors. Perhaps the best illustration I can give of his ardent efforts to promote the success and general application of the discovery, is the following:

He located himself on Long Island, a few miles distant from Brooklyn, on the most public thoroughfare, in a small cottage, with the significant sign of "WILLIAM VALENTINE, LAND DOCTOR." The inscription, from the enormous size of the letters, apart from its novelty, attracted the attention of all persons, by producing much comment and merriment. He could not have taken a better position for the carrying out of his reformatory plans, for certainly no part of the country more required the supervision and advice of an intellectual farming physician, for the land was poor and exhausted by an indifferent and careless people. The doctor resided here for a long time, a martyr to science, only one person having conversed with him upon the subject, and that by mere accident. A farmer passing by his door with a load of hay, had the misfortune to break his wagon, when the doctor appeared and offered his assistance. The farmer inquired if he was the "land doctor."

"Yes, sir, I am the man; what can I do for you?"

"Well, doctor, what is to be done for poor land?"

"Have you any that does not yield?"

"Yes, indeed, one hundred and fifty acres."

"You know what ails it?"

"Yes; it is worn out."

"Well, it wants medicine; it's sick—needs the doctor."

"Medicine; what kind?"

"Well, bring me a sample of the soil, that I may analyze its properties, and advise you what chemicals to apply for its renovation."

"Now, doctor, I don't understand your chemistry; our family always farmed by the almanac and moon."

Here the doctor left hurriedly in disgust, observing he believed there never were more stupid and dull agriculturists than the Long Island farmers,—and it was literally true, for after a residence of six months in a most inferior and unproductive country, he returned to New York without being once consulted or realizing a single dollar in return for his time and expense in his attempt to give wisdom to the uneducated agriculturist.

A WISE PHRENOLOGIST.

The doctor's knowledge of phrenology was marvellously truthful, for he had devoted much time and inquiry to its philosophy. He loved the peculiar and general index it gave to character. The appearance of every head invariably gave him a perfect type, mould, or representative of feeling and action; it enabled him to arrive at conclusions most satisfactory and indisputable, and thus, in many instances, his engagements and business transactions were guided upon this knowledge.

This characteristic was so prominent a feature in his daily intercourse with the world, that his views and opinions were more frequently correct than theoretical, occasionally producing the most fortunate results.

So positive was his faith in phrenological developments, combined with the expression of physiognomy, that the most important movements of his life were controlled by them. Frequently he would refuse to take passage on board a steamboat, unless he had previously taken a general survey of the captain's and engineer's heads, and if he entertained the least doubt of their care and skill, no inducement could prevail upon or urge him to travel with them. So, likewise, was the caution he exercised in regard to conductors and engineers on the railroads, making it a rule to sketch their phrenological formation before procuring his ticket. This prudence, on several occasions, preserved him from accident and loss of life. At Cincinnati he had engaged a passage on the steamer "Moselle," but a glance at the officers convinced him of their recklessness, and he immediately ordered his baggage to be taken on shore. His sagacity probably saved his life, for, shortly after leaving the city, the boiler exploded, killing and wounding one hundred and thirty of the passengers! I remember being in company with the doctor at Natchez, Mississippi, *en route* for New Orleans. When the boat arrived on which we were to take our departure, he obstinately refused to proceed in her.

"Why?" I inquired; "what is the trouble?"

"A great deal," he replied. "I do not like the looks of the pilot and engineer; they have villanous heads and features, and I will not risk myself with them."

So we remained for the next steamer, the officers of which indicated more care and system in their characters. Notwithstanding my feelings were vexed for the moment, at the loss of time, the doctor's precaution proved correct, for, some miles below, an accident occurred to the former boat, by which several lives were lost, and many injured.

Another remarkable instance of his admirable knowledge of phrenology took place in my presence. Many years

since, at the Masonic Hall, in Philadelphia, where I was giving entertainments, in conjunction with the doctor, a girl of
some twenty years, during a cold winter's morning, opened
the door and entered, asking permission to warm herself by
the fire, near which I was in conversation with a gentleman,
who soon after left. Not thinking of the girl's presence, I
was attending to my necessary arrangements, when I was
disturbed by the return of the gentleman, who excitedly inquired for her, when, to my surprise, I found she had disappeared. He stated she had stolen his purse, containing
twenty dollars This greatly astonished me; and not having
heard her go out, we at once commenced a search over the
building, and ultimately found her secreted behind a door
in the cellar. We took her upstairs and accused her of the
theft, which she persistently denied; but feeling assured,
from her actions and appearance, that she had committed
the act, we threatened her with the law unless she returned
the property. She declared her innocence, with tears, and
gave us permission to search her person, which we accordingly did, but without discovering the purse or money. At
this instant the doctor made his appearance, and, without
being informed of the circumstance, was requested to examine the character of her head. Removing her bonnet, he
commenced to ascertain her peculiarities, and exclaimed,—

"Why, girl, you are a natural thief!"

"Me, sir?"

"Yes, you!"

"No, I am not!" she replied, weeping.

"It is no use crying, girl; you cannot help it; you are
constituted one; whatever you see, your hands will take."

Here we were interrupted by the entrance of an officer,
at the sight of whom she made a confession, and gave information as to the whereabouts of the purse, after procuring which, we permitted her to depart; the officer inform-

ing us that she was constantly before the courts for pilfering, and known as the greatest expert in the city.

We were amused with the correct description of the girl given by the doctor, illustrating the truthfulness of his favorite study. He has gone to his long rest; peace to his memory! A greater combination of oddity, genius, and generosity never existed.

THE GUN TRICK.

All professional duties are subject to incidental circumstances, some of a character more or less agreeable than others, in reference to which I will relate a most disagreeable occurrence which happened while in the City of New York, and which might have proved fatal. One of my principal feats of attraction at that time, was the permitting a person to bring his own gun, powder, and ball to shoot at me, as hereinafter stated.

The gun was tested as a precaution that it was not charged, after which the parties were desired to load, with the usual quantity of powder. This being done, two or three balls of a large size were marked by different individuals, and dropped into the barrel of the gun, to the satisfaction of the audience. These preliminaries being passed through, I solicited the person in charge of the gun to take his position and fire at my left hand, which was extended from my body. This he did, but not without some apprehension, as his tremulous movement indicated. The words, "One, two, three—fire!" were given, when the discharge took place, lodging not less than a dozen carpet tacks in my hand, and about forty in the wall, causing the blood to flow freely from my wound, and creating no little alarm and indignation on the part of the audience, especially as I was unable to conceal the pain I was enduring. The poor man, in his belief of my immaculate powers, slipped a handful of tacks into the muzzle of the gun as he turned to take his aim. It was an exciting scene, and all present manifested so much feeling, that had I not interceded, some fatal consequences would in all probability have taken place, for their disposition to commit violence on the person firing was very determined; but happily it was averted by my explaining that there was more thoughtlessness in the affair, than premeditation to do me bodily harm.

CAUGHT IN THE ACT.

On another occasion, when performing the same experiment in Philadelphia, the person holding the gun for the purpose of shooting at me, was detected in dropping something into the barrel. Several of the company called my attention to the fact, and on being accused he denied so doing, and as it was a matter too serious to rely upon his veracity, I removed the weapon from his hand and turned it downward, when a brass button fell out. He was then groaned and hissed at as a reward for his dastardly conduct. He excused himself by stating that he supposed I possessed the supernatural power to protect myself from injury.

While exhibiting the same feat in the theatre at Savannah, a gentleman in the house drew his loaded revolver and earnestly requested to shoot at me, stating I could as easily catch the contents of six barrels as one. So determined was he in his desire to shoot, that it required much effort to prevent his firing, and to convince him my feat was only a deception.

But it is pleasant to know that others manifested a different disposition. A sailor jumped upon the platform in New York, and loaded the gun with powder and ball, and when requested to shoot, shook his head, and in an excited and earnest tone declared he would do no such thing.

"Why not?" I inquired.

He answered, "I don't wish to murder you."

"I don't understand you," I said.

"Because," he continued, "the balls, I am satisfied, are inside."

This created great laughter and applause, in which I participated, and observed that I thought he was afraid to fire a gun.

"No, indeed," he replied. "I belong to the navy, and fire cannon; but I'm —— if I want to kill a man for nothing, especially as funny a chap as you."

His remarks drew cheers, and I found it necessary to procure another person to fire; and when the sailor perceived I was unharmed, he rushed up to me, and shaking both my hands, expressed his pleasure that I was safe.

This feat was the most adroit in my performance; and, while it created a marked sensation and interest to the rough and unpolished, it was never popular with the refined and feeling; and, finally, it became attended with so much danger, that I found it necessary, for self-protection, to abandon it.

Once upon a time, being in Jamaica, Long Island, in company with a friend, whose humor never ceased to flow whenever opportunity afforded, we visited a farmer a few miles from the town, who had that day missed a scythe, which he suspected had been taken by a negro. Upon telling us this, my companion naturally asked if it was not the same negro who, a few minutes before, he had seen cautiously peeping from the door of the barn. This put the farmer on the *qui vive*, and rushing into the building, he heard quite distinctly some one beneath the hay, and occasionally a stifling noise, as if a person, intent on burying himself beyond reach, was half choking. He at once called in two of his laborers, and ordered them to fork off the hay, and to catch the "black thief." The forks were at work, and

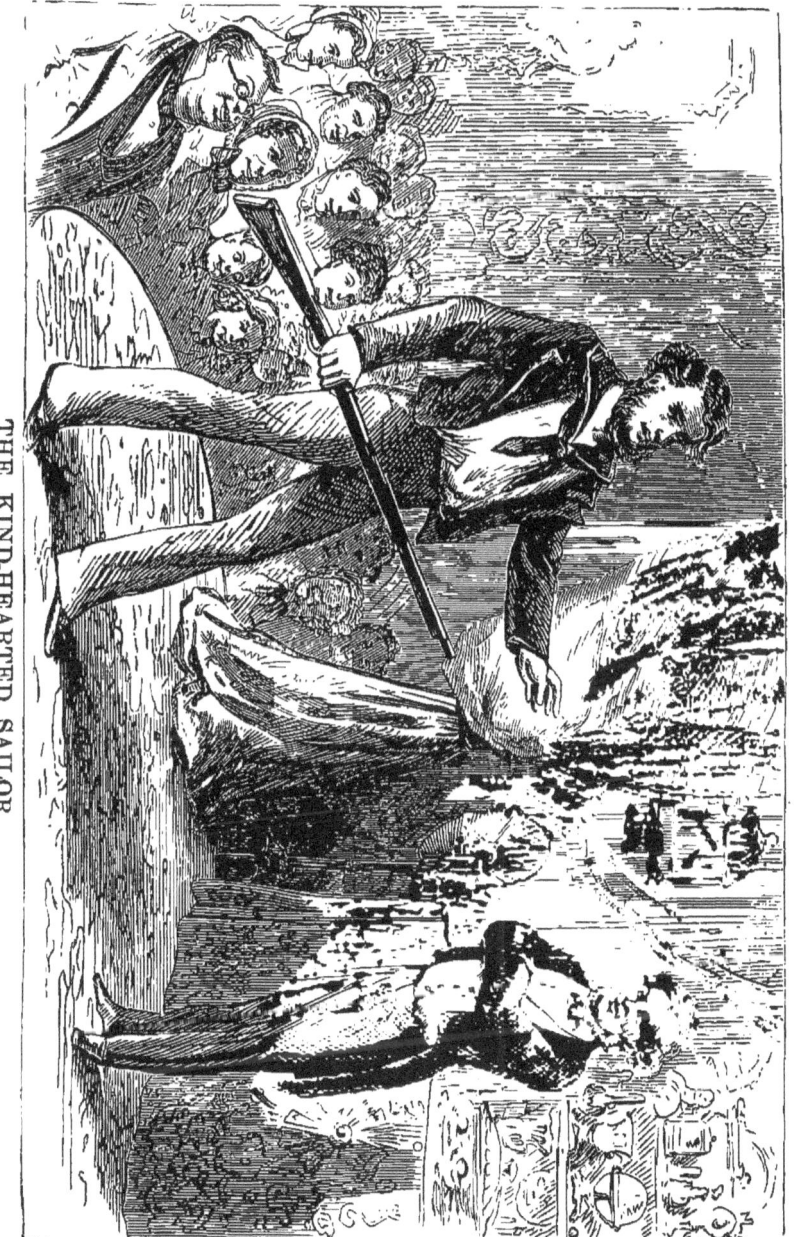

THE KIND-HEARTED SAILOR.

shortly the cries and ejaculations from the culprit in the hay began to grow more and more distinct, and the "don't, master," was repeated in rapid succession. But the men made the hay fly right and left, and scattered it in admirable confusion over the floor, when suddenly the negro shrieked "Murder! you have stuck the fork in my leg. Oh, don't, master! I'll give you back your scythe. Oh, murder! murder!"

"Catch the black rascal!" was the only reply of the enraged farmer, who, in a full glow of excitement, was urging the capture of the supposed thief, until a couple of tons of hay had been tossed on the floor. But the negro was gaining ground, and was evidently ahead of the pitchforks. The window had been reached, and the door creaked on its hinges; then a noise of a heavy fall to the ground was plainly heard, and a long and continued yaw! yaw! yaw!— such as a negro only can make—came ringing upon the ears of the farmer and his two men, who, in an instant, springing from the mow, rushed into the open air, ready for a vigorous seizing of the "villanous African;" but, alas! no person was to be seen in any direction.

My friend and myself showed by the twinkling of our eyes how much we enjoyed the effects of ventriloquism upon the farmer and his two men. By degrees the truth began to flash upon the mind of the benighted man that something had occurred, but he scarcely knew what, except by the confusion which had taken place in the hay, and the yaw! yaw! of the supposed negro ringing in his ears.

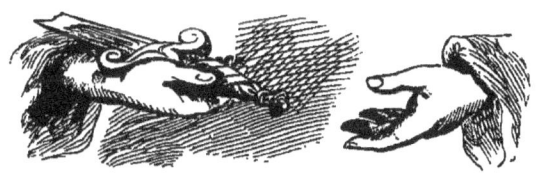

CHAPTER XV.

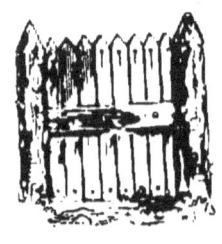 AVING completed all my engagements in New York, I took passage on a steamer, with nearly four hundred other passengers, for Boston, which was a greater number of persons than I had previously seen collected on board any one vessel.

An American steamer is·an excellent school for observation, and during the few hours I was on board, I obtained more knowledge of the American character than in the four months' previous residence in New York.

Immediately after the boat had left the wharf, nearly one third of the male passengers assembled around the office of the clerk to·pay their passage-money, each struggling to be first. But despatch being an active auxiliary in the American character, influences all their actions, and is the universal motto of the country. In one part of the vessel were grouped the merchant, politician, mechanic, and farmer, discussing the condition of the people and affairs of the nation—laws, trade, and general matters of interest; others were below in the cabin, engaged at cards; others were at the bar, indulging in liquor; while numbers were seated at tables, scattered over the immense saloon, deeply occupied in reading magazines, newspapers, and periodicals. On the middle deck a printer was stationed with type and ink for stamping linen or printing cards; a boy was wandering up and down with canes and portfolios for sale.

In the ladies' saloon were grandmothers, mothers, daughters, infants and their nurses; also a beautiful bride, apparently under twenty years of age, accompanied by her bridesmaids, journeying to her new home, under the protection of him to whom she had given her heart and hand, to participate in every joy and sorrow of the uncertain future. The sides of the boat were burdened with bales of cotton, and thousands of boxes, casks, crates, stoves, baskets, cases, demijohns, and other miscellaneous freight—a narrow passage through this immense freight being left open to the bow of the boat—and upon many of these packages were sleeping men, women, and children (deck passengers). Some were lying prostrate upon the deck, in some small enclosure, with their little all of furniture collected around them, while forward were horses, private carriages, and other baggage. The effect of all this incongruity gave much food for contemplation, and to a stranger, like myself, appeared strange and unnatural. The rules and regulations of the boat, printed in large capital letters, suspended in a gilt frame, appeared uncommonly singular. One of the rules read as follows:

"Gentlemen are particularly requested not to sleep in their berths with their boots on."

After my astonishment on reading this bootish notice had somewhat subsided, I inquired of a gentleman if it was customary for travellers in America to sleep in bed with their boots on? He replied that formerly such instances were of frequent occurrence, but that of late years the practice had greatly diminished; that he recollected an instance of an individual being in bed with his boots on, and when requested to remove them, obstinately refused, and upon the printed rules being produced, quaintly remarked "that the regulation did not apply to him, for he *wore shoes;*" that, finally, it became necessary to call upon the captain and clerk of the boat in order to compel him to submit to the requirements of decency.

The evening we left New York was very stormy, and the captain being a prudent commander, anchored for the night opposite New London. In the morning I arose early, and rapidly paced the deck, enveloped in a blue cloth cloak, for it was December, and bitterly cold.

In a Hurry to Reach Boston.

Breakfast at length being announced, I started for the cabin, and on entering it, found much difficulty in obtaining a seat at the tables, they being densely crowded; but finally succeeded in placing myself between two gentlemen—a position that I soon found far from agreeable. The rapidity with which they swallowed their food—being perfect gormandizers—caused the most frequent evolutions from the elbows of each, so that it required considerable attention in watching their movements, in order to protect myself from receiving blows of considerable force in my side. Finding no escape from their attack of arms, I sued for quarter, entreating them to entertain some compassion for my person. But the indifference they manifested was equal to the violence endured by the rapid exercise of the knives and forks, their apology being—"Crowded boat; very little room; hurry to get to Boston, sir; lots of people, but I guess you will get along, sir; nothing when you are used to it!"

As all should possess the philosophy of submitting to occurrences which are inconvenient and obnoxious, I took no further notice, but made the best progress I could. Observing some fried potatoes in a dish within reach of the person on my left, I requested him to pass them. Making no attempt to oblige me, I repeated my wish, when, half turning his head, with a huge piece of meat on his fork, replied,—

"Excuse me, sir, but I am in a great hurry to get to Boston!"

When I consider the extent of my travels, and the variety of society I have met with, I record with pleasure the above as a solitary instance of the most perfect selfishness.

Immediately after the morning meal, the boat pursued her course, passing Point Judith, and having left a number of passengers at Newport, we arrived at Providence, R. I., landed at the depot, and in a few moments were seated in the cars. The hours I remained on this route allowed me ample opportunity to reflect upon the extent and variety I had witnessed in so short a period, combining men, manners, peculiarities, and customs—national and original. I was aroused from my reverie by the announcement of our arrival at Boston, where, in a few days, I completed arrangements for my exhibitions. The only place or hall available was the Art Gallery, then occupied on Sundays by Abner Kneeland and the Society of Freethinkers.

This room was admirably situated on Summer street, the entrance being at the extreme end of the store of Jones, Ball & Poor.

The popularity of my performances secured me large and respectable audiences; citizens and strangers crowded the hall nightly for many months; and while there may have existed a disposition on the part of some few persons to be sceptical, or disposed to accuse and denounce me as being identified with the powers of darkness, they made no betrayal of their feelings or apprehensions.

At first I could not comprehend the peculiar characteristics of the Bostonians; but I readily observed a striking contrast between them and the citizens of New York.

7

Boston was, comparatively, an old-fashioned English city, with crooked streets and short corners, difficult for strangers to pursue their way without constantly inquiring their whereabouts. The citizens had not yet commenced to reveal their sagacity and capabilities for improvement; neither were the merchant princes or the practical minds prepared for that progress which shortly followed; but the inhabitants were at this time noted for their manufacturing and railroad enterprises, for their encouragement of the arts and sciences, their institutions of learning, the homes they had provided for the poor and afflicted, for their intellectual and moral character, and for all that was elevating and refined.

A Temperance Governor with a Bottle of Whiskey.

One morning I paid my respects to Governor Briggs, at the State House. I found him engaged in consultation with several gentlemen, but he courteously arose from his chair, expressed his pleasure at my call, and politely introduced me to those present.

His excellency was very popular, with an unblemished reputation, pure, and incorruptible, and was a leading and earnest advocate of temperance, his public and private life exemplifying the high moral, Christian gentleman.

In the course of an animated and interesting conversation, the governor made a special allusion to my profession, complimenting the educational effect it had upon the age, and the wonderful success with which it had corrected supernatural belief.

As I was about leaving, he requested, as a personal favor, that I would exhibit some trifling skill in my art.

"Certainly," I replied; "will any gentleman loan me a hat ?"

"Take mine," said the governor, presenting it to me, from which I immediately drew forth a bottle of whiskey, labelled "Old Rye."

At this, his excellency was not less astonished than his friends; and I doubt if more hearty laughing was ever heard in the executive chamber. In the midst of the merriment I remarked that "it was a bad omen for a temperance advocate to be found with a bottle of liquor." The governor good-naturedly answered,—

"True, Signor; bad for my reputation, but brilliant for yours."

A BOSTON MERCHANT.

Josiah Bradley was one of the wealthy merchants of Boston, a liberal and popular gentleman of the old school, a lover of mirth, with a pleasant smile for rich or poor.

At one of my entertainments I found considerable difficulty in procuring a gentleman to assist me, especially as it was requisite for the person to lend me his coat. No one consenting to appear, Mr. Bradley arose from his seat and walked upon the platform, proffering his services by taking off his coat and handing it to me, which I placed in a tripod, with a number of detached pieces of red cloth.

In a few moments the coat was taken out, one half red, the other black. Mr. Bradley immediately put it on, and promenaded back and forth, to the great amusement and laughter of all assembled. I took the coat once more, and passed it through a second process, and returned it in its original condition, which Mr. Bradley put on and resumed his seat, receiving long and loud applause, with immense merriment.

The audience comprised the *élite* of the city, among whom was the late Daniel Webster, who not only enjoyed the scene, but, at the close, shook hands with Mr. Bradley, and congratulated him that it was not the State Prison livery he had on. This little circumstance was the occasion of much conversation and laughter, and made my exhibitions more popular than ever.

FANEUIL HALL MARKET.

Shortly after my commencement, I made a visit to this celebrated market, which at this time surpassed all others in the country, not so much for the luxuries it supplied, as for its cleanliness, conveniences, regulations, and general respectability.

There were also many other reasons for its celebrity, and one, not the least, was the order everywhere observable, and the intelligence of those occupying stalls.

After a pleasant ramble around, well pleased with what I had seen, I arrived at the outside of the building, where it was customary for the country people to display and dispose of their produce. Seeing a barrel of apples, I inquired the price.

" One fifty," said the owner.

" Are they as good as they appear ? " said I, taking one in my hand.

" Yes, sir ; they are picked fruit."

" I do not believe a word of that ! " seemingly spoke a man, in a gruff voice, who had just stopped with a basket of eggs.

" Neither do I ! " said a tall, thin-looking woman, in a squeaking tone, as she walked up to the apples, a basket on each arm,—one containing a calf's head, and the other a variety of vegetables.

" I do not care what you believe, sir, or what you think, madam," answered the apple vender, looking angrily at the parties.

At the close of the latter sentence, the loud cry of a

child proceeded from the barrel, which produced no little amazement, all parties starting back with affright and surprise.

The woman declared that any man who concealed a child in a barrel of apples was a brute.

"That is my opinion," said the egg man.

Here the apple dealer protested against these insinuations; but, unfortunately, at this moment a cry of "Help! help! take me out, I shall smother!" came from the barrel.

"He is a villain!" squeaked the woman, appealing to the crowd that had in the meantime collected.

"Turn out the apples!" said one.

"Upset the barrel!" cried another.

"Send for the police!" suggested a third.

"On my honor, there is no child among the fruit!" exclaimed the countryman, evidently alarmed at the appearance things were assuming; but he had scarcely spoken these words, when the child was heard sobbing aloud.

"It will die!" exclaimed several voices.

At the same moment the barrel was upset, the apples rolling in all directions, and, of course, no child found, much to the comfort and joy of the owner, and disappointment of the lookers-on.

"Well, that is odd!" observed the woman; "we all heard the child."

Here the calf's head in her basket commenced blating, which she immediately dropped with alarm, when the apple man, who had been relieved from his difficulties, retorted on his female accuser, by calling her "Beelzebub's wife."

"I am no such person!"

"You must be," said the egg man, as he stooped to take the head, which again blated, when he quickly withdrew his hand, to the amusement of all.

"She is a witch, and should be arrested!" he exclaimed,

when he was again interrupted by the clucking of chickens among his eggs.

"Halloo! what is here?" cried he. "More witch's work?"

"A fine fellow, you, to talk of witches," chuckled the woman.

"Cluck, cluck, cluck," went the chickens; the calf's head blating, and the child crying; when, amidst this confusion, the police appeared, and demanded the cause of the disturbance; but immediately perceiving and recognizing me, laughed uproariously, and pointing at me, shouted,—

"Halloo, Signor Blitz! Up to your tricks, eh?"

At the announcement of my name the people gave three cheers, and separated.

CAMBRIDGE.

Long previous to the close of my engagement, I was invited by several professors and students to visit this classic location—the seat of Harvard University—noted for its beautiful residences, and distinguished for its assemblage of *literati*. The people of Massachusetts, and the alumni of the college, regard "The Institution" with much reverence and pride, which they are fully justified in doing, for no place in the country has been blessed with a more brilliant combination of professors, or a collection of works more valuable and numerous.

My exhibitions were flatteringly successful. The ready wit and volubility of the students at times elicited much laughter, especially when written communications were handed me, which I read aloud for the benefit of the audience. Some were exceedingly ludicrous, as the following:

"Signor Blitz is requested to swallow himself."

JUDGE STORY.

One of my patrons was Judge Story, who attended the first evening, and the many times that I subsequently appeared, seldom failed in being present. No one seemed more amused and delighted than he; and it was his usual habit to seat himself upon the front bench, surrounded by boys, and when I was in need of their assistance, he would urge them forward upon the platform. He always came prepared with silver and paper money to supply what I might require for any special feat.

At the close of one of the entertainments, the judge told me that he had laughed away much dull care and anxiety, and on his return home he intended to write until morning, for that nothing was so restorative to the brain as a good, hearty laugh.

The judge was a most agreeable man, his generous countenance and winning smile endearing him to friends and strangers; while ever ready with a humorous story, he could not be otherwise than the favorite of all.

AN AMERICAN GENERAL.

For a long time after my arrival in this country, nothing surprised me so much as the number of titled persons I was constantly introduced to. Every other man seemed to be either a colonel, major, captain, doctor, judge, governor, or deacon!

When I considered how many of these were mechanics, and in moderate circumstances in life—carpenters, shoemakers, tailors, landlords, etc.—it was a pleasant feature to witness the simplicity with which these honors were appreciated. Nevertheless, these distinctions are uncommonly ridiculous, not so much from an inability to represent the duties, as the frequent want of dignity to maintain them. When I first visited Lynn, it was not, as at present, a busy and prosperous city, but a flourishing town. The only place adapted for public amusement was the Town Hall, to obtain which it was necessary to apply to General DeWitt, the Chairman of the Board of Selectmen, or town officers. Accordingly, I procured his address, and started in search of his residence. Not observing any house suitable in style for a general, I inquired, and found I had passed it, and on retracing my steps in company with the person, he pointed out a one-story, dilapidated frame building, on entering which I expressed my desire to see General DeWitt.

"That is my name, sir," replied a stout, elderly gentleman, who, without coat, vest, or necktie, was occupied at a bench cutting out shoes, his shirt-sleeves rolled up to his shoulders, a pair of carpet slippers on his feet, and huge round silver spectacles on his head, tied with a stout leather string!

He politely granted my request, and I left him with a new idea of an American general's *equipments!* As all titled positions in Europe are held with much etiquette and dignity, I must admit my astonishment at his odd and business-like dress, combined with plain and unsophisticated manners.

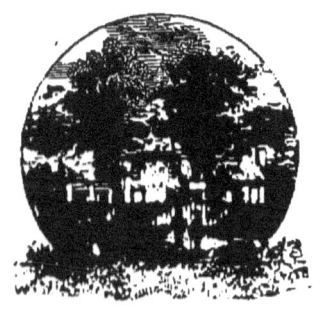

CHAPTER XVI.

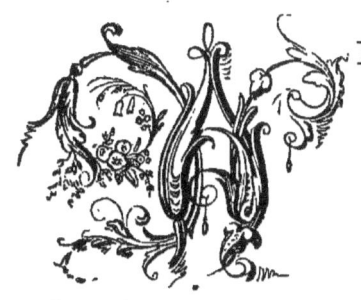ILL any one think me incorrect in saying, that of all the towns and cities, in either the Old or New World, there is none so celebrated for the extraordinary infatuation, intolerance, and superstition of its inhabitants as Salem?

Witchcraft in New England was more potent and presumptuous in its principles, and far more serious in its subsequent effect and consequences upon the public mind, than in Europe, where persecution likewise prevailed with the most unlimited license, without regard to the innocence or guilt of the accused, or character and truth of the evidence.

Fanatical influences have invariably spread with electrical rapidity, repudiating in their progress the judgment and sense of those who are practical and sound, producing the most lamentable and tragic results to the people at large.

All mankind are more or less superstitious, for it is a part of our nature, and forms a powerful element in character. From the earliest ages to the present time it has been subservient to circumstances,—sometimes smouldering in apathy, and at other periods awakened to fury by its powers. The senses are at all periods predisposed to the promotion of wonder and mystery, magnifying with immeasurable belief the most unnatural events.

7*

In the Old Testament we find the Jews reveal their prejudicial faith in soothsayers and astrologers, for which they were rebuked and denounced by the prophets.

In the eighteenth chapter of Deuteronomy, Moses especially exhorts the people to avoid all communications and consultations with familiar spirits, wizards, or necromancers.

Isaiah, in the twenty-ninth chapter, addresses the Jews respecting a voice having been heard in a case of divination.

The Saviour and His Apostles also frequently refer to the ready confidence of the people toward those who pretended to be gifted with supernatural powers, and strictly admonished all who exercised them, condemning witches and wizards as aspiring to the wisdom of the Creator.

St. Paul, in the thirteenth chapter of Acts, punishes a sorcerer with blindness, and in the sixteenth chapter following, in alluding to a woman from whom he had removed a familiar spirit, observed: "She is announced as a young damsel possessed with the spirit of divination, which brought her master much gain by soothsaying."

Josephus, the learned Jewish historian, to an extent shows the Witch of Endor to have been a ventriloquist, and consequently capable of conveying (by her art) to Saul the assumed replies from the shade of Samuel, the representation of which was most probably a phantasmagorial effect, or some illusion to serve the object.

In the records of the ancients, mention is made of the deceptions that existed in regard to supernatural inclinations; how those professing the spirit of doing good or bad, and pretending to a knowledge of the past and future, were countenanced by the people; and even since the Christian era, the mind has been much more perplexed and agitated as to the truth of the demonstrations of wonder-workers. In the thirteenth century Roger Bacon was looked upon as a professor of magic, and recognized to be in direct communication with the emissaries of the devil, so mysterious were his experiments.

In 1305, many educated people were burned at Padua. In 1480, Pope Innocent VIII. issued a bull, requiring the arrest and imprisonment of all people suspected of witchcraft. From education and the early direction of our thoughts, we derive more or less of the superstitious character with which we are associated. But ignorance is, doubtless, the positive foundation for all that is marvellous and unaccountable, and it is thus conclusive, that the mind is the stereopticon by which the objects we reflect upon are photographed, yet it is surprising that with all the capabilities and advantages we enjoy, we find the people of the nineteenth century equally preposterous by their support and recognition of Spiritualism, the professors of which pretend to hold intercourse with the dead, and record the thoughts of those within the realms of heaven, professing to receive and convey communications between families and friends, of a character as nonsensical to the understanding, as it is offensive to the moral appreciation of the Divine law; and in principle and imposition, greater in delusion than the witchcraft that existed in the various periods mentioned; for while we condemn the actors who participated in these dramas, we cannot do the injustice to accuse them of having been interested and instigated by pecuniary rewards, as the bold pretenders of the present fanaticism, who, singular to state, are countenanced and defended by the intellectual and wealthy, the example of which, to the ignorant, is dangerous and pernicious.

In all my perambulations, I never encountered such perverse people as the Spiritualists. Blind to the convictions of truth, and uncompromising in their belief of phenomena, they defend fiction, and emphatically ignore the Divine laws. Their principles not only conflict with the doctrines of all religion, but invade the domestic happiness of homes and peace of families to an alarming extent, the character of which has established nothing tangible in science, or, on investigation, to encourage or satisfy the inquirer, and the whole subject is unprofitable and dangerous. It is truly but a factitious effort to combat and unsettle the laws which God, in His wisdom, has proclaimed as eternal.

The wonders they profess to accomplish, and the extraordinary miracles they witness, are more the effusions of an impaired brain, than any real, earnest desire to impose on the world. This, however, may be qualified in a measure, in regard to those who are interested from pecuniary motives. These persons generally disturb the mind, by announcing the most fabulous events as having taken place, so there can be but little reliance placed on what they do and express. But the wild and absurd scenes frequently related by those innocent of guile and imposition, betray a powerful evidence of how effectually the imagination converts the senses.

What special good has Spiritualism provided since its advocacy to the present time? Who can designate a solitary practical advantage mankind has realized from its doctrines, or what are the solutions to the manifestations and interviews experienced with the departed?

No disciple of the theory, however capable or learned, can explain or enlighten even themselves, or explain what power or force these pretended wonders emanate from, or the demonstrations they behold and undertake.

Indeed, the source from whence these declarations originate, are so completely at variance with reason, that it accounts for the ridicule so unhesitatingly lavished upon all matters pertaining to the invisible world, in the sense of Spiritualism, for it is totally impossible that any rational intellect can admit the power and wisdom of the Supreme Ruler to be called into requisition at any time, for the most trifling purposes.

Man has always been a lover of the marvellous, susceptible of conversion to every extreme policy that combines novelty and mystery; and the effect of Spiritualism on the mind has a powerful tendency to disturb the thinking faculties, and engender the fruits of insanity. Very few escape its allurements; the very best of citizens have become martyrs to its folly, either as monomaniacs or lunatics.

The estimated number of Spiritualists in the United States, it is surprising to say, is one million; the greater portion of whom are invalids, or of a temperament better known as wanting in a positive strength of mind: a class that are dreamy and inactive in their propensities,—more ethereal than sublunary. The result of this infatuation has unfortunately deprived many hundreds of their reason, who have been necessitated to find a home and protection (on account of this peculiarity of thought) in the asylums,—a melancholy and final proof of its detrimental operation upon the brain; and yet, with all these accumulated facts in regard to its alarming tendencies, it has not been diminished in its worshippers, nor has it destroyed the faith of those who are still occupied in promulgating its teachings in every portion of the country. What a sad reflection, that, with all the intelligence of the age, the infirmities of mankind should be so conspicuously inclined to grasp a shadow!

The subject of Spiritualism has no foundation to recommend itself to the attention of the student, or the researches of the masses. It has nothing of a scientific or philosophical bearing to support its claim as a modern discovery. It never can reflect a particle of good upon the destiny of the human race. And what, then, must be the result of its teachings, and of its extravagant assurance to penetrate into the Creator's privacy, and make Him accessory to their insulting impositions?

That the majority of Spiritualists are sincere in their belief, I will not deny; indeed, I unhesitatingly admit such to be the fact, but the acknowledgment is no excuse for their singular views and positive complicity with those, who, by artificial means, delude the masses, for it is known beyond contradiction that philosophical instrument makers have been employed in manufacturing spirit-rapping tables and magnets for the production of concealed sounds, which are arranged in the halls, or under the floor, in the most ingenious manner, to produce the raps at the will of the operator. That we live in an age of progress and extraordinary discoveries in science, and useful inventions, all will concede; but in seeking to enter the shades of death, and the heavenly realms, to give vitality to inanimate objects, we undertake what we cannot perform. It is a great undertaking to comprehend our own destiny in this life, to adapt our capacities to a proper and faithful development of them, but let us not endeavor to ravel that which is not only above comprehension, but forbidden. Such is Spiritualism.

Rev. Dr. John Prince.

When I first visited Salem, it was my good fortune to be introduced to the Reverend Dr. Prince, a very learned and talented divine, and the inventor of the American Air-Pump, with many other useful additions to the arts and sciences. At the time I became acquainted with him he had arrived at the venerable age of eighty years, and was then the pastor of the First Unitarian Church, over which he had been the faithful shepherd for fifty-three years.

His mind was clear and unimpaired, and, with the exception of a slight physical debility, was in good health and condition.

The doctor was greatly interested in my art, and seldom failed during our many pleasant interviews to urge me to astonish him with some one of my favorite tricks. His admiration was philosophical, and for the moment he would reflect and reason, and ultimately explain the principle by which I accomplished the deception, and then he would enlarge upon' the relation of modern magic, with the intelligence of the times, and describe its usefulness and moral influences on the mind.

He related to me many amusing instances of superstition on the part of the citizens of Salem, which he had witnessed, and assured me that if I had made my appearance at Salem, in the early part of his ministry, I would have been subjected to serious trials, my exhibitions prohibited, and myself personally expelled.

In corroboration of his views he stated the following remarkable incident pertaining to himself:

PRODUCING FIRE FROM GLASS.

The summer after his connection with the Church, he imported the first electrifying machine that came to the country, and in the fall of the year, at the close of a Sabbath service, announced his intention of delivering a lecture on chemistry and electricity, studies to which he was ardently devoted.

On the appointed evening there was a large attendance, and the doctor illustrated his lecture by producing the electric spark, and many other experiments of a similar character, which appeared so marvellous and alarmingly incomprehensible to many present, that a large number of the male audience arose in haste and hurried their families from the church, looking at the doctor, as they made their exit, with eyes distended with horror. The lecturer continued his discourse until the close, when the remaining company, composed of clergymen, doctors, lawyers, and private gentlemen of intellectual minds, collected to discuss the motives which induced the parties to leave the church. Some ascribed it to ignorance, others to a want of interest, and some to other causes. A few days following, a party of gentlemen waited upon the doctor at his residence, and informed him that at a meeting held the previous day by his parish, they were delegated as a committee to communicate to him their anxious desire to dissolve the connection between himself and the Society. On hearing which, the doctor manifested the utmost surprise, and desired an explanation for so sudden a resolve.

"Well, doctor, the dissatisfaction arises from the wicked power you exercised at your lecture; in fact, sir, your congregation consider a man who extracts fire from glass, as totally unworthy to have charge of their moral and spiritual welfare."

The doctor remarked, "that they had misinterpreted his lecture, that he had only defined causes and effects, and the same knowledge was practicable to all who became proficient in the science." This, however, did not satisfy the committee, so urgent were they for his removal, by reason of their ignorance and superstition.

"Well, gentlemen, give this matter serious consideration for a few days, and probably you will change your views," said the doctor, on terminating the interview.

The matter became of general interest to the inhabitants; but by the influence of the more intelligent, the doctor's practical efforts triumphed over the superstition of his flock.

Salem contained numerous mementos of the wonderful and terrible events alluded to. In the court-house were preserved iron bolts, nails, and pins, with the depositions of the accusers. These instruments of torture were said to have been extracted from the flesh of the bewitched, and were produced as evidence against those who were so unfortunate as to be pronounced witches. The method of establishing the guilt of the accused was singular, and ofttimes proved fatal to the parties, for they were frequently thrown into the river,—if they swam ashore they were unfortunately condemned as witches and wizards, and were immediately sentenced to be hung; if, however, the poor creatures drowned, they were not regarded as such. In either case, their lives were sacrificed.

Codfish Aristocracy of Marblehead.

A few miles distant from Salem was the small and interesting town of Marblehead, where I made my next appearance.

The inhabitants of this place are, to a great extent, dependent on the fisheries, generous in nature, and a hardy race, well adapted to the locality.

I gave my exhibitions at the Academy, and I must here relate an incident which will, in a measure, illustrate the peculiarities of the people.

During the day of my performance, numbers inquired if I intended to receive fish—the merchandise of the place—in payment for a ticket, or the admission fee. To this I replied, no, I could not. When the hour arrived for commencing, there was scarcely a dozen persons present, while hundreds were collected outside. On observing to the door-keeper my surprise and disappointment, he remarked that if I would take fish in payment, he could fill the room in a few minutes; to which I consented. This fact being communicated to the assembled crowd, caused a general dispersion, but they soon returned laden with one or two fish, of the value of the ticket. To my astonishment the house was soon crowded to overflowing. The following evening the attendance was equally large, all parties bringing the necessary amount of fish to procure admission. Previous to my leaving, I disposed of more than two cart-loads of fish to a merchant of the town.

A similar circumstance has probably never taken place in the history of amusements, and notwithstanding my Marblehead friends have since experienced considerable chagrin that their mercantile traffic at the ticket-office had become known abroad, it does no dishonor to their integrity or worth.

A LODGING AT THE EXPENSE OF THE TOWN.

Perhaps of all the numerous and laughable incidents in my professional career, none was more so than that with which I was connected at Braintree, in Massachusetts.

The day was an exceedingly stormy one; the snow had fallen the previous night to a great depth, and, the Town Hall, at which place I was advertised to give my entertainments, was located a mile from the hotel, which distance, with bad walking, prevented me from taking my regular meals.

After the close of the evening's entertainment, which was witnessed by a numerous company, I concluded to content myself with a lodging on a settee, especially as the night was cold, and there was an ample supply of fuel. The janitor, observing me making preparations for sleeping, said he would be happy to accommodate me with a bed. I accepted his offer, and in a few moments accompanied him to a large and spacious building, where I was shown to a neatly furnished bedroom. At the break of day, I was awakened by numerous footsteps and loud talking, but could not conjecture the character of the place. At last I arose, and when the breakfast bell sounded, partook of an excellently cooked meal, and having eaten but little the previous day, it may well be supposed I did not deny my-self any of the good things provided. When I was about taking my leave, I inquired the amount of my indebtedness of the janitor.

"Oh, nothing," he replied. "There is no charge."

"How is that, sir? I expect to pay."

"Why, you have been entertained at the expense of the town. This is the poor-house, Signor Blitz!"

"The poor-house?"

"Yes, the poor-house; and you will always receive a welcome here, Signor."

My readers will naturally conclude I was astonished at being an inmate of the town asylum; my temporary abode, however, was pleasant, to say the least; for a softer bed or more palatable breakfast I never enjoyed, and only hope that all who may become necessitated to seek food or shelter from the parish bounty, may experience the like good fortune.

I appeared in all the towns and villages of importance in this State, New Hampshire, Maine, and Connecticut, being the recipient of much attention, and meeting with good success. I could but admire, everywhere, the prosperity and progress of an industrious and intelligent people, marked for their moral, energetic, and persevering character, eager as they were earnest in those pursuits which contribute to the greatness and improvement of the age.

This is but a just tribute to Yankee character; for, politically, intellectually, scientifically, and inventively, the New England people are surpassingly distinguished.

In the course of my progress West, in the spring season, I found it convenient to take passage in a canal packet, at that time a popular mode of travel. The passengers were numerous, and a greater incongruity of character could not have been assembled. The discussions on politics, law, religion, and commerce, were highly entertaining, and significantly instructive; the social distinctions were also not less perceptible.

Immediately upon the discovery of my profession, a polite and earnest appeal was made for me to give an entertainment in the evening. Finding it impossible to withstand the solicitations, I consented. The long, narrow cabin of the boat was not available to exercise my art to any startling effect, and so I selected those displays which, if less in representation, were more lasting in impression.

A Minister in Trouble.

One of my fellow-travellers was an orthodox divine, of strong puritanical predilections, serious in demeanor as he was reverential in countenance. During the exhibition, he gazed upon me with an indignant surprise that attracted every eye. At each feat he would exclaim, "Wonderful! remarkable! surprising!" and expressed his firm belief that the kingdom of heaven would be closed against me. One of the audience—a wag—perceiving the reverend gentleman's amazement, procured from the steward of the boat a silver teaspoon, and, by the assistance of one of the company, dropped it into the coat-pocket of the gentleman.

When about to close, I stated my tricks were all deceptive, and their success depended less upon the rapidity of execution than on the absence of the sight to the object at the precise moment, which was invariably caused by the talk of the performer; but there was one of the company whose tricks savored more of mystery than did mine, and though silently performed, had not escaped my observation. I also stated that I referred to the reverend gentleman; and to satisfy the spectators that he was as much a juggler as myself, I requested him to remove from his pocket the silver spoon he had so adroitly secreted.

Here all looked at the clerical individual with intense

merriment, as he arose to protest his innocence. "Feel in your pocket!" was the simultaneous demand. This he proceeded to do, and immediately drew forth the spoon, with evident nervousness. The applause was boisterous, and when it subsided, the clergyman found breath to denounce me as the personification of Satan himself.

Millard Fillmore was also a passenger, then on his return from his first session at Congress. He was a pleasing and affable gentleman, respected and admired for his bland and courteous demeanor, and appeared highly to enjoy the scene in the cabin. Some years afterward, I was exhibiting at Washington, when he was the executive of the nation, and took the opportunity to pay my respects to him. The interview was a very agreeable one, during which he remarked, "Little did I expect, Signor, when travelling with you on the canal, I should ever become the President of the United States."

I continued my western tour to the remote parts of the country, performing in all the principal cities and towns with my usual unexampled success. The residents of the then "Far West," did not enjoy the facilities and advantages of the present day. Their communications and business transactions with the older States were long and tedious; the conveniences which add comfort and produce refinement were not available; yet, while occasionally the polished emigrant might be discovered, the people as a whole were intelligent, though rough and uncultivated, but a degree of happiness prevailed through their arduous duties. The condition of all new settlers is varied, and fraught with incident; for, limited in society, and absent from the common attractions of life, they necessarily encounter many hardships. This endurance is combatted with zealous efforts, accompanied with a cheerfulness of disposition, admirably worthy of emulation. Surely, such advantages for man as the Great West afforded, could not otherwise than attract, as it has done, not only the natives of the New World, but a large number from foreign shores, who were developing, in an energetic manner, the immense resources of their adopted land; since which, new states, territories, cities, and increase of population have accompanied the prosperity of the country.

The immense products annually exported, with vast internal improvement in the arts and sciences, navigation on the lakes, and transportation by rail, testify to the enterprise of the inhabitants of the Great West.

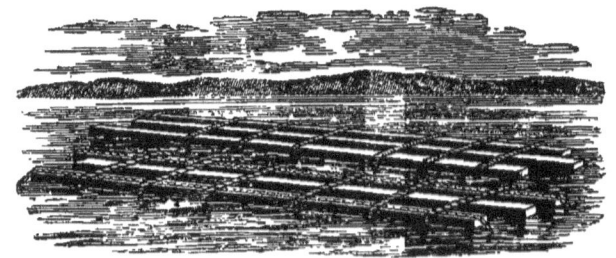

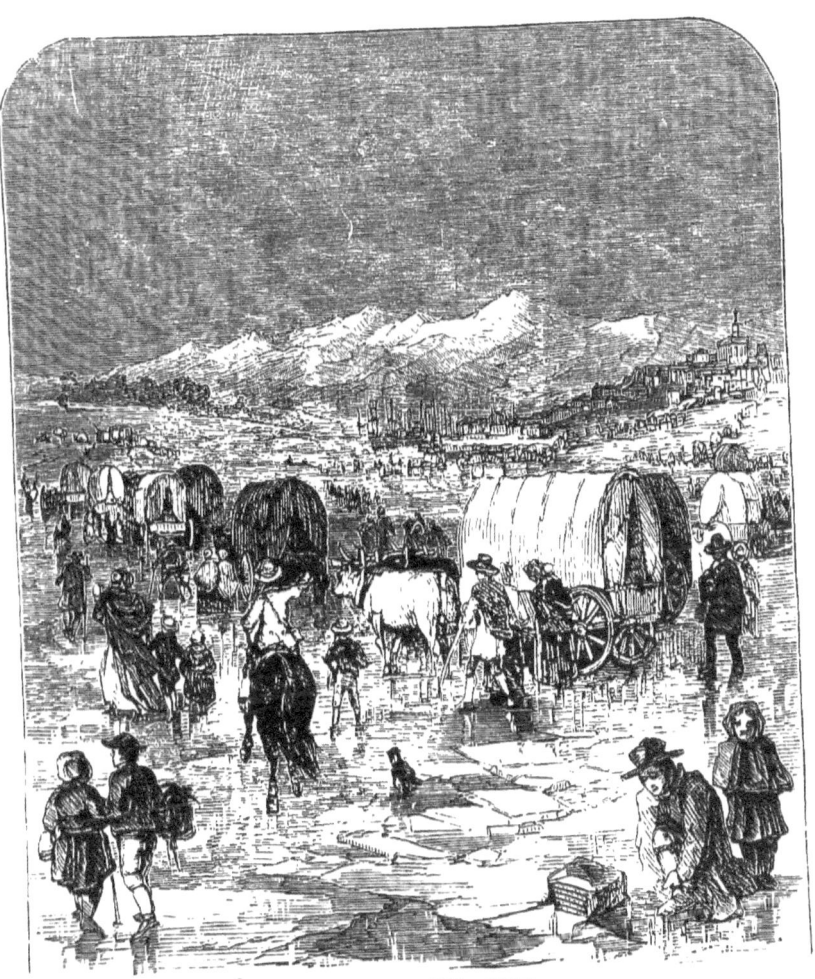

WESTWARD, HO!

CHAPTER XVII.

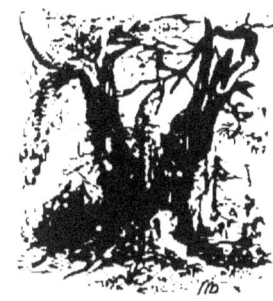 ERY well pleased with my visit to the West, I returned to New York, and accepted liberal terms from Mr. Maelzel, the proprietor of the celebrated Automaton Chess-player, the Burning of Moscow, the Automaton Trumpeter, and the Wonderful Rope-dancer, with other musical and mechanical mysteries, to visit Philadelphia, and appear in conjunction with his entertainment, which he gave in a new hall, on the northeast corner of Eighth and Chestnut streets.

This city was then large and flourishing, second in the Union for population and the importance of its trade, and highly admired for its cleanliness, regularity of streets, the neatness of its private dwellings, and also for the symmetrical squares which characterize the Quaker taste.

It contained numerous historical mementos, reminiscences, and associations connected with Penn, Franklin, and other learned and wise men of the olden times.

I found Philadelphia a model city: her markets—unequalled—were supplied from the rich and fruitful counties in the immediate neighborhood, and those of Delaware and New Jersey.

It also afforded admirable facilities and advantages for poor people: small and neat residences, with every convenience, were especially built for this class, so that it was a rare instance to find two families occupying the same house —a significant contrast to other large cities.

Pennsylvania is possessed of vast and important natural advantages, with mineral resources not less varied than unbounded—surpassing all calculation. It may be presumed that Philadelphia could not otherwise than increase and prosper, and what she must ultimately arrive at, when time fully developes this great wealth, the mind can scarce imagine.

THE GREAT AUTOMATON CHESS-PLAYER.

Our success was ample and flattering. Mr. Maelzel was a native of Germany—a large, phlegmatic man, extremely irritable, yet very kind, and he displayed great taste and refinement in all his arrangements, without regard to cost.

"It must be correct," was his constant observation.

At the close of my first evening he came to me, and placing his immense hands on my shoulders, said,—

"My dear Blitz, you are an excellent performer, but you must not make the people laugh so much. It is not shenteel to make them ha! ha! They laugh too loud; that's not shenteel."

At the breakfast-table the following morning, and during the day, he often reminded me not to forget his advice to "make the audience laugh shenteel." When the hour announced for opening the door in the evening arrived, he was whispering in my ear, "Remember to make them laugh shenteel, Blitz, and not them big ha! ha! ha's!" When the curtain rose he disposed of himself in one corner, and there remained the whole time I was before the company, and whenever they became merry he would whisper, "Blitz, Blitz, there's too much laughing ha! ha! Make it shenteel." And so he continued during my engagement, urging me to control the muscles and risibles of my audience—incessantly enjoining me to make the people laugh "shenteel."

Maelzel was a man of splendid attainments as a mechanic and musician, a fine linguist, and superior mathematician. The latter was absolutely an important auxiliary to the success of the chess-player. Enjoying superior knowledge of the game himself, he was fully capable of anticipating with almost certainty the success or defeat of his famed automaton. To those acquainted with his peculiarities, there could always be formed an idea of the state and prospect of the game; for when Schlomberg—being the absolute chess-player concealed in the figure—was *non compos* from the effects of wine, Maelzel's fingers became electrified and telegraphic, plainly interpreting defeat; and these symbols never failed to indicate adverse results. Schlomberg was very accomplished—could talk French, German, English, Spanish, and Italian with great fluency; most unobtrusive in his manners, with little or no dignity in his personal appearance. His position was a responsible one, for he superintended the out-door business, and in a great degree directed the exhibitions.

Occasionally his love of genial companionship would betray him into habits of indulgences which, however slight, unfitted him to compete with the masterly minds opposed to him in the game, yet there were instances, strange to say, when under the influence of stimulants, he would triumph over his adversary. Maelzel and Schlomberg were, in their time, the great living representatives of chess; their hearts and feelings were so identified with the game that they dreamed of it by night and practised it by day. At every meal, and in all intervals, a portable chess-board was before them; they ate, drank, and played, while not a word escaped their lips. It was a quiet, earnest, mental combat, and the anxiety of every pause or move was defined in each

8

countenance, their features revealing what the tongue did not express.

The chess-player was ingeniously constructed—a perfect counterpart of a magician's trick-table, with a variety of partitions and doors, which, while they removed every possible appearance of deception, only produced greater mystery, and provided more security to the invisible player. The drawers and closets were so arranged as to enable him to change his position according to circumstances: at one moment he would be in this compartment; the next, in that; then in the body of the Turk, which permitted Maelzel to open all parts at one time; when *the figure* was vacated he directed special attention to its skeleton character. There was a considerable display of superbly-finished machinery in the box or ball, of a complicated appearance, which diverged in various directions, the object of this being to distract attention, and impress the mind with the conviction that the mystery was in the mechanism. In this opinion I am confirmed by Maelzel himself, who, whenever he perceived the probability of defeat, withdrew the chess-player, stating to the audience that the machinery was out of order.

The attention that was created by its appearance and success has never been equalled by any invention. Not only the lovers of the game, but those of refinement in all parts of the world, were interested in the highest degree. It was an enigma, which even to this day, with all the explanations, has lost but little of its novelty; yet it has always been a wonder to me how the public, upon reflection, could seriously entertain the idea that a machine could compete with the human intellect.

In the winter following I met Maelzel in Havana, Cuba. He had visited the city previously, and was highly successful; but this, his second venture, terminated most unfortunately, for his business failed, his exhibitions were less attended, while his pecuniary matters became desperate and gloomy. While thus discouraged and surrounded by difficulties, Schlomberg died of a fever. Maelzel was now an old man, reduced in circumstances and involved in debt, obstacles unknown to him before; his pride and spirit could not battle with the change. He secured a passage for Philadelphia, but grief produced a severe illness, which terminated in death during the voyage. Poor man! he was buried in the sea, and his effects sold at auction, to liquidate the cost of passage and other claims. The chess-player was purchased by several liberal gentlemen as a memento of the renown it had acquired in Europe and this country, and was occasionally used by amateur players in its original capacity, until it was destroyed by fire at the Chinese Museum.

The trumpeter is now in the possession of a Philadelphia gentleman, and by his kind permission appeared under my direction at the Great Central Fair, located in Logan square.

My next engagement was at McArran's Garden, a spacious and popular resort, capable of containing many thousand people. The proprietor was a native of Ireland, and an active politician, which gave him considerable influence among his countrymen. At this time the *morus multicaulis* engaged all minds and pockets; fortunes were made in the morning and lost ere evening; many became rich, but more poor, the same day; speculators knew no bounds; so fabulous were the reports of the realization of great wealth by this and that person, that many were induced to invest their all, in the hope of obtaining a hundredfold in return. No class could resist the temptation of embarking in the general speculation. McArran was deeply interested. I remember his taking me to look at a field of some acres planted with the trees, and his remarking he had refused an offer of fifteen thousand dollars for them. I inquired what he expected to receive? He replied, "Double that amount;" but his hopes failed, for in a few days following the bubble exploded, and he not only lost all he had invested, but seriously involved himself. Not unlike the petroleum era, it produced ruin and desolation in homes where comfort and plenty had previously reigned.

I next occupied Masonic Hall, and afterward the lecture-room in the Chinese Museum, where I remained many years, enjoying the patronage of all classes, until its destruction by fire. I next opened at the Columbia House, and in a short time removed to the Assembly Building, where I have continued to exhibit at intervals for a long period.

My business success has been triumphant. All the above halls were limited in space, so that nightly many could not obtain admission. I have, I believe, gained the respect of all, and the ill-will of none; and I can number among my personal friends many, very many, of the first citizens of Philadelphia.

There are many interesting incidents connected with my professional and social intercourse in the city of Philadelphia, during these years, now long since buried in the past, a few of which I will transcribe from memory as accurately as possible.

A Truant Husband.

During an engagement at the Chinese Museum, I was attracted by a lady who was a constant visitor at my performances. Her face was of singular beauty, Grecian in model, with finely-formed features of classic shape. No smile lighted her handsome countenance—not even when the whole audience was convulsed with laughter, could the slightest cheerfulness be observed to animate her. It was apparent some sad and hidden secret was destroying the happiness of her heart, and overwhelming that peace of mind so much desired by us all.

At the close of one of my evening exhibitions she remained until after the audience had retired, and requested a few moments' interview, at the same time looking around with cautious apprehension lest we should be disturbed; and trusting, she said, to my generous honor to excuse the present step, and keep secret what she disclosed.

"My story, Signor, is a sorrowful one; no tongue, however eloquent, could express the anguish I have experienced. Human nature when provoked beyond endurance, operates in all the wild emotions of the imagination.

"At the early age of sixteen I loved and became the fiance of one I deemed worthy of my heart's warmest affection. Our joys were mutual; the sun was not brighter than our anticipations. We truly existed for each other, and time was annihilated by the bright vision of the future. We married, and lived for years happily in the society of each other; but alas! too soon our bliss was changed to grief, for Edmond, the chosen of my youthful affection, attracted by the fascinations of the gay and festive world, became enamored with the sparkling wit and silvery laugh of one whose vows bound her to another. Day by day his affections were weaned from me, the rightful possessor of his heart, and he seemed only to live for her, the gay and brilliant devotee of fashion. My love, my entreaties, were of no avail; this syren had estranged him in the very meshes of her existence —and now, Signor Blitz, I am alone in the dreary world, an orphan, deserted by my husband, with no one to look to for love or protection. You may consider it unwomanly in one, a stranger, to intrude upon you in this manner with a tale of domestic grief, but you know Edmond personally, and that, combined with your reputation for

:

necromancy, leads me to seek your aid in regaining the love I have lost. You, with your potent spells, can most assuredly work the charm of returning a truant heart to its original love."

"Madam," I replied, "I fully appreciate your feelings, and sympathize with you in your suffering, but I do not possess the ability to afford the relief you desire. True, I am a magician, but my art does not pertain to matters of the heart. The one to whom you refer is an acquaintance of mine, yet I have no magical influence over the personal feelings of any friend whatever. I promise you, however, my aid in all natural, not magical means, to restore to you the object of your love."

Here her disappointment was visible in the increasing gloom of her countenance; she had evidently depended so much on my reputation as a magician, that she believed me capable at once of restoring the lost love. After some moments of hesitation she arose, and urged me to employ all my powers, natural, magical, or otherwise, in her behalf, and bade me adieu with mingled feelings of relief and anxiety in her expression. Previous to her leaving, however, I requested her to meet me at the same place, the next afternoon, at four o'clock.

Early the next morning, I directed my steps to the office of Edmond, who, although young, had for some years been a distinguished medical practitioner. Gifted with great natural attainments, combined with the advantages of a careful and polished education, brilliant in his acquirements, he had obtained a popularity that few possessed; but the intoxication of social life had surrounded him, and disturbed his domestic relations. I found him so deeply engaged with a patient, that I entered unperceived and seated myself. In the course of a few moments the gentleman retired, when I received a hearty welcome. After a desultory conversation, I commenced the subject of my visit, which required great prudence and management. I stated to him that the spirit of his love—one whose image must be engraven upon his heart—had revealed itself to me in an angelic form—a vision, a dream, of purity and beauty.

"Who, Signor—who is the lovely being you describe? is it an optical illusion, or a romance?"

"It is not one or the other: it is a real, tangible being."

"And interested in me, Signor?"

"Yes, immeasurably so."

"Can I see her?"

"Yes, if you will meet me at my hall a few minutes past four this afternoon, I will introduce you."

He promised to do so, impressed with the belief that I was about to play upon him one of my magical or ventriloquial tricks.

Pleased with my success so far, I attended to the duties of the day, waiting impatiently for the hour to arrive.

At the appointed time Mrs. —— presented herself. I explained my interview with her husband, and his desire to be present, "which will be instantly." These words had scarcely escaped my lips, when the door opened and he entered. No artist could picture his confusion, or her touching expression; suffice it to state that the surprise had accomplished my purpose.

With open arms he embraced the devoted one, and, in broken sentences, renewed his former love and vows to return to his allegiance. The scene was a most happy one; their countenances beamed with pleasure, and joy, and honor to come. Both thanked me with feelings of gratitude, and went their way a wiser and happier couple. Time has since proved him worthy of her purest affections. Need I assert the pleasure I realized by this singular event, and its agreeable termination was highly gratifying to me.

A Prophecy.

During the existence of the United States Bank, I was in the habit of visiting the institution on matters of business, frequently paying my respects to Mr. Biddle, the President. A little circumstance occurred on one of these occasions that must not be passed unnoticed.

One day, after amusing him and friends with a few trifling feats, he remarked, "I hope you will not *conjure* all the money out of the bank, Signor."

"Oh! no, Mr. Biddle, I will leave that trick for others to do."

This retort, in a few years, proved I was prophetic, and that many a truth is spoken in jest.

Doing a Judge.

Legal science is broad and complicated, which many profess to understand, but few comprehend.

Law is known to be a tyrant, peculiarly and distressingly so, for it adheres strictly to its own interpretation, which, however singular, and emphatically contradictory to common sense, is nevertheless termed "according to law." It is to this, in a great measure, that arises the general antipathy to become involved in its uncertainties, disappointments, and expenses.

Probably no class of people are the recipients of so much vituperation, or whose honesty is so much impugned, as the legal profession.

These ungenerous charges are, as a general rule, expressed either from ignorance or without reflection, for we may as well doubt the honesty and integrity of every person engaged in any other profession or occupation in life, and feel impressed that all mankind are promoters of discord.

The true idea, and undoubted fact in regard to law, is, that until man becomes less contentious, and more amiable in the perplexities which surround him, he must necessarily expect to contend with the law, and abide by its consequences.

The disciples of Coke and Blackstone compose a numerous body of gentlemen, refined and intellectual, as they are honorable and truthful, with abilities largely diversified, combined with a practical knowledge of human nature and its phases. I can safely assert that no other profession can produce men more honorable, more energetic, or more persevering.

Philadelphia has always enjoyed a special fame for the legal acumen and sound knowledge of the members of her bar, who have added much dignity to the jurisprudence of the country.

Mr. Gibson, at the time of his death, was Chief Justice of the State, a position his impartiality and virtues honored. Being humorous in nature, and instructive in conversation, his popularity was unbounded.

Dining one day in company with him and a party of gentlemen at the United States Hotel, then situated between Fourth and Fifth, on Chestnut street, an animated discussion arose as to the correctness of testimony, as generally given in court, where the facts mainly depend upon the accuracy of sight. The whole party declared that, as seeing was believing, every possible doubt became removed.

"Not in all instances," replied the judge; "for we frequently believe what we do not see; and, further, my experience on the bench, and the attention I have given to the subject, not only compels me to be sceptical, but suspicious of human testimony, and confirmatory of my position, Signor Blitz will please favor us with a few tricks."

To this I readily assented, as I had anticipated the re-
8*

quest, and was prepared accordingly. "What character of feat would you prefer?" I inquired.

"Take the judge's money out of his pocket," said one.

"Oh, yes, do!" was the ready and unanimous request of all.

"I hope not," said the judge, smilingly; "for I have but little. I prefer that the Signor should place some in. Taking money out of people's pockets is a serious matter."

At this moment I arose and observed: "I am a victim of the judge's extraordinary manipulating abilities. He has my wallet, with its contents, now in his pocket."

"What! what!" shouted the judge, amidst the laughing applause and delight of all. "I have your pocket-book? Why, it is impossible; our present distance disproves the accusation."

His hands now fumbled in his pockets, drawing out the wallet! the appearance of which drew forth the most hilarious shouts, clapping of hands, and stamping of feet. The judge's countenance exhibited great amazement; but soon his face assumed its usual pleasantness, while he declared that the senses could be provoked to believe that which was not true.

EGYPTIAN MUMMY.

The Egyptian mummy brought to this country by Mr. Glidd, the American consul at Cairo, was opened in Philadelphia to the eyes of the curious, who desired to see the mortal remains of a human being who existed two thousand years before the Christian era. Previous to this proceeding, however, there were gathered round a collection of bald-pated gentlemen, whose thoughts seemed to have little to do with things modern, and, from their air of mystery, they appeared to be lost in the gloom of ages. These ancient gentlemen were inspecting the characters on the case of the dried specimen of antiquity, when suddenly they were startled by a voice from amid the folds of the linen which wrapped the mummy.

"Open the box! open the box!" said the voice.

"Who are you?" inquired one of the learned Thebans, whose curiosity had the advantage of his astonishment.

"I am a descendant of the Pharaohs," answered the voice within.

"Are you a genuine mummy?"

"Yes, genuine and no mistake—regularly manufactured in Egypt by some of the first artists."

"Did you come from Ham?"

"Ham? No! I am a better specimen of dried beef."

"What do you want here?"

"Ask yourself; your confounded prying Yankee inquisitiveness has waked me up from a slumber of ages."

A thought struck the scientific questioner, and he determined to settle a mooted question.

"Were the Egyptians black or red men?"

"Red as the knave of hearts."

"What caused the decline of the Egyptian nation?"

"It didn't decline! Like the modern Celt, the Egyptians emigrated to America."

"To America?" inquired the doctor.

"Yes. Open the box! open the box!"

"Then the pyramid at Cholulu is—"

"Exactly; it is nothing else."

"And you are—"

"Signor Blitz."

"Signor Blitz!" said the astonished inquirer.

The doctors looked at each other, and the words, "Done for," was distinctly heard issuing from the box, as if the dried descendant of Mizraim was laughing in its sleeve at the credulity of science, which could not tell a living ventriloquist from the dried remains of a burnt monkey's skeleton,

CHAPTER XVIII.

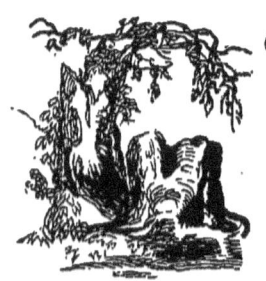 OING south from Philadelphia, I arrived at Baltimore, at which city I made a brief stay, exhibiting to large and enthusiastic audiences, at the close of which I commenced an engagement in Washington, meeting with the greatest success; for night and day the hall was literally crammed with people, whose upturned faces beamed with surprise and laughter. The more intelligent class of the community took a reasonable, common sense view of my feats, while others looked upon me as an emissary from the dark shades of Hades, sent to tantalize and deceive poor humanity with my deeds of sorcery. To the colored people I was an especial attraction of wonder and alarm. They could not associate me with other mortals, for their ready belief in my supernatural qualifications was amusing and entertaining.

Washington has always contained much to interest and instruct, being the capital of the United States, and the residence of the head of the nation. All the Government departments and public buildings are substantial and free of access. Apart from these attractions, and those arising from national affairs, it is a city which few admire.

Its peculiarity of streets, hotel discomforts, and extravagant charges, with constant mud or dust, renders it far from being an agreeable place. The society I found of a varied character, at times admirable for its refinement, as at other times it was unpleasant for vulgarity. This marked feature combined in its sphere much of the elective wisdom of the nation, where positions are obtained, with few exceptions, more from their political affinity to party, than any necessary reference to personal elegance.

DANIEL WEBSTER.

During the ·presidency of Mr. Tyler, I had occasion to call on the Secretary of the Navy on personal · business. When I arrived, as I supposed, at the department, I found several gentlemen awaiting an interview. After the expiration of a few moments I accompanied the attendant, and to my surprise, found myself in the presence of Daniel Webster, then Secretary of State. Glancing at my card, he turned and readily extended his hand, with—

"Welcome, Signor! No hocus-pocus among my papers!"—covering them with his arms.

"No, sir," I responded, "I am the one tricked this time: I was seeking the Secretary of the Navy."

"Perhaps I can answer the purpose," he replied.

After explaining to him my object, I received the requisite information. We laughed and chatted a few minutes, and I was about to retire, when I mentioned that as I had unexpectedly visited him, I would make known a matter of interest to me, namely, that I was an applicant for office, and hoped I could rely upon his influence in the matter.

"You, a magician, an office-seeker, Signor?"

"There is only one, sir, I aspire to; all others I should refuse without regard to their emoluments."

"Well, what one is that?" questioned the great statesman, in his deep and powerful voice.

"Count the treasury notes, Mr. Webster."

"The treasury notes, Signor?"

"Yes, sir. You might give me one hundred thousand to count, and watch closely, but you would find only seventy-five thousand when I returned them."

"Signor!" he exclaimed, with lively animation, "there is no chance; there are better magicians here than you, for there would not be *fifty thousand* left after their counting!"

Learning from such an authentic source that there were more capable conjurors in the employ of the government, I retired, without further urging my claim.

PRESIDENT FILLMORE.

When Mr. Fillmore was President I again visited Washington, in my professional capacity. I waited upon him, and he received me in his genial, courteous manner; and, pleasantly running his fingers over my hair, observed, "Signor, your locks are somewhat silvered since we travelled on the canal together; at which time, little did I anticipate becoming President of the United States."

In return, I replied that I hoped he would remain another term, to which he gave a smiling bow.

HENRY CLAY.

This gentleman was an occasional visitor at my exhibitions. At the close of one, he told me, in a happy and laughing manner, he wished I would come to the Senate, Chamber, and, by the aid of my ventriloquial power, send my voice among his democratic friends, so that they might vote for the measures they had opposed. He said, "It would cause a glorious excitement among the democracy!"

My journey South was pleasant and successful. The whites and blacks were alike eager and zealous to enjoy what appeared marvellous in my entertainments, for both

betrayed evident apprehension in respect to my conjura-
tions. The rich, poor, and sick consulted me as to past
events connected with life, liberty, and death, with an un-
hesitating confidence that inspired me with a sympathy for
their simplicity and superstitious delusion.

Richmond.

In many respects this is a delightful city, beautifully situated. The contrasts between the higher and lower classes
were more marked than at the North, and a haughtier tone
of character prevailed among them.

The most objectionable feature was slavery, the influence of which predominated above all other considerations.
It was also perceptible that this institution gave origin to
many of those high-handed actions so common in their civil
and political history, inspiring its admirers with a devotion
far more constant and sincere than any reverence for God,
or patriotism toward the Government.

Charleston.

As I continued my travels, I discovered even a more
determined regard for this idol of their love, surpassing
every moral and natural expression of the just and good by
insult and outrage. It is difficult to understand how singu-
larly infatuated the minds of people can become to a wrong,
which not only inflicts pain upon the sufferer, but must
ultimately recoil upon themselves. In a national point of
view, the North was inexcusable to the world for its ready
and silent acquiesence to slavery; for the political policy of
the free States very generally governed itself to meet the
acceptance of the South, and thus, to a great degree, not
only strengthened the evil, but gave them the power to defy
those who disputed it.

Charleston then contained no attractions; nothing to

amuse, instruct, or impress the mind, with the exception of a few handsome residences on the Parade or Battery.

The majority of buildings were old and dilapidated, without the least assumption to architectural taste. Decay and indolence presented themselves at every footstep, and if the grass did not literally grow in the streets, it was not attributable to any energy put forth to prevent it.

In their business habits, there was a conciliatory and generous spirit that favorably impressed strangers.

As a matter of course, the African race exceeded in population that of the whites. I was frequently amused with their unsophisticated expressions, and the animated wonder displayed in their countenances. How the broad features would distend, the protruding lips expand, as the mouth opened and eyes rolled in that peculiar manner so expressive of surprise and amusement!

"DE DEBIL ABOUT, SURE."

As two athletic negroes were engaged in tumbling about a bale of cotton on the dock at Charleston, a mysterious voice, appearing to come from the middle of the bale, exclaimed,—

"Don't toss me about so hard."

"Bress de Lord! who dat? w'ar you?" spoke one of the darkies, as both let go their hold and stood aghast.

"Inside the bale," responded the voice.

"Joe," said one of the negroes to his companion, "de debil is about, sure," and then collecting himself somewhat, he thus addressed the sewed-up man. "How cum you dar?"

"Put in at the plantation, to made out the cuss-bale," replied the voice inside.

"I golly, Joe, you hear dat, what'll buckra man do next? Wal, you've got to go along wid de bale to de cotton press, and you will be packed den, sure," said one of the knights of the hook, and both set to work again at their job.

Just then loud cries of "Murder! murder!" proceeded from the bale, when the darkies, convinced that "de debil" was really about, dropped everything, and took to their heels. The comedy was highly enjoyed by some friends who were standing around me, as I was looking after a cage of canaries that came out by steamer from New York.

A Runaway Slave.

Conversing one afternoon with the proprietor of a grocery store, my attention was called to a loquacious negro named Jack, who, after inquiring the price and quality of almost every kind of goods, seated himself on a barrel containing rice. At this moment a voice from within halloed,—

"Stop dat; you sitting on my head, Jack."

"Who is dar in dis cask?" inquired Jack, as he quickly jumped off.

"It is me, Tom, from the plantation; massa whipped dis nigger t'other day, and I am going to de North where de men are all free."

Here Jack's face assumed an indescribable picture! Holding up both hands, he uttered with much earnestness,—

"You be going to de North, Tom?"

"Yes, where everybody do as he like. Sam and Joe nailed me up, but keep your mouth shut, for if massa finds dis boy, he will be the death of me."

"But how is you going to breathe, and what you got to eat, Tom?"

"Why, I am in de middle of the rice, and de air comes through de little holes. I want you to take me to de wharf."

"Can't do so, Tom, my principles are of dem sort dat does de right with my brother man, and I will not run off any nigge."

"Den, by golly, I cum out of de cask and stick you," loudly threatened Tom, with a sound of commotion.

"No, you won't do dat," replied Jack, and in an instant darted out of the store with the speed of an antelope, indifferent to every effort to stop him. The reader can judge how much we enjoyed the incident.

Savannah, Columbia, and Augusta, were prettily arranged, with streets broad, and laid out with much taste.

The agreeable acquaintances I formed were courteous, and hospitable in their attentions, free from all servility of speech or manner. Occasionally an allusion would be made to the negroes, and their happy condition, which I could not see, and of course my relation as a stranger forbade me to comment upon.

During my temporary residence at Savannah, the city was surprised by the phenomenon of a snow-storm!

A Southern Snow-Storm.

This was certainly as terrific as any I had seen at the North, the appearances the night previous indicating no such event; but the morning testified not only to the fickleness of the climate, but recognized the truth of the adage, "We know not what a day may bring forth." The oldest inhabitant had no recollection of anything like it in severity.

The scene was one of great interest and amusement, the white population gazing with wonder, and the blacks looking spell-bound, as they scrutinized the heavens to discover whence came the feathery deposit. Finally, old and young of both colors, mingled in a tumultuous affray of snowballing, no one escaping if he chanced to be near.

In Pulaski square, two figures of life size were erected, representing General Jackson and Mr. Van Buren—the latter at the time being President—and if not perfect in feature, were admirable in design.

The bustle and activity on the part of the citizens to procure sleighs called into activity their inventive genius. Temporary runners were made, on which tubs were placed, and on some, boards were arranged for seats. To these hastily improvised sleighs, horses of greater or less speed were attached. But the most singular sight, and beyond description, was the appearance of the negroes, with their heads of wool and shining faces covered with flakes of pure white snow. It was ludicrous in the extreme, as they gayly tripped along, laughing at and ridiculing each other.

I next visited Milledgeville, Macon, and Columbus, cities limited in population, the former the capital of the State.

Affection in Animal Nature.

On my journey I was necessitated to remain over night at a hotel, on the line of the railroad. When I arose next morning I found my rabbits—which were requisite to my business—had increased their family. I removed the young, and gave them to the son of the proprietor of the hotel. After an absence of two days I returned, when, to my surprise and delight, I found the little creatures alive, happy, and contented in the care of a cat, who had adopted them in lieu of her own progeny, which some one of trifling love for brute life, and of blunted nature, had drowned a few nights previous in a neighboring pond. I often relate this fact of kind pussy, and draw a moral from animal nature.

Indian Raid.

On reaching Columbus, I found a great excitement and alarm prevailing, for the town was threatened with an attack from the Indians of the Cherokee nation, who had made their appearance on the opposite side of the bridge which spanned the river, producing the greatest apprehension. The inhabitants were all armed, and cannon placed in position to check them if they advanced, which the Indians perceiving, they concluded to retire some distance.

This tribe of Indians had committed many depredations, murdered the planters, destroyed property, and only a few hours before my arrival had killed the stage driver, and burnt the mail. The city was greatly crowded with strangers, so that accommodations of the humblest character were scarce and expensive, especially at the hotels.

After many days of uncertainty, information was received that the Indians had dispersed in bands, and the right of way again open, which created a general exodus among the travellers, who, in large parties, proceeded on their route. My own fears were not so much allayed as to justify my accompanying them, so I remained a few days longer, and entertained the joyful and relieved citizens with my performances, which they generously patronized.

During this time many travelled the public road, but not without bringing tidings of men, women, and children being butchered, their homes set on fire, and their cattle slaughtered or driven away.

After considerable hesitation, I arrayed myself in the armor of courage, ordered my horses and wagon, and with a loaded single-barrel gun, my agent and myself wended our way through the disturbed country, resting nightly at planters' houses, which were usually well filled with travellers. At one of these places the proprietor, previous to our retiring, distributed among us a number of muskets and ammunition, in order to be able to defend ourselves from any sudden raid of the Indians, which he said might be possible, as they were known to be prowling in the vicinity. This announcement unbalanced my nerves, and pictured to my mind a variety of war-whoops and yells, accompanied by savage visages. All sleep was banished, as I vigilantly watched, with my weapon in hand, in dread expectation of the cruel red men. The night was one of a solemn and fearful character. The heavens were dark and gloomy, and with the exceptional twinkling of an unpretending star, there was not a single gleam of relief to cheer our hopes. Every breath of wind and rustling of the leaves, or the howling of a faithful hound, gave an increased terror to the mind.

So the hours passed until morning arrived, with its bright and welcome sun. Each heart congratulated itself, and experienced that inward acknowledgment which all feel to the Protecting Hand after a miraculous escape.

We breakfasted at an early hour, and immediately active preparations were made by all parties for leaving. Our path was through a thickly-timbered country, romantic, and at times grand and inexpressibly awful, particularly so when penetrating the dense swamps that we encountered on the route. In the afternoon I arrived at a plantation, where I located, and was kindly received. To my delight, a few hundred yards from the house was stationed a company of State militia, ordered out to capture the Indians.

During the night the place was visited by one of those thunder-storms so common to the climate, which none unaccustomed to their severity can estimate. The wind assumed a herculean strength and defiant tone. Giant trees of many years' growth, and those of tender structure, were uprooted and strewed around in utter ruin, while the rain descended in frightful torrents, creating a temporary lake of water. Amidst the most sublime and terrific roaring of thunder, with rapid flashes of lightning illuminating the sombre heavens with brilliant lustre, each element betrayed its utmost fury, and contended for the final superiority of power.

We arose at the break of day to arrange for our departure. All again looked calm, happy, and quiet; the birds were gayly hopping from twig to branch; the cattle snuffed the air with a seeming delight, while a fresh perfume pervaded the softness of the atmosphere. When the horses were ready for the wagon, what was my astonishment on finding a wheel, missing. This was a detention I had not anticipated. Search and inquiry was everywhere made and instituted without success. My difficulty may be easily imagined. Soldiers and negroes were employed in every direction, but failed in its recovery. The day had nearly passed without a knowledge of its whereabouts, when the planter intimated it was not impossible but that some of the soldiers were the perpetrators, as they had been guilty of many provoking acts to travellers, and he would advise me to seek an interview with the captain, and suggest to him the inconvenience of my position, the loss of business, and the propriety of his communicating these facts to his command.

Without delay I proceeded to his quarters, when I found he was absent with most of his men, and would not return until sunset. In the interval I reconnoitred every bush and mound without effect, until the time arrived for meeting the captain. I found him, when we met, to be a rough, unpolished man, with little or no refinement for the sensitive feelings of others. He was of middle stature, with a countenance dark and fierce, intimating much determination; an eye sharp and penetrating, which was almost buried amid his shaggy locks and bushy beard. I stated my trouble to him, and in a pleasant manner told him I had heard his men were in the habit of amusing themselves by practical jokes perpetrated on passers-by, and he would confer a great obligation by interrogating them in regard to the wheel; that I should be willing to pay a reasonable sum for its return, in order that I might pursue my journey.

A WHEEL WITHIN A WHEEL.

"Wheel gone, stranger? That's nothing. Didn't take your horses, did they? Just like my boys; I'll have a talk with them for you."

This was poor consolation, but I had to submit. After a little time the men were collected, and addressed—near as my memory will serve—as follows:

"Soldiers, this stranger from the North lost his wagon wheel last night; now, if any man here knows about it he will say so, and receive the reward, which, I conclude, will be treating the company."

All shook their heads, or verbally denied any knowledge of it. I now despaired of ever recovering the wheel, and was about to return, when the captain, who had been conversing in a low tone with several of the men, came toward me and stated he understood I was a showman, a magician, and ventriloquist—a person that could make something from nothing, little things big, shoot with an empty gun, and the very fellow to entrap the Indians by my voice ; that I had better join the company; or, if I would give an exhibition of my art, I might rely upon the return of my wheel.

I assented, repaired to the house, unpacked a trunk, and selected apparatus for an entertainment, which I gave in the open woods, in the presence of the soldiers, planter's family, and many negroes. The feats produced a good-natured result, and I was considered worthy of the return of my wheel, which was produced and presented to me, accompanied by hurrahs and cheers. The hour being late, I was obliged to defer my departure until the morning, when I arose at an early hour and rode with all despatch to Montgomery, where I arrived at twilight, without the loss of my scalp.

Before bidding adieu to this tribe of savages, I will add

that they, like many ignorant whites, were very superstitious, and everything strange or unaccountable they attributed to the supernatural. An interesting illustration of this is related by Mr. Richardson, in his "Beyond the Mississippi." The substance of it is as follows:

An Inventive Genius.

The history of the Cherokees has one very remarkable character. His Indian name was Sequoyah. He was born in Northern Georgia, long before the tribe removed beyond the Mississippi. His father was a wandering German pedler, named Guest, and his mother an untaught Cherokee woman, whom the peddler married, and soon abandoned. Young Guest showed much mechanical aptitude, becoming an expert blacksmith, and made his own tools and bellows. He also learned the silversmith's art. The Cherokees had no written language. One day, several noticing a white prisoner in the act of reading a letter, raised the question whether the "talking leaf" was a special gift from the Great Spirit, or a mere human invention. Sequoyah, though scouting the suggestion that it was miraculous, grew interested in the subject. A lameness, caused by a white swelling, kept him from active pursuits, and he labored for years collecting the words of the Cherokee language, and designated symbols to represent them from birds, beasts, and trees. He had neither pens or paper, but wrote upon bark with nails or sharp wire. At length a glimpse of the only practical mode dawned upon him. He did not know a word of any language but his own. He had no help from the accumulated experience of other races and other men of genius, but alone in the wilderness this untutored half-breed discovered the great principle, which it had taken civilized nations centuries to ascertain, that arbitrary signs must not stand for ideas, but for sounds. He found the vowel sounds of the

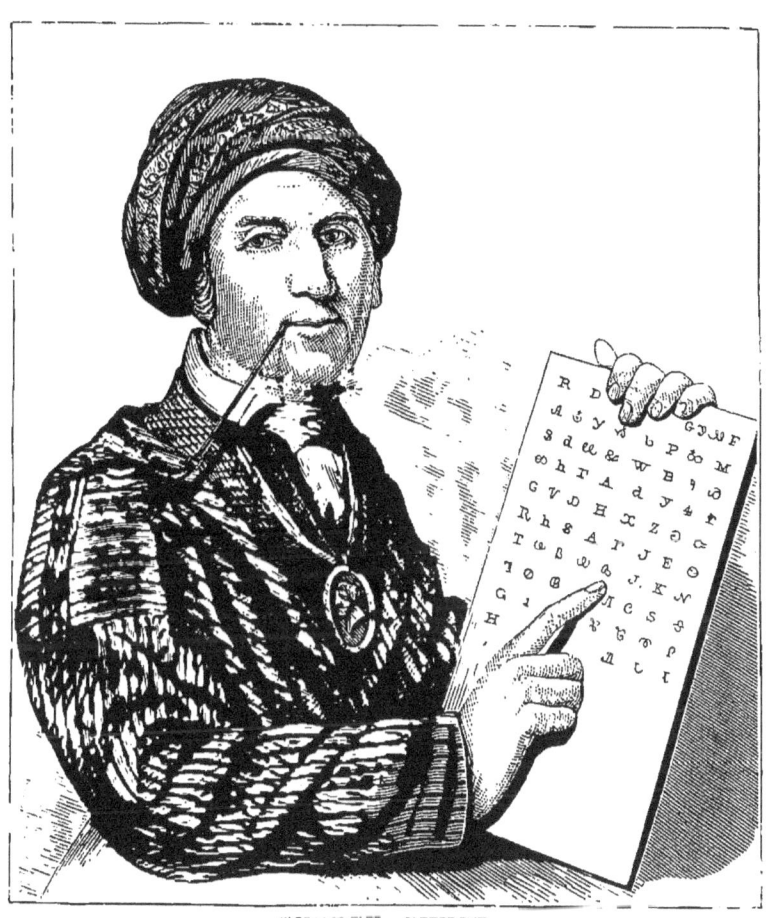

GEORGE GUEST.

Cherokee language to be nine. These he multiplied by the consonant sounds. He made use of an old English spelling-book which fell into his hands, and adopted many of its letters, and invented new characters to fill out his list, thus forming a complete syllabic alphabet. At first his tribe were utterly incredulous, but having taught his little daughter, he sent her away and wrote to her such messages as they dictated, and when she read them the stoutest braves were awe-stricken, and fancied it must be necromancy; but having taught it to others, they confessed his triumph, gave him a great feast, and subsequently held him in high honor and veneration.

9

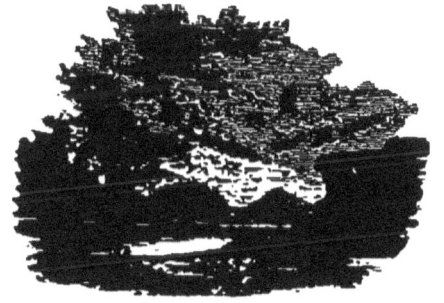

CHAPTER XIX.

A DANGEROUS CUSTOMER.

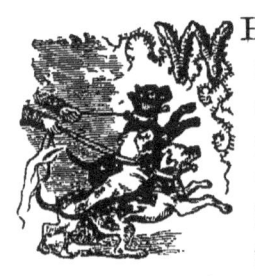 HY Montgomery should have been selected as the rallying-point or place of meeting of the persons appointed to make arrangements and perfect schemes for the dissotion of the Union and the formation of a Southern Confederacy, I cannot fully determine. At the time of the convention, it was a city of some sixteen thousand inhabitants, on the Alabama River, and over three hundred miles from the Gulf of Mexico. When I visited it, on my southern tour, I found it clean and pleasant in appearance, with many fine buildings, streets wide and regularly laid out, the citizens manifesting much interest in improving and ornamenting the place. It had, however, been long noted for its unparalleled murders and outrages, and those criminal acts which insult and defy the law. Men were shot at or stabbed on the public walks, and the guilty wretches permitted to escape, brandishing their pistols and knives with threats of death to any one who should attempt to arrest them.

How the widow and orphan have wept at their sudden bereavement, their own lacerated hearts know best.

Bad Men and Worthless Money.

While here, I myself was connected with an affair that

at one time appeared alarming. A resident of the place paid me ten dollars, which proved to be worthless, and shortly afterward we accidentally met. Showing him the note, he at once recognized it as the same he had given me. When I informed him that it was a bad one, he coolly replied that he knew it was. I then asked him if he would exchange it for good money.

"Oh, yes," he replied; "come to the Planters' Hotel after dinner."

I called, accompanied by Mr. Hutchinson, proprietor of the Montgomery *Advertiser*, and found him in the public bar-room, and upon my presenting the note, he remarked he did not intend to take it back.

"You are aware I can compel you to do so?" I said.

"What do you say?" he impetuously shouted, with a malignant scowl, drawing a huge bowie-knife.

"I will take a glass of sherry wine, sir; what will you drink?" I replied, my presence of mind not deserting me.

Here my friend, Mr. Hutchinson, lost his equanimity, and with a hand of iron grasped him by the neck, and declared if he had a pistol he would shoot him for his attempt to insult and take advantage of a stranger. In a moment several were presented to him by the excited lookers-on, who, in a remarkable degree, were interested in the anticipation of a fight.

In order to avert bloodshed, I at this scene exerted all my powers to a removal of the arms from my defender, which, to my satisfaction, I succeeded in doing, much to his reluctance and the opposition of the lookers-on, who were eager, beyond measure, for an affray. The parties retired to an adjoining room, the one taking with him his knife, of which I endeavored to deprive him, contrary to the wishes of Mr. Hutchinson, who had no weapon. Soon they returned, my debtor holding in his hand a ten-dollar note, which he extended toward me. This I declined receiving, for, from appearances, I entertained the thought that my gallant. friend had advanced the money to satisfy my claim; and to prove to him that I considered the debt cancelled, I here destroyed the counterfeit note.

Toward evening of the same day, I was returning to the hotel, when a druggist appeared at his door and called me by name; and on my entering, he directed my attention to a rifle and shot-gun, advising me, without delay, to take one and shoot the man I had the controversy with.

"You surprise me, sir!" I exclaimed. "Take the life of a human being?"

"Why, yes; waylay and kill the rascal; you are justified by law. I am a witness to his saying you should not leave this place alive. Take this; it is loaded"—offering me a double-barrelled gun.

I refused, saying I was not one that placed so little value on human existence, however bad the creature might be, and, to his disappointment, left without accepting his offer or following his advice.

I now proceeded to Mr. Hutchinson's, informing him of the threat uttered by the person from whom he had so generously defended me. He assured me there was no danger or fear of any injury from him. "For he well knows that if he murdered you, Signor, we would kill him."

I considered the affair as one that might have become, in many ways, fatal in the extreme, though to my great and good fortune, it was avoided, though not without the kind assistance of Mr. Hutchinson.

At Wetumpka, a little, stirring, active place, situated at the head of navigation on the Alabama River, a similar exhibition of that reckless disposition to take life, so common in the South, and in which I was also unintentionally a participant, occurred.

A SHOT FROM BEHIND.

I gave my arm to a gentleman who was suffering from lameness in his feet, and while walking down the main street, a person deliberately ran up, and, from behind, discharged a pistol at us, but without causing any injury, with the exception of my being deprived of a portion of my hair above my ear.

This unexpected salute caused me, quick as lightning, to take refuge in a store, which occasioned much mirth to a large crowd. Sword-canes and bowie-knives, however, were offered to my friend, who was the one upon whom the attack was intended, but the parties retired without bloodshed.

This attack resulted from a political difference, and provided a topic of conversation for the people, in which I had to bear considerable ridicule for being frightened and running away.

The most singular conclusion of this *mêlée* was the assaulting party being summoned before the authorities, and fined five dollars! I expressed my surprise at the smallness of the sum, when a gentleman remarked that he was only fined that amount because he failed to kill; but had he taken life, there would have been nothing to pay.

MOBILE.

I now shipped my horses and carriage on board a steamer, direct for Mobile, as I supposed, but we were frequently delayed at various landings, to take in cotton. The *modus operandi* of shipping this freight provided amusement and lively interest, especially at night-time, which was picturesque and romantic. Bale after bale was tumbled down a declivity of several hundred feet, to the bow of the boat, which, with the glaring light, and the cheerful activity of the negroes as they despatched the cotton, and the animation displayed by the crew as they rolled it on deck, accompanied by the coarse and violent language of the mate, which appeared to be his prerogative, materially compensated for the monotony we should otherwise have been subject to ere we reached Mobile.

This city contained a population large and increasing, with a profitable and important interior and export trade; yet those advantages did not invoke the exercise of those faculties that promote improvement and bestow health. A slumbering propensity prevailed that made evident how little disposed or ambitious the citizens were for developing their many resources, and especially so in the removal of obstructions to navigation. My entertainments created pleasure and surprise to the intelligent, and fear and doubt to the ignorant; many grave feelings of suspicion were indulged in as to my birth, parentage, and belief in the Divine laws; and notwithstanding my presence at church on the Sabbath, which was an omen of some goodness in me, yet it did not dispel the doubts and fears of this serious and thoughtful people.

I was, as usual, consulted by those in love, and others whose thoughts and hopes of the future was the sole object of their hearts' approval.

EXPERIENCE AS A DETECTIVE.

One morning I was waited upon by a venerable-looking gentleman, with gray hair. He proclaimed his unlimited confidence in my knowledge of astrology and those sciences by which light and darkness are penetrated, and the evildoers discovered. He had been the victim of some thief: his watch, diamond ring, and several hundred dollars had been taken from him, and he had failed to discover the perpetrators.

I declared I was not the potent person he accredited me
to be; that I could only distinguish the evil from good by
those influences that were true and above doubt. After a
few additional remarks, I accompanied him to his residence,
where I was introduced to his family, when, in a moment
of inspiration, or some spiritual -manifestation which the
senses cannot define, my eyes encountered the object of the
inquiry. A nervous emotion attacked the guilty party, who
was not unconscious of my victory.

With a success so unexpected and complete, I returned
to the hall to give the matter my attention. I had scarcely
arrived, when a young gentleman, from whom I had but a
few minutes before separated, entered and confessed himself
the offender; that, by an unfortuitous circumstance, he had
become an *habitué* of the gaming-table, whereby, in regular
and desperate play, he had become deeply involved, and to
save his honor from reproach, he had purloined the missing
articles; but last night fortune had favored his efforts; he
had recovered the watch and ring—which had been left for
security—and a larger amount of money than all his previous losses, and as he had the intuition to perceive that I
was aware of his guilt, he had come voluntarily to me, with
a heart full of contrition, in hopes of avoiding the damaging consequence of exposure, by the restoration of the
property to his father, in some manner whereby the secret
might forever be unknown.

His story needed no confirmation, for my first impression, from his appearance, gave me the assurance of his
complicity in the matter. I entertained a sympathy for his
position, and felt it a duty to relieve his embarrassment,
and probably enjoy the proud satisfaction of preserving
him from destruction. I addressed him on the evil path he
was pursuing, the ruin and disgrace that must eventually
follow. I desired him, by all those principles which endear

us to manhood, and the sacred ties that bound him to his family, to avoid the sin and destruction of a gambler's life; that I would convey the valuables to his father by means that would appear equally inexplicable as was their removal. He gave both hands as a pledge of hereafter adhering to my advice; and, placing the effects he had taken upon the table, instantly departed, with a conscience greatly relieved. After brief reflection, I despatched a note to his father, expressing the importance of his presence at my exhibition in the evening, as I entertained pleasant hopes of obtaining for him his missing articles. At the hour of the performance, I observed him, in company with his son and daughter, seated in the hall, and when occasion required the use of a hat, I procured his, remarking that there were many things of value which he had forgotten to remove, and I would take the liberty to do so, which I proceeded to accomplish by removing the notes, watch, and ring from thence, much to his astonishment and that of the audience, who, not understanding the circumstance, considered the hat a receptacle of wealth, and the owner thereof a lucky man. The thanks I received from the gentleman were many, and his entreaties for an explanation not less urgent.

It will be an interesting fact for my readers to know that the son faithfully adhered to his determination, and never afterward entered a gaming saloon, but became an honest citizen.

New Orleans.

My next remove was to the Great Gulf City, noted at home and abroad for the proclivities of her citizens to that unlimited license of feeling, which their actions so frequently developed.

Society here formed a very opposite character to that of other large towns or cities, combining every variety of foreign and national element, conflicting and predisposed to fatal consequences. Yet it must be admitted that the numerous drinking-saloons and gaming-tables inaugurated, in a great measure, most of the cases of shooting and killing that have been so frequently recorded.

The importance of the city in a commercial aspect cannot be over-estimated, for, while all comprehended her position, few could realize her inseparable connection with the immense agricultural productions with which the Mississippi and its tributaries abound, or imagine the increase which the progress of time would prove. What New York is in importance to the North, such was New Orleans to the South. Both are cities of immense combinations and advantages, each ardent and spirited rivals for the trade and commerce of the Western and Middle States. Nature—always just and wise—could not have been more liberal or less economical in her generosity to these extreme geographical points, which, in union with those arts and sciences that provide facilities, remove obstructions, annihilate space, and immensely multiply the resources and wealth of the country, could not otherwise than give a metropolitan stature to the city of New Orleans, such as would attract the ambitious and enterprising from all parts, whose habits were rapidly imparted to the quiet impulses of the natives.

One portion of the city was occupied by the French population, who, if not favored with that progressive spirit to the same extent as their American fellow-citizens, were far more happy and contented, and disinclined to dispute the advance they advocated; and, although their business relations were frequent from necessity, socially they were to a degree limited: the vivacity and peculiarities of the French being, as I suppose, little adapted to the Anglo-Saxon race—otherwise, a perfect harmony existed.

For a stranger to be impressed with the commercial

9*

status of New Orleans, it was at this period only necessary to observe her levees, crowded for miles with ships and steamboats, and mark the untold amount of exports and imports with which they were lined; and how this commerce annually increased until the commencement of the war, it would . be almost fabulous to describe. But a new era in her history has taken place, which, however disastrous in disturbing her progress, or embarrassing to the spirit and pecuniary matters of her citizens, will in a brief period replace her in a position infinitely surpassing her days of former greatness.

My entertainments were well patronized by all classes, without distinction of color, and it would be a question of much doubt to decide whether the wise or ignorant were the most interested and amused, for many of the former consulted me respecting hidden events—buried treasure by the pirate Kidd, their future success, marriage, health, and wealth, so earnest were they of my gifted powers to divine their progress through life. It may not be out of place to assert that in the many thousands of inquiries of this character, I never gave a single encouragement that a possibility existed on my part, or that of others, to foretell coming events, while I regret to state that in all the principal cities the newspapers contain many advertisements by a class of people professing their knowledge as fortune-tellers.

An Over-Zealous School-Teacher.

During one of my exhibitions in this city, a lady, proprietress of a boarding-school, attended with her pupils. She was of a nervous, quick temperament, difficult to please, and did not hesitate to criticise openly all my feats. A singular scene occurred, owing to her forward deportment, which, while it did not add to her display of wisdom, produced much merriment in the audience.

I had borrowed a lady's silk cloak—at that time fashionable—and cut a large piece from the centre, replacing it again without injury, to the no small astonishment of the company. But the "schoolmarm" pronounced her dissatisfaction with the trick, and was anxious that I should repeat the experiment with her own cloak. To this I assented; but as she desired to *cut it herself,* I declined, stating the feat was a mere deception, and that her cutting and mine would not produce the same effect. After much tantalizing and entreating me to allow her to cut it, I consented, and gave her the scissors, when she instantly cut a piece large enough to admit the head of a person, and holding it up to view, remarked: "There, sir! repair this."

"Madam, that which I do not cut myself, I am unable to restore!"

The excitement and laughter my words produced can be imagined. The poor woman paid dearly for her interference. This scene was a theme of gossip for many days.

JEALOUSY AND LOVE.

One morning a gentleman entered my room abruptly, and signified his intention of shooting me, at the same instant presenting a pistol to my head. I demanded an explanation of his unwarrantable course.

"Why, sir," he hurriedly replied, "at one of your exhibitions, a few evenings since, your automaton figure accused me of being in love with more than a dozen ladies, which, to my misfortune, is readily believed by the lady who accompanied me, and to whom I am engaged, and I hold you, sir, responsible for the destruction of my happiness."

"Why did you not assure the lady it was only a practical joke?"

"It may be to you, sir, but to me it has had a most

damaging effect, and the only reparation you can afford is to visit the lady with me, and convince her of the truth."

"Most certainly," I replied, seizing my hat, and immediately walked with him to the home of the disquieted one, who, after an explanation, banished her suspicions, and confirmed her faith by impressing a kiss on the lips of her innocent lover. A peaceful conclusion to a stormy beginning.

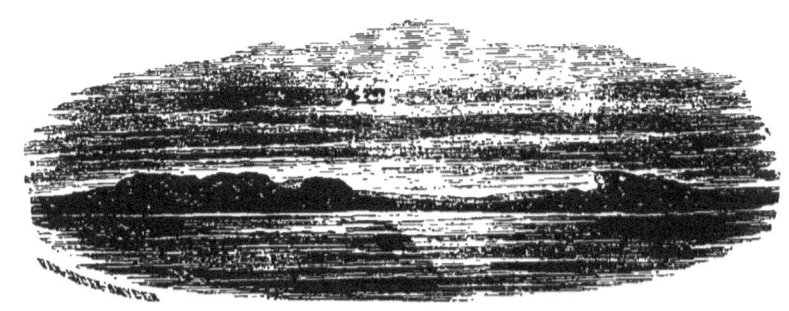

CHAPTER XX.

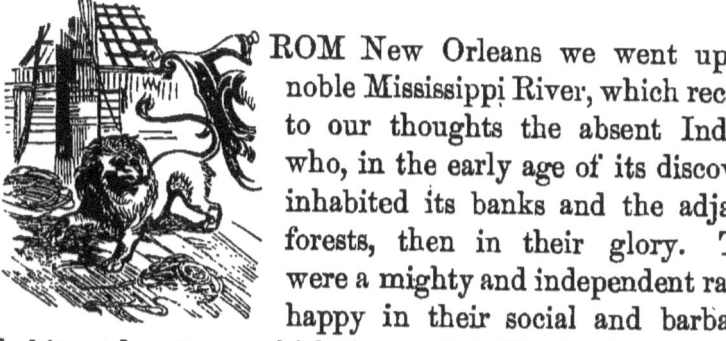

ROM New Orleans we went up the noble Mississippi River, which recalled to our thoughts the absent Indians, who, in the early age of its discovery, inhabited its banks and the adjacent forests, then in their glory. They were a mighty and independent race—happy in their social and barbarous habits and customs, which time and civilization have partially conquered—and are removed to a new home in the far west.

In my progress I exhibited at all the cities and towns with my customary success, creating strange impressions as to my origin, and the manner in which I obtained my mystical and ventriloquial acquirements.

The stories which had preceded and accompanied me, greatly alarmed the minds and imaginations of the colored inhabitants, who speculated as to my nativity and claim to humanity. They had been given to understand that I was a wizard in the true sense; that I could metamorphose black people white; and if I was not a lineal descendant of the magicians who lived and operated in the days of Pharaoh, I must be fully equal to them, for by what natural process could I accomplish the wonders they had heard of and witnessed? -The more they inquired, the greater were they perplexed. So earnest were they in their faith that many came with large sums of money, and entreated me to change their color. This ignorance was the more readily excusable than that frequently displayed by their masters and others.

At Natchez I encountered a party of the Cherokee tribe of Indians, several of whom were squaws. In company with a friend I visited their wigwams or tents in the immediate vicinity of the city. I found them inquiring and subtle to a degree unmistakable. In broken, yet comprehensive English, they complained of the aggressive power of the Government in removing them from the land of their childhood, and driving them to the far-off territories, where the rivers and streams, the rocks and woods, were all strange!

I remarked to one, whose countenance betrayed an indignant feeling, and who violently denounced the vindictive acts of the Government toward their people, "that they would be far happier in their new region of country, and less exposed to the intrusions of their white brethren, who were only influenced by that Great Spirit who giveth wisdom, and whose sun and moon warms and lights every part of the earth with His glory." To these words he shrugged his shoulders, and replied, "Me no think so."

I communicated my wish for them to witness a few experiments which I proposed to show them. Immediately they all collected around me, and watched my movements with the most unremitting scrutiny. Their surprise and astonishment I have never seen equalled; for their eyes bespoke what a wonderful person I appeared to them—especially so, when I declared my intention to eat one of their babies, which the mother refused to part with, much to their joy and satisfaction. But when I exercised my ventriloquial powers, by imitating and conversing with various voices under the ground and in their baskets, they became wild and alarmed, and precipitately fled, leaving myself and companion alone. We followed and called aloud for them to stop, that I might explain; but this only increased their speed, giving the most unearthly yells and screeches in reply.

Perhaps nothing in the course of my travels produced such a continual smile of wonder, or afforded an equal amount of enjoyment to all parties interested, as the horses I drove. They were sold to me under the cognomens of "General Jackson" and "Martin Van Buren." They were a tall, well-matched, finely-proportioned pair of bays, and admirably did they represent their illustrious namesakes. A determined energy prevailed in the former, and a sagacious spirit predominated in the latter. They were known and celebrated as the

GIFTED HORSES.

I found from experience that ostlers in general devoted but little care and attention to their necessities. Frequently they were without food and water, and in order to insure better treatment, I resorted to stratagem. On my arrival I invariably communicated to those who had charge of them that they were gifted with the powers of speech, and if they were in any manner neglected they would announce the fact to me; and to convince the people of this truth, I would converse with the horses, and inquire how they were taken care of at their last stopping-place. They would reply, "Excellent; never better; good feed and water." Then those present would utter their amazement, with a disposition to retreat. At other times they would express delight, and collect their friends and the inmates of the house to see the wonderful horses.

At Vicksburg I greatly doubted the sincerity of the ostler. On questioning him in regard to his unkindness, he stoutly declared it was not so. I stated to him that the horses had complained to me. He insisted that he had been faithful. "If you have, they have not spoken truly," I replied, and proposed that we walk to the stable and inquire. The man followed with a look of assurance, asserting that he had done his duty. When we reached there, I said,—

"Well, General, how is it? How is the grain?"

"Plenty, but no water."

"How with you, Martin?"

"No water, no water."

At this point the ostler shook his fist in rage, accompanied by an oath, exclaiming,—

"It is false, you brutes!" and hastened to fill their troughs with a needless supply of corn and water, sufficient for several days.

The animals neighed, "Good! this is what we wanted."

He did not stay to listen further, or to behold the gusto with which the horses ate and drank, but made a rapid exit, expressing his belief "that they were the d—l's horses."

This little episode was the theme of much jollity, and during the remainder of my stay, the horses were well provided for. Many similar scenes of this character were constantly occurring, which afforded much merriment, and insured the best offices of care for the "General" and "Martin."

I continued my journey, receiving constant ovations and courtesies, which provided me with a gayety of disposition that did not fail to impress me with a thoughtful spirit. I could not help comparing my happy position with the poor, sick, and unfortunate. At times, indeed, I may assert that my mind was occupied with an expression of acknowledgment to that source from whence we receive all the love and goodness we enjoy, directing me on all opportunities to contribute to and assist the distressed and deserving. I gave freely, and performed gratuitously for all societies and deserving objects, and realized an inexpressible happiness thereby.

At this period—1837—the monetary affairs of the country were sadly inflated; the banks had everywhere suspended specie payment, and issued an unlimited amount of paper currency. Fabulous sums in shinplasters, from five cents to a dollar, were circulated by the people, so that to a considerable extent every man was a banker, and distributed his own notes, promising to redeem them in bank bills whenever a certain amount was presented.

In this manner every State was crowded with all descriptions of worthless paper. Property and merchandise became subject to the influence it produced, creating an artificial value beyond belief. Many amusing instances to me resulted from the exorbitant sums which storekeepers desired for their goods.

At Natchez I was looking at several pairs of boots suspended at the door. When I inquired the price, the owner replied,—

" Thirty-eight dollars."

" For the lot, sir ? "

" No, sir, for one pair."

One storekeeper demanded eighteen dollars for a hat, and when I observed it was an enormous price, answered,—

" That is not high, sir; I gave twenty-one hundred dollars for that nigger's head you see there."

A Financial Crisis.

While in Mississippi, I had collected seven hundred and fifty-five dollars of the Hinds County Bank at Clinton. There were fives, tens, and twenties in post notes, including thirty dollars in ones, which were payable in specie on demand. The post notes were, like those of other banks, at a great discount and almost valueless out of the State. I retained them until I arrived at Clinton, thinking I could make better terms at the bank where they were issued. I called with the expectation that I could purchase a draft on New York, or some other northern city, but my hopes were sadly disappointed when I was informed that they would only redeem the one-dollar notes; the others they could not give specie for until they arrived at maturity. I observed that it would be impossible for me to keep them, especially as they were of different dates, and I intended in a few days to leave for St. Louis, where their money was foreign, and it would be of little value. Therefore, I presumed that they would discount them.

"Could not do that, sir. We should soon break."

"What! not purchase your own notes?"

"No, sir; not prepared to."

"That is singular," I replied. "Is there no one in the town that would discount them?"

"Yes," one answered, pointing to a dry-goods store. "If you call upon the proprietor, I think probably he may oblige you."

I received all my pay in gold for the one-dollar notes, and walked to the store mentioned, where I found the owner, a polite gentleman, but possessed of a sharp countenance.

After naming my business, he said he would exchange for specie.

"At what rate?" I asked.

"I will give you one hundred and twenty dollars for your paper."

The reader may imagine I was a little more than surprised at his offer.

"Did you not make a mistake, sir?" I inquired.

"No. I will give you *one hundred and twenty dollars* in silver for your seven hundred and twenty-five in paper, and I don't care to take it even at that."

Finding it impossible to make better terms with him, I left and returned to the hotel, with the supposition that I should be fortunate enough to meet with some person disposed to be more liberal. I found several gentlemen willing to accommodate me, but at no less rate than the former. After remaining in the place two days, I made a sale of it for one hundred and thirty dollars, that being the highest sum I could obtain for it. This sacrifice was nothing compared with the insignificant value of some paper.

The destruction and loss entailed upon almost every one was enormous. None escaped the terrific consequences that ultimately resulted in bankruptcy. Counterfeit notes, and those of broken banks, were circulated with the same freedom as the genuine. Extravagance and delusive wealth predominated without limit, and when the explosion occurred, it was like the eruption of a volcano, leaving few rich and many poor. As to the intrinsic value of money at this period, I will give an instance:

The profits of my business during a journey of seven months, amounted to thirteen thousand dollars, from which I only realized *thirty-seven hundred dollars!* Such was the character of the financial affairs of 1837!

I continued my peregrinations, and arrived at St. Louis, a city occupying an important position in the commercial history of the West, and although limited in point of population, there existed an indomitable energy of character and business qualifications in the citizens at large, who, prompted by a liberal policy, gave encouragement and freedom to the interests of trade; and to those principles, combined with her extraordinary advantages, natural and geographical, may be ascribed her present unbounded influence. A large proportion of the products with which the boats on the Mississippi, Missouri, and Ohio rivers are laden is taken from her levee.

The rapid growth of the city has indeed been marvellous and gratifying. Her firm and untiring advocacy of those issues that are unrestricted and benign, and which accord so truthfully with the progress of the age, attract the special admiration of all devotees of wisdom and liberty.

I gave my exhibitions in the ball-room of the Planters' Hotel, and was obliged to erect my own seats. For this purpose I made a contract with a respectable master carpenter. The following morning he came with five black men, who performed the work under his direction, but in a slovenly and imperfect manner. At this time the mechanics were mostly of the colored race, but when I again visited the city, seven years after, I likewise had occasion to make my own accommodations, and once more procured the above person, who made his appearance with German carpenters, and finished the work in an admirable and expeditious manner; and so, as emigration pursued its course westward, the colored people gave way to the skill of the foreigner, and in a short period the white citizen and laborer monopolized every employment, by which means slave property became unprofitable, and obliged the owners to dispose of them.

The city was pleasantly situated on the Missouri River, with convenient and spacious streets, and all the opportunities for the display of taste and refinement. Pleasant society and generous hospitality were the characteristics of the inhabitants: a prevalent feature in western life.

A NERVOUS TRAVELLER.

I left St. Louis for Louisville in a new iron steamer, called the "Ion," in honor of Miss Ellen Tree, the charming actress who so exquisitely personated this character in Mr. Talford's classically beautiful tragedy of that name.

The boat was making her second trip. Shortly after

leaving, I became acquainted with one of the passengers, a very pleasant Virginian, who had been in the interior of Missouri to purchase land, and was now returning home to take his wife and children to his new estate.

He was a man of good sound information, well acquainted with the history of his country, spoke of her in terms of praise, whenever the subject deserved it, and condemned that which all sensible Americans consider is not compatible with her interest and honor.

Literature found in him a firm advocate, while the arts and sciences animated his feelings as he discoursed of them. His patriotism glowed with that quiet sensitiveness that charmed every ear. He was good-looking, though corpulent. After a few hours' association with him, I discovered that, with his amiable qualities, he was extremely nervous, for whenever the boat stopped to replenish her stock of fuel, he would say, "My friend, let us hasten to the extreme end of the boat; for if an explosion should occur, we should have a better chance of escape." And whenever I attempted to dismiss his fears, he would reply, "Friend, there is much danger in the boat's stopping. I am always fearful until a few moments have expired on her course."

The "Ion" had an innumerable quantity of life-preservers suspended in various parts, for the protection of the passengers, and my quondam acquaintance would constantly promenade the deck with me, with one over his arm. I do not ever remember to have met a person so apprehensive of accident.

The second night, as we were steaming up the Ohio River, we were thrown into great consternation by the boat running upon a snag or tree buried in the river, one portion of which was just beneath the surface of the water. The shock was violent, and many others, as well as myself, were precipitated from our berths, receiving numerous bodily bruises. The shouts of voices, the rushing of the steam as it escaped, the noise and confusion of passengers as they frantically ran to and fro, greatly excited my apprehension as to our situation.

Partially dressed, I hastened on deck, inquiring what had happened, where we were, and what was to be the result.

No one was capable of affording the least information, and all were looking after their own preservation. Observing many with life-preservers, I ran to the place where I had previously seen them, when, to my utter astonishment, they had all disappeared. At this instant the clerk of the boat passed by, and assured me that there was no ground for alarm, for the "Ion," instead of running against the snag, was lying across it, and, in a short time, would be able to proceed.

My anxiety being relieved, I turned to seek my Virginia friend, who I discovered on the lower deck, enveloped in life-preservers. He was a perfect pyramid of them, for scarcely a particle of his body was visible ; a more comical effect was never produced or witnessed. He looked Falstaff, complete. It was so grotesque that I laughed immoderately. He had placed four around his waist, two on each arm, and one attached to each leg. When the passengers beheld him so equipped, their mirth was unbounded and their wit unlimited. I inquired if he had entertained any serious fright.

"Yes, indeed!" he replied, with much excitement; "but I was determined to float, as you perceive!"

During the continuation of our journey, the event was a constant source of amusement, rendered especially so as the author of our mirth kept possession of his preservers until our arrival at Louisville, where I left the boat. My nervous friend gave me his address, with a pressing invita-

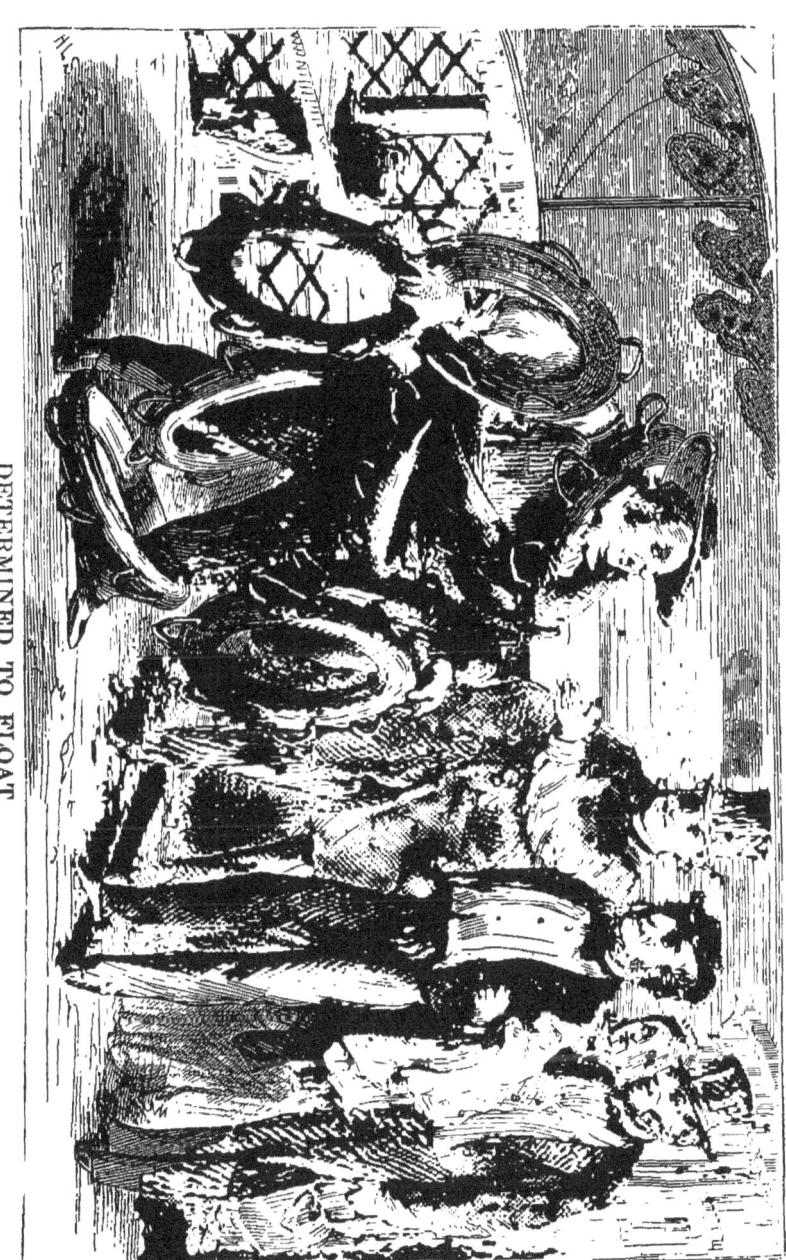

DETERMINED TO FLOAT.

tion to visit him, and talk over the—to him—wonderful events of our voyage.

I have never had the pleasure of again meeting him, but I frequently picture to myself, and describe to others, his ludicrous appearance.

Louisville was a neat, moderate sized city, the inhabitants pleasant, social, and refined. Many families were immensely wealthy, and not less liberal in their expenditures, and encouraging the most expensive taste and splendor, with gayety in life. My professional exploits secured me great popularity and success. A little incident happened to me here, which gave delight to the citizens, at my expense.

A Quick-Witted Irishman.

While conversing in a grocery store with the proprietor, an Irishman came in to make some purchases. The trader was extremely anxious for me to astonish him by performing some feat, which I complied with. Before concluding, I requested the loan of a quarter of a dollar from the Hibernian, which he at first refused, and even when the storekeeper pledged himself responsible for it, he reluctantly gave it to me. I desired him to close his hand, and hold the money secure, and I would change it to a five-dollar gold-piece.

"Faith!" he muttered, as he grasped the quarter, "it is just as I would like ye to be after doing, but I don't believe ye can coin money so aisy. Let me see if you can do it!" he excitedly exclaimed.

"It is already done," I said. "Open your hand and look."

The man cautiously relaxed his fingers, and, at the first glimpse of the gold, jumped and hurrahed wildly, as an Irishman only can; but when his curiosity was entirely satisfied as to its reality, he carefully deposited it in his pocket, with many thanks, declaring me to be the most wonderful man in the world.

I here desired him to replace the money in my hand, and I would again convert it to the original quarter.

"Sure, after Mike being rich, would ye make him poor again?"

"But you know it is only a trick," I answered.

"A thrick? Divil a one! Sure, man, it is a rale piece of goold,"—thrusting his hand into his pocket, to protect it from any sudden or unperceived effort on my part to extract it.

"You know it is but a joke," I repeated. "Return me the gold, and I will astonish you by transforming it into silver, once more."

"By St. Patrick, you had better not do that!"

"Yes, you must give me back the gold."

"I would not part with it if priest McDermott bid me."

Finding my efforts to procure the money a failure, I resorted to artifice by alarming his fears of my power to do good or evil. I assured him that unless he returned the piece of gold, he would be a miserable man all his life, for it was Satan's coin, who was always around in search of his own, and would take him away with the gold.

"Och! sure, your honor, the Holy Father will save Mike, and if ye want any more silver quarters to change into goold, come to Michael McCarty. He is the man for you." And with these consoling words he walked rapidly away, leaving me minus my half-eagle, while the storekeeper laughed immoderately at the magician being outwitted by a son of the Emerald Isle.

All Louisville became cognizant of "the joke," as they called it, and hugely enjoyed it at my expense; but I could not see it as such.

When I revisited the city, I learned that the smart Irish-man frequently inquired after the man who made the five-dollar gold-piece!

A Man on a Pleasure Tour.

The peculiarities of travel in the United States singu-larly impressed me, as it must all foreigners who visit the country for profit or enjoyment.

In railroad cars, steamboats, and hotels, you are assuredly certain of meeting some acquaintance. In many instances I encountered very singular evidences of American business and pleasure travelling combined—some so remarkable and incredible as to produce admiration and wonder. Giant efforts are undertaken, with a unanimity of thought and action, only applicable to themselves. Naturally a people of great fondness for pleasure and sight-seeing, their wan-dering spirit has no limit, but, coupled with a desire to see and learn, they view distances and adverse circumstances as an impulse rather than an impediment. This characteris-tic is truly and laughably established by the following:

On my travels in Kentucky I met a gentleman with whom I was acquainted in the North.

After the usual congratulations, I inquired if he was resid-ing in this State. "Oh! no," he replied, with *sang-froid* expression, "I am on a pleasure tour." Encountering him a few days after in the street, with a huge bundle of papers under his arm, he remarked "that the times were very pre-carious; no money; every one appeared to be insolvent; did not know what means he should resort to."

"What troubles you?" said I. "Surely a person in pur-suit of pleasure need not meet impediments in regard to the character of the times."

"Yes, sir; but I have several hundred bills to collect," answered the pleasure-seeker, "and I have been unable to

10 *

procure as much as will suffice to pay my ordinary expenses, although I have traversed this and three adjoining States, the past six weeks, with accounts amounting to no less than forty thousand dollars."

"Why, I really imagined you were on a pleasure tour."

"Oh, yes, I am," he replied, "with the exception of making these collections, and searching after titles, and holding commissions for five commercial houses."

Such is a man of pleasure in the United States, and I do not doubt he spoke the truth, for I am convinced you cannot discover the American who does not mingle business with his pleasure travel.

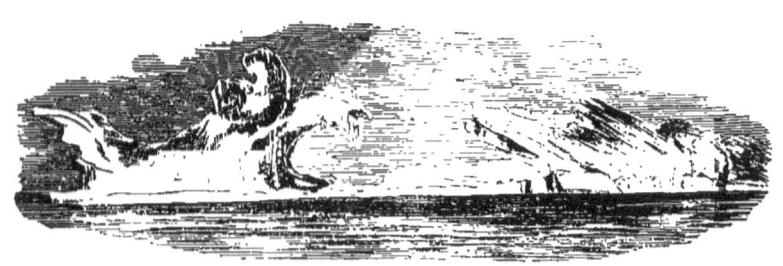

CHAPTER XXI.

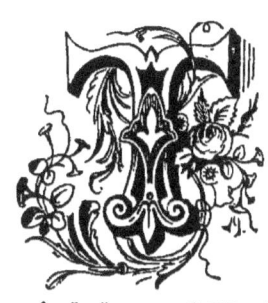HE provinces of New Brunswick and Nova Scotia being desirable points to visit, I proceeded thence, direct from Boston, in the autumn season, per steamer "St. John." There was a large number of passengers, composed of all nationalities, classes, and ages. It reminded me of Noah's Ark in miniature, for there were not only men, women, and children, but goods, wares, and merchandise of all kinds and descriptions, with household furniture of every variety, besides cattle and other four-footed animals, without number.

In a few moments, I formed an affable acquaintance with nearly all who desired or entertained any inclination to be communicative, which enabled me to learn the antecedents and past history of many, also their future prospects and expectations in life.

They comprised pleasure seekers, business men, adventurers, and lovers; and for a miscellaneous assemblage, their views were above mediocrity. An American gentleman inquired of a Nova Scotian, how he was pleased with his visit to the United States?

He replied, "Very much, except its political character."

" Why, it is our pride; the admiration and hope of mankind."

" But there is an excess of freedom; no restraint to thought or action."

" These are the cardinal principles of our institutions. Our forefathers fought vigorously and victoriously for them, and they remain to-day an example of freedom, prosperity and happiness."

" While I admit you enjoy many excellences, which other nations would profit by adopting, yet this equality is untenable, and unnatural. Society and authority demand a line of demarkation."

" This prevails abundantly, for the social elements of life are not amenable to political jurisdiction."

" While I admit the latter may predominate to an extent, yet there is something in republicanism that is equalizing, without regard to merit or worth."

" Quite the contrary, sir. We regard our warriors and patriots with popular veneration. We believe in our hearts that Washington never had his compeer as a statesman or General."

At this moment he was interrupted by a Frenchman exclaiming,—

" Sir, excuse me, you make mistake; the first General of the world was Napoleon. Ah, sir! you forget he conquered kings and kingdoms. My dear sir, I admire Washington; but I love, reverence the Emperor Napoleon."

" It is but natural that you are endeared to Napoleon. All history acknowledges his military genius; but never-theless, in my own estimation, he was inferior to Washington in those attributes which give perfection to man; for in his efforts to abolish monarchs he did not abolish monarchy, while Washington, in establishing a republic, made every citizen a nobleman, or gave him the means to become one."

"You wrong the Emperor; his glory is bright as the summer's sun; he fought the tyrants of Europe for civil and political liberty."

"You must remember, sir, America was very differently situated; a new country, unaccustomed to the influences of wealth and a powerful aristocracy; the circumstances and positions of each were very different; both were great men, but the exception in Washington's favor was, he was a great and good man; his life pure and unsullied, without a single blemish upon his character."

These remarks evidently provoked the Frenchman, for he drew up his shoulders, shook his head, and with much excitement replied,—

"Pardon me, sir, I cannot acknowledge your opinion for the honor of France; pride for the grand Emperor, and my own consideration forbid it."

Here he turned away, and the party dispersed.

A Myth—One of the Smiths!

A few moments before leaving the wharf, there was a sharp controversy between the captain and a genteel-looking man, who, it appeared, had on several occasions travelled on the boat without contributing the passage-money. Flattered by his former success, he believed he could again repeat the imposition; but the clerk, not being desirous of granting him the opportunity, demanded his fare. Smith observed he would pay it when ready. The clerk then requested him to leave the boat.

"No, indeed! I would like to see the man who could put me off."

After an angry exchange of words, the captain was called, and promptly requested payment, not only for his present passage, but for all previous ones.

"Now, captain, there is no need of your being so provoked. My name is Ezra Smith, son of Ben Smith, and nephew of Joe Smith, the Mormon prophet."

"I don't care for all the Smiths in ——. Pay your money. We have no room for dead-heads."

"Let us talk the matter over, captain. The world will not explode if a man's pockets are empty, and he don't always have ready money to pay his way. Why should he be called a dead-head?"

"There, now, leave the boat, or I will throw you overboard," at the same time pushing him toward the plank.

"Captain, hands off, or I'll take the law on you, sure as my name is Ezra Smith."

"I don't care for the law; come, walk ashore," said the captain, at the same time calling several of the crew. They landed him on the dock, amidst much laughter, he vehemently shouting,—

"It is an outrageous insult to the Smith family."

The night was soft, and the moon brightly illuminating and cheerful. The whole horizon presented the remarkable feature of a prismatic curtain—not a speck or cloud, while the vast space was one spectacle of harmony and beauty. To insensible minds the splendid magnitude of the sight would fail to attract admiration or reverence, for the potent power of a benign hand would be invisible to them, and they never behold the glory and wisdom which give birth to all that is magnificent and good, but gaze without a reflective thought or an inward praise.

Old Neptune was in the best of humor; not a ripple disturbed his ocean bed; the vessel fleetly moved over the calm sea, emitting from her bow the phosphorescent light in dazzling abundance. The captain of the boat was a wag—at least he pretended to be such. He had related several singular adventures he had participated in, such as the removal of doorsteps, unfastening of bells, and exchanging sign-boards, with other similar midnight depredations, arising from his love of a good joke, as he said.

Fortunately I was unknown to him; neither was he aware that there was a magician on board, which enabled me to test his qualifications for encountering one of those pranks he was so fond of enjoying at the expense and ridi-cule of others. For this purpose it was necessary for me to act with precaution, and then only as opportunity pre-sented, especially as ventriloquists depend as much upon favorable circumstances as upon science, or the artist's skill. Nearly all the passengers had retired for the night, with the exception of a few who could not resist the temptation of strolling on deck, to enjoy the noble sight the heavenly bodies afforded. For several hours I paced every part of the vessel, with the hope of meeting the captain; but be-coming weary and feeling fatigued, I was about proceeding to my berth, when I perceived him coming from the cabin. Preparing myself for an interview, I saluted him, remark-ing on the loveliness of the night.

"Very fine," he replied, also remarking that he had been suffering the past three hours with an excruciating headache.

I stated that I had in my carpet-bag a peculiar powder, a pinch or two of which would probably relieve him, as its efficacious character had so frequently been tested. With the utmost despatch I procured the restorative and gave it to him, and after partaking liberally of the same, he de-clared he had experienced much benefit therefrom; at all events, he was decidedly more lively and loquacious. We at last descended into the cabin, where he seated him-self upon a large travelling trunk, when, to his great amaze-ment, a voice proclaimed from the inside,—

"Halloo! captain."

In a moment he was on his feet, inquiring, with looks of intense interest, who was secreted there.

"It is only me," said the concealed one.

"Who are you?" demanded the captain, excitedly.

"Only an old friend—a dead-head," was the response.

"Have you not paid your passage-money?" questioned the captain.

"Pay! I never pay," retorted the unseen.

"What is your name?"

"*Ezra Smith.*"

The captain's countenance was petrified with astonishment, and he observed to me that he thought he recognized the tone at first, but he said, "Well, Ezra, you are a scamp. I thought you were put off at the wharf?"

"So I was, captain, but I managed to get here, and unless you give me something to eat, I shall die from starvation."

"A good thing if you do."

At that moment groans and moaning issued from the trunk, which so affected the captain that he called for the steward to bring a hatchet and some brandy, quick as possible; but it is needless to say that upon his opening the trunk Mr. Smith was not to be found. The noise awakened many from their sleep, who came rushing to the spot in their night-garments, in time to witness the success of my ruse. The mystery greatly perplexed and disturbed the captain's mind; so much so, that he emphatically declared he believed some fearful calamity had occurred to Smith, of which he was the cause, and that his spirit had truly appeared.

The following morning the event was a theme of general discussion, all unanimously agreeing that Smith was then on board, or a fatal tragedy had overtaken him. Nothing of a special character engrossed attention, until our arrival at

Eastport, where the steamer was detained several hours discharging cargo, and a vigilant watch was kept to discover Smith, which was a source of great amusement to me.

The boat again proceeded on its journey, after a complete and indefatigable search had been made for Smith, whose whereabouts, living or dead, was of momentous consequence to the captain, who, being of a speculative disposition in regard to spiritual manifestations, could not divert his thoughts from the conviction he entertained of Ezra Smith's death, and his own complicity. It was evident that a few hours had effected an extraordinary change in his appearance, for in his movements there was a total absence of that vivacity and self-possession which at first impressed me. Every footstep betrayed less activity, and a gloomy care pervaded his countenance, as if some sad and portentous event awaited him.

With mingled feelings of satisfaction and sympathy for his present unhappy condition, I concluded my object had been attained, and the proper time had arrived for removing his fears and embarrassment, by acknowledging myself the sole author of the misery and suffering he had endured. This was the more necessary from the rapid pace at which we were approaching our destination, when we should in all probability separate forever. There was but little time to execute my purpose, for the passengers were all busy collecting their baggage, preparatory to landing. My first step was to arrange for an interview. This was soon accomplished, and without ceremony I proceeded to discharge my mission. At the commencement he was reticent and guarded, which was only relieved by the gradual development of the whole plot, and my mischief.

"What! do you mean to assert that Smith was not in the trunk?" he indignantly demanded.

"I do, most emphatically."

) 10*

"Is it possible my senses have so deceived me?"

"Precisely so, captain."

"But how am I to account for the conversation, and the disappearance of the man? If not Smith, who was it?"

"A myth—one invented for the occasion. To be explicit, captain, I personated Smith by my powers of ventriloquism."

"Who are you?"

"Signor Blitz, at your service."

"What! the celebrated ventriloquist I have heard so much of?"

"I am the person."

"Then I am indebted *to you* for all the torments I have experienced?"

"Truly so—I was a witness to the altercation between you and Smith—and I had the presumption to exercise my professional abilities upon your credulity."

"Well, Signor Blitz, you succeeded admirably, and forgetting all I have had to contend with, mentally and physically, on account of your roguery, I freely forgive you; only promise not to mention the subject to any person during your stay in this part of the country, and be assured I shall never hear the name of Smith again without being reminded of you and my friend Ezra."

I promised, and faithfully kept it during my sojourn in the town.

Shortly after my disclosure to the captain, we arrived at St. John, a peculiar, quaint town, void of any attractive feature. The houses were mostly built of wood, with no pretension to architectural rule or taste whatever.

The inhabitants I found to be a rugged and unpretending people, genial and hospitable in their feelings toward strangers, and unquestionably happy and contented in their civil and political enjoyments, devoted in their attachments to the mother country, depending more upon the imperial legislation for justice and material aid, than the wisdom of their own provincial parliament, and those beneficial requirements which should emanate from themselves, as a people anxious and desirous of securing such legislation as might be necessary to the development of their resources, and a permanent assurance of prosperity for the future.

National blessings are the results of energy and judgment, and may not always be secured without an indomitable struggle; yet, when consummated, they display a pride and glory in behalf of the nation, whose discernment lost no time in anticipating and realizing them.

The business of St. John was important, consisting principally of large exports of lumber, ship-building, and fisheries, which, if proper means had been used in giving encouragement and opportunity for the development of these and other advantages, the extent of trade would have been infinitely greater.

The soil, for the most part, is unproductive, and the climate uninviting, especially so to emigrants who dislike cold and severe winters of five months' duration. Yet there are tracts of land of great fertility, which, with skill and industry, make amends for the unfavorable seasons. Iron, coal, and other minerals abound in immense quantities, which, of late years, have become a source of wealth, and if the American spirit of progress was only imbued in the character of the New Brunswick people, their trade would be immense.

My professional exertions were bountifully rewarded, for a crowded audience was in constant attendance. By my patrons I was looked upon with anxiety and dread—suspicious of my ability for good or evil.

It was declared that armies of mice infested every house, as all the cats had been driven to distant localities by me;

also, the cows failed to give their customary milk, much to
the discomfiture of every family. These, and other diabolical visitations, were attributed to my influence, so that the
grave looked upon me with misgivings, and the young with
fear and anxiety.

At the close of my engagement, I proceeded by steamer
up the St. John River, a beautiful and picturesque stream,
with lovely and interesting scenery,—a miniature resem-
blance of the majestic Hudson, in its grandeur and magnificence,—to Fredericton, the capital of the province.

I found Fredericton to be a small inland city, void of
every significant claim for its extent of commerce, or any
effort on the part of its inhabitants to promote it.

A silent submission yields to existing circumstances,
namely, a total indifference to progression, or that spirit
which buoys up hope and effort, and conquers even when
despair appears triumphant. This trait is a distinguishing
feature in the people of the British territories of North
America, in whom there is not that intuitiveness that marks
the nervous sanguinity of native Americans, whose happy felicity to embrace advantages have given them their
present greatness. To account for the inertness of one and
the energy of the other is an enigma which embarrasses
the mind ; and when we refer to the rapid transformation
of wildernesses into States, with the growth of cities and
towns, we are impressed with amazement, yet we cannot
otherwise than premise that their immense strides toward
civilization and power must be based upon the liberal influences which the United States manifests toward emigrants,
a policy that inspires man with ambition for wealth and improvement. Bad government restrictions, and the multifa-
rious impediments which surround settlers in the English
possessions, must be the index to the tardy increase of their
population,

JOHN Q. ADAMS.

My visit was a very agreeable one, and highly interesting, not especially on account of my enthusiastic reception, but from several pleasing incidents.   One was the arrival at the hotel where I was stopping of John Q. Adams, accompanied by Mr. Curtis, of Boston, who had been on an extended tour through Maine and Nova Scotia, travelling in that quiet simplicity which gives dignity to greatness wherever it is known to exist, and which was so conspicuous an element in the character of Mr. Adams, who was an impressive conversationalist.

His years, experience, learning, and statesmanship gave confidence to his words.   He exhibited no erratic verbosity of language, but, with a Greek and Roman earnestness, personified wisdom in its various attributes.

American politics was a theme discussed with special interest, occasioned by the approaching election which was to take place in a few weeks—Mr. Van Buren and General Harrison being rival candidates.   Mr. Adams warmly advocated the claim of Mr. Harrison, with eloquence and argument, and declared that public opinion was so absorbed in his favor that he would annihilate all opposition, and be elected by a tremendous majority, which prediction history has verified.

A gentleman inquired of Mr. Adams if he did not believe the slave oligarchy of the South would fall from its own influences; remarking that their illiberal and dictatorial spirit disquieted public sentiment, assumed an antagonistical form to the great principles of true liberty, and that the issue between slavery and freedom was fast approaching, and God, in His righteousness, would visit retribution on Southern institutions.

"Exactly so," he replied.   "The intelligence of the age

is provoked by the assumption of their public men, and the toleration given by the convention of political parties in the free States, to emolument and power. But the time is not very remote when the combat between truth and error will occupy the nation's mind; and however great the struggle may be between the existence of a free government or one of an arbitrary and repugnant nature, I feel confident justice and wisdom will triumph."

Twenty years after these opinions were expressed, the battle for human rights and liberty broke forth, and for a period of four years was signalized by the most noble and daring deeds of bravery and heroism, with immense sacrifices of life and property; but in the death of slavery, and the great glory of universal liberty for all races and all time, surely our anticipations have been realized to the fullest extent.

Mr. Adams, in company with His Excellency General Sir John Harvey, the governor of the province, Lady Harvey, and a distinguished party, attended my performance. On their entering the hall, the whole male portion of the audience arose out of respect to the distinguished personages. The following morning Mr. Adams left for the United States.

Sir John Harvey was an extremely popular man, and much admired for his kind and benevolent nature. His administration of public affairs was marked by a liberal and conciliatory spirit, and he was noted for his hospitality to Americans.

To his wise and just policy may be attributed our amicable relations with the English government during the warlike excitement pending the boundary negotiations between the State of Maine and New Brunswick.

CHAPTER XXII.

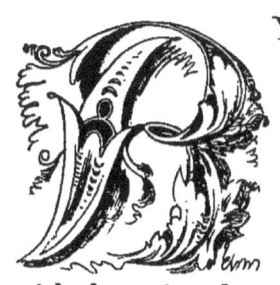 Y returning to St. John, I could leave by steamer for Windsor, Nova Scotia, *en route* for Halifax. We set sail at midnight. A dense fog, such as is known only in this climate, was prevailing; not an object was visible to the sight; the air was chilly, which, with the quiet gloom, engendered the most anxious thoughts of awe and solemnity, and unaccountably impressed the feelings with impending danger.

Fortunately the sea was unruffled, and the boat enabled to pursue her course under a moderate pressure of steam, piloted by the captain, whose watchful eye was ever upon the "mariner's hope"—the compass—or endeavoring to penetrate the thick atmosphere, while contending against the fluctuating tides, which are so frequent in the Bay of Fundy, whose waters we crossed, but we arrived safely, at noon the following day, at our destined port, favored by a kind Providence and a skilful commander.

Windsor was a pretty little place, and its commerce rapidly increasing, arising from its immediate vicinity to vast mines of coal, plaster, and limestone, with many other important minerals.

It contained a university, and was the residence of Judge Haliburton, the author of "Sam Slick" and other works, that obtained for him, at that time, a popular celebrity, and which were unquestionably written for the purpose of picturing the inactive habits of his countrymen, the Nova Scotians, in comparison with the busy and progressive Americans.

After a pleasant ride by stage, of forty miles, over an excellent and interesting road, I reached Halifax, the capital of Nova Scotia, a garrison town, containing several barracks and a dockyard, an extensive harbor, with large military and naval fortifications. The town was clean, and neatly built, with commanding streets and many spacious and commodious houses. The harbor is one of the finest on the American continent, and, in the summer season, is remarkable for its romantic, picturesque scenery. The effect upon the traveller, as he enters from sea, is most grand and imposing.

Much nobility of character prevailed here, and few places can claim a more refined society, partly attributable to its being the residence of the governor of the province, and the rendezvous of the admiral of the British fleet, who, with the army, navy, and government officials, gave a lively tone to public and private affairs.

The commerce of Halifax is principally fish, consisting of salmon, cod, mackerel, herring, and alewives, dried, pickled, smoked, and preserved, numerous quantities of which are exported.

A few miles distant, on a popular and fashionable road, was the former summer residence of his Royal Highness the Duke of Kent, the father of Queen Victoria, who was at one time the governor of the province of Nova Scotia. It was beautifully situated, and no doubt originally of great elegance and magnificence, with all the adaptations for royalty; but when I visited the place, it was a ruin in the completest sense of the word. The roof, doors, shutters, and frames were all a monument of wanton destruction and dilapidation. The interior of the once gay and animated halls was the home of the owl and rook. A trifling sum, annually, would have preserved this agreeable and memorable spot as a suburban resort for future executives; but I presume the Nova Scotians were not more overburdened with a spirit of liberality than with pride.

Many of the inhabitants remembered the Duke with great affection and regard, and they invariably spoke with admiration of his various traits of kindness, and other noble attributes.

The success I experienced was more than my hopes anticipated. All classes vied with each other in patronizing and extolling my efforts. The old and infirm, and the residents of the country for miles around, attended my *soirées ;* and, as they had never had any previous opportunity of witnessing entertainments similar to my own, they enjoyed amazingly the wonders of magic and the ventriloquial modulations of the voice. I was, however, credited with every variety of roguery and mischief, which, if not absolutely of a kindred character with the misdoings of the evil one, were at least able personifications of his power.

The horses had become drones and refused to eat; the most faithful dogs were stupid and reluctant to obey; housemaids careless and inefficient in their duties, so that a general grievance and disorganization prevailed in the domestic arrangements of the people. These and similar absurdities were attributed to my professional skill and sinful alliance. To judge humanity severely for its excess of simplicity in matters of apparent mystery, would be inconsiderate and ungenerous; yet it is impossible to avoid complaining of the great amount of marvellous ignorance that is attached to circumstances and events that are subject to a rational explanation.

GOLDEN ORANGES.

A lively and highly entertaining scene occurred in this place, between a vender of oranges and myself. She accosted me on the street, with a basket of this delicious fruit, importuning me with no ordinary praise of their superior excellence.

"What is the price?" I inquired.

"Three shillings a dozen, and cheap at that, sir."

"Are they sweet?"

"Yes, like honey."

"If so, I will purchase some."

Taking my knife from my pocket, and cutting one into two pieces, a golden sovereign lay in the centre, to the amazement of the seller, who looked alternately at me and the money with wonder. A similar coin appeared in another, at which her conntenance betrayed the most intense surprise and delight, exclaiming, in an excited tone,—

"Golden oranges, by St. George!"

A third orange was cut with the same success, when the woman suddenly stopped me, and commenced squeezing her fruit, refusing to part with any more of her valuable commodity: "They were not for sale; that her fortune was made." With great animation and agility, she hurried to a secluded spot on one of the wharves, where she cut up all her oranges, without realizing a single golden hope. The disappointment was beyond her endurance. She came to me, expressing her indignation and contempt, and applied to the mayor of the city for a warrant to prosecute me for being instrumental in destroying her prospects. I sent for the deluded woman, and more than compensated her for the loss she had sustained.

This transaction becoming known, created intense excitement. The hall was constantly filled until the close of my engagement, by pleasure-seekers and others interested, although by some I was condemned and stigmatized as a representative of sin, from some bottomless pit, and a persecutor of the human race.

My appearance was a special object of interest to the poor, unwise believers in witchcraft, and, although I earnestly endeavored to convince them of their unphilosophical and erroneous ideas, and that my feats were natural experiments, my reasonings were powerless. The bad assailed me, and the self-righteous shook their heads with suspicion, and thus I was treated until my departure.

After a profitable and agreeable visit to Pictou and Truro—certainly the most interesting, fertile, and promising portions of Nova Scotia—I returned to Halifax and took my departure by steamer for Quebec, in Lower Canada, passing through the Gut of Canso, up the St. Lawrence river.

During the passage, the coal on board the vessel ignited, and produced no little alarm among the passengers and crew, but, by the blessing of Providence, and the increasing diligence of the captain, officers and sailors, the fire was extinguished. The weather was favorable, which materially assisted in preventing any serious disaster, as it enabled the seamen to labor with little or no difficulty.

When all danger was removed, and every countenance beamed with cheerfulness, I was solicited to exercise my ventriloquial powers in the cabin, to which all disengaged from duty were invited. The steward, a Canadian by birth, declared that I had control of all the fairies on sea and land, for they sang and conversed with me at command.

QUEBEC.

Quebec was an ancient city, with all the antiquated principles of the past, with opportunities for improvements in comfort and wealth; a lingering spirit prevailed for old land marks and business propensities that neither enriched or assimilated with the times. No one could sojourn a day in the place without observing the lamentable inconveniences and deficiencies. Perhaps this insensibility to public and private welfare may, in a measure, be assigned to the opposite elements that exist in the French and English character, which greatly predominates here, and whose nationalities have frequently been embittered and provoked, so as to create little or no sympathy or union of feeling. To these and other causes is to be attributed their slow progress and dim faculties; for, favored with an immense producing country, and highly important water communications and privileges, there are few of those practical combinations that give success to commercial enterprise and manufacturing spirit. A complete laxity of resolution and energy exhibits itself, and a comparison with the extraordinary enterprise of their American neighbors cannot but startle the reader with amazement, and impress the mind with conjecture at its unaccountability.

Quebec was settled in the year 1608, two hundred and thirty odd years previous to my visit, in 1840. It then contained a population of thirty thousand, with a trade light and less in importance than that of hundreds of towns of one fifth its numbers, and not a quarter of a century in existence.

American energy and perseverance, combined with industry, has so far outstripped their Canadian brethren, as to stamp them their superiors for those practical purposes which give a standard to a nation.

This truth is confirmed in the numerous States that have become a part of the American Confederacy, many of which were an uninhabited wilderness thirty years since, whose population to-day are numbered by millions, with cities of several hundred thousand inhabitants; people of genius and force, marching onward in the great advance of the world's progress, building up a vast empire, and expanding those influences that promote virtue and happiness. This powerful energy is continually developing itself, without limit or exhaustion, and, although occasionally these efforts may fail from some untoward circumstances, or by over-reaching and speculation, the persevering march continues unabated.

If Canada, a hundred years since, had become independent of British alliance, her present history in the world would have been far more glorious—greater in the arts and sciences, her commerce immense, and her enormous tracts of unpopulated, uncultivated land improved and settled upon, with commanding towns, secure for all time, no matter what political faith her citizens may have adopted.

My appearance in public was hailed with extraordinary expressions of delight and wonder. All classes attended my representations, many of whom manifested frightful thoughts as to my abilities and the exercise thereof. Others, again, of wiser philosophy, admired my exhibitions for illustrating how successfully the senses were capable of being deceived. Yet, I was accused of committing every form of mischievous pranks. Infants were sleepless, pianos out of tune, and lights burned dimly ; and one poor, feeble-minded woman called and beseeched me to have ·compassion upon her child, whose eyes had not been closed for nearly a week. Such instances of folly awakened the most unpleasant thoughts, and unhappy regrets that ignorance should be so prevalent among them.

My notoriety had become so general, that the curiosity to witness my marvels was not confined alone to the lovers of amusement. The clergy, and devout of all sects were more than ordinarily interested. They could not conceive me to be the representative of error, or that my art was pernicious to the morals, and, in giving countenance to my necromancy and ventriloquial powers, they supposed it would operate to disabuse the minds of the believers in the evil of my wonders, and convince them that my exhibitions were of a natural character, and their success attributable to the adroitness and perfection I had arrived at, in the art.

BEFORE THE BISHOPS AND CLERGY.

While these views were entertained and expressed, I was invited to give a special performance at the Roman Catholic Seminary, an institution valued for its high repute and scholastic attainments.

The event was peculiarly gratifying, as my audience was composed of two bishops and sixty-five gentlemen in "Holy Orders," besides several hundred scholars and domestics. A more joyous and happily excited party I cannot remember. The prelates were pleased, and laughed incessantly, and cheerfully loaned me their rings and handkerchiefs to manipulate with. The person who assisted me was an honest son of Erin, who had charge of the cattle necessary for the establishment. He was the subject of frequent mirth, especially when a calf blated seemingly from him, which convulsed the company with the most uproarious laughter.

The scenery and views from every part of the city was magnificent, the public squares and walks handsome in the extreme, containing monuments to Wolfe and Montcalm, generals in the French and English armies, who fell at the taking of Quebec, in 1759.

MONTREAL.

My next move was to Montreal, which presented the opposite impression from Quebec.

The people were more active, as a locomotive pressure

animated every pursuit; hands and minds were on the alert, engaged vigorously in the construction of railroads and manufacturing establishments, extension of commerce, or other progressive movements tending to prosperity. The upper part of this city is admirably laid out, with fine streets and conveniently-constructed houses of gray stone; the public buildings spacious and numerous; the quays, locks, and wharves were of cut stone and heavy masonry, unequalled on the whole continent of North America for extent of structure, durability, and grandeur. Montreal has within herself untold evidences of future greatness.

My exhibitions assumed more than a marked notoriety, as the whole population at once became interested therein. I was the object of every eye, and the mark of the curious. All grades of society crowded the theatre, manifesting their applause and astonishment. Reports were circulated as to the strange things I had accomplished in the progress of my travels; how I healed the sick and enriched the poor; that the natural laws yielded to my purposes; old people became young; the ugly beautiful; signs disfigured and misplaced; these and other extravagances were fearlessly asserted by many citizens of a credulous nature to be my diabolism, and immensely enhanced my success.

At this period the political tranquillity of the country had become perplexed by the annexation of Upper to Lower Canada. Party feeling was bitter and personal. The consummation of the act was opposed as unwise and detrimental to public interests, but this fallacy has been disproved by the material happiness, great prosperity, and increase of population since its accomplishment.

THE GOVERNOR-GENERAL.

Lord Sydenham, who was at this time the Governor-General of Canada, encountered much opposition in passing the measure. The sarcasm of the press and the people was violent beyond reason. As a proof of this, I quote the following passages from the papers, which honored me by a connection with his lordship:

[*From the Montreal Messenger, November* 2, 1840.]

"SIGNOR BLITZ.

"We have more than once alluded to this renowned magician, who, during the last week, has been astonishing the senses of the citizens of Montreal. We learn with surprise, however—for we did not know that he was a Hercules also—that he draws great houses nightly.

"It was with much greater surprise we read the following, which we copy from the Montreal *Herald:*

"Signor Blitz's performances at the Theatre Royal continue to attract good houses, in spite of the inclemency of the weather. We understand he is to exhibit his *diablerie* at the Government House, on Monday evening.

"There is some mistake in that, 'for sure,' as the boys say. Who tries to sell wooden nutmegs to Yankee peddlers? Who throws pearls before——?—(it would be vulgar to say what, therefore we forbear putting the *animal* into print). Who carries coal to Newcastle? Who gilds refined gold? Who paints a lily? Therefore, we say, there is, 'for sure,' some great mistake in the announcement of our typographical chum.

"There is already a great deal of *diablerie* of one kind and another going on at the Government House, or else the world is sadly given to — (another word which it is impossible we should use). This Canada of ours is remarkable for the number of magicians; our French call them *sacrés astrologues!* We believe they have the impudence to call Her Majesty's Representative by that name. That Signor Blitz should go to the Government House to exhibit his

diablerie is a thing we will not believe, any more than
that the moon is made of green cheese.

"Why, Signor Blitz would be ashamed of himself before
he had been five minutes in the saloon. What should we
have thought of Major-General William Henry Harrison,
of the United States army, although a very *remarkable*
military hero, if he had ventured to *instruct* the conqueror
of Marengo and Austerlitz in the art of war? What,
then, should we think of Signor Blitz? No, no, Mr. Blitz
is not quite so green as that.

"When the magician we allude to got the *French* to
agree to the Union of the Canadas, about a year since, *all the
French—vide* the despatches—was not that wonderful?
Did he not get the 'family compact' of Upper Canada to
agree to it too? Was not that wonderful? He has done
more than that, however. He has converted into thick and
thin admirers of Whigs and Whiggery (those atrociously
vulgar persons and that thimble-rig thing) the rabid, high-
flown Tories of Canada! What do you think of that, Mr.
Blitz? Go to Government House to exhibit your *diablerie!* The thing is impossible! If it had been announced that Signor Blitz was going to — (that is really too
vulgar a place to print), we might have believed it, although
to exhibit *diablerie* there would have been, in truth, wast-
ing sweetness on the desert air; but the going to Government House for such a purpose—Ha! ha! ha! ha!"

"Signor Blitz exhibited his wonderful sleight of hand
tricks yesterday evening, in presence of that illustrious political conjuror, the Governor General. Surprising as are
the Signor's optical illusions, they are immeasurably surpassed by what has been performed by his excellency by
way of Jim Crow change in politics, on the part of the inhabitants of Upper Canada,

11

"We know not what may have been the respective feelings of the aristocratic and plebian conjurors on beholding each other face to face; but we suppose they both laughed in their sleeves, at each other and at the public, and admired their mutual dexterity on their own peculiar stages."— *Montreal Herald,* Nov. 3, 1840.

The entertainment at the Government House was a brilliant affair. The heads of the various departments, and a select number of the *élite* and fashion of the city were present. The next morning I received the following letter:

"The aid-de-camp in waiting is commanded by His Excellency the Governor-General, Lord Sydenham, to state that Signor Blitz performed at Government House on Monday evening, November 2d, to the satisfaction of his lordship and a numerous party.

"GOVERNMENT HOUSE, MONTREAL, Nov. 3, 1840."

Lord Sydenham was a quiet, unassuming gentleman, the first and last of his title, originally an eminent merchant of London. He entered Parliament in early life, and in the course of a few years, became distinguished for his practical knowledge of Commerce, which procured him the appointment of President of the Board of Trade. Ultimately he accepted the governorship of Canada, and was made a peer. The mental and physical labor connected with his administrative duties, and the bitterness with which his assailants assaulted his government, so overtaxed his endurance that he shortly died.

TORONTO.

Having concluded my prosperous engagement, I enjoyed a brief vacation, and next appeared at Toronto. The numbers who attended were immense. Soon the usual exaggerated stories were in circulation, concerning not only my professional skill, but which attributed to me exploits far more wonderful than those related of Agrippa, Dr. Faustus, and other mighty professors of magic in the olden time.

These rumors greatly interested the admirers of mystery, as well as those of a more pious nature; and whenever I attempted to vindicate myself from such ridiculous tales, the more inclined were they in the belief of my guilt. As might have been expected, my audiences were immense, and the enthusiasm extravagant.

I was invited to give an entertainment at the Government House in this city, and received the following letter after the same was concluded:

"GOVERNMENT HOUSE, TORONTO,
11th February, 1841.

"The aid-de-camp in waiting is directed by Sir George Arthur to express to Signor Blitz the great satisfaction felt by His Excellency, Lady Arthur, and a numerous party of friends, with his performance at Government House this evening.

"To Signor Blitz."

Sir George Arthur was Lieutenant-Governor of Upper Canada, a plain, practical gentleman, of retiring habits, with no extreme political principles or special characteristics, but honestly disposed to promote the happiness and welfare of the people.

Toronto is beautifully and advantageously situated on Lake Ontario, and certainly one of the prettiest places in Canada.

The city contains numerous attractions in its public buildings and benevolent institutions; also, fine and spacious streets, and well-built houses. Its population and commerce have increased with amazing rapidity, outstripping all other cities in British America, and fully equalling in growth the most successful ones in the United States, and her citizens have favored all the various projects for advancing in the great van of human progress.

I continued my perambulations, visiting all the principal places in Upper Canada, meeting with the most liberal patronage and the cordial welcome of the public at large.. A large portion of the country was well adapted to agricultural pursuits, the soil being fertile and productive, and the people engaged in cultivating the same appeared to be contented and industrious, and their minds were but little disturbed either by the vagaries of politicians or the ostentation of fashion.

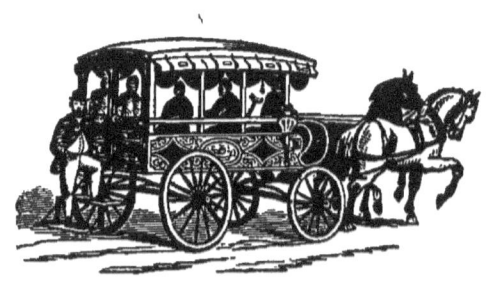

CHAPTER XXIII.

IVING my whole time and attention to my profession, I soon completed my engagements in Upper Canada, and returned to Boston, *en route* for New York, and, as usual, met with many laughable incidents on the way, which may interest the reader, and therefore I will relate a few of them.

THE WISE TURKEYS.

At one place a marketman had some fine turkeys in his wagon, and was selling them quite rapidly, when I stepped up and inquired the price.

"Twelve and a half cents a pound," said the owner.

"Twelve and a half cents!" I exclaimed; "why, that's an extraordinary charge for stale poultry," effecting a slight uplifting of the nose, as I uttered the last words.

"Stale!" shouted the farmer; "you're no judge;" and placing his arms akimbo, he eyed me with a fierce expression.

"Keep cool," I replied; "this matter can be soon settled without a quarrel, for the turkeys know how long they have been killed, and I have the power of giving them voice to tell, if you will but submit to their verdict."

The farmer, at this, laughed immoderately, and seemed now to regard me as just out of a lunatic asylum. I, however, retained my gravity, and pertinaciously insisted upon putting the question to the turkeys, offering to give twenty dollars for the six which were in the cart, if one of them did not confirm the charge I made.

"Well, you're one of 'em," replied the farmer; "I'll do it; put up your money."

I took four eagles out of my pocket and placed them in the hands of a spectator—a large crowd having now collected—telling him that if the first turkey I lifted did not say he was killed last fourth of July, he (the farmer) was to have the gold.

All was now arranged, and I grasped one of the largest of the turkeys, and said to it, in a solemn tone of voice,—

"When were you killed, old gobbler?"

"On the fourth of July last," said, or seemed to say, the turkey.

The farmer's eyes stood out about two inches from his head, as he cried out, "It's a darned lie!"

To be brief, I was soon recognized, and the whole mystery was speedily explained, entirely to the satisfaction of the farmer, for the last words he said on my leaving him were,—

"I'll be hanged if I don't take all my folks to see Blitzen, if it costs me the whole six of the talking turkeys."

THE ASTONISHED CLERGYMAN.

While chatting with a few friends, one Saturday afternoon, in the United States Hotel at Hartford, a clerical gentleman, of mild demeanor, entered and examined the register, for he was expecting, as he observed, a brother minister, to officiate in his pulpit the following morning. One of the gentlemen present, of humorous character, remarked to me that the stranger was the Rev. Mr. ——, of a neighboring village, to whom he was desirous I should be introduced. I

endeavored pleasantly to decline the honor, as I concluded
the introduction would not be profitable or agreeable to
either of us, on account of the decided impression I entertained in regard to his physiological developments, which
ultimately proved my sagacity; but my friend B——, one of
the old Knickerbockers of Hartford, was irresistible, and I
was formally presented, and at the same time requested to
perform, for his gratification, a particular feat, to prove by
my skill how the mind and vision could be deluded in the
open daylight, independent of all preparations and fixtures.
I consented, and succeeded admirably; but the effect upon
him was such, that without the least hesitation, and in the
most abrupt manner, he commenced declaiming against my
pursuit, and expressed his opposition to all amusements,
considering them frivolous and dangerous to the welfare of
mankind. His words were so unwelcome and ungenerous,
that I endeavored to convince him to the contrary; and
while engaged in this object, my attention was directed
to a slight pressure upon my back, and, placing my hand
there, a pack of cards were dropped into it. This was
ammunition I little expected, and I determined to use it to
the best advantage.

"Why, sir," I said to the domine, "you are the last
person to take exceptions, or speak unfavorably of innocent
recreations, when you, a minister of the Gospel, carry cards
about with you, to play your games in some sly corner, perhaps for drinks and money."

"What's that you say, sir! I have cards? you are
insane!" he spiritedly replied.

"Oh, yes! you are entirely mistaken, Signor," cried the
wag, my confederate; "for Mr. —— is a strict, unwavering, orthodox preacher."

"That may be," I answered; "but he plays cards, nevertheless; he has them in his pocket now" and to prove my

assertion, I drew a quantity from the shawl round his neck, and with great rapidity deposited the balance in his pocket.

The reverend gentleman looked confused and serious; my droll assistant, Mr. B., again declared I was in error, and at the same time put me in possession of the back-gammon box and dice.

"Will you satisfy all present, and myself, that you have no cards in your pocket," I resolutely demanded.

"Oh, yes! with pleasure; I despise such articles," he reiterated, as he thrust his hand into his pocket, from whence he drew the cards, the appearance of which overcame him with amazement and fright.

I excitedly exclaimed, "I knew I was right! and that is not all, you are an expert gambler, for look here," I continued, taking the hat from his head, out of which tumbled the box and dice.

This so completely nonplussed him, that for a few moments he was powerless of speech. Recovering himself, however, he moved toward the door, and, speaking in a severe tone, said,—

"You'll do, sir! you'll do!" and quickly left for the street.

The effect upon all was intensely rich and memorable, and no one better appreciated the incident than myself; but, without the voluntary aid of my mischievous friend, I could not have triumphed so successfully. The story spread far and near, and gave rise to great mirth; and an editor of one of the city papers published in his daily issue that the clergyman would not have been more surprised if he had found a sheep in his pocket.

While in New Haven, Connecticut, I spent an evening at the Tontine Hotel, in company with several gentlemen of that city. Quite an animated and interesting discussion arose, respecting the theory and practice of picking pockets.

Of course, the opinions given were materially opposite, yet their conclusions and inferences were not totally void of truth. One declared that success was entirely attributable to nimble fingers; another, to the absence of mind on the part of those victimized; a third maintained it proceeded from the robber's instinct and knowledge of mankind, as invariably the pocket-books were valuable and usually well filled; finally, I was solicited to state my views. I replied it was a business, and the people who pursued it made it the exclusive study of their lives, and that few were safe from their depredations. One of the party, a vain and positive person, joined issue with me, by emphatically announcing that he defied any one to extract his pocket-book from his pocket.

"Why, the Signor himself can do it," said one of his friends.

"I greatly doubt it," replied the gentleman in question.

"Convince him, Signor!" all exclaimed.

I jocosely said I could not at the present time, from the simple fact that he had neither money or pocket-book about his person.

"Yes, I have," he sharply retorted, at the same moment producing from his pocket one of an uncommon size, which created a general smile. "Here it is," he continued, "containing two hundred dollars; and if you can remove it from me, you are welcome to it and its contents."

To this I replied, "I seldom exercise my abilities upon friends, although there are occasions when circumstances compel me to vindicate my professional powers in opposition to my feelings."

"I scarcely think, Signor," he responded, "that you have the ingenuity,"—at the same time placing his pocket-book on his knee, beneath the table. The conversation assumed a political turn, and, during the excitement it pro-

11*

voked, my friend forgot all precaution in regard to his pocket-book, which neglect was taken advantage of by the gentleman occupying the adjoining chair, who gently abstracted it from its position, and passed it to me. This I little anticipated; however, it gave me the opportunity of triumphing over my obstinate companion. We separated late at night, and when I was confident he had retired to bed, I repaired to his residence, and rang the door-bell with energy, until he threw up the window, peevishly inquiring who it was, and the object of the visit.

"It is only me—Signor Blitz—bringing your pocket-book."

"What! my pocket-book?" he cried. "Oh! that's a joke!"

"Not in the least, for I have it here. Shall I throw it up to you?"

"No; I'll come down," he answered; but first he examined his pockets, when the fact became apparent that, with all his shrewdness, he was as capable of having his pocket picked as others who were less pretentious and defiant.

When he appeared, he looked bewildered; and, being but half dressed, presented an exceedingly ludicrous picture. It was a late hour, and I did not pause to answer his questions, but wished him pleasant dreams. Early the following morning he came and urged me to relate by what means I had become possessed of his pocket-book—for it appeared to him a complete mystery.

In thus announcing my views as to pocket-picking, I do not wish it to be understood that I am a professional in that line, especially as in this case I was simply a receiver.

A FAMILY BEDROOM.

At one of the hotels in a western city, after being lighted to my room in the fourth story at bed-time, I retired to

THE FAMILY BEDROOM.

rest; the room, although elevated, was commodious, and in a distant corner was another bed. The moon, although full, could scarcely, with all its penetrating powers, force its inflected rays into my room, owing to the cloudiness of the atmosphere, and the bleached domestic hanging before my windows. I had been in bed, perhaps, half an hour, when I heard footsteps approaching my door, which was opened noiselessly, and two well-dressed men entered. I could see there were two—only when moving, however—and my first thought was one of apprehension; but upon their going silently to bed, I concluded to play off a little joke upon my neighbors. I began to imitate an old man of the country, with a cracked voice, and a long, spitting cough. By his side, apparently, lay his beloved companion, offering a word or so of advice, whenever an opportunity permitted. Even the innocent infant was not forgotten; for, awakened by the restlessness of its parents, it manifested its vexation by plaintive wailing. "Old beloved" became furious at the disturbance; mamma vented her spleen upon baby, and confusion was fairly rioting over in my corner. About this time, I noticed a head pop up from the other corner.

"Bob! Bob!" whispered the head. "Bob! we have made a serious mistake, and got into a family room."

"Old man," whispered the old woman, "didn't you hear some one open the door?"

"No, no! go to sleep; you are always thinking about ghosts."

The head brought out from under the cover a body and thin legs.

"Bob," said the head, "you can stay if you are a mind to, but I am going." And out came the head and legs, followed by Bob, now aroused to consciousness of the peculiar delicacy of his situation; but little time was taken to clothe themselves, for the door was immediately opened, and the head and Bob disappeared, with the balance of their clothing. It required all the nerve I possessed to restrain my laughter while they were hastily decamping, yet I kept up the conversation between the "old beloved?" and mamma, and the crying of the child.

But a few minutes elapsed ere the door was again opened, and the clerk, followed by the head and Bob, entered and approached my bed, as I feigned heavy sleep.

"You see, you are mistaken," said the clerk.

"I tell you," replied the head, "that Bob and I were in that bed yonder—see where we occupied it—and we heard a man, his wife, and I don't know how many children, over in this corner."

The muscles of the clerk's cheeks began to twitch, and Bob seemed touched with awakening intelligence. As profound as was my slumber, I could scarcely resist laughing aloud.

"Do you think that fellow has been playing a trick on us?" asked the head.

"Well, it kinder looks so," said the clerk.

The head approached my bed, laid its hands roughly on my breast, and shook me violently.

"Stranger! stranger! where's that woman and baby?" it inquired, in a loud voice.

I yawned and rubbed my half-opened eyes, and appeared astonished at the unexpected visitation.

"Where's that woman and baby you had here?" repeated the head.

"What woman and baby are you speaking of?" said I, in utter amazement.

"Ah! poor innocent young man! how suddenly ignorant you are. Rise from your bed, and follow us instantly."

"Oh, excuse me."

"We cannot," escaped from Bob's lips.

I half rose, yet hesitated. The look of the head was grave, yet the clerk and Bob were smiling.

"Be quick, and don't keep us here all night," remarked Bob.

I was a little irritated at this, and springing to the floor, demanded the cause of my being disturbed at that hour of the night.

"No harm will befall you, stranger," said the clerk, with a half-suppressed laugh.

"For hiding that woman and baby," said the head, with a smile struggling at the corner of its mouth.

"What do you wish of me?" said I, hastily dressing myself.

"Follow us," commanded the head, in a deep, sepulchral tone; "you are to meet the fate of the Royal Beast—drowned in a butt of wine."

Having finished my toilet, I followed my curious visitors to the bar-room of the hotel. I was called upon in the presence of the landlord, who presided behind, to make a full confession of my capital offence. Bob exploded; the clerk swallowed his tobacco in trying to save his breath, while the landlord closed his eyes in ecstasy. "Give us," said the head, in an authoritative command, "some wine: let it be dark for the criminal, that it may drown his recollection of the deed of darkness; give us also wine, that we may hide the frightful vision that drove the very blood from our cheeks, as well as sleep from our eyes."

SMUGGLING A PASSENGER.

I was superintending the operation of transferring my luggage from the porter's truck to the car at the Old Colony depot, in Boston, when the baggage-master threw on its end an important box of mine, with the usual force for which they are distinguished, when he was startled by a voice crying out,—

"Don't—don't stand me on my head!"

The baggage-master—who, by the way, was a country fellow—stared in round-eyed wonder, while the occupant of the box repeated, with some impatience,—

"I'm on my head. I tell you, turn me over, quick!"

The frightened baggage-master, with considerable trepidation, placed the box in a horizontal position, when the voice cried out,—

"That won't do; you've put me on my face—Oh! oh!"

The manipulation of trunks and carpet-bags reversed the position of the troublesome box, when a sort of grunt of satisfaction at once issued from it, and wiping the perspiration from his brow, the baggage-master addressed me,—

"I say, look here, you must pay fare for this young gentleman in the box."

"Oh, no," I replied, "I have carried him more than one hundred thousand miles upon railroads, and never paid his fare yet."

"Can't help it," he replied, "you can't smuggle nobody over this 'ere road; and if you don't fork over, I'll set him out on the platform, and leave him standin' on his head; you kin depend on that, old fellow."

The incensed official was about suiting the action to the word, when the conductor of the train approached—who had frequently witnessed my performances—and inquired, "What's the trouble, Signor Blitz?"

I explained; and when he understood that the only occupant of the box was my automaton boy, "Bobby," that figured in the ventriloquial scenes, he readily allowed him to pass as a "dead-head."

After the train left, the perplexed baggage-master found

' in one of his vest pockets a silver quarter, which he declared must have been placed there by magic.

A Child in a Carpet-Bag.

Since people have got to carrying dogs, bundles, kits of tools, loaded market-baskets, and such like truck inside of omnibuses—at least they did so at the time this occurred—we presume no regular patron would be much surprised to hear of a baby being transported in a carpet-bag, bundled into a Broadway stage.

The day was rainy, and everybody out of doors in bad humor, of course; particularly such as, after waiting under a dilapidated awning, or in a dripping doorway for half an hour, rush out into the rain and mud, and run the risk of their lives to get a stage, and be told by the twelve inside, that it's "all full." As a general thing, persons thus bluffed off work their way back to the pavement the best way they can, and wait for another chance; but there are some who will not stand it, and force their way into the vehicle, no matter how many object.

One of these won't-be-refused persons paid dearly for his boorishness, as the story will show. A stage, filled with its compelment of twelve, was hailed by a big man, in a wet, shaggy coat, and carrying a large carpet-bag. The driver stopped, of course—who ever heard of "coachee" fancying his stage full?

"All full! Go on, driver. There's no room here, sir," and a dozen other exclamations came from the insiders, but the driver sat still on his box, and the dripping stranger pulled away at the door, which a man was holding together by the strap. The outsider was too strong for the insider, however, and, pulling the door open, jammed in, and passed roughly along, over boots and gaiters, to the front of the stage. Here he deposited his carpet-bag upon the feet of a lady passenger, and crowded about one third of his huge person upon the bit of spare space on the opposite seat, and faced the audience.

"A pretty idee, to keep a man standing out in the rain and mud, wasn't it?" exclaimed the angry intruder.

The ladies looked at each other and smiled, while the men laughed outright.

"Maybe I've been amongst civilized people some time in my life," said the now fairly riled stranger, "even if they didn't have painted stages and painted people in 'em."

This drew a deprecating glance from the ladies, while the gentlemen looked as if they wouldn't mind pitching the fellow out.

"A–h! a–h! a–h!" came from the carpet-bag.

"Halloa! what's that?" asked a short, fat man, with big hair and a thin voice.

"A baby in a carpet-bag," shouted another.

"A–h! a–h! a–h! a–h! a–h!"—from the carpet-bag.

"Take it out!" cried the man with the thin voice.

"There ain't any child in my bag," roared the shaggy coat. "Them's my clothes, and nothing else."

"A–h! a–h!"

"The deuce there ain't!"—from the fat man. "Turn him out with his baby! Turn him out!"

"Let 'em try it!" roared the shaggy man. "Who's a-goin' to do it?"

"A–h! a–h! a–h!"

"Gentlemen, we cannot stand this any longer! Go out with your baby, you brute!" said I, assuming immense indignation.

"Stop the stage and let me out!" called out one of the ladies.

"I tell you I ain't got no babe in this bag," growled

the shaggy man. "I'll bet ten dollars on it. The critter is somewhere else,—in some of the seats, maybe."

"A–h! a–h! a–h!"

Here the alarm of the ladies began to be intense. Several insisted on getting out; one improvised a very good feint at a faint.

"Sit still. I'll go out and see the driver. This nuisance is not to be borne any longer!"

The stage was stopped and I got out, and did see the driver long enough, at any rate, to hand him a quarter, and then walked straight into Stuyvesant Institute, giving a quizzical look at the people in the stage.

"Who is that fellow?" growled the man with the shaggy coat, after I left. "I've a good mind to get out and thrash him. The idee of *my* having a child in this carpet-bag!"

"That man?" answered the person addressed. "That is Signor Blitz, the ventriloquist and magician."

"*The devil!*"

"No, not quite, but rather a near relation. You can go on, driver."

THE MYSTIFIED QUAKER.

In Nantucket I had occasion to visit a bank, on entering which, I inquired of an elderly Quaker gentleman if I could be accommodated with a draft for three hundred dollars, for which I would give him the specie. He requested George, a tall, gaunt, and serious-looking man, who acted as paying and receiving teller, to count the coin, which he carefully did, placing it upon a tray, on which there was already a considerable sum. Finding the amount correct, he informed the Quaker, who inquired of me to whose order I wished my draft made payable.

"My own name, sir,—Signor Blitz," I replied.

"Art thee the man?" he asked, in great surprise, darting his full, hazel eyes through the corner of his spectacles at the money. "Art thee truly the veritable Blitz? Can thee deceive me as thee do others?"

"Oh! Yes, sir, with pleasure."

Whereupon I performed some feats that appeared so mysterious to him and his assistant, that the latter moved the tray, with its contents, to a shelf in a distant part of the bank. The Quaker became so absorbed and interested that he urged me to repeat my tricks, saying, "I think I can detect thee next time;" but I baffled him so completely that he turned round, calling on George to take away the silver, pointing his finger at the tray. The latter lost no time in doing as he was directed, and immediately deposited it in the immense iron safe, which he locked, and planted himself with his back against the wall, holding the key in his two hands behind him, with a timorous and watchful countenance.

"Do you think, sir"—addressing myself to the Quaker —"the money is secure because he has locked it up and holds the key?"

"Can thee take it out now, friend?" he asked, with anxiety.

"Yes, all the money I paid you, and as much as I wish besides, which I will return on your allowing me ten per cent. of the sum."

"No, no, I beg thee will not do it! I am confident thee can do anything, after what I have seen thee perform."

There were many citizens in the bank at the time, who deeply enjoyed the earnest manner of the Quaker and his assistant.

CHAPTER XXIV.

DURING my western and southern tour, several other laughable occurrences took place, which might as well be related here, lest they be forgotten. One of them happened in Cincinnati, and created quite

AN EXCITEMENT IN THE MARKET.

About eight o'clock one morning, there was considerable excitement in the Fifth Street Market, on the south side. A middle-aged German woman was earnestly engaged in disposing of a choice collection of fresh vegetables. She was as busy as she well could be, measuring out her produce and receiving money in return. Among other articles, she had a barrel of fine, large beets, which a gentleman seemed disposed to purchase; and while he was examining them carefully, he was astounded by hearing a pig squeal in the bottom of the barrel.

"Why, madam," said he, "you have buried a pig beneath your beets!"

"Vat?" asked the astonished woman.

"There is a pig in this barrel," replied the would-be purchaser.

At the same moment, a pig was distinctly heard giving smothered grunts and squeals beneath the beets. This, of course, attracted the attention of all, and soon the barrel was surrounded by a crowd of inquisitive men and women.

"Mine gracious!" exclaimed the female vegetable dealer, "mine poys have covered von of mine leetle pigs mit der beets!" and she instantly went to work, removing the vegetables with speed. The nearer she came to the bottom of the barrel, the more distinctly was the pig heard. Faster and faster were the beets tumbled upon the sidewalk, until at length the bottom was reached, and no pig was there!

"That's strange," said the purchaser. "I positively heard the pig squeal."

"So did I," responded more than a dozen voices.

The woman was bewildered. She examined the barrel and the beets, yet could not account for the phenomenon. The crowd grew larger; the circumstance was related over and over again, but no one could account for it.

But a few moments after, incidents stranger still occurred in another part of the market; for the same gentleman who wished to purchase the beets approached a butcher's stall, where a lad was in attendance as salesman.

"What do you call this?" said he, catching hold of a pickled hog's head.

"That's a hog's head," responded the boy, as he whetted his knife. "Do you want to buy it?"

"How long since it was killed?" asked the purchaser.

"About four weeks," answered the boy.

"What a lie! You only killed me yesterday," came from the hog's head, in a grunting sort of tone.

The lad was so startled, he dropped his knife.

"Why, the hog ain't dead yet!" said the purchaser.

"That's a fact, old fellow," sang out the head.

The stupefied boy looked at the man, and then at the head. The butchers gathered around, and the head, to the amazement of all, gave a series of very natural grunts. At last the countenance of the butcher-boy suddenly brightened, and, with a broad grin, he said,—

"What great fools we are! I knows you, sir,—you're Signor Blitz,—the man who did all them funny things."

He was right. I acknowledged my name, on hearing which the butchers enjoyed a hearty laugh, and no one was better pleased than the boy, who laughed boisterously.

"Ha! ha!" I said to him, "you're a singular boy, to come to market without your breakfast, and carry your vegetables in your bosom!"

"What's that?" he pertly inquired.

"Carry your vegetables in your bosom. Ah! I knew you were a remarkable boy."

At the same moment, I drew an immense carrot from beneath his white frock. Another shout of laughter followed, in which all joined.

"Don't laugh so," said I to his master, "for you are as bad as your boy. See here!" I exclaimed, as I pulled a huge beet from under his jacket, amid a perfect roar.

Advising the butchers to look out for their meat, I left the market in the best humor.

Another Market Scene.

In going through Sixth Street Market one morning, I observed a middle-aged Dutchman leaning against a lamp-post, with a basket of clean-looking eggs before him. He seemed anxious to sell out, and constantly kept up the cry,—

"Bure eggs, shentleman and vomans. Sheap, sheap, sheap!"

"How do you sell your eggs?" I inquired.

"Fourteen cent a tozen."

"Fourteen cents, eh? Well, now, that is not dear, if they are all good."

"Goot!" remarked the Dutchman, rather indignantly. "I sells noting but fresh, goot eggs. Der isn't a pad egg in all dem vat's in de basket."

"Not a bad egg?" said I. "Now, my good sir, if I was convinced of that, I would instantly purchase the entire lot at your own price. Good eggs are what I want, and I will not stop at a cent or two a dozen."

"Shoost look at that, mine frien," said the egg dealer, as, with a sort of pride, he picked up one of the eggs, and, shading it with his hand, held it between his eyes and the sun; "clear as vasser mit a well-bucket, eh?"

I took the egg, and, holding it in the same position, declared it was not fresh.

The Dutchman examined it again, and then reiterated his former assertion, when, to settle the dispute, it was agreed to break the egg. I broke open one end of the shell with my knife, when lo! a feathered head came peeping through the aperture. The Dutchman started back with affright, while much merriment arose from the mixed crowd which had gathered around.

"I thought that chap's eggs wasn't good," muttered one.

"Arrah! an' it's chickens he's selling, and not eggs," chimed in an Irishman, with a smile.

"La, me, I was just goin' to buy some of them," exclaimed an old lady, as she put on her specs and looked at the bird.

"And the darling thing is alive," said a young lady, as I caught the unhatched chicken and drew it carefully out.

The Dutchman was too much struck with wonderment to heed the numerous jeers which came from the crowd, and with his hands crammed in his breeches pockets, and his eyes fixed on me, he seemed transfixed as a statue.

"Now, my friend, you see you cannot deceive me with your eggs. If they were really as you represented them, I would have taken the lot, but as it is, I can only have the one I broke open. The chicken is worth something—what do you charge me?"

"Two cent," replied the Dutchman, with a heavy sigh.

"Cheap. I will pay you," running my hand into my pocket. "But stop—may be I can get the money out of another egg."

Picking a sound one out of the basket, I broke it open, and to the great amusement of the now very large crowd around me, and to the stupefaction of the owner of the eggs, I pulled out from it a ten-dollar bill.

"Ah!" said I, "that's better than chicken. I will try another."

I reached down, and was about to select a third egg, when the Dutchman seized his basket, and covering it with his body, shouted,—

"Go way mit you! you spile all my good eggs mit your tam fool tings!"

Laughingly, I tossed him a half-dime to pay for the two eggs I had used, and pushing my way through the crowd, made off. The eyes of all followed me, for more than one thought I had some connection with the evil spirit; but, learning who I was, Mynheer said I might come again, if I would only put ten-dollar bills, instead of unhatched chickens, into his eggs.

A Conscientious Doctor.

The difficulty I labored under in New Orleans was in not being able to procure a hall, for at that period minstrels, lectures, concerts, and other evening entertainments were not so plentiful as they are now, and owners of property were cautious about changing the architectural arrangement of their buildings for such purposes. It happened, however, that Dr. Plough, an eminent dentist, had converted the third story of a large building into a museum, with a stage or platform erected at the extreme end for scientific lecturing purposes. I called upon him in relation to the room. Now, the doctor was an earnest Christian gentleman—one of that class of men very strict and sometimes over-zealous in the cause of religion. He was thunderstruck when I gave him an insight into the nature of my performances.

"No, sir!" he exclaimed, "I will not let my room for any such purpose. It would be blasphemy; I will not aid the d—l in his works."

His decision placed me in a dilemma, from which I knew not how to extricate myself; but remembering there was in the city a gentleman engaged in mercantile pursuits, who had frequently attended my entertainments at the North, I at once referred the doctor to him, in regard to the moral character of my exhibitions. The doctor consented to see him, and the interview between them was really amusing. I give it in form:

Dr. Plough (addressing the merchant): "A certain Signor Blitz is anxious to rent my room for demonstrations in magic. I call upon you, who, I am told, witnessed his performances in New York, to inquire whether they are of such a description as to justify me, a member of a Christian Church, to grant his request, as magic, you know, sir, was one of the vices of the people of the city of Ephesus—a city it took St. Paul three years to save from destruction."

"I consider that the magic spoken of in Scripture was very different from that practised by the Signor. The study of magic in that age of the world was resorted to for evil purposes, and to gratify the licentious habits of its inhabitants. The Signor's magic, on the contrary, is merely sleight of hand, aided by mechanical genius, and peculiar conversations of art and science."

"I am informed he can throw his voice into a horse or a figure, and even make animals speak. Is not this sinful?"

"No, sir! some say that it is a peculiar gift, but in my opinion it is simply imitation; and this, doctor, is the most interesting part of the Signor's exhibitions. It is termed ventriloquism—meaning, literally, speaking from the stomach—a word derived from the Latin *venter*, the stomach, and *loquor*, to speak. This, doctor, is purely legitimate, and closely allied to philosophy and science."

"Yes, I perceive—I see; but his tricks of legerdemain?"

"Simply mechanical. He is a follower of those learned men, whose genius in mechanics and art flashed over the earth, and actually went out in the dark ages of the world, but now they are revived in the nineteenth century, and Signor Blitz is one of the students in the art."

"Can you name some of those disciples?"

"Certainly: Cornelius Agrippa, Paracelsus, Cagliostro, Michael Scott, Dr. Faustus, Bacon, Dr. Dee, and many others."

"You have raised my curiosity, and I should like very much to be present at his representations."

"Let him have your room, and take my word for it, the clergy will be the first to witness him."

"He shall have it, sir. Can I use your name to Parson Clapp as an authority for the character of the Signor and his mysteries?"

"Most certainly."

I was thus successful in getting the room, and to this day enjoy a pleasant acquaintance with the doctor, who, I will add, attended my exhibitions, and seemed much pleased with them.

12

In St. Louis I was accustomed to patronize a cigar store, the proprietress of which was a sharp business woman, who attended to the sales in person. I was invariably disappointed in obtaining the article represented; and, as the imposition (for such I considered it to be) continued, notwithstanding my complaints, I came to the conclusion that, as I possessed the power to detect and punish, I would embrace the opportunity, more for the public good than my own advantage. Entering the establishment after closing my entertainment, I inquired if she had any particular brand of cigars.

"Oh, yes, sir," she replied, briskly opening the showcase, and pointing her finger, "here they are, imported Havanas."

At this moment a voice was heard to issue from a brick flue,—

"Oh, widow Jones, what a fib!"

Hastily turning her head in the direction of the sound, she demanded who dared impeach her word, and by what means he became secreted in the chimney.

"Why, you know, I'm Ben, and those cigars were made in Connecticut. Why not tell the truth?"

"You are a scamp, or some thief," replied the widow. "How did you get in there?"

"Why, widow, that's a good joke, pretending to be so innocent; I'm not the first man you have concealed here. How about Sam Baker and Old Perkins?"

This excited the widow's wrath beyond measure, and she declared she would send for the police and have the wretch arrested.

"Before executing your threat, madam, what about the cigars?" I asked.

"About fifteen cents each," she replied.

"I'll take four."

Here the voice in the chimney cried,—

"Signor! Signor! take my pocket-book out of the snuff-jar and pay for the cigars, and keep it until I call for it."

The widow lifted the lid, and to her horrible surprise removed from amidst the snuff a handsome porte-monnaie, and, handing it to me, I paid her the amount and left the store, while she hurriedly tied on her bonnet to proceed to the Mayor's office, with a countenance black and vengeful.

Hours with the Insane.

It is a Christian and generous feeling to turn from the dazzle and bustle of daily life to seek the unfortunate objects removed from the world's mirror; and where is there a better or rarer opportunity for cultivating it, than in a visit to an asylum for the insane, to behold poor humanity in its saddest garb—a household of wrecked minds, of all ages and sexes? From some, occasionally a gleam of wit and rational thought will emanate, while in others a complete darkness of mind prevails. Each sufferer has his own peculiar phase to dream and dwell upon, which is a source of pleasure to his diseased imagination; yet these afflicted patients are not without that strong anchor—Hope; it is to them as the bright sun to the earth, and flatters the hearts of families and friends. The gentle and benevolent are devoted to the inmates, and the surroundings of these institutions are arranged for their pleasure, benefit, and improvement.

In my professional visits I never failed to attract their attention and amuse their feelings, and if they had not the sharp and observing traits of people free from the infirmities they experience, there was invariably a quiet cunning, a philosophical emotion, which revealed an expression of their comprehension and enjoyment—a temporary freedom from their mental ailments, was indicated by their gloomy faces becoming radiant with smiles and mirth. Possessing the faculty of rendering the unfortunate happy, I improved it on every occasion, and my own heart was delighted in seeing how they could appreciate the most dexterous of my feats, and ofttimes their critical and witty remarks were both sensible and amusing.

I remember while performing the egg-bag feat, at West Philadelphia, one of the audience—an elderly man, confined for his religious views—rose and said, in a loud tone,—

"You are the very man wanted here, sir! We are all fond of eggs, but seldom have them."

This matter-of-fact view of my abilities created, as one may suppose, a general laugh, in which the steward, who was present, joined, promising to provide a better supply of them thereafter.

On another occasion, a female patient, whose maniacal laugh interrupted my entertainment, when requested by the doctor not to laugh so loudly, replied,—

"I cannot cry when nature makes me smile; I wish you were as funny a man, doctor, then we should always be merry and happy."

I once accompanied a visiting committee on their tour of inspection, and upon leaving one of the wards, a bright, healthy-looking woman nervously pulled my coat and beckoned me toward her. On approaching, she begged me to take her to her husband and children. I replied that I regretted I had not the power to do so.

"Oh! yes, you have; you can take me away and no one will ever know it. You can spirit me out of this place," she continued. "I believe you can do anything, after what I have seen you do to-day."

To soothe her, I told her the doctor would no doubt take her home to those she loved.

"The doctor!" she uttered, with emphasis, and a face of scorn, drawing herself up in a dignified manner. "The doctor! I would not believe him on his oath; he has promised to do so the last three years. He don't keep his word, Signor. Oh! it is cruel of you not to take me away when you can do it. I want to be with my husband and children so badly!"

I left the poor, afflicted soul, and followed the party, but not without a flow of tears, for her request and urgent appeal were very touching.

One day, on leaving an asylum, I shook hands with several, one of whom said,—

"Are you going, Signor?"

"Yes; there is no further necessity for my presence."

"I wish there was," remarked another, "for we would like to have you here all the time."

"Under what circumstances?" I smilingly inquired.

"As a crazy man," they all cried out; "for then we would find out your tricks."

This I thought was not bad, although severe upon me.

The canary birds were always an unfailing source of pleasure to the patients, who appeared to realize the wonder of their performance, the sagacity they displayed, and the patience exercised.

The day succeeding an exhibition I gave at the Worcester Asylum, Massachusetts, I received the following letter, written in a neat and beautiful style:

"WORCESTER ASYLUM, MASS.,
"October, 1850.

"DEAR SIGNOR BLITZ: The lady patients of this establishment owe you a debt of gratitude for the charming entertainment you gave them yesterday. The sweet little birds were so pretty and astonishing, that we wish we had them as companions; they would occupy our time while passing the tedious hours of our confinement. We feel assured you love the dear little creatures, and are good to them. Your visiting us in our solitude proves you have a good heart. Pray come again soon.

"Your Lady Friends."

I recollect being introduced to a gentlemanly person from the South, whose father had been, a few years previously, governor of the State in which he resided. He was very melancholy, and much given to despondency. He remembered my name and profession, and remarked that I called to see him at a most desirable time, for he was a prisoner against his will, and that I was the one to give him his liberty.

"By what means?" I inquired

"Why, your magic art," he re

I shook my head seriously.

"Do you refuse?" he sadly questioned.

"No; but I am not capable. I should suppose you would be happy and contented here, away from the cares of the world, surrounded as you are with all these lovely flowers, brought to you by kind friends."

"What are all the beauties of nature," he remarked, "without liberty? Look at these bars and bolts; is this a free country?"

"Your confinement will doubtless prove beneficial, and you will return to your home, reconstructed in health and strength."

He looked upward, and drew a long sigh, softly exclaiming,—

"I hope so."

Here we separated.

On another occasion I was invited into the ladies' parlor, for the purpose of hearing a young lady inmate of the asylum sing, accompanying herself upon the harp. She was very prepossessing in her appearance, with a countenance chaste and intelligent. Her pliant fingers gracefully ran over the many strings of the instrument with extraordinary rapidity, producing the sweetest strains, combined with a voice rich and melodious; when suddenly, during the execution of an air from the opera of Norma, she frantically threw the harp from her, and relapsed into a wild distraction of mind. It was the most distressing scene I witnessed in all my intercourse with these people; but it is gratifying to relate that the young lady subsequently fully recovered, and is now an ornament to society.

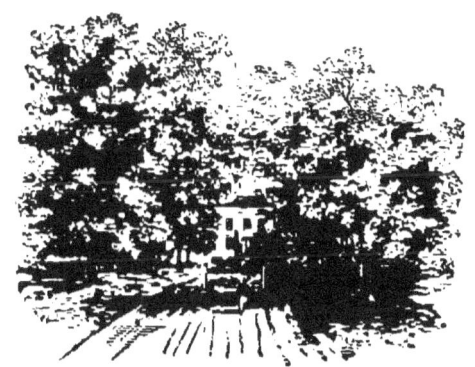

CHAPTER XXV.

FTER returning from Canada, I remained a short time in New York City before my departure for the West Indies. Looking back, thirty-five years ago, when I first landed at the Battery, and contrasting New York as it then was with its present appearance, I am filled with surprise and astonishment at the great changes that have been made. It is truly wonderful! There was then but one man in New York reputed to be worth over a million of dollars, and that was John Jacob Astor, who previously, when he was a young man, eighteen years of age, peddled cookies, cakes, and tea rusk, which he carried around in a basket. Then a very few wealthy men resided above Canal street, but most of them below Chambers street.

Fernando Wood, about this time, resided at 37 White street, and was a leader at the Tabernacle Church, in Broadway, and one of its deacons. Arthur Tappan & Co. were doing the largest silk business in the city, their store being at No. 122 Pearl street. James Gordon Bennett, about this time, from a small dilapidated basement in Ann street, near where his marble building now stands, issued the first number of the *Herald*, using a board on two barrels for his editorial desk; and having but little money, he did all the editorial work himself. It was a small, inferior sheet, on poor paper, but has proved an immense success. Only six years previous to this, Horace Greeley, with $10 in his pocket, and all his worldly goods tied up in a cotton handkerchief, was wandering up and down the streets, looking for work to keep himself from starvation. He set type, and wrote, and labored on, poor, but not despondent, till, in 1841, he issued the first number of the *Tribune*, which, like the *Herald*, has grown famous, and proved a wonderful success.

At the time spoken of, the Battery—the great promenade—was in all its glory, for here were congregated the aristocracy of the city, in all their wealth and magnificence. And Broadway, too, how changed! What architectural palaces have been constructed; what immense wealth has been expended in erecting stately and magnificent structures. At the time spoken of the old jail stood at the east of the City Hall, on the very ground now occupied by the Hall of Records. It was a plain brick building, and had on the top a cupola and bell, and in this cupola the poor debtors used to sit for hours sunning themselves—imprisonment for debt being not then abolished.

When I first came to New York there were but four daily papers, the *Commercial Advertiser*, *Evening Post*, *Journal of Commerce*, and the *Sun*, which was then sold for a penny; but what an immense increase! The dailies are very numerous, and the weeklies—devoted to the various interests and kinds of business—are said to number at least one hundred and fifty! In the little triangle bounded by Park Row, Nassau and Beekman streets, at that time stood the old brick church wherein Dr. Spring officiated, which fronted on Beekman street, and extended back to the place where the *Times* building now stands; but it has passed away, with all its sacred associations, and where its entrance once was, the editorial and publishing rooms of the *World* now are.

12*

Fronting the *Times* building is Printing-house Square, and within a stone's throw are published and printed the *Tribune, Times, Sun, World, Democrat, Day-Book, Rural New Yorker, Christian Union,* and other papers, making the name of the locality a very appropriate one.

Dame Fortune seems also to have been a necromancer, for the many changes in the city have been effected as if by magic. The old police—leather-heads, as they were called —with their pea-jackets and firemen's caps, have disappeared, and gentlemen in blue, with gilt buttons, trimmings, and white gloves, drilling and marching with all the regularity and precision of veteran soldiers, have taken their place. The old fire companies and fire-engines have become things of the past, while steam-engines and paid men have been substituted; and these may soon disappear, for inflammable, wooden buildings are being transformed into brick, and brick into iron, granite, and marble, so durable and perfect as to be not only fire-proof, but proof against burglars.

What changes, also, in individual affairs! Forty years ago Nat Prime, the banker, was considered the richest man in New York, and yet he was not worth a million. John Jacob Astor, at eighteen years of age, a poor boy, peddled cakes as before stated; and although he inherited nothing, he died leaving an immense fortune. A. T. Stewart came to this country very poor, and taught school for his support, but he is now represented as worth $50,000,000! Cornelius Vanderbilt was the son of a Long Island farmer, in moderate circumstances, and received but a limited education, but being energetic and saving, he succeeded in becoming the owner of a small sloop or periauger, and at twenty-three years of age had saved $10,000; he is now considered worth about $25,000,000. Daniel Drew was born on a small farm also, and received but a limited education. He

PRINTING HOUSE SQUARE.

began business in a small way by driving cattle to market and selling them, and for fifteen years was a cattle drover; then he became speculator, broker, and banker, and is now worth his millions. David Groesbeck was apprenticed to a shoemaker, and had a hard struggle with fortune, but is now worth $10,000,000. Jay Cooke, without the knowledge or consent of his parents, got a situation as clerk to enable him to support himself, has been very successful, and probably is worth $10,000,000. Mr. Hatch, of the firm of Fisk & Hatch, was, ten or twelve years since, the cashier of the Jersey City Bank, in New Jersey, at a salary of $1,200 per annum, and with this salary he supported his wife and several small children. He lived on the second floor, over the bank, which was in a small brick building. Receiving governmental favors during the war, he can now be looked upon as one of the millionaires of the city. James Gordon Bennett, in 1835, had but a few hundred dollars, but his fortune is now estimated at $7,000,000; but why go on with this digression, for thousands could be named whom Dame Fortune has equally blessed. Let the city of New York continue to increase in population, wealth, improvements, and architectural splendor, for thirty-five years to come, as she has for thirty-five years past, and she will have outstripped even London, and stand as the Empire City of the world, while her Broadway, in the language of another, will "glitter in continuous marble, from the Battery to Central Park."

Having procured a passage for Barbadoes and the West India Islands, I finally set sail in a bark, the master of which was a Virginian by birth, an intelligent young man, but opinionated, arbitrary, self-conceited, and arrogant. The passengers, five in number, were constantly irritated and provoked by his tone of conversation, which frequently was personal and offensive. He persisted that he was familiar with all professions and pursuits, knew their virtues and failings, declared he could detect error from truth without failure, allowed no merit to genius or character. In his own judgment the world was one commonalty of bad people, and himself the personification of wisdom and perfection. He assailed the most distinguished men with an ungenerous spirit, and his manner toward humanity, in every phase, was contemptuous and unpardonable. He defied man to deceive him, or act upon his imagination.

Of course we all considered him the most egotistic of men we had ever met, but these peculiar traits of character were only displayed on special occasions. Usually his demeanor was bland and courteous, but whenever excited, or engaged in argument, his disposition was betrayed. One afternoon, while conversing with him upon deck, the sails trembled for a moment, indicating the vessel slightly off the wind. With the alertness of an antelope, and the strength of a lion, he ran and seized the man at the wheel, throwing him down upon the deck, and then, with his knee on his chest, and hand grasping his throat, expressed the most horrid imprecations—blaspheming the name of the good and gracious God in language so wicked that I was paralyzed with terror. The abuse and violence he gave the poor man grieved my feelings sadly. The submissiveness of the sailor was extraordinary, for not a murmur or word of complaint escaped his lips as he resumed his duty at the wheel.

These exhibitions of cruelty by captains and officers of vessels are constant and numerous, and in general result more from a violent temper and love of domineering than necessity. Very few know or can imagine the outrages and injuries inflicted on sailors. No class of people are subject to such degradation and unnatural treatment, and when they appeal to courts for redress, judgment is in almost every instance decided in favor of the transgressor; so there is but little hope for the poor sailor of obtaining justice from the law. Yet we need not live without anticipation of a change, for in these days of civilization, when societies are continually being inaugurated for the protection of animals, why should not a lively interest develop itself in behalf of the mariner?

Independent of the incident referred to, our voyage was a pleasant one; favorable winds and a placid sea accompanied us during the passage, which was short.

For two days previous to our arrival, the captain was anxious and unremitting in his endeavors to ascertain his position, especially as he had no chronometer, and from early to late his efforts were directed to avoid the embarrassment attending the passing of the island, or encountering the perils of a tropical shore. The evening previous to reaching our destination was a serene and lovely one; the ocean appeared as a glassy lake, with the bright full moon dispensing her mantle of light, in its glory of beauty and wonder; the passengers and men were on deck, in eager anticipation of hearing the joyous sound of "Land," when suddenly the prevailing tranquillity was disturbed by loud cries of distress from beneath the forward part of the vessel.

"Ship ahoy! ship ahoy!"

"Heave a line!" shouted the captain, as he sprang toward the unfortunate sufferers. "Where are you?" bending his body over the vessel's side.

"Here—under the bow," a voice replied.

"Heave over!" he commanded, in animated tones.

"Ay, ay, sir, she is gone!"

"It fell short," answered the shipwrecked men, despondingly.

"Haul in smart—let go again!" ordered the captain.

"Look out—catch!" hallooed the mate, as his brawny hands threw the coil over.

"Missed!" mournfully returned those in the water. "Don't let us drown."

"Hold on a little!" exclaimed the captain, as he hastily placed a rope around his body, and a heavy one over his shoulder, prepared to descend to the rescue of those who were crying for help. "Hang on, you are all safe."

"But we are faint and sinking."

"I don't see you," he uttered, in disappointed tones.

"We are below the keel—the vessel is running us under!"

"Come abaft, I'll be with you!" he loudly remarked, as he climbed on deck and hurried to the stern, followed by the passengers and crew, whose countenances betrayed deep and solemn interest. "Whereabouts, men?" he lustily inquired, as he looked over the rail.

"We are clinging to the rudder; lower your boat, we are exhausted."

In a moment the captain and two sailors jumped into the boat, vehemently excited, giving the order to let go easy.

"Steady! steady!" he repeated, as the frail messenger approached the water's surface. "Come, now, boys, give us your hands," himself and men looking eagerly over.

"We haven't any."

"What!" he muttered, with amazement, "no hands!"

"No; nor feet."

"Is that so? Who are you, spirits of pirates, or ghosts of land monsters?"

"Neither," a voice broke forth above; "it is but a ventriloquial illusion."

"Is it possible!" he cried out. "Haul in on deck there;" which, on reaching, a loud burst of laughter greeted him.

But this reception was in no way flattering to his boasted claim for shrewdness and judgment; yet he had the magnanimity to acknowledge his being the dupe of art, and himself as vulnerable as other men. It was a satisfaction and a triumph to me, that I had gained my point in proving to him, before those he had so frequently insulted, and whose intelligence he so little estimated, that if not his superiors in knowledge and practical information, they were fully capable of judging as correctly as himself. The circumstance also enabled me to rebuke him, in my own peculiar manner, in return for his barbarous and tyrannical course as a captain.

BARBADOES.

Early the next morning land was reported in sight, which was found to be the place we were destined for. We dropped anchor in the roadstead, there being no harbor, and immediately after landing I proceeded to the Clarence Hotel, so named in consequence of His Royal Highness, the Duke of Clarence, taking up his abode there while on a visit to the place when a midshipman.

A ROYAL BED.

The landlady was a corpulent, masculine mulatto woman, known to all travellers as Betsey Dawson, not less renowned for her peculiarities than her exorbitant charges. When she showed me my room, I was surprised at the magnitude of the bed, its dimensions in height, length, and breadth exceeding anything I had previously witnessed or heard of.

"What a bed!" I exclaimed.

"It is a good one," said Betsey.

"No doubt of that," I replied.

"None equal to it on any of the islands, sir."

"But its size!"

"Why, is it not large enough?"

"Yes," I answered, laughing; "there is room for a regiment."

"Well, sir, that is a royal bed."

"Yes, it looks royal."

"The King of England has occupied it."

"Ah, indeed! Which king?"

"William the Fourth."

"Is that possible?"

"Yes, indeed."

"Well, how am I to reach the top?"—it being not less than nine feet from the floor.

"Good gracious!" she remarked, directing her eyes toward a recess in the corner of the room, "you have not examined the furniture. Don't you see the steps?—the precise ones His Majesty made use of."

Turning to the spot, I beheld the indispensable article. Retiring to, and arising from, this bed, was an adventurous undertaking! The like history of a bed was never before known to me.

The dense population, confined in so small a space, compelled all to be occupied. There was no idleness, nor a rod of unimproved land on the island. A model community, a busy little world, of more than one hundred thousand people.

The surface of the country was greatly varied, and occasionally very beautiful.

Of the 106,470 acres which it contains, 100,000 are under cultivation, and, with a rich and attentively tilled soil, produces, in bulk and valuation, an enormous supply. The products are sugar, aloes, arrow-root, cotton, rum, and molasses.

The island is girded by numerous coral reefs, of a dangerous character. Bituminous coal, potter's clay, ochre, and petroleum are found therein. The woods and forests had been nearly all cleared away, so that the land could be occupied for agricultural purposes, much of which is annually planted with sugar-cane, the remainder appropriated to pasturage and provisions.

In 1842, 21,545 hogsheads of sugar were produced, and the quantity has increased in ratio with each succeeding year, till the product has reached 60,000,—a notable fact that the colored race, when encouraged and compensated, are neither indolent nor indifferent to their own or their employers' interest.

The churches have accommodations for 40,000 persons, and schooling is provided for 10,000 children. In addition to this, all the churches and chapels have Sunday schools attached. There are five weekly newspapers, one of which, the Barbadoes *Mercury*, has been published more than one hundred and twenty years.

The attachment of the natives to their home is warm and sincere. No nation can possibly be prouder of their country than the islanders, especially the colored race, who declare themselves to be the true Barbadians. Indeed, this devotion is not confined to the latter, for an eminent law officer of the Crown asserted, at a public dinner given in honor of his return from Europe, that he would prefer being a dog in Barbadoes, to a Duke in England.

It may, however, be presumed that in his desire to flatter his countrymen, the gentleman was far from particular in the delicacy of his comparison, or the graceful selection of his language, saying nothing respecting his veracity.

The confidence which has always prevailed in the minds of the inhabitants as to their power and strength, and the loyalty they entertain toward the English Crown, is proved by the fact that when Napoleon contemplated an invasion of England, they invited George the Third to take up his abode with them, promising him protection from his enemies; at the same time the island did not possess a single gun or fortification for defence!

Bridgetown is a plain city, with no palatial residences, but many of a comfortable character.

Hospitality abounds so universally that a stranger is the recipient of constant attention, and the citizens, white and black, are noted for their industrial habits, and good order is everywhere preserved. While all other islands, since the emancipation, have diminished in wealth and prosperity, Barbadoes has rapidly advanced. Her agricultural resources have increased abundantly; at the present time exporting double the amount of her productions annually that she did any one year during the period of her slavery. This pleasant feature is a powerful rebuke to all who are illiberal and opposed to the merits and claims of freedom.

The benevolent institutions of the island are numerous, and the hearts of the residents charitably disposed, contributing a large amount of good in a quiet and unobtrusive manner.

The political and civil administration of the government was so admirably and faithfully conducted, that I never heard a single murmur or complaint.

During the winter months the tropics are subject to severe storms and hurricanes, but no island experiences its severity so much in the destruction of life and property as Barbadoes. Its position as the most windward island exposes it to the sweeping vengeance of Neptune's ill-humor. In ordinary seasons the atmosphere is pure and clear, but excessively hot during the day. The mornings and evenings are refreshing, and delightful breezes prevail.

My professional appearance was a success. The wisest shook their heads with amazement, while those more ignorant, particularly the colored population, appeared grave and impressed: they could not possibly understand the philosophy of magic to be the emanation of art. Their education, associations, and limited intercourse with the world gave them no comprehensive ideas, no penetrating spirit or strength of mind, and they looked upon my feats as the off-spring of a gifted and unholy power.

No portion of the entertainments given excited so much wonder as my ventriloquial exercises. They were unacquainted with any explanatory principle to admit of its acquirement, but unhesitatingly proclaimed that no person could represent so many human voices and natural tones without being an accomplice of His Satantic Majesty!

Concluding a profitable and satisfactory engagement, I bade adieu to Barbadoes, bearing with me a lasting recollection of the gracious reception I had received from the people.

GRANADA.

From Barbadoes I proceeded to Granada, once a flourishing island, but at that time it presented a sad and melancholy spectacle of dilapidation.

The produce of sugar and other resources had declined to a serious extent, and apparently the ambition and industry of the residents accompanied it. The Granadians extended many greetings to me. They were deeply interested, and particularly anxious that my visit should be both pleasant and advantageous. This was fully attained, for crowds attended my exhibitions, and the unqualified attention they gave me in private, inspired me to please and entertain them. Nothing could exceed the delight and laudatory expressions my feats procured for me. The whole community were unquestionably believers in astrology, and the traditional accounts of the early ages. They considered my powers more than human, and consequently many were the demands made upon me to revive the sick, remove diseases, restore property, and banish trouble.

An Uninvited Guest.

A number of gentlemen invited me to dine with them at their hotel. The party was a very pleasant and agreeable one, marked for that affability and geniality desirable in social life. Suddenly, in the midst of anecdote and song, the company was disturbed by a voice from the closet.

"Who is there?" several gentlemen inquired.

"Only me."

"Come out," said one of the guests.

"I wish I could," the man replied.

"What do you want?" another asked.

"Have you any wine?"

"Plenty," was the answer, "but none for strangers; you had better go home."

The unknown one responded,—

> "Fill up the cup, the cheerful bowl,
> And drink long life to each good soul."

At the close, two of the party arose and opened the closet, and to their surprise found no one. This created an interesting discussion. Every variety of opinion was given, and the closet examined and reëxamined. A few declared it was an acoustic illusion; others that a person had secreted himself to annoy them, and disturb their pleasures by occupying some unknown retreat. This argument was considered indisputable, from the fact of the voice and conversation being so distinctly heard, and the closet so thoroughly examined. After much exchange of sentiment, it was admitted to be a mystery that none could unravel, and all resumed their seats at the table, when they were immediately attracted by the same voice in the closet begging for wine.

"It is some discarded spirit from the infernal regions!"

declared an elderly gentleman of the party, with a dismal frown.

"What do you come here for?" called out one.

"Wine," answered the invisible visitor,—

> "It makes a man so jolly and free—
> Give, oh, give a bottle to me!
> Fill a bumper, and drown all sorrow,
> Live to-day, and heed not the morrow."

All acknowledged that, whoever the rogue was, he had a poetical taste.

"Wine, I say—bring wine!" reiterated the intruder.

In a moment a number proceeded to the closet, and several to the outside of the house, where they stationed them-selves to prevent an escape, but their ingenuity and expectations were again baffled—the closet was unoccupied, as before—not a shadow of humanity was seen therein. On reassembling, the landlord and his family were summoned and questioned, without eliciting anything to solve the mystery. It was evident I had sufficiently confounded and confused my entertainers, as they were beginning to show signs of vexation. I therefore explained my wantonness, and confessed myself the guilty party, alone responsible for imposing upon their credulity; but they were far from impressed with the truth.

"It is ridiculous! Ha! ha! That is amazingly preposterous! Certainly you do not expect us to believe what you have said? Do you consider us crazy?" These were but a few of the various exclamations in reply to my statement.

"I repeat, gentlemen, that you behold in me the interrupter of your festivity, the object of your search, the culprit you were so anxious to secure; the wine man in the closet is your humble servant, and it needs but the simple experiment for you to take your former positions, and I will amuse you with a repetition of the wonders of the human voice, and the great power of ventriloquism, by which you were misled."

A second invitation was not required. Eager and curious, they once more gathered around the table, and with surprise pictured upon their countenances, listened to my rendering a second edition of the closet scene. A great shouting accompanied the close; hands and feet applauded; every tongue congratulated me; extra bottles of wine were called for, and my health toasted as Blitz and his *double*.

St. George.

The capital of Granada was a peculiarly-constructed place. Nothing fanciful or in any way pertaining to elegance in its buildings, public or private. Yet the character of the island, in many of its parts, is not without beauty and picturesque scenery, especially its mountains, a portion of which are wild and interspersed with numerous rivers and brooks, produced from time to time by volcanic eruptions. There are also several bays and creeks, besides a lake of more than two miles in circumference, situated in the interior. The climate is healthy and salubrious—one of the most agreeable in the tropics.

My next voyage of a few hours landed me at

St. Vincent.

Here I found the people no less kind and liberal than those of the preceding islands.

My appearance awakened an interest and curiosity that was universal, and increased by the many fanciful stories which reached them in advance of me. I promptly perceived that the public mind was incorporated with the imaginary world and its impracticabilities, for I was importuned to accomplish greater marvels than ever were achieved by pagan or Christian.

Their belief in sorcery and its works was evidently sincere; and all important or remarkable events, either in public or private life, were ascribed to the presence of the magician.

The reception accorded me was novel in its excessive laudations. The masses were jubilant with my fame, and many hundreds were nightly present, enjoying with amazement the thaumaturgical efforts of the hands, and the fascinating mysteries of ventriloquism.

KINGSTOWN.

This city did not present a flourishing condition. Dwelling-houses and business places revealed decay and neglect; consequently agricultural returns were gradually declining, while trade and commerce, so dependent on the former, necessarily experienced reverses, with little hope for the future.

In contrasting the present time with that period, called the "golden era," when slavery existed there, we discover nothing strange or unexpected. The magnificence of the one, compared with the desolation of the other, is but a legitimate consequence. Its significance dates back to the original wrong,—the base of an institution fortified by power and might, whose odiousness subverted every moral principle, permitted by law to annihilate all good, and degenerate the generous impulses of character. Should any one complain of this decline, when they consider that during the "golden era" men, women, and children were treated like brutes, obtaining no other remuneration than a meagre sustenance and the whip, enduring a life of misery and wretchedness, in order to enrich their profligate and ungrateful masters, was it reasonable to expect that when their happy deliverance from bondage arrived, that these persons, without the least education, or having any idea of industry, economy, or love for God or man, would become at once useful and capable citizens, gifted with that ambition and thrift their masters never exemplified ?

It is to the selfish evils they tolerated, that the inhabitants of the West Indies owe their present condition; to recover from which, they must incite their colored brethren, by personal example and word of mouth, to organize schools and crowd them with pupils, must encourage learning amongst them, and never fail in public to impress upon their minds the value of education and industry. Then will their lovely and sunny land be filled with an abundance of the earth's good, and all colors and conditions of men made comfortable and contented. Those islands, so naturally beautiful, will smile with renewed grace; the rivers, rocks, and streams, those sweet valleys and noble woods, with towering mountains, will appear as never before, —spots of enchantment.

St. Vincent is one of the most charming places in the tropics, the soil uncommonly productive, and the scenery majestic and beautiful,—the mountains and groves especially so. Near the summit of one is a volcano, which underwent a terrible eruption in 1812. Its height is nearly 3,000 feet above the level of the sea, its crater three miles in circumference and 500 feet in depth.

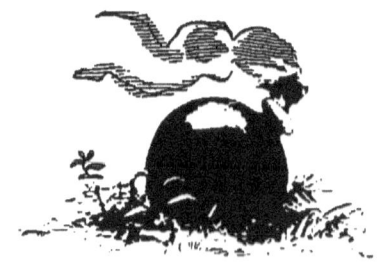

CHAPTER XXVI.

HEN I sailed for Trinidad, it was in a small sloop; and having left at 5, P.M., we arrived there shortly after sunrise the following morning. The captain and two men were negroes, and comprised the entire crew. The size, uncleanliness, and miserable accommodations generally, of the sloop, impaired my confidence in her safely crossing the water. This unpleasant apprehension was largely increased by imagining base intentions on the part of these three men toward myself.

I was the bearer of a package, entrusted to me by the manager of the West India Bank at Granada, to deliver at the bank in Trinidad. I was notified that the contents amounted to several thousand dollars in current bills, besides many notes of large amount, and as I was particularly requested to guard it safely against loss or theft, I was anxious and watchful.

The night was purely tropical, the air sweet and balmy, fragrant with the perfume of flowers wafted by the wind from the shore. The stars were twinkling brightly in the azure canopy, while the gentle swell of a fair sea floated us merrily on our course. My enjoyment of the noble sight was marred by my anxiety, and the attention I gave the skipper and his men, respecting whom I had so

13

strong a suspicion. Perceiving the three collected together and conversing in low tones, as I imagined for no good purpose, I approached them with some hesitation, and commenced a friendly conversation with them, which, to my surprise, they understood and appreciated from the beginning. I talked of the deep and its mysteries; the glories of heaven, and its imperishable gifts; how the promises of God were fulfilled, and the hopes of all believers realized.

"Blessed is the name of the Lord," cried out the skipper.

"Amen!" came from the two men.

"How gratified and thankful I am, captain," said I, looking in his face, "that you acknowledge a kingdom of eternal bliss for man!"

"Why, sir," he replied, "when I was a boy, my mother used to pray with me, night and morning, to 'Our Father in heaven.'"

"Is she living?" I inquired.

"Yes, sir,—in heaven; she left this earth for that happy land four years since. Her body is buried under a palm-tree on the plantation where she was born and died. I walk out every month to her grave, to take out the weeds and water the flowers; and before leaving I pray, and sing the hymns she loved."

"She must have been a good and pious woman."

"She was truly so, always singing praises to her Redeemer, and I love to do like her, and so does George and Joe,"—now addressing his companions, who acknowledged the truth by bowing. "Their mothers were slaves, and had no opportunity of knowing the Saviour like mine, who was a free woman; but I read the Scriptures to them, and prayed with them, until they, too, loved the Lord."

"Glory! glory!" they shouted.

"Amen!" said the skipper, and continued by remarking that "slavery never failed to oppose religion. It was Satan contending with the Lord; he had combated with Him in Egypt and all corners of the earth; but the day of deliverance was at hand. Our Redeemer, the true Lord and Master, came in the armor of Power and Justice, stretched forth His hands, and broke the chains of the enslaved."

"Praise God for ever and ever!" cried the seamen, in ecstatic tones.

"Amen!" reiterated the skipper, proceeding with his harangue. "Then the fathers, mothers, and children beheld the light of Christ, Christians came as did the Apostles, preaching and explaining the Word, giving hope and comfort. You see, sir, the advantages my people now have; all this they were not permitted to know before, for, as I stated, it was considered unwise and dangerous for slaves, with few exceptions, to recognize their Maker. Oh! my heart is full with song. Let us sing and return thanks. Perhaps you will join?"

The effect was impressive. A devoted tribute of love and gratitude arose from voices admirably harmonious, whose sweetness was materially increased by the melody of sympathetic minds. In tones that faintly trembled in the gray morning clouds, hymns and songs of praise were sung. My fears were turned to joy, for I found the skipper a man of enlarged intelligence, and possessing the Christian virtues, and whose thank-offering I am sure God was pleased to accept, notwithstanding his color and race.

The mountains of the island soon commenced to be visible, and they were soon followed by the sun's golden rays, stealthily penetrating every cliff and craggy precipice. A strong tide at the entrance of the Grand Bogus delayed our speed a trifle, but we shortly afterward came to anchor close to the landing at Port of Spain.

TRINIDAD.—PORT OF SPAIN.

For a few moments I reflected upon the agreeable manners of the captain; my good fortune in being a passenger with a man of so many excellent traits of character—a truth that was afterward corroborated by many of the leading merchants of the place, who regretted there were no more people, black or white, of the same spirit.

I was so anxious to be relieved from all further responsibility attending the money I had in charge, that, notwithstanding it was but five o'clock in the morning, I proceeded immediately to the bank, but found it closed. I ascertained, however, that the upper story of the building was occupied by the manager, as a dwelling. I proceeded to a side entrance, and knocked at the door, which was opened by a negro, who, vigorously rubbing his eyes, and with a mouth extended at extreme angles, inquired, in thick-tongued speech,—

"Who's thar?"

"A stranger."

"What's your business dis soon?"

"Can I see Mr. Finley?"

"Yes, sir, he opens the bank at ten o'clock."

"I would like to see him before that hour."

"Him asleep, sir."

"What time does he breakfast?"

At this moment, a gentleman, awakened by our colloquy, looked from a window above, and requested me to walk in and be seated until he came down. On his appearance he introduced himself as Mr. Finley. I informed him that the occasion of the early visit was owing to my eagerness to deliver to him, in person, a large amount of money, committed to my care for him.

He broke the many seals and tape which bound the

wrapper, examined the contents, and pronounced them perfectly satisfactory, and then cordially invited me to the hospitalities of his house, during my residence in the city.

I returned to the vessel, obtained my baggage, and established myself at the best hotel on the island. When I entered the breakfast-room, I found some half-dozen black men, and as many white, collected around the table. I paused at the sight, and drew back with a hesitating feeling as to the course to pursue, which, from the smiles depicted on the countenances of the party, assured me was fully understood by them; but a keen appetite, and a disposition to conform to the customs and usages of the place, induced me to take my seat, which was between two of the colored men, whose politeness was more natural than artificial; and I cannot but admit that I was favorably impressed with this temporary amalgamation. The dignified tone and refinement of the conversation, its versatility, questions discussed, and opinions given in the French, German, and English languages, gave a decided superiority of mind to my colored associates, and temporarily abolished the inequality of the races.

The colored population of Trinidad, numerically, have produced many eminent and solid educationists, with spirited purposes, aspiring to all the noble traits of the Saxon character. Every island contains very many of like culture and accomplishments, which procure for them distinguished positions in civil and political life. These persons, with slight exceptions, were favored with special advantages, having been students at the most celebrated seats of learning in Europe.

This nobility of intellect was not applied to the amelioration of their own masses. There was no semblance of unity or sympathy toward those whose suffering ignorance needed the advice and guidance of the better informed. No great effort was made, or wealth contributed, for improving the schools, and giving the necessary instructions for their moral and spiritual welfare.

The English government, and that of the West Indies, are equally responsible for the manifold evils and general diminution of trade, and of those productions which are the source of wealth and prosperity. Their policy exhibited an abandonment of all concern—a complete sacrifice of that protection which duty, wisdom, and philanthropy expected when slavery was abolished. No suitable laws were passed by the British parliament, or the native legislators, to encourage labor and frugality, and to elevate those whose minds and souls were sadly benighted.

How unlike is the melancholy history of these islands to the Christian measures of the American nation, which, with freedom, gave light and truth, and those other auxiliaries so indispensable and necessary; as, for instance, the immediate establishing of schools for old and young, protecting and instructing all in their rights and privileges; appointing the fit and proper ones to office, and permitting them to participate in the reconstruction, and unite with their fellow-citizens in the discharge of all their political duties and privileges; advising every one to emulate their neighbors and friends in industry and thrift, to ignore idleness and extravagance, and prove to the observing world, by their conduct and daily life, how justly they deserve immunities.

My advent was, to a remarkable degree, a fortunate one. The favorable notice and attention I received from all parties, and influential citizens, gave a tone and character to my position as a stranger and possessor of an art involving so much mystery. Shrewd and penetrating minds were invoked to determine as to the natural merits of my exhibitions in public, and those ascribed to me in private, and as they were unable and failed to enlighten the inquirers, my renown became more and more extended. It would be impossible, even if memory permitted, to give a full and proper account of my rumored achievements. Bars and bolts yielded explicit obedience, by which means I had disgorged numerous iron safes of their contents; the bills and notes I had deposited with Mr. Finley, on my arrival from Granada, were spirited away by me, with other moneys from the bank, in defiance of every human precaution. None contradicted or denounced these falsities; the very parties named as victims of my deeds became themselves accomplices in imposing on the credulity of the people. Such was the confidence I had secured, that several visited me in regard to family matters, of the most secret and delicate character; any undertaking appertaining to my business prospered; I was the triumphant and roving monarch of my profession.

Port of Spain is unquestionably the most perfect and handsomely built city in the British West Indies. With regular, well-paved streets, and houses imposing for their durability, also small and pleasant squares, that gave a tasteful appearance, the whole character of the place disclosed the evidence of a substantial and dignified community.

My letters of introduction gave me the *entrée* of the best society, which was superior and highly refined.

The · Masque Ball.

During my sojourn I attended a grand fancy dress ball, given at the Government House by His Excellency Sir John McCloud, in honor of Queen Victoria's marriage. It was but natural that the interest in a youthful sovereign should be loyal, and of an affectionate and devotional nature. Invitations were extended to the adjacent islands, and hundreds of the distinguished and fashionable were present.

The event was a successful and graceful homage to the young queen. The sweet and lovely faces of the young, the happy cheerfulness of the old, the animated appearance of the officials, combined with the elegance and costliness of the costumes, produced a scene of brilliancy seldom seen. The whole affair was liberal and expensive, and afforded pleasure and gratification to the generous host and his guests, and the occasion has never been effaced from my memory.

My character in the ball-room was in the dress of an astrologer or magician, composed of a black domino, covered with playing cards, and a high, conical-shaped hat, covered with hieroglyphic and mystic symbols. A large board was in front of my person, supported by a strap from my shoulders, on which I exhibited various demonstrations in legerdemain that bewildered the bright faculties of the merry group that surrounded me, and who could not unravel the spontaneous growth of bouquet after bouquet of matchless flowers, which I distributed in endless numbers to the fair observers.

One countenance surprised me at this assembly. It was that of a tall black man, handsomely dressed in a suit of black, with white kid gloves. He was promenading with a lady of Saxon beauty, clear blue eye, and a complexion exquisitely fair. They were acknowledging the bows and recognition of all they encountered. I was informed that this gentleman was Dr. Phillips, a person of fine literary attainments, a member of the Governor's Council, and in every respect a nobleman—educated abroad, possessing a fine mental capacity, and, in his personal appearance and manners, highly cultivated. The lady who accompanied him was his wife, whom he married in England.

There were many others of like color and similar accomplishments, with large wealth, but whose dark complexions

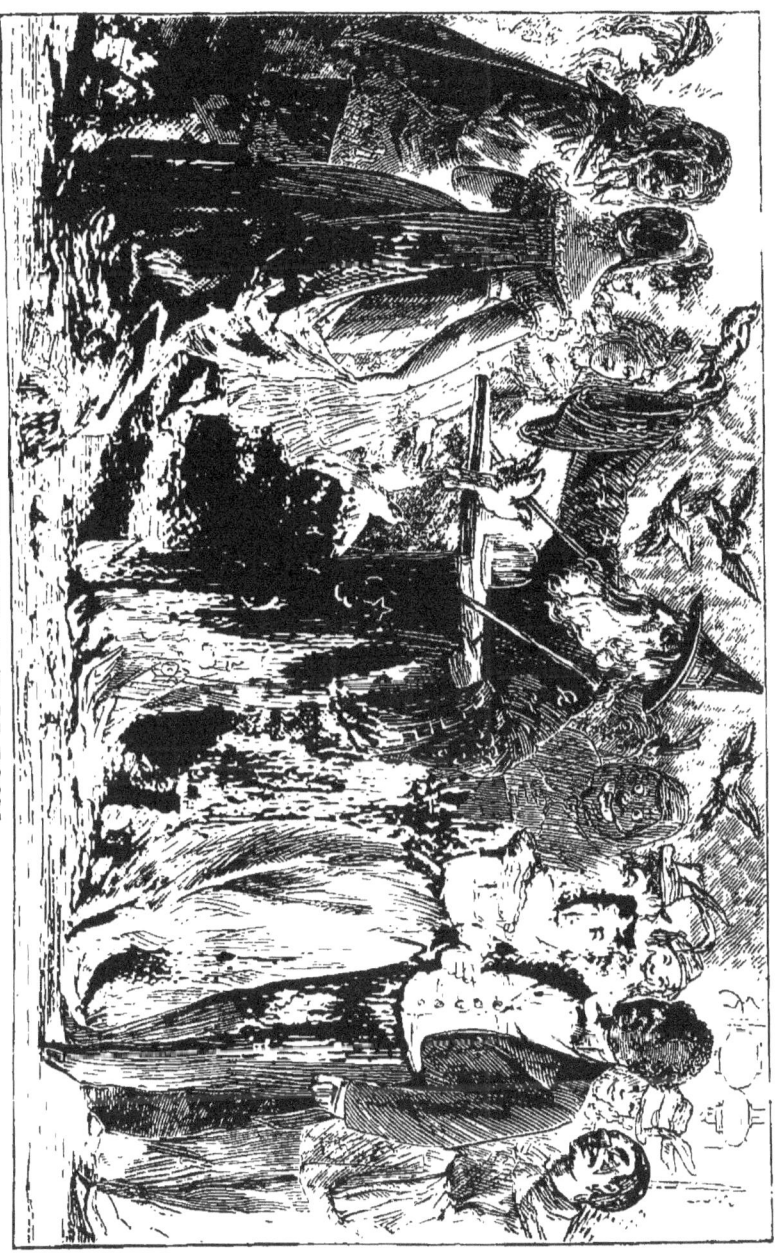

MAGICIAN IN A BALL-ROOM.

did not deny them a reciprocal intercourse with their fairer friends.

Trinidad contains a variety of natural wonders not found elsewhere. Its many volcanic actions of the past and present; the tall mountainous scenery; the hills, valleys, and fertile plains, with odorous plants, bounded by sweet rivers and placid streams, charm the eye with delight. The mud and submarine volcanoes are numerous; the largest of the former is between one and two hundred feet in diameter, with mud continually boiling and bubbling, which never overflows the surface. Some give heavy discharges of water, impregnated with earth, and burdened with earthy matter. The latter frequently emit petroleum, with loud explosions, accompanied by fire and smoke, shooting out unctuous matter of bright black fossils. But of all the objects, none is so impressive as the Pitch Lake, to which I made a visit in company with several gentlemen. We provided ourselves with refreshments, and engaged a party of negroes to row us down the river, a labor of some hours' duration. For many miles before reaching our destination a strong sulphuric odor greeted us, increasing in strength as we approached our destination.

The sight of the lake astonished me, and I stood contemplating the phenomenon with a feeling of awe and amazement. My friends, more intimate with its security, walked at once upon the surface. At first I refused to follow, which created a hearty laugh, but their freedom and total indifference to danger gave me resolution to join them. At every advance I found its bituminous substance less solid, and experienced, as we gradually neared the centre, a slight undulation—an elastic feeling, such as is realized on the sand at the sea-shore; a sensation which, if it did not entirely overcome my bravery, at least gave it a temporary check. I followed my companions, however, pausing at

13*

intervals to admire the lovely quietness of the silver waters
of the innumerable streams that diverged from various
points, and the sulphurous springs ejecting their boiling
liquid. We penetrated every nook and corner, examining
the few isolated trees and brush, whose vitality was so singu-
larly sustained, and all other objects, with deep interest.
Nothing escaped our observation; the most minute trifles
supplied us with interest and reflection; a burning sun of
intense heat did not prevent our perambulating the circumference of the lake and its vicinity repeatedly. Our labor
of pleasure was continued until time intimated the necessity
of our return, after one of the most enjoyable of days.
The lake is on the leeward side of the island, more than
seventy feet above the sea, and one and a half miles in circumference. It is a deposit of asphaltum, bituminous secre-
tion, and earth, united in a compact body. On its border
the pitch is firm and cool; in the environs are to be seen
several layers of cinders. Its depth is unknown, although
several attempts have been made to fathom it. The pitch
has been extensively exported to Europe, to be used in connection with other compositions for asphaltum sidewalks,
pavements, and roofing, but, I believe, not with profit.
Whether this results from the expense of procuring and
shipping, or its imperfections, I am unable to state, although
it had been applied and practically approved of for paving
and other purposes. Its most remarkable feature was, that
however great the excavation, even if made by one hundred
negroes per day, the next morning the whole surface of the
lake would be upon a level. For miles around the soil contains a mass of this matter; dead bodies have been exhumed
after twenty years' burial, and found without the least de-
composition—an evidence of the preservative qualities of
this composition. To the scientific the island is one magnificent field for exploration, for there is scarcely a step that

does not develop some interesting subject for the mind to dwell upon.

Trinidad is favored with a healthy climate, and the mortality is less than in other islands. The constant dews and vapors ascending from its inland water-courses and the ocean are greatly beneficial to vegetation, and furnish a pleasing and-cooling atmosphere.

The island has an area of 1,292,800 acres, but only 30,000 under tillage. The soil is unusually rich, capable of inexhaustible supplies, with extensive woodlands, valuable for ship-building and other uses, but the want of industry and development is disheartening, and has an embarrassing effect upon the community.

My mission to Trinidad having been completed, I sailed for Antigua. My visit had been pleasant and profitable. The patronage, kindness, and hospitality were more than I could have anticipated. It was not possible to take my departure without strong feelings of regret, and earnest good wishes for the happiness of the inhabitants, and a speedy development of the wealth and resources of their beautiful and unequalled island.

The brig in which I took passage was built and owned in Connecticut. The master, first and second mates, cook, and one seaman were all natives of the same State, and a part of the cargo was also manufactured there. There was a fair sprinkling of New England influence, which was perceptibly displayed in the discipline and management of the vessel.

The master was shrewd and parsimonious, and extremely careful of the odds and ends. He would say that many little stones would build a house. If he was not the king of arithmetic, he was its great admirer, and a constant student, for he never failed to record his faith in the proposition that one and one make two. He "reckoned" and "calculated" by rule in all matters. When I called to inquire if I could take passage with him, he replied,—

"I reckon so."

"What will be the charge?" I inquired.

"Thirty-five dollars, I calculate, for there are the fixings and extras."

"That is so. When do you leave?"

"At daylight in the morning. You had better sleep on board; it will be no extra expense, 'I calculate.'"

During the evening, a party of friends accompanied me to the vessel, and, after much hand-shaking and bestowing on me their best wishes, returned, saluting me with hurrahs and waving of their hats until they had reached the shore.

An Expensive Pet.

I then retired to my berth and slumbered, unconscious of my whereabouts, until morning, when I arose, and found we were miles on our journey, dancing over the waves, under full sail, and with a strong breeze in our favor.

The deck of the brig was encumbered with horses, shipped in the States for the market, and besides these the captain had a pet monkey, which was the special favorite of nearly all. He was continually playing his pranks; some droll and amusing, others mischievous. He would jump upon the backs of the horses, go through the evolutions of a circus-rider, or he might be seen climbing to the highest point of the mast, bearing with him as a trophy a cooked chicken, or a large piece of beef or pork. This propensity drew upon him the extreme anger of the cook, who was responsible for all losses and waste, as the captain said this was the only way to make people "calculate." The cunning of the monkey more than equalled the shrewdness of the man, and a warfare always existed between the two.

The least absence from the galley enabled "Sam"—who never failed to watch his opportunity—to enter and commit sad havoc: the tea and coffee were upset, and all the preparations of the culinary department scattered around, or carried away by this imitator of humanity.

For two days these exploits were continually enacted, the monkey escaping up the rigging, with the sailors in pursuit, but to no purpose. The third morning events reached their climax, and "Sam's" misdoings brought him to an untimely end. While the captain was taking an observation, he slyly crept into the cabin, and was seen absconding with the captain's gold watch. A hue and cry was raised, all hands endeavoring to capture the culprit, who ascended the ropes and masts to the highest point. All the shouting, cursing, and chasing was of no avail; there the monkey remained poised in mid-air, chattering his teeth in ridicule and triumph. The captain, perceiving that there was no possibility of recovering his property, became much excited, and lost his forbearance. He procured a gun, took deadly aim, and fired; the watch dropped upon the deck; but with a spring "Sam" fell shrieking into the sea, where he was soon lost to sight.

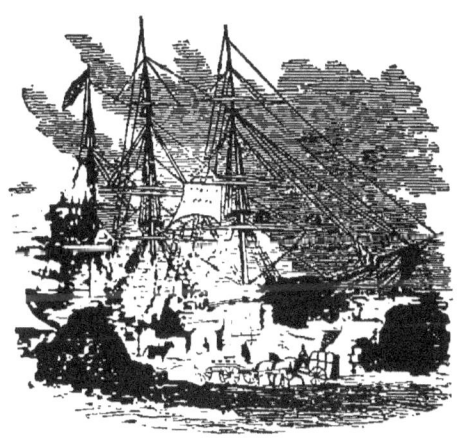

CHAPTER XXVII.

ANTIGUA.

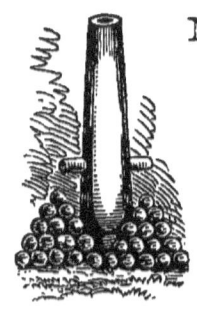

N the course of the afternoon we arrived off the Island of Antigua. The rocks and surf, with a fresh wind and heavy sea, for some time baffled us in our attempts to reach the wharf. The pilot, a loquacious man, notwithstanding his natural agility and constant custom of boarding vessels, found much difficulty in getting over the side. As soon as he reached the deck he bowed and assumed charge, observing, "De most labor I eber experienced, Cap, was to climb dis vessel's side."

"I reckon so," was the reply.

He now, upon duty, sang out,—

"Take in the topsails! Haul up the fore-tack! What's the news in the States, Cap? Steady! steady! that's it— keep her so. Have you any corn beef, Cap?"

"I calculate so; reckon you want to beg a piece?"

"That's queer—both of the same mind. Fools often are. There is nothing foolish in a piece of American corn beef, Cap."

"Work the vessel in before dark, and you shall have some."

"Good! Don't let her fall off; brace the main yard; easy. Brig don't steer well, Cap. She is not trim. Ah! she is slipping in fast. Ever on the island afore, Cap?"

"I reckon I have made twenty voyages here."

"Thought so; face familiar."

"Why, *you* have taken me in several times."

"Glad of that; better to have old friends than new. Let her luff; clew up the foresail; keep her off a point."

The action and energy of the pilot soon placed the vessel alongside the dock, when he declared he never before carried a vessel in with the same despatch. The pilot, having discharged his duty, received his fee, and was rewarded with a large joint of meat, which he accepted gratefully, acknowledging his thanks in a comical vein of language.

THE EDUCATED HORSES.

When leaving for the shore, and passing the horses on deck, one of the latter spoke, saying, "Pilot, I would like to dine with you to-morrow."

"Halloo!" cried the pilot, looking with surprise.

"I would like a slice of your beef," said the horse.

"What kind of horses are these, Cap?"

"Very fine ones," replied the latter, as he approached them.

"Not exactly fine," spoke one of the animals, "we are old and worn out."

"Who made that observation?" said the captain, with a degree of amazement that was unmistakable.

"I did," retorted a gray horse.

"Dem wonderful critters, Cap!"

"Yes, I reckon they are. I am astonished and thunderstruck. I never heard them speak before."

"What a story, captain!"

Here the skipper drew up in a rage toward the one he presumed had accused him.

"Don't be rash!" exclaimed the other horse.

"Well, Cap, they beat all I have ever seen."

"I calculate they do. What made you so long silent?" addressing the horses.

"No one noticed us till now. It is not polite to intrude. Our education is more refined."

"I should like to know where you obtained it?" demanded the captain.

"At home."

"Where is that?"

"With the spirits."

"I don't believe a word of it."

"You don't? Then you are a heathen."

"If you talk, I'll throw you overboard."

"You had better not; we cost too much, and you would lose your freight."

"I reckon I should; but you cannot be horses, unless you have the Old Boy in you!"

"If our Great Spirit was here, he would turn you into one."

Here the captain seized a billet of wood, and was in the act of striking, when a loud guttural tone cried, "Beware! beware!" The captain dropped the wood with fright, started back with fear and indignation, threatening to procure his gun. At this I interposed, and professed myself the evil spirit that had perplexed his mind.

"You?"

"Yes, me, captain; I have done all the talking."

"What kind of a man are you?"

"Dat child don't belong to dis world," the pilot remarked.

"Not different from other people, except I am gifted with the power of throwing my voice."

"You are a ventriloquist, then?"

"I am."

"What is dat?" inquired the pilot.

The captain attempted to explain, but the pilot shook his head, and said it was a language he did not understand. Here I imitated the barking of a dog at his heels,. when he made a rush for the shore, shouting,—

"Dat's too much for me!"

This restored the captain's good nature, and giving me a hearty shake of the hand, admitted I had the best of him.

THE KIDNAPPED NEGRO.

The following morning, while removing my luggage to the hotel, the porter—a negro—was unexpectedly astonished by a sound from the trunk he was carrying,—

"Be careful—be very careful."

"Who's dar?"

"A man."

"What man?"

"Colored boy."

"Who put you dar?"

"Master."

"What for?"

"To save passage-money."

"He is a mean man. What is he going to do with you?"

"Take me to the Southern States of America to sell for a slave. He says I'll bring twelve hundred dollars."

"I would not go."

"I don't intend to, if any one will help me."

By this time several persons had collected, and demanded his release.

"Where is the owner of the trunk?"

"Break it open."

"Who has a key?"

"It is a wicked thing; the man will be stifled. Here, let us have him out," giving the trunk a vigorous kick.

"Halloo! that thumped my head!" shouted the man.

Perceiving there was a determination to force the lock, I drew the key from my pocket, and inquired if he wanted his liberty.

"Yes, I do."

"Well, you shall have it."

On opening the trunk, the suffering man was missing; but his voice was distinctly audible penetrating the ground, saying, "I am off to the other world!"

This unexpected result produced the greatest sensation and suprise.

"He is the devil!" cried every voice.

The countenances of the bystanders proclaimed the interest they felt for the man, and their inability to solve the sudden exit and whereabouts. They declared, as they walked discontentedly away, that I must be the Old Nick, and those who lingered near the spot made vain attempts to discover some opening in the ground through which he had disappeared. So great was the excitement attending this occurrence, that it was some time before I could induce any person to take my trunks to the hotel.

St. John.

This is one of the chief towns of Antigua, and although the capital, yet it presented a gloomy spectacle, for it was destitute of those encouraging influences which stimulate the energies and mind to industry, and give character to a prosperous and independent people. The gorgeous sun never revealed its smiling rays upon an island more rich and luxurious; but Nature, however prolific and generous, not only relies upon man, but expects him promptly to develop and diffuse her gifts, and whenever there is no determination or disposition to exercise the physical and intellectual powers and faculties, to improve the advantages so uncommon and rare, desolation and pecuniary suffering must be the inevitable fate of all such communities.

My public representations here were also successful. Nothing could exceed the interest they created. "Such wonders," as the Antiguans expressed themselves, had never before been witnessed on the island. They had heard and read, to some extent, of the supposed miracles said to have taken place in the early ages of the world, and even in later times; but in this enlightened century, when the mind is capable of grasping with every important subject of science,—of penetrating into the wonders of the heavenly bodies, to unravel their mysteries,—of employing lightning as an agent of speech, connecting continents by its mighty action,—of compelling steam and machinery to do that which was formerly the labor of the hands, and when the natural effects of genius predominates in every department of life's busy scenes—how strange it is that the vision and reasoning of thousands should fail to detect and explain the secrets of my art; but on the contrary, its development confounds and perplexes their imaginations, and gives to me an unwarrantable greatness of character. Were I endowed with powers above all men, it would not be possible to commit such immeasurable and extravagant marvels as I was accredited with in this place. The intense heat, scarcity of water, dull times, and all other local grievances, were attributed to me. Such was the belief of the ignorant; and even those unaccustomed to be impressed by romance, could not resist the pressure of opinion as to my complicity with the evil one, and final destination to his regions.

This was singularly developed in various instances. Many avoided my presence; others refused to hold any interviews on business matters with me; and even the most eminent divine on the island, the pastor of a large and influential congregation, declined accepting two hundred dollars, being the profits of a benefit given for the poor! and when rebuked for his unwise course, justified himself on principles of religious morality in the following language:

"What! receive alms for the poor from a wizard—a bewitched hand? Oh! no. What spiritual grace would flow upon the objects in distress? No good can possibly come from such a source, any more than the presentation of the Bible to Satan, with the expectation of his becoming pious and prayerful."

So said this godly man; but a majority of his parishioners, more truly Christian in character, and with broader philanthropy, disgusted by the reverend gentleman's mawkish sensibilities and inclination to acquiesce in the current gossip of the day, at the expense of the poor and distressed, in opposition to his opinions, appointed a committee for its proper distribution.

From most of the intelligent I received respect and attention. Their uniform kindness greatly diminished the injurious effects of the many and conflicting statements connected with my public and private life, which, with a self-consciousness as to my innocence of any evil motives, encouraged me to invent more startling mysteries. The only serious difficulty I encountered, was in the procuring of a hall; but a wealthy and popular gentleman, with a liberality seldom exhibited, placed at my disposal the spacious drawing-room of his elegant mansion, to which the public were admitted.

Antigua is a pleasant island, with an unusually dry atmosphere; the coast remarkable for its ruggedness, but the interior especially rich and diversified, which is frequently beautiful beyond description. Usually, sufficient grain is produced for the requisite want of the inhabitants, being the only island in that section where the soil and climate are favorable to its growth.

After a few days of quiet retirement from professional exertions, I prepared to make my adieux to many pleasant acquaintances; but previous to my leaving, I received the following letter from His Excellency Sir Charles Fitz Roy:

"Sir: The Governor-in-Chief desires me to say that he has been highly gratified at witnessing your very surprising performances, during your visit to Antigua.

"I am, sir, yours,

"G. H. FITZ ROY,

"*Private Secretary to the Commander-in-Chief.*"

Sir Charles and Lady Fitz Roy were connected with the best and most aristocratic families of England, but in pecuniary matters they were less distinguished; yet there was a liberality in their characters which they exercised even beyond the resources they possessed, and which gave them popularity and respect.

NEVIS.

This is one of the small but beautiful groups of the Antilles, delightfully situated, containing various objects of geographical and scientific interest, with special advantages of a medicinal and curative character for invalids. Numerous sulphur-springs, and baths of varied temperature, attract to its beneficial soil numbers inclined to pulmonary or consumptive complaints.

If the facilities for reaching the island were only better, and the hotel accommodations more extensive and convenient, with the necessary comforts attached to them, the increase of visitors would be large, and of pecuniary benefit to the citizens; but the same want of energy, so conspicuous in the tropical character, prevails here. Here is a vine-yard rich and profuse, without laborers to plant or gather the golden treasures. They prefer contented poverty to the more exalted physical employment and ingenuity of the mind, for which there are ample opportunities, with a fair prospect of success.

I gave two entertainments, that were liberally patron-ized, and created an immense *furor*. Not a few declared that I was an escaped imp from the fold of darkness; that my walk, actions, and speech were not in common with other men, and my constant dress of black was considered an evidence of the truth of their opinions. Others, less speculative, and not disposed to admit my friendship with beings of the invisible world, praised the dexterity with which I exercised my art, and regarded it as the very best evidence of the unreliability of the sight, besides being an excellent medium for enlightening the timid and supersti-tious, to awaken their dreamy thoughts, and give liberty to rational impressions.

I concluded a short engagement, and proceeded to St. Kitts, or St. Christopher, a charming spot, with healthy, fresh air—in fact, a little Eden; for here grows exuberantly, fragrant exotics, and all the luscious fruits and productions of a warm earth and glowing sun. Nature, in all her fruit-fulness and loveliness, betrays a happy greeting, a solicitude for all who live in this genial clime, the excellences of which are not, unfortunately, made available.

My presence and wonder-working were the occasion of much commotion, for I was flattered and feared without reference to truth or merit, and obtained great popularity, and a crowded attendance. Few understood me, or cared to reason respecting me. They beheld with astonishment the wonderful effects produced by the mechanical action of the hand, its promptness of execution, and superiority over the mental and optical organs. They doubted nothing, but admitted everything; to them, seeing was believing, in the positive sense. No explanation of facts could convince the islanders, particularly the uneducated, as to my mortal bearing. "How is it possible," they asked, "for a man to transform white to black, extract the choicest wines from empty bottles, and produce all the supplies of a vegetable garden out of a borrowed hat? Surely, these things, observed with our own eyes, are confirmations beyond all conjecture!"

These, and similar expressions, were indulged in freely. The proprietor of the hotel was a notional and remarkably unhappy man. He feared his house would be ever after haunted, and spirits make it their rendezvous, for he had, more than once since my arrival, been awakened from his slumbers by wild and fearful cries, to gaze on features of the most ghastly hue. These nocturnal visions were told to friends and neighbors, and naturally increased the general speculation.

BASSETERRE.

This is the capital of St. Kitts, a plain, forlorn place, with no striking beauties in its buildings or streets, or ornamental squares; but an exhibit of unconcern appeared in all the minor and important duties of the town. The absence of the most trifling conveniences was very marked. Contentment, however, governs the feelings of the people. The scenery of the island is unusually grand and imposing. The lofty ridges, descending magnificently toward the sea, presents a charming picture; the soil, rich and fertile to the highest degree, and cultivated woodlands and pasturage reach the mountain tops, near which is the remains of what was an active volcanic crater. Salt-ponds afford valuable advantages, while sulphur and silver ore are also found to some extent. The island is subject to fearful hurricanes, and one occurred in 1722 that nearly destroyed the whole of it.

My engagement completed, my patrons and myself were united in reciprocating those amenities which are so pleasant on all occasions, and in every degree of life.

After waiting several days in vain for an opportunity to procure a passage, I found it necessary to charter a vessel, as the only possible means of continuing my journey. The skipper and his son (colored people), proud of their contract, and the confidence reposed in them, washed and scrubbed their sloop to a praiseworthy extent, and decorated her rigging with some half-dozen flags, of different nations, which floated their tattered drapery on the gentle breeze. All preparations being complete, a delegation of friends accompanied me to the water's edge, and dispensed their farewells and good wishes, the mellow tones of which lingered long in my ears. The swan-like sails were spread, and the little boat floated on the blue waters, with a fairy grace, toward St. Thomas.

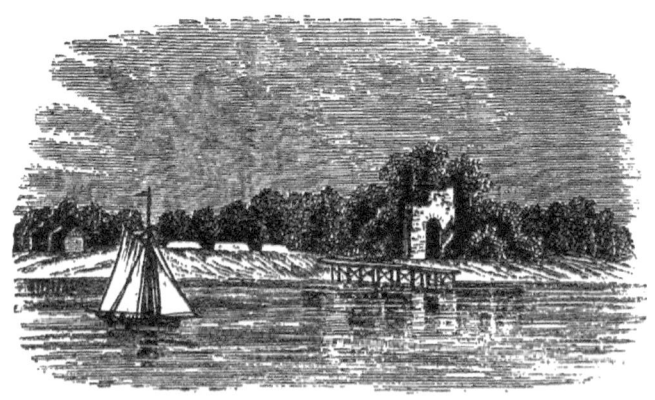

CHAPTER XXVIII.

A SEA VOYAGE.

HE vessel looks quite gay, captain," I remarked, "with so many national emblems flying."

"Oh! yes. I did not know which one was yours, so I set them all."

"That was very kind and complimentary of you. I am an American by adoption. I see you have the English one at the top."

"Yes; because it is the only flag under which all men are free."

"Not more so than the American, eh? Does not that defend all who seek its protection? Any political refugee is safe under its banner."

"That may be, so far as concerns the whites; but the English flag does not admit of difference in color,—it is just to all."

"So is that of the United States," I said.

"No, there is a great difference in that country. The laws are unkind to the colored race—very much so; in some parts of it they are neglected and despised, and in others, oppressed and enslaved."

"But that is not so as a rule. Of course there are exceptions; but as regards the institution of slavery, it was admitted as a compromise, at the formation of the constitu-

14

tion, but it has millions of opponents, and, in a few years, will be abolished."

"I hope so,—the sooner the better. The Americans, I see, are wise and sharp."

At this moment our conversation was interrupted by the announcement of dinner. I descended, and entered a small, confined cabin, and seated myself to a well-prepared meal of turtle soup and curried chicken. While dining, I employed my eyes in examining the surrounding objects. The first and most imposing one was a large and apparently well-used family Bible, on a small carpet-shelf; over which was painted, in large white letters,—

> "Blessed is he who often looks
> Into the best of all books."

Above this was suspended a spy-glass and several maps, a silver watch, and lithographic portrait of Lord Nelson, in a tasteful frame, entwined with oleanders and roses; and from this handsome adornment I concluded the admiral was held in high esteem. There were also a table and bench, which comprised the whole of the furniture. The bench I was to sleep upon!

"Do things please you, sir?" inquired the man who waited upon me.

"Very much. You appear to understand cooking."

"A little, sir; most West India people are good cooks."

"How do you account for it?"

"The climate, sir."

"Is that so?"

"Yes, sir. Food has not the same taste here as in cold countries. We have to season it well, to sharpen the appetite."

A whistle from above was a signal that assistance was needed. The man hurried upon deck, and I followed.

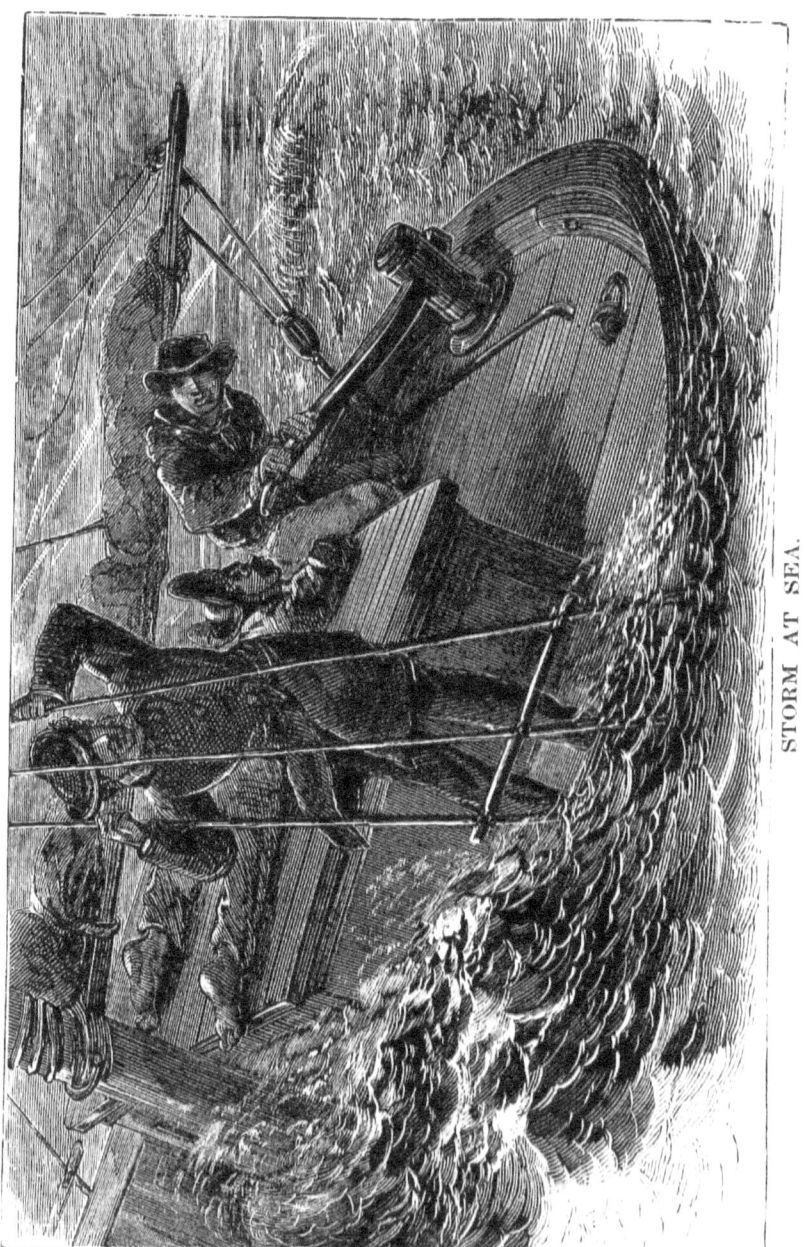

STORM AT SEA.

"Joe, take the helm," said the skipper. "The wind has shifted to the southeast, and I had better take in sail, and make all snug. It looks dusty-like to me; we shall have a heavy sea."

He now let down and furled the mainsail, and reefed the jib. By this time the storm had commenced in earnest, and the vessel combated the angry waves with a defiant spirit; the more it blew, the more zephyr-like the little craft danced over the strong and undulating waters.

"Now, Joe, I'll steer. You close the cabin door and lash it."

"Bad weather," I remarked.

"Very; but it will soon be over."

Gradually the whole horizon became dismal with a gloomy darkness. Occasionally the fierce and rapid flashes of lightning illumined for a moment the sable dome, while the thunder echoed a mighty chorus. The wind and rain were fearful, and the sea terrific. I held on to the slender rigging with a frightful feeling, as now and then a raging billow would break upon the deck. The tiny boat betrayed no weakness, but, like the ark in the deluge, rode out the gale in safety.

"Well, captain, that was a hurricane with a vengeance."

"Nothing to what we sometimes experience. The sloop has been in much heavier weather, by a long shot."

"She worked nobly."

"Yes, she is reliable; I well know her qualities; a better piece of work never floated."

Slowly but gradually the elements became peaceful; the glorious sun penetrated once more the sombre clouds, and prismatically distributed his golden lustre around heaven's vast curtain, and as every vestige of the tempest vanished, the sky smiled with a rich mellowness—a transformation so lovely and exhilarating, that no artist's pencil could sketch the grandeur of the scene. Once more the boat was under full sail, and apparently aware of her superiority, pursued her course with unprecedented speed, bending the whole burden of her canvas to the pressure of a yet strong but settled breeze.

"She is leaping!" exclaimed the captain, with a smile of satisfaction.

"Yes, she is sailing fast; she is a racer."

"Nothing equal to her in these waters; yon know her name is the 'Dart,' sir."

"I think you should have called her the 'Fairy.'"

"I could not christen her that, for I have seen too many ocean spirits—as some call them—and been frightened by their wild and antic capers."

"When and where?"

"At all hours of the night—sometimes dressed in the colors of the rainbow."

"Were you not asleep and dreaming?"

"Not I, sir; I never close my eyes when at the helm; and I have often beheld the whole surface of the water appear as a lake of silver, and have observed the Queen of Fairies upon a golden throne, surrounded by her court; their beauty and graceful homage toward her, the music of their sweet voices, ascending from their coral beds in the boundless depth of the ocean, and their crystal laugh, rippling the gentle waves, appeared truly enchanting."

"These charmed melodies must have entranced your senses."

"Yes, I cannot express the sensation; it seemed as if I were at the gates of Paradise."

"Was the dance you mentioned equally fascinating?"

"Yes, more so; their little feet skipping on the foam-crested wave, with a bewitching velocity, every attitude of their extraordinary motions was, by some reflecting conjuration, increased to millions of shadows, countless as the stars—a perfect jack-o'-lantern."

"How did they close their festive gathering?"

"Always, at the dawn of day, they grew more mystical and fanciful, and gradually sank from view."

The shades of night had now approached, and as the moon deepened her broad and beaming light over the solemn quiet, with unlimited generosity, I could not but think of life's varied and dramatic character. How cheerful to some, and tragic to others! Its influence on the universal mind; the joy derived from hope and affection, blind to every fault, shoots its love with unerring aim; its struggles, triumphs, and miseries, combined with a thousand incidents, mark how strange and wonderful is the lot of man.

A DREAM OF HEAVEN.

In my reflective mood, I remembered all dear to me in heaven; and those united by family ties and friendships, in this mundane sphere, were equally pictured to my memory.

After thus exhausting my mental feelings, I became wearied, bade the captain good night, and retired to the cabin to seek repose. I found my bed was composed of a light hair mattress, stretched upon the settee before alluded to.

"Hope you will rest well to-night, sir," said Joe, the attendant; "and if you need more clothing, there is a blanket at the foot."

"Thank you."

My couch was hard and uncomfortable in every respect, but I closed my eyes, and without difficulty was soon wrapt in slumber. I little realized the frail support between me and the mighty deep. I dreamed of walking in fields and gardens laden with flowers; the paths were paved with pearls, and the trees filled with birds of every hue, warbling their songs of joy and welcome; there were magnificent palaces, and grand castles built of sparkling gems, with majestic turrets, extending their brilliant spires, with splendor and dignity, far heavenward. The more I wandered, the more beautiful and grand were the objects brought to view; and I also saw innumerable happy-looking people, of noble and courteous demeanor, apparently of a nation unknown to me. I asked one, in flowing white robes, whence he came, and who were the beings that surrounded me.

"We are inmates here; this is our final home," he replied.

"Well, who are you, and where am I?"

"This is the righteous world—the eternal home—the great city of the good—where the spirit of life never becomes extinct; angels minister to the wearied their holy comfort; the sweetness you inhale is the essence of a dew that descends from the Throne of Grace, and gives everlasting vitality; the air is constantly impregnated with its rich and precious blessings."

"What are these superb structures?"

"They are Temples of the Lord, where He administers His Divine Will, and where millions of voices with mingled praises, vibrate gladness and honor to His glory."

"Is this happiness perpetual?"

"Yes, it is for ever and ever."

"You are greatly favored."

"Divinely so."

"Is the prospect all so bright—not one dark and obscure spot?"

"No; the light of heaven is never dim. Beyond this boundary, however, is a yawning pit, bottomless and unfathomable, which contains masses of beings whose mortal career unfitted them for the unfading bliss of this spot."

" Are there many convicted ones ? "

" Their numbers are countless, yet this domain is filled with precious gifts; the spirit of immortality is provided for old and young. There is also a great book, wherein are written and recorded the names and deeds of all, and it is kept near the Throne in the judgment-room. I cannot take you to it, for no hand is permitted to touch its golden clasps; no eye note its revered contents, save *He whose love is Justice!* '

" Why this prohibition ? "

" You must not question the wisdom of the command."

" Is it not natural to seek to learn our destiny ? "

" To those who doubt the truth, but not to the faithful."

" Is there no appeal—no hope ? "

" Yes; belief."

" Will that secure the treasure ? "

" Triumphantly so; for, without you are fortified with it, there is no salvation, and bitter is the wrath that punishes those whose hearts are unregenerated. Go thy way, and teach faith, hope, and charity; scatter thy good deeds around, that a life among the saints may be thy reward."

As the last words were spoken, the illusion was dispelled by the entrance of Joe, who inquired if I had rested well, and how soon I would be ready for breakfast. I made a hasty toilet, and after regaling myself with a hearty meal, proceeded to the deck, where I found the captain steering his craft with pride, and a capability deserving a more important command. After the usual salutation, I remarked how bright the morning was; that a happy loveliness, a laughing joy, bedecked the horizon and mingled with the rays of the cheering sun. There was much to admire, and nothing to mar the beauty of the scene; indeed, the whole prospect was the counterpart of an Italian lake: the more the eye surveyed its magnificence, the more it increased, and our boat bounded over the gilded ocean with the swiftness of the wind.

"Was the night a pleasant one?" I asked the skipper.

"Yes, beautiful, with a light wind and quiet sea, while hundreds of water-nymphs were tripping their shadows on its surface, like the will-o'-the-wisp."

"Captain, you must be a ready believer in witches and phantoms."

"How can I be otherwise, when I see them with my own eyes!"

"Do they ever molest you, or desire to come on board?"

"Oh, no," he replied. "They hold no communication with the children of men. I only wonder for what purpose such mysterious beings were created."

"Well, captain, we will not moralize upon their presence or usefulness; but tell me how long you have made the sea your profession."

"Since I was a boy."

"Then you must be well acquainted with the different islands?"

"Yes," he replied; "there is not a mountain-spot but that I am familiar with, a harbor or inlet that I cannot navigate in the darkest night. My father, for fifty years piloted in these waters, and was famed for his care and knowledge. He carried me with him to sea from boyhood, so that I had a good master, and he, I hope, a faithful apprentice. But the Jones family, for generations, have all been noted as skilful pilots and captains; and Joe, I feel assured, will take my place. For our predilections we are dubbed 'sea dogs'; but a man is not a fish, even if he can swim."

"When do you expect we shall reach St. Thomas?"

"I think we shall make the run by to-morrow morning, sir. The vessel is skipping her best."

"She appears to do so, most certainly. I presume, captain, there is a great falling off in the trade and wealth of the islands?"

"Very much. The imports are nothing in extent now to what they were in former times; their value is insignificant in comparison."

"To what do you attribute the great change?" I asked.

"The result is owing to many circumstances. First, the climate is better adapted to the colored people, who, when they were slaves, were never encouraged or coun. tenanced, their only worth being their labor; hence they were neglected in every instance. Their moral and mental condition was of no importance to their employers, com, pared to their physical developments. No care or attention was given to instruct the mind, or to improve those natural impulses that are essential to a man, however low or degraded his position may be."

"Captain, how could you expect the advocates of slavery to adopt those measures you speak of? Would it have been wise and philosophical for them to have done so?"

"Most assuredly, sir; for intelligence, in any capacity, strengthens and stimulates the actions."

"But such a course might have been dangerous in its effects, might have engendered discontent, and been detrimental to the relation existing between master and servant."

"Not in the least, sir. Knowledge has always alarmed tyrants, but in principle it is just and reasonable; and had the slave-holders established schools for the children during the day, and relieved the labor of men and women an hour or two earlier, and thus have afforded them an opportunity to attend a night school, both parties would have experienced the advantage in a wonderful degree, for time never fails to exhibit the results of knowledge. In this case, both the master and slave would have been benefited, and, as circumstances and occasions arose, the latter could have

14*

purchased their freedom, and with other advantages which would have arisen, and the saving of their earnings, they would have become landholders, and our islands, to-day so distressed and impoverished, though rich in soil, would be cultivated with success and profit by a happy, industrious, and prosperous population, prepared also for self-government."

"There is much truth in what you have stated, captain, for no doubt, if such a course had been pursued, the most important benefits would have been experienced; but, doubtless, such a measure was opposed by the advocates of slavery, who lived in an age less refined, and their liberality was not disposed to destroy—as they supposed—their pecuniary interest."

"Exactly so; they were deficient in wisdom, and could not penetrate the future. Their selfish nature predominated in every thought and movement."

"Do you entertain any hope of a better condition of things ?"

"Not, sir, until more earnest efforts are given to educational purposes; for it is impossible that wealth, industry, or comfort, can emanate from ignorance. A man without a mind capable of directing his habits and actions, cannot advance in the scale of civilization. It will take a generation to produce the good ·I have named, for the most devoted exertions will be required from the government, and from humane and philosophical people, to render it a success."

"Do you consider that emancipation has been 'a benefit ?"

"Yes, it has removed an aristocracy, whose hearts were insensibly hardened to the sufferings of a captive race, deprived of enjoying the natural love and possession of their own families, and who were ofttimes punished and cruelly tortured for exhibiting natural affection."

Thus we conversed, upon various topics, the day long, broken only by the hour for our meals; and when night came, with the splendor of a tropical clime, and the lustre of countless stars, our thoughts and language turned upon other subjects.

The captain spoke of witches and miracles on land and sea, their influence upon different minds, how some recognized the invisible spirit, and others doubted the existence of any power beyond the present, being evidently a sceptic himself respecting those events which his judgment could not unravel. I concluded, therefore, to test his sincerity and confidence in ghosts, and the unreal objects he had spoken of.

An Old Maid on Board.

Suddenly, a female voice called "Joe!" who, springing from his position on the deck, replied,—

"Ay, ay, what is it? Who are you?"

"It is a woman's voice," said the captain; "some of the water witches."

"You are mistaken, sir; I am an honorable woman."

"If so, why here at this hour of the night?" said the captain.

"I have been sadly abused, driven from my home, without friends or protection."

"Excuse me. We don't hold intercourse with dwellers of the mystic regions," replied the skipper.

"My people are as good as yours."

"What do you know of me?" asked the captain.

"A great deal."

"You do?"

"Yes; everybody has heard of the Joneses,—the sea dogs."

The latter words produced a marked effect upon the

captain's mind, and, nervously placing the vessel in Joe's charge, he rushed from one side to the other, to discover the stranger, and question her identity more closely, but she was invisible.

"What's become of you?" he sharply inquired.

"Don't you see me?"

"No!"

"Why, here I am."

"Strange, then, not to see you."

"No, not at all; you've been drinking."

"You are an impertinent creature; I'll pull your ears if I get hold of you."

"I am sure I am right, or you would not talk so unlike a gentleman."

"Do you mean to say I am intoxicated?"

"I do."

The captain, turning to me, remarked he had a good witness to the contrary.

"But that man is no better than you; he has been drinking, too!"

"You are outrageously insulting."

"What can such as you expect?"

The captain's eyes wandered in every direction to find his accuser, but without success; and he then declared it was a mystery unexplainable.

"Facts are unwelcome things to those whom they concern," said the woman.

"She is evidently some mischievous old maid concealed about the boat," I observed.

"Pretty shrewd guess for you, sir; but fortunately, Jones knows who I am, and all about me. I am where he placed me, and he can find me in a moment if he wishes."

"Is that so, captain?" I asked.

"No, sir!" he declared, in a great rage; "I am as innocent as you are, and ignorant as to who she is, and her whereabouts."

"Ah, Jones! you are a wicked man to fib so. Didn't you conceal me in the store-room?"

"Ah, captain! the affair is explained!" I cried out.

"Do you believe it?" he fiercely asked.

"Of course I do; so trot out your ghostly passenger."

"There is no one there, living or dead, to my knowledge," he answered; "but we will see. Joe, take the helm, while we look for ourselves."

We descended, and the captain took a key from his pocket, with which he unlocked the door of a small store-room, encumbered with paint, pitch, ropes, sails, blocks, and implements of hardware, a barrel of flour, one of sugar, and coffee, with other necessary provisions for a vessel.

"Hallo!" shouted the captain, with herculean lungs; "if you are here, come out and let us see who you are!"

"I would like to do so, but I am so squeezed in, I am unable to move."

"If so, it is no one's fault but your own; what did you go there for?"

"Why, you know well enough. What is the use of your pretending innocence?—you behave shamefully!"

"You are crazy; but come out—I'll not ill-treat you."

"I don't know about that—but remove your goods."

The captain tumbled out his stores, but no shadow of humanity appeared. Gazing at me, he inquired what I thought of it. I shook my head, and said it *appeared* incomprehensible.

He replaced his goods, and relieved Joe; when, for a whole hour, he discoursed upon the strangeness of the event, when I explained that he had been the dupe of the power of a ventriloquist.

"Well, well—is it possible!" he replied. "It is a great art, capable of turning a man's brain. How is it done?"

"By knowledge of tone and modulation of the voice."

"You must be a perfect master of it, for you completely embarrassed me."

Here Joe notified us that the Island was in sight. We soon arrived there, and found a large fleet of vessels at anchor, whose flags, with one or two exceptions, represented every nation. The magnificent and romantic harbor, and the beauty of the scene, can only be imagined by those who have visited the spot.

Soon as it was possible, I landed with my luggage, and pleasantly located myself in the best regulated, and most comfortable hotel in the tropics.

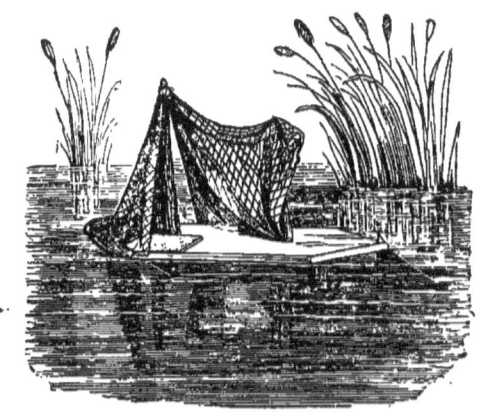

CHAPTER XXIX.

N my arrival at the Island of St. Thomas, I found it to be a pleasant place, but confined to a small geographical area. The inhabitants were composed of Germans, Spaniards, Americans, English, French, and West Indians, besides a large number of colored people.

The trade and commerce transacted here with Europe and the United States, likewise with all the sister islands, was immense. The number of vessels from all parts of the world, that daily arrived and left, was wonderful. This traffic was owing in a great measure to the port being free—the wisdom of which explains itself.

The island is seventeen miles in length, and four and a half miles in breadth. The mountains are rough and elevated, which occasionally decline gradually, but near the shore are frequently very steep. Much inconvenience from the want of an ample supply of water prevails; and little attention is given to the productions of the soil, which is sandy and barren, the greater portion not being under cultivation. The island formerly abounded with wood, that protected it from the excessive heat.

My entertainments were held in the dining-hall of the hotel, and attracted large audiences, who laughed, and betrayed their emotions and feelings in doubting their senses, and at times broke forth in the most excessive bursts of merriment. Each day increased my celebrity; few could understand the philosophy of my art, for my operations were not classified with the ordinary actions and doings of man. Rumors and speculations entered largely into the imagination of the people. By some I was supposed to be the king of a gypsy tribe, travelling in search of new subjects to connect with my race; by others I was judged to have been a descendant of the master spirits who practised their skill in ancient days; for such impossibilities as I seemed to perform, they imagined demonstrated the truth of their opinions.

Reports of my movements and actions were constantly given, which old and young, in their simplicity and excitement, believed, from the effect of what they themselves had seen and witnessed.

Jamaica.

After the close of a prosperous engagement, I proceeded by the English mail steamer for Jamaica. The establishment of this line of vessels has been invaluable in every degree to the inhabitants of the tropics. Not unlike railroads, they have afforded facilities of equal importance— annihilated time and space, connected as they are with the whole group of islands by branch lines extending to all the principal seaports in the Gulf of Mexico. The approach to Jamaica is very beautiful. The elevation and grandeur of the mountains, whose peaks are almost invisible by the misty drapery that surrounds them, is romantic and gloriously magnificent.

Port Royal harbor, which we enter, is guarded by forts of powerful construction; its navigation is difficult and precarious, requiring much judgment, which is overcome by the masterly efficiency of the colored pilots.

KINGSTON,

The largest city of all the British West India Islands, is built upon a sandy soil, with streets of fair pretentions. The houses in general, are erected with convenience and comfort, those of the wealthy especially so; but since the decline of the prosperity of their owners, have become magnificent ruins.

The public buildings are not remarkable for their importance or special character, either in appearance or structure.

Jamaica excels all the other islands, not from any particular superiority, but on account of the magnitude and variety of its productions, natural advantages and scenery, combining in the general productions all the excellences found beneath a tropical sky. Yet, with all its resources and advantages, the greater portion of the land is still in its normal state, which, in a measure, is attributable to the scarcity of labor to improve it; but a far more notable impediment is the lamentably inactive, unenergetic character of all classes, who, notwithstanding many disadvantages, have had abundant opportunities of improving their condition. Why is this prevailing feature so prominently observable in every island, with the exception of Barbadoes, where the population is dense? Is it a want of sensibility, or the enfeebling habits that arise from habitual indolence, or an indifference to the great blessings that arise from intelligence, labor, and an active life?

The paramount obstacle is doubtless the general character of the climate, and its depressing influences upon the system, together with the evil effects arising from the institution of slavery, the radical errors of which are permanently engrafted upon the masses, and which time and education, combined with good laws and a correct estimation of industry, can alone change.

My arrival was hailed with general satisfaction, and an anxious desire to witness my performances. For this purpose I engaged the theatre, which was nightly filled with all classes, who were astonished and elated beyond description. My notability increased to a remarkable extent, for the scenes were never before so emphatically bewildering. The oldest inhabitants had not witnessed during their lives such manifestations, which, if not absolute miracles, were not less so in mystery; neither had the hearing ever been charmed by such a variety of tones, emanating from one voice. Gray heads and youthful faces looked upon me with fear and trembling, mingled with curiosity, and at times provoking me to exercise my profession on those they were hostile to, or tantalizing some well-known wag whose local pranks were an annoyance to their quiet propensities.

The whole community became inquirers as to my relationship with "the great master of sin," from whom many believed I received all my knowledge; and not less perplexing was the natural disposition I assumed, for I laughed and talked like other people, and even conducted myself as one free from all pretentions, so that in some measure my virtues counterbalanced my evil doings. But this view was confined only to a limited number of the thinking class. The majority, however, were less liberal in their opinions, for they considered me as one to be avoided, and much of this feeling arose from the diabolical spells it was said I had invoked and inflicted upon the inhabitants since I had made my appearance, and a multitude of absurd stories did not fail to excite the imagination and develop their superstitions.

These peculiarities sadly demonstrate how inferior intellects can be imposed upon, and the evil effects possible to result from their convictions; for of such instances the history of the world has an abundance of unfortunate proofs. Those that we read of in the Dark and Middle Ages, we can generously afford to pardon, but now, since Christianity, science, and learning are universally disseminated, we feel deprived of that sympathy, and express our feelings of pity and disgust.

A Haunted House.

In one of the principal streets was an untenanted house, from which, at divers times, day and night, were heard issuing the most unnatural and distressing noises, so that the premises had, far and near, acquired the character of being haunted, which the people declared had, under my direction, become a rendezvous for all heaven's rejected spirits, that revelled therein at midnight.

Sober minds smiled, as I did myself, at the inventive source that connected me with such imaginative acts of wantonness, but neither their denial or mine could convince to the contrary; so I determined to *fairly deserve* the credit so profusely bestowed upon me.

One afternoon I procured the keys, and in company with a few speculative friends, and some who doubted my innocence, directed our steps toward the house mentioned.

The moment we entered the door, great commotion was heard in all parts of the building, similar to a number of people endeavoring to escape discovery.

"Hallo!" I shouted, "here is a company called to make your acquaintance."

"We have no desire for acquaintance with our enemies."

"Why not?"

"Because our hearts warm for kindred spirits, whose delight is in the midst of a bewildered atmosphere, where dreamers reign."

"Are there any here?"

"Several; but we do not wish to be disturbed in our duties," replied a deep, hollow voice.

"What are they?" was asked.

> "We want the blood of wicked men,
> To light the lamp of our gloomy den;
> Where skulls and bones are scattered around,
> In our home beneath the silent ground."

The whole party now exhibited an earnest desire to leave.

"I am going," said one; and "I feel afraid to remain," observed another; "Let us all immediately depart," said a third; "We shall all be murdered," uttered the fourth, trembling with fear and emotion.

"You had better leave, and save your lives, before we come down," spoke a most unearthly voice.

I now proposed that we should all go up and attack the imps!

A spontaneous reply of "No! no!" proceeded from every mouth.

"We knew you were cowards," muttered the disagreeable spirits.

I again urged my friends to ascend the stairs with me, but I entreated in vain. I then announced my intention of proceeding alone.

"We shall not permit you to risk your life," responded the gentlemen.

"I am bound to face these embodiments of Satan!" I replied, and darted up to the next story with lightning speed, followed a step or two by my frightened friends, whose desire to prevent my sacrificing myself I firmly believe was sincere; but after a second thought they retreated. When I reached the floor above, I produced a tumultuous uproar of voices, stamping, fighting, and every species of noise,—I seemingly contending with a host of invisibles,—which gradually ceased, and quiet was restored.

Thus victorious, I descended and found myself alone, for those I left had hastily fled to the street, where they impatiently awaited the result of my boldness, and when they beheld me free from injury, without a solitary scratch, they were more than amazed, and congratulated me upon the courage I had displayed. Their inquiries as to who I met or came in contact with were so numerous, that I was wearied with giving my experience.

They all agreed that the authorities should burn the house, and thus relieve the city from the carnivals of hobgoblins and their attendants.

"You are a superstitious people," I answered. "Why, there are no such creatures in existence. The uncouth sounds, noises, and battles, said to have taken place are all fictitious, mere inventions of the imagination; for on our visit *I* was the only evil one present, and I hope my ventriloquial powers gave you a satisfactory evidence of its being a fact."

My companions looked at each other with a singular feeling of ignorance and shame, admitted how little they knew of this world and its wonders, and the folly of their presuming to discuss their knowledge of the mysteries that shadow the future.

I was subsequently invited to an entertainment, where mirth prevailed to an unusual extent, at the expense of the haunted house.

THE SINGING AND TALKING MULE.

Observing a dingy African standing in charge of a mule and cart, I inquired if the mule was for sale.

"No, sir," the man replied.

"I regret it, for he is just such an one as I want."

"Missis wouldn't sell him for de world."

"Why not?"

"Bekase him belonged to massa, who am dead. You can find plenty of 'em."

"Yes, I know that myself; but I cannot find a *singing* one."

"Dis mule don't sing."

"Yes, I do," said the mule, shaking his head.

The man's eyes looked wild at this announcement, and he screamed,—

"Dick, is de debil in you?"

"I knew he was a singer."

"Well, I neber heard him talk before now; I think it's funny."

"I suppose he knows you are not musical."

"Exactly—he has no soul for it," said the animal.

"Golly, Dick! I am frightened to hear your tongue wag so. Are you turning into a man?"

"That's just what I have done;" and the mule commenced singing as follows—

"Long time I've been a drudging mule,
I am now no longer such a fool."

The negro shuddered with fear, rolling the whites of his eyes with rapidity, and stammering—

"Why, dis be very curious."

"It is true, Tom—I am a beast no more. I shall never go into the stable again and eat corn."

"Then you'll die," said Tom.

"No; I'll live on beefsteak and the fat of the land."

"Come Dick, you are bewitched, and I tink we had better go home," said Tom.

"I have no home, no family dear,
No heart to love, no one to cheer."

"Why, you sing as good as a bird. Who was your master?"

"The Spirit of the Mountain. Shall I send him to you?"

"No, I don't want his acquaintance. Let's go to the plantation, Dick."

"I am not going."

"It takes two to make a bargain, Dick."

Here the negro caught hold of the bridle, when the beast said,—

"Tom, drop that; I'll not move a foot."

"You am a stubborn creature."

"*All my family are!*"

Tom appealed in vain, but the mule insisted to the contrary. The crowd had now largely increased, and were much edified by the scene, which terminated in Tom's conquering and driving up the street at the utmost speed, firm in his conviction that Dick would make his "missis" lots of money, for it was the only mule he had ever heard sing and talk.

Such incidents were not, probably, calculated to correct the sentiments prevailing in regard to my affinity with midnight genii and their host of dependents; yet, to comprehensive and educated minds, especially those possessed of worldly knowledge, they were not only amusing features, but acceptable for their meritorious perfection; while, to untold numbers, encouraged by their fanatical and natural inclination to believe in incredible facts, it tended to increase their faith the more.

After visiting Spanishtown, the seat of government, and enjoying a pleasant residence on the island, I bade farewell to many friends, whose hospitality and general indulgences are most gratefully remembered.

DEMARARA.

I embarked for Demarara, British Guiana, by steamer, the approach to which presents nothing pleasing or encouraging. The flat surface of the soil, as you pass up the river, is not broken by a single object far as the eye can reach. The only extraordinary feature is the total absence of mountains, rocks, woods, and hills. Not a tree-top, church spire, or a commanding building could be recognized, and the low and uninteresting appearance of the land is a matter of uncommon surprise. The most singular attraction is the sudden discoloration of the water immediately after leaving the ocean to enter the harbor.

GEORGETOWN.

The capital has the appearance and character of a Dutch settlement. The houses are capacious, and erected upon piles, to reach which it is necessary to pass over canals or drains. The streets, in many instances, are spacious, and the public edifices erected with taste and elegance. It was evident that a general understanding prevailed on the part of the inhabitants to ignore antiquated styles of buildings for those more modern, with valuable improvements and sources of comfort, to the extent of their means. The country in the immediate neighborhood is extremely low, and to reach the grander portions, it is necessary to traverse some distance into the interior, where plains of great magnitude, and elevated spots, betray pleasant and agreeable views.

It would be impossible to describe the satisfaction and applause with which my entertainments were received, or the considerations and reflections of the gay and thoughtful; the former acknowledged my acquirements with graceful compliments and unsurpassed patronage, while the latter were captious and less sanguine as to my merits and claims upon society. It was a matter of discussion with them how far I was deserving of their friendly salutation, by what process I became intimate with the character of my doings, for they eagerly believed in what they did not see, and the exaggerated accounts they heard enhanced this feeling, so that I became the general topic of conversation during my stay, which was frequently accompanied by the most unwarrantable faith in my achievements and dependencies on the powers below. They unhesitatingly asserted my name was recorded in the black book, for no one of Christian virtue was ever known to exercise such evidence of gifted traits. Dame rumor charged me with provoking an increase of sickness, unusual annoyance from insects, while fragments of broken pastels filled the air. Disagreeable as these accounts were, I pursued my career with more than my accustomed ardor. Experience had by this time removed all sensibility of feeling pertaining to such intolerant fancies. Sceptics and fanatics have flourished in every clime where the mind is imperfectly balanced, or education is neglected.

My out-door feats procured me great popularity, for whenever a suitable opportunity presented itself, I did not fail to make use of my dexterity of hand and ventriloquial powers, which were generally of a momentary creation. The intense interest and pleasure my roguery would supply to the gazing crowd, was alone a compensation; but this *modus operandi* invariably resulted to my pecuniary benefit, by the numbers who patronized my appointed *soirées* at the hall.

The Prolific Eggs.

Early one morning I visited the market, by far the most neat and commodious one I had seen during my travels in the tropics. A clean and orderly air prevailed in all its ar-

15

rangements. The women were neatly attired in light muslin dresses, and their heads decorated with fanciful cotton handkerchiefs, while the men were not less particular in their appearance. I came to a dealer in eggs, and inquired the price per dozen.

"One shilling."

"Are they fresh?" I asked.

"Dem laid dis morning."

"How do you know?"

"De hens cackle when de sun rise, and den me get um."

"Then there are no chickens in these?"

"No; no chicks in dese."

"Are you sure of that?"

"Why, yes; what make you think dere any?"

"Because I ate some yesterday which contained several, and they are alive in me now, for I feel them."

Here a number chirped, and the woman shrank back with terror, saying,—

"Why, bless you, massa! I think they kill you. Ain't you sick?"

"Yes, they trouble me a great deal,"—the chickens making themselves heard again, and the woman evincing her previous alarm.

"I think I'll take one of yours, and try it," said I, when, taking one in my hand, a sound proceeded from it, which produced additional fear.

"Well, dere is one in dat, I am sure;" and she commenced turning over the eggs in her basket, when a whole brood of chickens greeted her curiosity, by a vigorous chirping, and she declared they were warm, and refused to part with a single one, as she intended to take them home and put them under the hen, which would pay her better. Of course, the different market people who had gathered around were greatly astonished, for their imaginations could not solve the phenomenon ; but a policeman who had been on duty at my hall the previous evening, being now a looker-on, relieved their anxiety by making known to them that I was Blitz, the ventriloquist—a queer fellow.

A Merchant Nonplussed.

In life we encounter every phase in the human character. Mankind are far from being alike gracious in their demeanor. Some are more difficult to please than others. Many are over suspicious and conscientious. They believe in no merit or righteousness but their own. To them the sun is seldom bright or warm, the flowers sweet or lovely, and nothing in nature is cheerful or pleasant. Such seldom or never contribute a smile or a joy to a single heart, however great may be its affliction. They live for their own sake, and their opinions are at war with every plan or principle that affords happiness to society.

There is a large class of such people in the world, one of whom it was my misfortune frequently to meet here. He was a merchant of good standing, but unpopular in his social intercourse, by reason of his parsimonious habits. I endured his waspish obstinacy and garrulous disposition without betraying the slightest degree of anger, believing it wiser to repay him in a manner that would render him ridiculous in the eyes of his friends, than by any rebuke or altercation, thus waiving all considerations in reference to my own personal feelings. The occasion was afforded me at the residence of a wealthy gentleman, where a large assembly had gathered, by invitation, to partake of and enjoy his munificent liberality. Luxuries were numerous beyond relation, being the products of all climes, independent of cost. The richness of the exotics, their perfume, the fruits and delicacies, the substantials, the variety and rare-

ness of the wines, the decorations, the valuable qualities of
the plate and china, the splendid dresses of the ladies, their
sparkling gems and animated countenances, radiant with
health and beauty, rendered the event a most brilliant and
interesting one.

The guests were constantly grouping around me, in the
hope and expectation that I would amuse them with some
experiments. Most eager among them was the individual I
have alluded to. Without hesitation I consented, and commenced operations by causing the disappearance of handkerchiefs, rings, and gloves, and the producing of an inexhaustible supply of bouquets, which were presented to the ladies.
The eyes of all looked electrified, especially those of the merchant, who, after endeavoring to account for what he himself and others had seen, remarked it was a happy faculty—
the obtaining the growth of flowers without owning a foot
of land. Why did I not supply fruit in like manner?

"Are you fond of it?" I asked.

"Yes, I live upon it," he answered.

"That, then, will account for the quantities in your
pocket."

"In mine?"

"Yes, sir."

"You have made a mistake."

"Oh! no; I'll take them out, if you will allow me."

"With all my heart, sir."

He turned his body partially around, while my hand
entered his pocket, and withdrew bananas, oranges, and
other fruits, one after another, not only to his consternation, but to the great merriment and glee of his acquaintances.

"Well, you assisted yourself liberally to-night," I said.

"No, sir! I never carry things away!" he indignantly
answered.

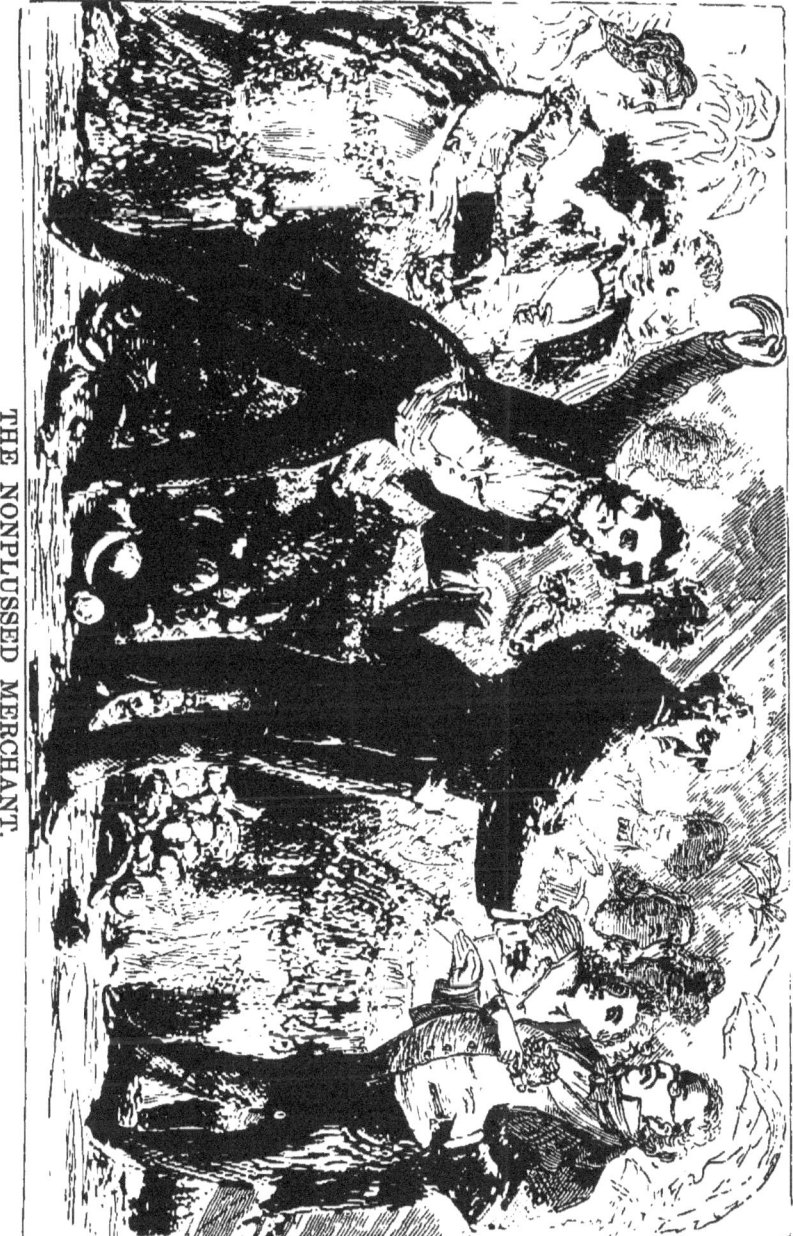

THE NONPLUSSED MERCHANT.

"But facts show for themselves," I retorted; "and here is a quantity more of things!"—taking from his neck ham sandwiches and grapes.

He appeared confused and ashamed at what had taken place, and, lifting his hands, protested he was not guilty of stealing, and by what magic means they came about him, his philosophy could not fathom. This, however, did not subdue the taunts and laughter he was subjected to, or prevent my realizing full satisfaction.

A Drunkard Saved.

Perhaps one of the most agreeable and happy incidents of my life occurred in this city.

A friend whose hospitality knew no bounds, and whose nature was most social and genial, became daily more and more addicted to intemperance. He was the husband of a lovely and intellectual wife, and father of three sweet children. His convivial habits naturally gave great concern to his friends, and especially so to her whose heart and love he had secured. The demon of liquor betrayed its destroying hand upon his constitution, to the appalling horror and unmitigating agony of her whose affection was unceasing as her hopes.

My intimacy with both was of the most cordial character. Observing his inclination for indulging to excess, and deeply sympathizing with his wife and family, at the same time lamenting that a mind so brilliant, with all the accomplishments and refinements of a gentleman, should become a prey to such sad influences—a most melancholy example of a noble intellect lost to family ties and the world—I considered it my imperative duty, if I possessed the power—which I believed I did—to rescue him from the dark pit to which he was approaching, and revive in him a conscious reflection of his own suffering, the evils and sorrows entailed upon his relatives, and the immoral effect upon society.

Without communicating my plans to any one, the day following my decision, I invited him to a quiet dinner with me, which he readily accepted. In the meantime, I prepared an ample supply of liquors, consisting of wines, brandy, porter, and ale. We took our seats at the table, and, soon as courtesy permitted, I invited him to take a glass of wine. "Here is sherry, madeira, and champagne; which is your choice?"

"Champagne," he replied.

A Portuguese waiter filled our glasses. My guest saluted me, and placed the wine to his lips, when a deep voice, as if coming from his glass, warned him not to drink. My friend seemed agitated, as he looked me in the face, inquiring who addressed him.

"That was singular. Did you taste?" I responded.

"No, but I will," raising his glass.

"Stop! It's poison!" a solemn voice exclaimed.

He betrayed an uncomfortable feeling, and gazed around the room for intruders, observing,—

"Why, this is a mystery, is it not?"

"It is a guardian spirit, with a warning, I believe."

"Do you think so?" he asked.

"I do, and would accept the advice."

"But suppose we try sherry?"

"With pleasure."

The waiter poured the wine, and each took a glass in hand to drink, when a grave voice again commanded him to beware! My visitor put his glass down again, and arose from his chair, lifting the table cover, which in a moment he dropped, evincing great disappointment and vexation, pronouncing it some incarnate imp, who desired to disturb our pleasure.

"Perhaps they have a good object in view," I remarked.

"What! in preventing my drinking?"

"That is my hope," spoke the invisible one.

"Who are you that made those unearthly-sounds?" he inquired.

"A friend that wishes to save you from a drunkard's grave," uttered the warning voice.

He decided to test the phenomenon by swallowing the wine in the glass, as his appetite was strong, but had scarcely taken the glass up for that purpose, when the same voice solemnly insisted on his not drinking it.

He had not the courage to drink it, but again put it down, demanding the voice to appear and prove its identity.

"It is forbidden. I come to plead for your wife and children, your family, your reputation; that joy and happiness may replace misery and bitterness."

"Excellent monitor!" said I.

After a slight hesitation, he broke forth with the following declaration,—

"Signor, there is something so singular in this circumstance that I am induced to give it attention. I shall forever abandon all liquor. I am resolved. Remember what I say."

"Bravo! bravo!" loudly echoed the unknown counsellor.

"What a fortunate affair this has proved!" I exclaimed.

We sat and chatted over the unaccountable episode until late at night, when the new disciple of temperance retired to his home, and singular to say, his sleep was one continuous dream of a home of pleasure, an affectionate family, a sober and respectable life, excepting for a moment, when he saw, as through a veil, the drunkard's family—his careworn wife, her starving, squalid, ragged children—marks of desolation and final ruin. This and more he told me the next morning.

How greatly I have rejoiced that I succeeded in my wishes none can imagine, for I am informed and believe that my friend has never violated his promise and resolution, and for more than twenty years I am assured he has been a devoted and consistent champion of temperance, and to this day knows not to whom to attribute his happy escape from degradation and the thraldom of liquor.

After a successful season, I visited several plantations, the proprietors of which were gentlemen of marked character and noble impulses, unfailing in their efforts to render my stay pleasant and agreeable. The sweet air, fragrant and perfumed, and nature sparkling all around with animation and luxury, increased the pleasure I realized, and my departure from which was a deep regret; but necessity, the harbinger of a wanderer's fate, so decreed it. The third day after my return to the town, I embraced the opportunity of leaving for New York, *via* St. Thomas, parting from many warm hearts and sunny smiles, with a sincere regard and interest for their future.

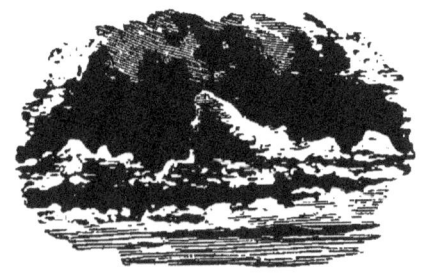

CHAPTER XXX.

N reaching St. Thomas, I received the pleasant greetings of my friends, and their unabated hospitality, until I sailed for the American metropolis, where I safely arrived, and passed the summer and a portion of the winter months in pleasant retirement with my family, whose care and education were to me of momentous importance. This education, though, was in a degree dependent upon the natural talent and ambition of the children themselves, yet they required, as all youthful minds do, paternal advice, domestic instruction, and home training, which duty I never under any circumstances failed to discharge. My whole attention was thus occupied with these and other matters up to the time of my leaving for Cuba.

I will not undertake to depict the sorrow occasioned by a separation from home and its endearments; how fond hearts are distressed, and dread to utter what they feel and fear. It is a picture common to every-day life, which nearly every one has experienced, and if any have escaped the scene, they know not what a test of pure love is mingled in the pain, or the cheering compensation it gives to every forward footstep; for there arises a sweet halo, an inspiration.above all earthly value—that which riches are unable to procure; it is the satisfying consciousness that you are beloved at, and missed from, home.

I had engaged passage on the " Christopher Columbus," a regular packet ship running between the cities of New York and Havana. Her figure-head was a majestic bust of the immortal discoverer of the New World, elaborately carved, painted, and gilded. The large number of passengers were composed of Americans, Spaniards, French, English, Germans, and Italians, who far exceeded the accommodations. Many were obliged to sleep on temporary beds in the cabin, and take their meals as opportunity might afford; but notwithstanding the abundance of inconveniencies, there were no complaints or ill-humor, but a general manifestation to divide all the comforts, and render each other comfortable as possible.

I resigned my berth in favor of an elderly Spanish gentleman who was sick, and accompanied by his daughter. His Castilian pride and politeness refused to deprive me of what I had contracted for, but I explained that he was advanced in years, while I was young and healthy, and better able to dispense with the luxury. "Very well, sir, I accept, and ever shall esteem you my friend," he replied, which he truly proved.

There was no paucity of life or character, for the voyage was such an one as might be expected from a collection of unselfish, yielding spirits, all hilarity and good-will. Night and day passed away without any apparent reserve or selfishness being exhibited, so that when the time arrived to separate, it impressed the fact upon my mind that any amount of annoyances can be overlooked, where the obliging traits of our nature develop themselves.

THE KING PIG.

I must not fail to give an account of an event which created no little commotion for the time, followed by a theme for mirth and wonder. Late one night a pig (several of which were on board), escaped from his pent-up abode and entered the cabin, where all was calm and quiet, in search of something to eat; but after reconnoitring and failing in his search, commenced squealing to the extent of his powers, which in a moment produced a scene not often witnessed on the sea.

State-room doors were thrown open, and the inmates stood looking, in their white robes, like ghosts, and the occupants of the cabin were on their feet, equally as odd in their drapery.

"Where ish de hanimal?" uttered a phlegmatic German.

A grunt answered, which occasioned the inquirer to retreat backward, amid much laughter.

"Dunder and blitzen! it ish under my ped!"

Here a general crowding commenced toward the spot, to secure the intruder, who, either defiantly or from alarm, grunted and squealed his best, which soon brought the captain down from the deck to learn what caused the excitement.

"A pig is in the cabin!" several exclaimed.

"If that's so, let us drive the rascal out."

By this time the steward and his assistants, who had been awakened by the excitement, made their appearance, when all present began to hunt for the pig.

The German laid flat upon his face, with his eyes and hands stretched in every direction.

At one moment piggie squealed here, and the next there, the hunters changing their positions accordingly.

"He is a devil of a pig!" broke forth mynheer.

"Vat you expect, sar, from one swine?" said a Frenchman.

Piggie grunted.

"Ha! ha! he understand ze language!"

The captain called the steward to know if he had seen him. He answered,—

"No, sir; I have looked in all directions—he must have gone out."

But the pig denied this statement by grunting in one of the state-rooms.

Every one made a rapid movement toward the spot; the captain entered first, with a pleasant smile, confident of success; but he was sadly disappointed. After looking and feeling beyond all doubt, he came out, exclaiming,—

"This puzzles my brain!"

Others were equally chagrined, for their efforts were not less fruitless.

I thought it time to own my complicity and roguery in the matter, and allow those I had so wilfully disturbed to enjoy the balance of the night in rest and peace.

Gradually all retired, but not without a peculiar dread of master piggie's reappearance. This feeling was heightened by the squealing which continued long afterward, and by degrees was lost in the deep waters.

The affair was a continued matter of discussion and speculation. The captain insisted that it was a general dream, until the day preceding our arrival, when a full-baked member of the pig family, that was placed before him for carving, commenced to grunt and squeal in the same manner as his midnight friend had indulged in.

"Where is the man-pig?" cried the captain.

I arose from the table and acknowledged the compliment.

"You have cheated us grandly," he continued. "Now give us a first-class imitation of a live pig, and let us see how you do it, and we will forgive you for our nocturnal adventure."

This I did, and I believe it gave a good relish to the

meal, for the hearty laughter must have greatly assisted digestion, while I secured the title of "King Pig!"

ḤAVANA.

The harbor, a fine one, presents an admirable view of the Moro Castle and other forts. The various buildings, from their prominent position and novel style, are quite imposing.

The large fleet of shipping, with their national colors flying, enlivens the appearance and increases the general interest.

The boats of the officials and those for the accommodation of the visitors that collect around the steamer, impart ·a momentary excitement, particularly as every one is anxious to leave for the shore.

One of the first inconveniences encountered is in regard to the baggage, which can pass an examination only at the Custom-house. This is frequently a tedious and annoying process, and the only course to ensure despatch is the free use of gold, which never fails to obtain promptness, with an excess of politeness. But the greatest inconvenience passengers have to contend with is the passport system. The general submission with which governments allow their subjects to be taxed for arriving at and departing from the island, independent of the imposition for land permits and the vexation attending them, is equally culpable and ungenerous, and betrays how little is the care and protection they afford.

It is not necessary or desirable to discuss the national right of Spain to regulate her internal affairs and those of her dependencies, or to enforce a law so obnoxious by exacting such sums from travellers, but it is not a policy in accordance with the spirit of reform which nations are almost everywhere exhibiting. If the Spanish government enforces the law from necessity and as a political safeguard, it is an evidence of a want of confidence in its own stability, and marks how corrupt must be the principles upon which it is based. Why should every stranger be considered with suspicion, as a revolutionist and political adventurer? My own convictions are that the mercenary laws of Spain, made for the purpose of obtaining means for its support, knows no bounds, recognizes no principles of justice or honor, and therefore it is the necessary and paramount duty of all governments, and especially so of our own, to remonstrate and demand the entire abolishment of taxation, and remove the impediments upon the temporary movements of their people.

The period has passed for the maintenance of laws so extreme and insulting. We find a better and even a more equitable vein of men's privileges prevailing in our intercourse with the Chinese or Japanese nations, who, with their alleged barbarisms, do not deign to tax the ingress of those who visit their countries. Surely Spain will not consent to be surpassed in the scale of liberality by those who have but so recently countenanced and inaugurated so broad a spirit of intelligence, and a desire to keep pace with the tendencies of the age.

If Spain, after a proper and respectful demand to abandon her tariff upon the footsteps of every man and woman who may enter her dominions, obstinately persists therein, claiming it as her legal right, then it becomes the duty of every government to peremptorily demand and insist upon the removal of all restrictions on personal travel; and should Spain refuse to comply therewith, then should the governments enforce such compliance by such means as may be necessary; for it is infinitely more honorable than submitting to a rule discreditable to the nineteenth century.

The splendor of the city, as it appears from the water,

disappears on entering it. The stranger is instantly astonished at the absence of the more notable attractions. Nothing meets the eye that is noble or grand; the streets are
contracted and badly paved, with a general uncleanly
appearance. The houses are gloomy in their external
arrangements, but comfortable and adapted to the climate and style of living, which, with attention and enterprise, could be immensely improved. My expectations
were greatly disappointed in regard to the beauty and
grandeur of the place, as I was sanguine of finding much
more elegance than the reality proved.

There were no magnificent structures of art, no tasty
displays in their public and private buildings, or the least
indication of modernizing to the current want of the times,
with the exception of the Plaza de Armes, a handsome
square, with finely-prepared walks, graced with several
fountains and choice exotics, which, in the evening, presents
a blaze of light. Near this resort is the government house,
and a large number of mansions belonging to the aristocracy and those possessing large capital; yet nothing reveals
itself that might be anticipated from its great wealth and
celebrity.

The universal feature, so remarkable in the habits and
proclivities of the tropical character, are no less developed
here than in those islands where slavery and wealth are extinct; for you will perceive all the associate evils that
linger around that gigantic institution, from whence their
riches are derived, without any qualifying preparation for
future wants. A brief residence in the city will strikingly
impress the peculiarities of the population upon the mind;
for each and all seek the immediate gratification of their
desires—no matter how limited or profuse may be the
extent of their means. They never deny themselves a
wish, or pause to reflect upon consequences, so that the

poorest at times appear the gayest and most gorgeously dressed. Indeed, there are no people that can surpass the Cubans in pride and love of ostentation, for they are seen in every movement, public or private.

In their business transactions they are more than punctual and suspicious, so that frequently one detects a species of meanness that almost destroys confidence in their integrity. There is a strong and undoubted avaricious feeling in their nature, for money never fails to exhibit itself in all matters of trade. While we perceive a similar inclination in the natural traits of mankind generally, there is nowhere that quiet, artful attempt to disguise it from observation, as is displayed in Cuba. There are invariably two or three prices to an article, so that it requires some knowledge and no little ability to purchase to advantage, even if familiar with the language. This I learned from experience. Yet there are, beyond doubt, numerous exceptions to what I write; but that a cunning and unflattering vein of their own interest is signalized in all occupations of every-day life, from the humblest trader to the wealthiest merchant, is indisputable.

The Governor, or Captain-General of the island, possesses the supreme power to rule. He is an autocrat in the true sense of the word—his judgment and verdict are absolute. There is no appeal from his decision, except in a very few peculiar cases which have to be carried to the "home government" at Madrid, with only a faint hope of success, unless the result is of more than special importance to Spain or the islanders.

The highest officers, the rich, the poor, the good and bad, the old and young, the innocent and guilty, are equally subservient to his interpretation of right and wrong; a sad and painful comment upon Spanish institutions. This almost unlimited authority being invested in one man, it is certainly important and necessary for the good of the people, that the ruler should be a person of rare genius and the most exalted virtue and integrity—with the principles and character of Washington—so as to serve his country with a fidelity of purpose, and add renown to the laws and the government.

Rulers may be honest, and fulfil their responsibilities with credit, and yet be of only ordinary capacity. It is the heart and intellect combined, which works, remodels, and presides for the amelioration of the masses. They should remove the burdens and unjust laws of antiquated date, so unsuitable for the present enlightened age, and substitute patriots for despots, that all may feel happy and confident in the paternal care of those who govern. This class of rulers, however, are not found in Cuba, where the administration of justice is but an apology for what it signifies, as it is universally admitted that, from the highest official to the lowest, in all departments of the government, they are the most corrupt persons known. The more elevated the position, the greater their peculations. It is a notorious truth that many of the governors have returned to Spain, after two or three years' residence on the island, with large wealth, a great portion of which has been obtained from an interest in, and conniving at, the landing of slaves, which is in direct violation of the treaty for the suppression of the abominable traffic, Spain being one of the contracting parties, and bound to punish all who countenance or participate in its extension ; thus, through the whole ramification of the laws, there is neither security or virtue.

Society is entirely controlled by the Captain-General. He may be despotic or otherwise, as may be for his interest, without a fixed principle for either course. Usually the executive character of the law is excessively procrastinating. The Chancery Court of England, at one time so famous for its lingering propensities, gave judgment with locomotive speed compared to the long and tedious course pursued here, excepting in cases of treason and fermenting revolution, of which disposition is made with despatch, as are some minor cases, subject to fines, which are imposed and collected with a nervous rapacity. Independent of these, there is nothing decided in regard to the guilt and punishment of parties, many of whom have been prisoners for years, unable to procure a trial, on account of influences brought to bear, or from personal aversion and indifference to their fate.

The prisons throughout the island are miserably arranged dens, crowded with people charged with every known crime, promiscuously incarcerated, and who have no possible expectation of their trial or hope of release. In my visits to these establishments, I have seen and conversed with gentlemanly-looking and well-dressed, intelligent men, who informed me of the untiring and fruitless efforts of themselves and friends to procure either a conviction or declaration of their innocence; for in the event of the former, their condition could not be any worse, and in the event of the latter, they would be entitled to immediate freedom, and could return, after their long absence, to home, family, and friends.

These are unpleasant and startling revelations, but nevertheless they are true; and if the attention of the humane could be attracted sufficiently to interest themselves in behalf of a class so abused, or Spain could be inspired to reform her criminal code, and to appoint judges of high legal knowledge and acumen, with the moral uprightness to decide faithfully, at reasonable periods, it would be happy indeed for the fortunes of all living under that government.

One cannot but lament the harassing despondency which the poor victims of Cuban injustice, under the rule of Spain, have to endure. I must not omit to observe that there is a civil court, at least one that has pretension to this character; but apart from the trifling cases intrusted to the Alcaldes—local justices—the law is entirely dispensed by the military commanders, who, in a measure, are absolute dictators. Of course, I do not charge them with a wilful dereliction of their duty, but it is wrong, both in theory and practice, to intrust them with such important responsibilities, the result of which must be, in almost every instance, adverse to the privileges of the people, and in favor of the government; for no personal rights are so secure as when the laws are administered by the civil courts, especially when the trial by jury is the palladium of every man's right—a prerogative not permitted in Cuba. It is a sorrowful sight to see Spain, strong in her proclivities for ancient usages, remaining a passive observer of the wonderful advance of civilization, and forgetting how importantly her own interest and the happiness of her subjects are identified in this utilitarian era.

To convey some idea of the military establishment necessary for the preservation of the island from internal disorder, and revolt from its allegiance, there was, according to an official statement made some few years since, the following number of troops: Sixteen regiments of infantry, of one thousand men each; two companies of picked men, one hundred and twenty-five in number; two regiments of lancers, of four squadrons each, comprising six hundred and two men and five hundred horses; besides four light squadrons, each consisting of one hundred and fifty-one men and one hundred and twenty-five horses; also a regiment of foot, with eight batteries of artillery, a brigade of five batteries, and a company of sappers and miners, together with a large reserve of chiefs and other officials, making the total number of the regular army as follows: Infantry,

17,500; cavalry, 1,800; artillery, 1,500; sappers and miners, 130. Total, 20,930.

This does not include the civil guard, which is also a part of the forces. In addition to the above, there is on the island one regiment of militia infantry, one of militia disciplined, and one of militia cavalry, of seven hundred and eighty-one horses; also, eight rural squadrons of two companies each, with one hundred horses. The Cuban companies of cavalry also number seven hundred and forty mounted men, making in all thirty-five hundred men, and the complete land force, 24,438.

The naval force consisted of 1 frigate, 44 guns; 7 brigantines, 104 guns; 11 steam vessels, 54 guns; 4 schooners, 11 guns; 2 gunboats, 6 guns; 2 transports: in all, 25 vessels, carrying 219 guns, manned by three thousand seamen. At the same time there were in construction two war steamers, for additional defence. But this immense military and naval force has largely increased, the expense of raising and supporting which is many more millions of dollars annually.

This only shows how weak was the loyalty of the islanders toward the government of Spain, and proves that independence or annexation to the United States would be joyfully welcomed. This perpetually surrounding a people with an extensive armament, and the taxation it imposes, must daily enlarge the prevailing discontent.

The great difference between a despotic and a republican government is remarkably illustrated: this island, having a population of 1,018,060, out of which 510,988 were white, 176,647 free colored, and 330,425 slaves, required a force on land and water of 27,438 men, fully equipped for war. This is startling compared with the government of the United States, embracing a population of upward of forty millions of inhabitants, and but recently emerged from a civil war, the most bloody and desperate known in the annals of ancient or modern times, with an acrimony of feeling predominating in the rebellious States, not only between political parties and the different races, but an unyielding hostility to the laws of Congress, accompanied with frequent demonstrations of cruel acts of bloodshed and murder toward each other, with an area of country extending from the Atlantic to the Pacific shores, with territories containing several hundred thousands of Indians constantly violating their treaties of peace, and encroaching upon the rights of border settlers and the path of emigrants, destroying life and property, driving families from their homes, and spreading fear and distress around them. With the ordinary supply of troops for her hundreds of forts, arsenals, dock-yards, armories, and other important points, Congress reported a bill for reducing gradually the military establishment to 29,300 men. This is the most perfect comparison between an absolute monarchy, whose sole existence depends upon the army and navy, and a republic, where the moral power only sustains the sovereignty of the law, and has given to her the glory and prosperity she enjoys, together with the immense civilizing influence for which she is preëminently the most in advance.

The educational character of the people is, in a degree, not less demonstrative of the benighted influence of the government, than is the general acquiescence of the Cubans themselves. There are but two universities or colleges. The primary schools are very few, and controlled by special boards appointed by the government. The whole number of teachers, according to the last census, was only 500, and the pupils 9,000. The more wealthy families have their children instructed at home, for which purpose a private teacher is engaged, who attends the house from one to two hours daily. It is not extravagant to state that four fifths of the children are without schooling. On the whole, the ignorance of the islanders is deplorable, for, in the rural districts throughout the country, the master, servant, and slave are alike unacquainted with the first elements of education. According to the statistics of the United States, published in 1860, there were 106,911 schools, 130,125 teachers, and 4,917,332 pupils attending school, being five times the whole population of Cuba. Besides these, there were 6,636 academies, with 15,763 teachers, and 455,545 pupils. There were also 455 colleges, with 2,772 teachers and 54,-969 students. There were 26,564 libraries, containing 12,-889,601 volumes, with an annual income of $33,990,405.

This array of figures, even ten years ago, appeared almost fabulous when placed in contrast with Spain and her subjects in Cuba at that time.

Of course there was no essential demand for newspapers, no deep interest for a knowledge of passing events in the world, no ambition or enterprise. On the entire island there were not more than six daily newspapers, and three weekly—not one of which was political, while all were under a censorship. In 1860, there were in the United States—daily newspapers, 387; tri-weeklies, 86; semi-weeklies, 79; weeklies, 3,173; monthlies, 280; quarterlies, 30; annuals, 16; grand total, 4,051. Of the newspapers and periodicals, 3,242 were political, 277 religious, 298 literary, and 234 miscellaneous. The unbounded patronage given to the diffusion of information has caused the number of papers and periodicals to increase rapidly, till their number is now legion. Surely, that people must be prosperous and mighty whose gates of knowledge are thrown so wide open for all their children, and where it is the privilege of all to become thoroughly educated in all the affairs of the government.

The moral and religious principle of the masses in

Cuba are low and degrading. One singular fact, on the part of the male population, is, that they are never known to attend church or evince any devotional feeling, their zeal being entirely engrossed by those depraved exhibitions of bull and cock-fighting—amusements barbarously disgusting and evil, in which the priests frequently participate. The females, however, are constant and earnest in their devotional duties, crowding the consecrated edifices at all times. Whether this emanates from a reverential feeling, or from custom, their own hearts know best. In all domestic and other desirable qualifications, they are sadly deficient; they have not those capable and requisite traits which give to a home those sterling assurances of comfort and happiness. Indolence in their habits is so proverbial that they appear but living automatons. To what extent education and climate has influenced this characteristic, I am unable to state; but the presumption is, that they are the effects which slavery, wealth, and a tropical temperature combined, produce.

Three fourths of the population are of the colored race; the balance is composed of Europeans and natives. Some few years since, an active emigration took place from the Azores, and the frugal and industrious habits of these people have been productive of much good to the old residents.

The geological character of the island has never been accurately investigated, but it is sufficiently known to be of a granitic gneiss sienite character, with a secondary and third formation, principally calcareous. The minerals are rich and numerous. Gold and silver have not been found in any quantities, yet there is no question but that they extensively exist. Copper is plentiful; several large mines have long been in operation, conducted with a degree of success and profit. Coal, marble, magnesia, iron pyrites, quartz, and slate, have been discovered, with many other varieties of the greatest importance. The floral character is magnificently grand and diversified, the sweetest flowers and plants are everywhere visible, and the air laden with their perfume, the beauty and fragrance of which are beyond description. The water lily— *Victoria Regia*—is indigent here, and is to be seen spreading its cool, broad leaves on the rivers. The scenery is varied—at times lovely and grand; vegetation exuberant and elegant in the extreme, in many instances presenting the most beautiful panorama of nature imaginable. The climate is damp and unhealthy, subject to fevers and other diseases of a serious nature, which the low position of the city greatly accelerates, but in the interior the air is more salubrious, and sickness less prevalent.

Earthquakes are frequently experienced in the southeast part of the country, but hurricanes are not of common occurrence.

The soil is good and fertile; perhaps not quite equal in quality to many of the islands, yet the productions are very abundant, and if cultivated on modern principles, and attended with the smallest approach to science, the return would be greatly augmented, for the capacity of the land and its resources are far from taxed; but the higher class of agricultural improvements are not a subject of any great interest, for the inference is, that that which is lost by ignoring these improvements, is gained by the compulsory toil exacted from the slaves. This wisdom of economy, however, results in a serious loss, for their physical energies become relaxed and feeble, which might otherwise have been largely strengthened and saved, so that in an economical point of view it is not less important. Many of the large and principal sugar plantations are managed with skill and system, and the proprietors exercise a fair treatment of their slaves. But the land for all other purposes throughout the island is wretchedly neglected, the owners depending entirely upon the natural growth more than any judicious exertion or attention to its necessary wants and capabilities. A perfect confidence or satisfactory feeling prevails, without reference to results, consequently every branch of farming is in a deplorable condition, and this in a country overflow= ing with milk and honey. But the love of ambition or desire for wealth cannot impress ignorant minds with the value and importance of industry; yet, notwithstanding this neglect, the crops are very large, and annually increas- ing. In many districts of the island there are vast tracts of uncultivated land, superior and excellent in character, well wooded and valuable, comprising mahogany, ebony, cedar, and others no less precious, which, from the scarcity of labor, remain unimproved. Much land is appropriated to the raising of cattle, which is quite lucrative. The prin- cipal productions are sugar, tobacco, coffee, rice, maize, indigo, molasses, and malloehlen grass. Honey, wax, on- ions, and poultry are largely produced. The supply of fruit is prolific, embracing the pine, oranges, limes, bananas, figs, strawberries, and other varieties of a delicious nature.

16

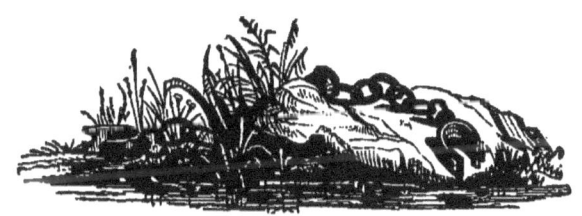

CHAPTER XXXI.

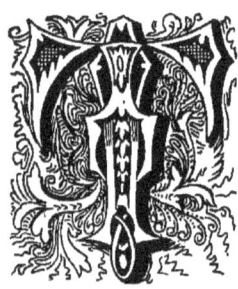HE greatest embarrassment I experienced was the want of a hall, but ultimately I procured a large room at the Tacon Theatre, which was at this time in course of erection. The carpenter engaged by me to prepare seats and other necessary arrangements, was a native of the island, and made a special promise to use despatch, but he pursued his work with the greatest leisure, although he had *twelve* persons employed. It took them a full week to do what two Americans would have accomplished in two days. Every few minutes the whole party would stop to smoke their cigarettes, and when they did labor, the scene was so amazingly ridiculous, that, notwithstanding my patience was tried almost beyond endurance, still I could not for the moment but forget the feeling, and laugh freely. I once saw a man take an ordinary hand-saw to saw a common board, which he could not do till a second man sat himself down on the floor opposite, and holding the point of the instrument between the thumb and forefinger, aided him in the work, while a *third* person balanced the end; and when a piece of wood or plank was needed, however small or light, it required *two* men to furnish it. This whole job seemed to me to be a complete farce, so that I became fatigued and disgusted with such indolent mechanics, and

to add to the annoyance, they did not labor but six hours per day. The more I complained and urged them forward, the less they accomplished, and to my inquiry as to the time they would finish, the reply invariably was, "Mayana, Signor!" which, interpreted, means to-morrow—a common and characteristic word among the Cubans; and so it continued "mayana, mayana, mayana," until they finally announced it completed.

I commenced my exhibitions with great expectations, which were fully realized. The hall was continually crowded with a sea of heads, combining the old, middle aged, and youth; also, the gay, and idle, and those of a morbid and sensitive nature. Nothing could surpass the excitement and interest created: some smiled; others looked solemn and agitated; what was engendered in their minds could only be imagined from their expressions, for there evidently appeared an uneasy feeling in their actions, as when it became necessary for me to approach any portion of the audience, to solicit the loan of any particular article, many would shrink back and shake their heads, as though I was the incarnation of evil. But this betrayal of superstitious belief prevailed continually; there was no release from its powers; their whole nature was impregnated with it; they were the personification of its principles, and yoked to its influences. An easy and simple feat was as equally unaccountable to them as the most complicated one; their organs of vision were not less contracted than those of their reflections—unable to distinguish by sight or reason, they were ever in a dream of amazement, and gave utterance to their emotions by exclaiming that I was a "Brugo!" In the hall, drawing-room, or street, I was pointed out, and even parents flocked to the windows, holding up their children to see the "Brugo," as I passed.

This popularity, however distasteful to my feelings, was

a tribute to and a confidence in my necromantic abilities, and very largely increased my receipts. The more sober and reflecting people were, with few exceptions, no less enthusiastic and interested. I was considered by some as the author of all misfortunes; yet the deaf, blind, crippled, and the afflicted of every kind, sanguine of my powers to benefit their condition, visited me constantly; from morning until night they crowded my residence, importuning me to prescribe remedies for their recovery—to exercise such potent spells as were at my command. Their entreaties were unceasing and earnest, and all efforts on my part to disabuse and enlighten their thoughts in respect to my vocation, its duties, and my powerless position over spiritual events, were unavailing. I told them that the Great Master of heaven and earth directed and distributed His favors agreeable to His wisdom; that it was to Him they must appeal, for no man could grant dispensations beyond the ordinary laws of science, or penetrate into the kingdom of peace and love. These and a thousand similar remarks made no impression upon their minds. The confidence they entertained in my powers and capabilities was beyond removal; it was a conviction arising from a religious superstition, always prominent in those whose views and peculiarities conflict with the common law, or attempt to render ridiculous those permanent principles which govern the world.

The incongruity of the mental organs has existed in all time. The most learned have been noted for their idiosyncrasies, so that it is more generous to sympathize with the feebleness of humanity than to decry and rebuke its intellectual derangements. While, however, there may be occasion, in some respects, for solicitude, there is ample prospect for future congratulations, for the sweeping progress of the age favors disencumbering the mind of crude

impressions which encompass it. These are pleasant hopes
for those familiar with the immense credulity that pervades
all classes of all nations.

My exploits lost none of their attraction, as no one pretended to account for the facts they saw, or bestowed time
to think of or explain them, or from whence appeared the
emanations of the mystic world. Men and women shrank
with fear, refusing to taste or accept the fruits and flowers
produced by the enchanted hand of the magician. "What!
eat your apples!" exclaimed a believer in *diablerie.* "No,
indeed! I should feel Beelzebub prowling around me." A
person more adventurous carried one—"the enchanted apple"—home, which he ate before retiring. During the
night he imagined he suffered intensely, and invoked every
infernal curse upon my head, and prayed forgiveness for the
sin of receiving the "Brugo's" gifts.

THE MYSTIC FLOWER.

A lady, whose love for flowers could not resist the
temptation of taking home a bouquet, in the morning
found, to her surprise, that the flowers composing it had
completely changed their character. There was no longer
the beauty and variety of the previous evening, but a mere
bunch of dry sticks, without a solitary leaf to be seen,
or even the appearance of there having been any. This
alarmed the possessor, whose imagination called up all the
peculiar fears and apprehensions prevalent with people
whose optics and perceptions are of a chameleon character.
The circumstance spread far and wide, and became the common discussion in high life and low. The bishop and priest
were consulted, who examined the dark and musty volumes
of the Church, but their anxious researches were unsuccessful. This failure on the part of the learned teachers to
reach a solution of the wonder-workings I was daily and

hourly exercising, materially increased my reputation, and the Cubans' belief in necromancy, to an unprecedented extent. Nothing was lost or found but that I was in some manner connected with it. This forcibly demonstrated itself in various instances, perhaps in none more so than the annexed incident:

The Thieving Soldiers.

Early one morning, before sunrise, I was notified that the hall door of my exhibition room was discovered to be open. I repaired immediately to the spot, and found the room in possession of a corporal and two soldiers, who had been placed there to protect it. I looked carefully over my apparatus several times, and missed a Spanish real—twelve and a half cents—a pack of cards, and a mechanical stick. I inquired of the soldiers if they had seen any of the articles. One of them replied that he had purchased a bottle of wine with the money, but all denied any knowledge of the cards or stick. "It is very strange," I remarked, "that no one should know anything of the matter. The cards," I continued, "were of no consideration, but the stick was of great value to me on account of its mechanical construction; and unless the person who had taken it from me returned it, I would haunt his dreams, and destroy his sleep." Each man shook his head and declared his innocence. I dismissed the men, locked the door, and returned home.

Many days had passed without any clue to the stick, and all hopes of ever obtaining it had vanished, when I was suddenly surprised by the appearance of one of the soldiers, who drew from his sleeve the stick.

"Here, Signor," he said, with much emphasis, having evidently a disturbed and harassed mind, "here is your stick, or the devil's rod; take it, and return me peace. I have been a miserable wretch since I committed the theft—

punished at night by restless sleep and grim phantoms, and during the day I experience an inward mortification and shame that destroys my happiness."

" Well, did I not predict all this to you ?"

" Truly so ; yet I expected to escape detection, and to operate with the stick, by summoning the genii of gold to lay before me his richest treasures; but your mighty power prevented this. Only bestow upon me my former comfort."

"I grant it freely, with the condition that you state what became of the pack of cards."

" Ah ! Signor, I concealed them in my shoe for safety, but before I reached the guard-house they were gone; you deprived me of them."

" What reason have you for so thinking ?"

" Because I feel satisfied no one but yourself could have taken them from me."

" Soldier, it is gratifying to hear you entertain so much confidence in my knowledge and skill."

"I have occasion for so doing."

" Well, truth will always triumph. I freely forgive you, and trust your future actions in life may be guided by those principles of virtue, that bring respect and consideration."

He bowed his leave, and took his departure with a relieved countenance, and, I hope, an unburdened conscience.

The world is a mirror, that reflects every ism and oddity of belief. The feelings of society are the premonitory foundation for good or evil. Circumstances may have much to do with the character of men ; but the teachings of a moral home, and the education of the early mind, is a solid structure to man. To him, the highest hills are easy of ascent, and his life, not unlike a green and verdant valley, pleasant to look upon and remember. Men of evil minds are always unhappy and discontented, and it is natural they should be so, for they are devoid of all love, blind to every form of beauty and worth, and impenitent to the last. They murmur at their condition, and express themselves dissatisfied with everything.

THE UNJUST FINE.

Frequently I was engaged to give my entertainments at private parties. On the first occasion, I was subject to much embarrassment, for, returning home one night between the hours of eleven and twelve,—after my performance at the residence of a wealthy Spaniard,—in company with my interpreter, having birds, rabbits, and trunks, the driver of the *volante* was stopped by the police, who desired to see my permit for being out so late. Not having the special document required, they stated that the whole party were their prisoners. They inquired my place of residence, to which we all proceeded. When we arrived at the house, they intimated that we could all retire to our beds, but they were obliged to keep the carriage, horse, and postilion in the court-yard. Happy to escape in this manner, I readily consented to do so.

In the morning we all had to report ourselves before the judge, who fined us three doubloons—fifty-one dollars. Not admiring his wisdom, or comprehending the justice of his decision, I requested to be informed of what I had been guilty. He replied that I had violated the laws of the island, and I must pay the penalty. I respectfully protested against this decision, pleading my ignorance of the law in regard to the necessity of procuring a pass from government.

"I accept your statement," said he, "and for that reason I have only imposed one half the usual sum."

At this moment a gentleman entered the office in apparent haste, to obtain his honor's signature to some papers. The interruption afforded me an excellent opportunity to make arrangements for astonishing the learned judge. I seized an envelope, in which I placed three silver dollars, and folded the paper, near as possible, to the shape of the coin.

After the gentleman left, I counted out three doubloons, but told the judge that the government treasury would not be benefited by the money.

"Why not?" he indignantly asked.

"Because it is magic gold, and will become silver the instant I leave your presence," I replied; and in proof of this, I requested to be allowed to wrap them in an envelope, to which he assented.

I dropped in the pieces, one by one, and shaped it closely resembling the one I had prepared with the dollars, when, in a second, I substituted the silver enveloped in paper, for that of the gold, notwithstanding the judge's sharp attention to my movements. Then I requested him to make some memorandum in writing upon the package.

"Yes, I will seal it with wax;" which he did, made an impression with a ring, and, further, wrote something upon the paper, then placed it in his pocket, remarking that "it was not in the power of man to change it." I assured him that he would find himself deceived.

"If you can abstract it," he defiantly exclaimed, "you are welcome to it."

Having discharged my obligation, the judge said I was at liberty to retire. I heard nothing in relation to the money deposited in the judge's pocket until the following day, when a message reached me from him, stating his wish to see me. I anticipated his object, and was fully prepared for his surprise.

I found him in company with many persons, whose di-

16*

lated eyes indicated their interest in what he was relating. His own countenance also evinced that peculiar expression which never fails to develop itself whenever the feelings are perplexed or severely troubled. With the silver and paper in his hand, he was explaining, in an excited manner, what appeared to him a miracle, the movement of his head, shoulders, and hands, keeping time with the volubility of his tongue.

All eyes turned to me as I entered. The gentlemen buttoned their pockets, as if afraid that I should relieve them of their contents. The judge received me graciously, and commenced by saying that after I left him the previous day, a strange sensation came over him, such as he had never before experienced. The blood in his veins began to throb, and shocks penetrated his system, which alarmed him much. I replied that there was no necessity for fear; that the shocks were only caused by the electric action on the metallic substance in his pocket.

"What length of time did the feeling you describe continue?" I asked.

"For several hours; but ultimately it subsided," he replied.

I explained to him that such was the natural result of those laws that appertain to science, that there need be no further apprehension, as the substitution of the silver for the gold was fully accomplished.

"What invisible source have you?"

"None but these," exhibiting my hands; "they are the crucibles by which I dissolve and recoin the metals."

"Then you have the faculty of making the rich poor, and the poor rich?"

"That depends upon circumstances," I answered; "for wealth, when fraudulently secured, only becomes liable to evil propensities; but when honorably acquired, it is harmless, even as against the magician's caprice. When did you discover the fact of the transformation?" I asked.

"While at dinner. I removed the package from my pocket, broke it open, and you can picture my amazement on finding the silver dollars. The effect was astounding. My brain became dizzy with fear!"

"You may remember, judge, that I distinctly informed you, at the time you fined me, that the money would never be of any advantage to the island revenue, the truth of . which you have realized."

"You speak truly; but how was it effected? It seems incomprehensible; for nothing has ever transpired in Cuba so decidedly beyond comprehension, and it even surpasses in wonder the renowned magicians of the East, the magic of India, the fakirs of China, and the feats of the Hindoo and Brahmin priests, who cultivated and practised their knowledge of necromancy with a stubbornness of mind incomprehensible."

"I am happy, judge, to hear you express so high an estimation of my abilities. I was operating only on my own money, but I am prepared at any moment to repeat the experiment by converting all the gold and silver in your residence into copper, without approaching the premises."

This proposition created the greatest consternation in the astute mind and feelings of the magistrate, who rose from his chair with the fearful expectation that I would execute what I had proposed.

"No, no, Signor, pray do not!" he cried, in a voice broken with fear, "I have several thousands of gold, and much family plate; I should be ruined!"

"I have no object," I continued, "beyond convincing you of the immensity of my art, and what it enables me and those who are its disciples to achieve; but even this is nothing in comparison to what I am capable of doing. I can remove the teeth from your mouth, the hair from your head, and the clothes from your back."

"I believe all you state, Signor; indeed, I think whatever you undertake will be successful—only spare my person and property."

"Yes, we are all confident," responded the judge's friends, "that there is no exaggeration in what you affirm. We feel assured you are the master and embodiment of a power miraculous and absolute."

I gave my word I would suspend all further action; that no future exercise on my part should molest the judge, indirectly or otherwise, for, as I had succeeded in establishing the wonders of natural magic, I could afford to be generous and forgiving. The judge hastened toward me, and shook me heartily by the hand, for what he termed my magnanimity, in which they all expressed their acquiescence.

In the evening a messenger delivered to me the following letter, written in Spanish, accompanied by a box:

"WONDERFUL SIGNOR! Please accept a souvenir of twelve doubloons as a memorial of my high consideration for your eminent—I might say, without impropriety, supernatural—talents.

"With wishes of friendship and esteem,
"Your sincere admirer,
"DON ———."

Of course the greater portion of Havana was greatly disturbed by the positive statement of the judge, who was overwhelmed and tormented day and night by eager inquiries from every grade in society, and to each and all he emphatically declared the truth of the report in regard to himself.

How marvellous is the imagination! How frequently a little unpremeditated circumstance will excite the mental faculties and create a marked sensibility for romantic extravagances, and those ideas that are associated with the invisible spheres! for so sensitive are the organs which direct our opinions, that we unthoughtfully become victims to the most improbable and ridiculous conclusions. This instability of character has always been conspicuous in man, and notwithstanding knowledge, and all the civilizing influences of life, it seems likely to continue. This declaration may appear strange, and not complimentary to the enlightenment of the age, and endless numbers will be prepared to deny and affirm to the contrary. No doubt such persons have their opinions respecting the decline of those follies which were so prominent in ancient periods; but if time has accomplished this object, it has been no less successful in the creation of countless frailties and follies equally absurd. This is fully established by reference to all the leading newspapers and periodicals, whose columns continually abound with editorial essays and discussions of the Spiritualists and their public lectures, and the advertisements of fortune-tellers and astrologers; indeed, there is scarcely any exemption from their influences. Society is painfully interested in seeking a faith that is untenable as it is injudicious and wicked.

Nothing could surpass my uninterrupted success. Applications were repeatedly made to me, by people of position and understanding, to awaken the dead from their slumbering graves, and excavate the buried secrets of pecuniary value on matters of family importance in regard to mislaid bills or papers. There was no description of fanaticism that did not daily reveal itself. This is illustrated by the

Box of Cigars.

In compliment to a friend, who had rendered me valuable services, I had obtained a box of the finest cigars manu-

factured on the island, which I forwarded, with my compliments. To my surprise he returned them, with a copy of
the Bible, and a note expressing his thanks, but stating that
he could not on any account—devoted as he was to a cigar—
attempt to inhale the perfumes of hell! and hoped the *good
Book* would guide me through life, and protect me from the
powers of Satan and his innumerable advocates. This gentleman was cultivated in mind and dignified in character,
but not without his idiosyncrasies.

A most remarkable illustration of how effectually the
physical system is affected by the mind, came at this time
under my observation, which I will here relate:

THE LIBERAL LANDLADY.

On my arrival in Havana, I settled at a quiet and convenient boarding-house. The proprietress was an invalid,
yet, in some degree, active and industrious. After attending my exhibitions, she frequently consulted me in regard
to her ailments, urging me to charm away her trouble, and
provide her with the health and strength of former days. I
regretted my inability to benefit her, as I professed no knowledge of medicine whatever, but stated that I had by me a bottle of mixture in the virtues of which I had the most implicit
confidence, and if she would take a teaspoonful at night
and in the morning, it perhaps might be of advantage to her.
To this she joyfully assented, and, strange as it may appear,
in the course of *one week* she fully recovered, and affirmed
she was well. My remedy was a bottle of Cherry Pectoral,
which I had by me. I explained it to her, but she attributed its healing power solely to my magic powers. The
gratitude of this woman knew no limit; there was no luxury
or comfort, however expensive, that she did not procure for
me; and I sincerely believe that this simple circumstance
alone would have enabled me to obtain any amount of patients

as a medical practitioner. From the time of my prescription up to the time of my leaving the city, she refused all compensation for my board, as she stated I had restored her to life and health. Of course I remunerated her in other ways, poor deluded woman!

My readers may correctly infer that my profession has subjected me to an infinite variety of events of a character developing all the singular traits and dispositions of the human mind. Charity for the infirmities of others should not fail to enlist our sympathy and forbearance, and remind us that we cannot see ourselves as others see us. So constituted are the faculties that the reasoning powers will become the dupe of their own senses, for it is extraordinarily difficult, if not impossible, to remove impressions produced by traditions and adventures. There are more people in the world wrong than right. To attempt to change their belief would not only be a herculean task, but in most instances a failure. There was no escape for me, either from the importunities of the illiterate or the demands of the wise and learned, for *all* looked upon me as capable of exercising my art either for good or evil.

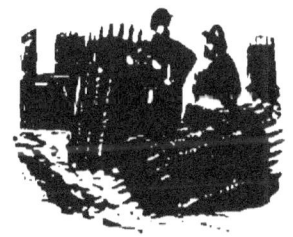

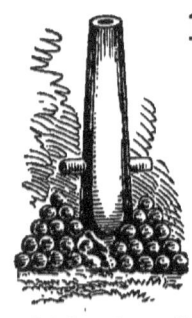 N the city of Havana resided a retired planter, Señor José Garcia, and his amiable lady, Señora Madelon. They were rich and influential, blessed with an only child, a daughter, who was the idol of their hearts, the flower and happiness of a palatial home. Few possessed such graces of nature, or enjoyed the advantages of so high a position, which she adorned with the beauty of her person and the brilliancy of a gifted mind. The most fabulous sums were appropriated to educate and accomplish this darling of their love, and teachers were procured proficient in all languages and sciences.

Señorita Inez Garcia was also the delight and idol of society, and was admired by old and young, for there was not in the city or on the island one so popular, or so much entitled to the universal homage she received. A smile and a kind word for friend or stranger, and an affability almost irresistible, accompanied at all times with a generous purse for the poor and afflicted, were the magic attractions of this fair lady. But as wealth, youth, and beauty are not exempt from vicissitudes, or independent of those trials which surround life, so in this case. Inez was privately betrothed to Señor Carlos, a young gentleman of ability and character, the son of an old Castilian, haughty and

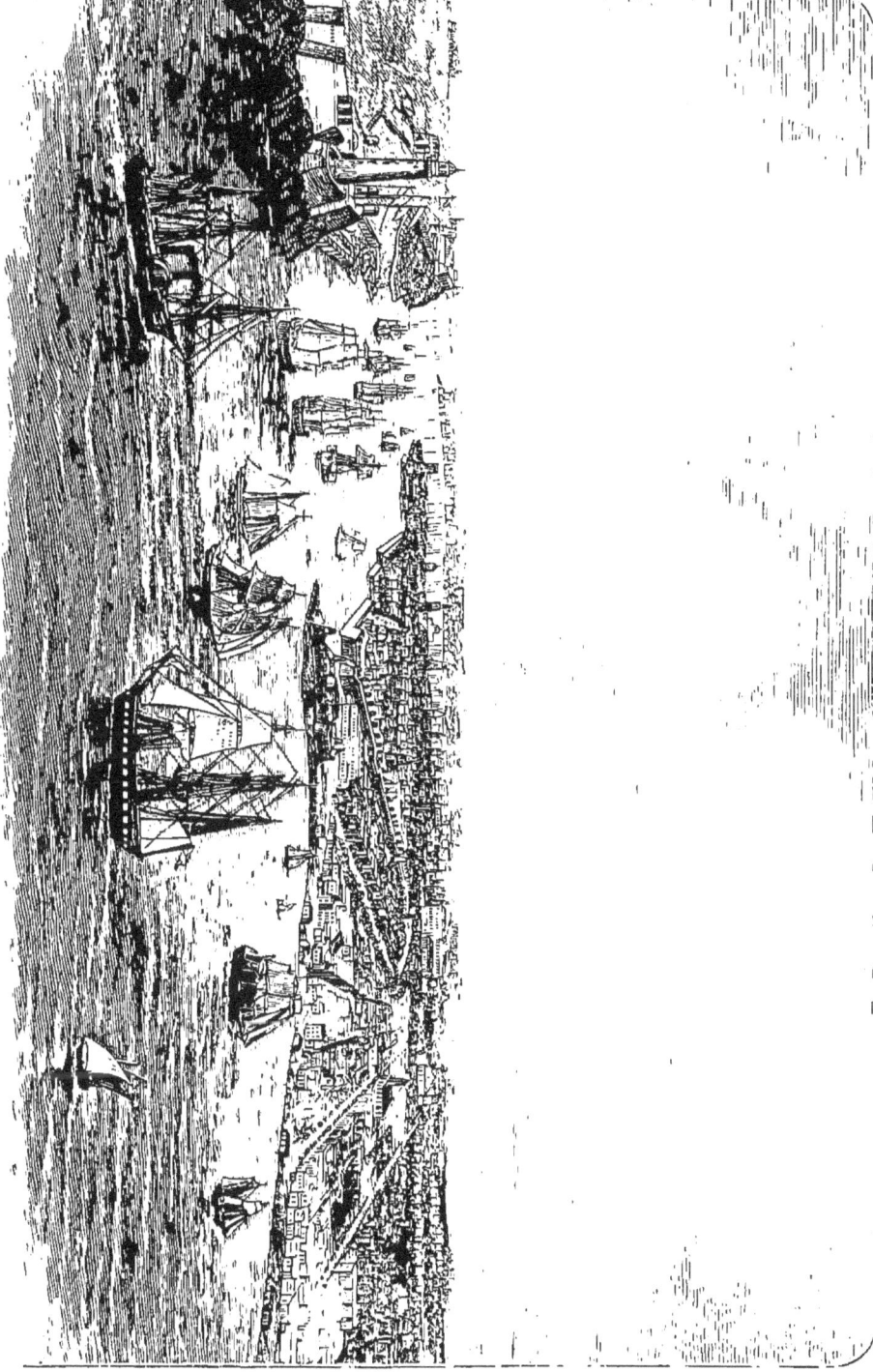

aristocractic as all natives of Old Spain are well known to be, especially as exhibited by those residing in Cuba, while between the fathers of the lovers a bitter and undying feud had for a long time existed, neither of whom was conscious of the engagement.

This enamoured couple met, conversed, and enjoyed each other's presence with that transport and delight so usual where love predominates. Thus two years passed fleetingly away, when our hero and heroine resolved to solicit the consent of their parents. This was an act of no ordinary undertaking, for both full well knew in advance the opposition and denial they would encounter; but true love suffers no defeat, encounters opposition in every form, and fights valiantly for its prize. This was the determination and feeling that inspired Carlos and his *fiancée*. But the repulse they met with was overwhelming. The grief and sorrow which from this day encompassed the two was not only distracting, but mingled with the most painful apprehensions.

The father of Inez, invariably a man of quiet and liberal impulses, became frantic with rage and curses.

"What! marry the son of a tyrant, an enemy to my beautiful country—earth's paradise! Never will I sanction such an alliance."

The father of Carlos was less impetuously demonstrative in his denunciation, but equally firm in his opposition. His antipathy to connect himself with a native Cuban in family alliance was unconquerable. From necessity, therefore, all secret meetings, as well as communications between the lovers, were for a period entirely broken off and discontinued. But not many weeks had elapsed before the inventive genius of love baffled all the precautions, of whatever character, taken by the parents, and their appointments and communications were again resumed and uninterrupted, there being a determination on their part to love the more, and brave every obstacle.

In this critical position of affairs I arrived in Havana, when my fame and wonders soon became known to the distressed Carlos and Inez, who immediately consulted me as to the truth of the reports concerning me, and of my willingness and ability to serve them, proffering to me untold sums of gold to interest myself in their present and future happiness; to relieve their difficulties by gaining the permission of their natural guardians to their union. I gave them no encouragement, as I was unwilling to undertake that which I could not accomplish. They retired dejected and disappointed at my refusal, but returned again in a few days, supplicating me to intercede and put in practice my powers of necromancy for the accomplishment of their desire. The more I urged the impossibility of my benefiting them, the greater was their persuasions and promises of gold. I assured them my feelings were deeply interested in their behalf, and if circumstances could be favorably arranged, I would place in execution a project that might not be without its influences, and possibly might affect their destiny.

I suggested that Inez should promenade with her father in the plazza during the evening, but if by any unforeseen occurrence she should be unable to attend, to communicate at once with me. With this understanding we parted. This course I considered the only plausible one to insure success, as it was a customary and usual place of resort for the people. At the proper time I proceeded to the promenade, and, after a few impatient moments, observed the fair Inez leaning upon the arm of an elegant-looking gentleman, in the prime of life, and dressed in a suit of white linen. I followed them closely, without a recognition from Inez. Suddenly a voice exclaimed,—

"Señor José Garcia! Señor Garcia here?"

Thus startled, he separated from his daughter, and turned toward the sound, inquiring who it was.

"Me, Señor; a member of your family from the invisible dominion."

"What do you require of me?" he asked, in trembling accents.

"Consent to your daughter's marriage with Señor Carlos."

"Never!" he angrily muttered.

"Your happiness in this world and the next depends upon it," was the response.

"Who are you that rebukes and advises me?" he asked.

"I am gone," was said, in receding tones, "but beware!"

I retreated some distance, and observed him directing his search in the vicinity of the spot whence came the admonition of the imperceptible monitor. Suddenly he took his daughter's arm, and walked toward his home, where he arrived much perplexed and troubled; he then related the strange event to his wife, who was equally bewildered, especially as she was of a superstitious turn of mind, and an advocate of all the isms of the age.

The night to them was a fearful one. All sleep was banished from their eyes; forms and characters of every description appeared to them; and thus they passed the hours of darkness, restless and sleepless, until the morning sun arose in its splendor and cheerfulness, when they arose and arranged their toilet for taking a carriage ride, and discussing the scenes of the night, the precise nature of which was a secret known only to themselves; but one thing soon became very evident to them, which was, that their sympathies were aroused, and hearts softened, for on their return to breakfast a reaction had taken place, and they embraced Inez, withdrawing their hostility to her becoming the bride of Señor Carlos.

The heart of the maiden throbbed with bright anticipations for the future. No butterfly was more light and airy. All this she imparted to me in the course of the day, with a countenance sparkling with animation and brilliancy. The outburst of her gratitude was touching in the extreme. My pen cannot convey the least approach to its excess.

"Now," she vivaciously exclaimed, "you have only to conquer the father of Carlos, and we shall then be united." I shook my head, and gave her no great hope of my further success, for all depended upon the probability of meeting opportunities, although I felt greatly elated at what had been achieved.

Day after day they visited me, to inquire what I proposed to do. My good fortune in my first attempt had inspired their confidence so much that their minds fully believed me invulnerable to failure.

During the week, a masquerade ball was to take place at the residence of Count Hormoso, at which Carlos informed me his father was to be present, and specified the disguise he would appear in, at the same time promising to procure me an invitation. This was a fortunate circumstance to further my scheme, in which I had become earnestly enlisted.

True to his promise, the invitation was received, and I repaired to the assembly in a well-chosen disguise, and soon perceived the old Castilian, the object of my search. Time was valuable, and I immediately commenced operations by using my ventriloquial powers in impressing his feelings with great alarm at the consequences of his refusal to his son's marriage with Inez, the lovely and virtuous daughter of Señor José Garcia.

"Give me your name," he demanded.

"Never!" I returned, in a hollow voice. "I am not of this sphere. Remember the advice you have received."

I then departed, and mingled with the gay and merry crowd. This second attempt was not less a victory over prejudice, for, in a few days following the masquerade, Carlos and Inez came with the glad tidings that Don Luis had complied, though reluctantly, and had removed all impediments to their alliance.

Carlos and Inez literally considered me their good genii, and loaded me with handsome presents, of great value.

In a few months, the nuptials of these lovers were celebrated with much pomp and magnificence, amidst great rejoicing. Long previous to the marriage, I received many pressing invitations to be present, but untoward events prevented the pleasure of my participating in celebrating an event to which I had contributed so successfully; but hundreds, however, did witness the unalloyed exuberance of those whose hearts were full with sweet joy and fond prospects in the union of the houses of Garcia and Luis, whose rivalry, once so implacable, has since mellowed into a bond of affection and interest.

Years have come and gone since this happy event, and many of those prominently associated with the narrative are beyond family feuds or pleasures. Their memory only remains. Carlos and Inez are still living, blessed with lovely children, and other of heaven's choice gifts to an unprecedented extent, much of which is liberally bestowed upon the needy and destitute; in return for which they receive the blessings of the recipients, and the smiles of numberless poor.

THE CAPTAIN-GENERAL OF CUBA.

It is totally out of my power to describe the intense feeling of excitement produced by the exercise of my art, for even the Captain-General was carried away in the vortex. He was a man of stern character, whose rigid system of government occasioned a feeling of much terror to the lawless and wicked, as it was grateful to the peaceful.

Strictly faithful to his duties, his rule recognized no distinction between the rich and poor. His administration demanded respect and obedience from all. Previous to his appointment, crime prevailed constantly; the daring hand of the murderer and robber knew no limit; society and the laws were alike demoralized; there was no protection for either life or property by day or night. Those who administered the government were influenced and silenced by the assassin's and plunderer's gold.

My fame and acts, combining truth and fiction, had been made known to him, for there was nothing unknown to his ear, that occurred in public or private life. His mind could not unravel the strange and exciting stories afloat in all classes of society, and, anxious to see and learn from myself, he despatched one of his attachés to me, with the request that I would visit him.

My interview was an agreeable one. I enjoyed it very much; to his Excellency it was at times merry and serious. He was sharp and cool in his questions, and betrayed much determination of character. His language was forcible and commanding, yet free from that presumption I expected. He seriously inquired if I was in possession of some controlling power over mind and matter; if I could invoke the saints and produce longevity; if I was a Mephistopheles in disguise—one ultimately doomed to the torments of perdition.

"Happily I am quite the contrary to that which your Excellency has expressed."

"I am pleased to hear this, for I had doubts of your claim to a natural life; yet your conception of coming events, and the practical success that attends your professional exercises, are mystical. They impress the thoughts and feelings with distrust."

"With ignorant people only; for I assume no supernatural qualifications. I only follow the strict principles of my profession," I replied.

"But where is the solution to the art of suppressing the organ of sight and other senses?"

"It is a knowledge of man's unguarded habit, his proneness to novelty and excitement, and surrounding circumstances."

"Do you pretend all men are victims to this principle?"

"They are, in a general rule."

"Can you convince me of this?"

"I think it is possible."

HE BECOMES A VICTIM.

This part of our conversation was disturbed by the barking of a dog in one of the ante-rooms, then the mewing of a cat in a closet. The Captain-General seized a stick and ran toward the cur (as he supposed), in a menacing attitude, but no dog was found! the only proof of his former presence was a deep, low growl. He returned, and made a plunge with the stick into the closet, which he had hastily opened, and from whence came the incessant mewing of the cat, whose antagonist belabored resolutely about, but in vain, for puss escaped his vengeance, and was last heard in a distant "mew, mew," down a staircase. The ridiculous scene quite overbalanced my gravity, and I burst into an uncontrollable fit of laughter, saying,—

"This is conviction, I hope. Is your excellency a believer in my power to deceive the faculties of man?"

In the utmost consternation he looked at me, and exclaimed,—

"I am satisfied of the fact that you are a perfect master of your art, and I have been the victim!"—when he, too, laughed immoderately.

Here we separated, much to our mutual satisfaction at the pleasant interview. During my residence in Havana I found him a warm friend and valuable patron. This incident soon circulated, and there was no little mirth produced at the expense of the civil and military governor of the island. It provided food for the gossips and busy tongues of the people. To the sceptics, as well as believers in *diablerie*, it was a source of great mystery.

MATANZAS.

After an unparalleled visit, mingled with good fortune and notoriety, I left for Matanzas, a neat and attractive city.

The people were prepared for my reception, for they had, long in advance, become familiar with my professional career in Havana. The whole community were not only interested, but animated with an inquisitive zeal, beneath which could be detected an unsettled feeling of insecurity. Why they did not openly avow their apprehensions was a question even among themselves. My own convictions were that they entertained doubts as to my origin, and the lawful nature of my pursuits. They importuned me on every point to give them that satisfaction which disordered minds invariably seek. My only response would be the enacting of some feat, or the exercise of my ventriloquial power, which startled them the more, and increased their anxiety; yet, notwithstanding, I was the recipient of their well-known courtesies and hospitalities.

The theatre I occupied was nightly filled to overflowing, and the sensation I produced was emphatically impressed upon all. Some manifested dismay and gloom; others grasped the hands of companions, and there was *no* detraction from the usual inventions in regard to my proceedings, which produced special effect upon the ignorant minded, who fully believed I had given a bond to the father of all sin, to serve his purposes, and enjoy and exercise a power strange and fearful, such as no Christian would undertake or covet. With this possession a terrible doom was supposed to await me, and at an allotted time I was to consign my body to the pains and miseries of purgatory. This idea extended generally, and some few fanatical individuals complained of me to the chief magistrate. They proclaimed me a dangerous person, and that the peace and good of society required I should be examined.

BATTLE WITH THE BEES.

The Alcalde, a vain, conceited man, whose brain comprised but little depth of thought, himself had faith in the rumor that so disturbed the public. This official at once enclosed his card, requesting me to call at my earliest convenience, which I lost no time in complying with.

I found this dignitary an emaciated, shrivelled up, elderly person, with a fierce expression of countenance, indicative of passion and tyranny. His first words were delivered with an assumed softness,—

"Ah! Signor Blitz; much pleasure in meeting you."

I replied, through an interpreter, "Happy to make your acquaintance."

Said the Alcalde, "Signor, you are turning the people's heads with what you term demonology. What master have you studied?"

"The only great and true one—Nature."

This discomposed his honor for a moment.

"But you must," he continued, "follow the rules that governed your predecessors in ancient magic, or how could you obtain such power over the senses? The cabalistic art

17

is, I know, an unearthly science—one that revels in the midnight choruses of the enchanter's councils."

"I never, sir, consulted the living or the dead. My success depends upon my manipulating qualifications and the failure of the observers to direct their reason and sight to circumstances as they transpire, which provides me with advantages so incomprehensible to you and others. All men are absent-minded, and as one faculty will betray the others, it is no wonder we hear and view deficiently of all facts."

"This may be so with those whose vision and hearing are impaired, but not in regard to those whose mental organs are harmonious and centralized."

"But those people are very scarce," I replied.

"I consider myself one of this character," he energetically, and with self-confidence, exclaimed.

"Well, sir, it is flattering to your perception."

"Yes; I am a man you *cannot* impose upon or falsely impress." Now at this precise time he was annoyed by the buzzing of a bee. "I only state," he continued, "my experience in matters that commonly provoke the world." Here the bee buzzed to its utmost capacity, and to the great annoyance of the speaker. "A bee is an insect I detest above all others," he observed, moving his hands with great velocity.

I remarked that they were unwelcome visitors.

Here there was an accumulation of bees, industriously humming and buzzing around his head and shoulders. This increased provocation obliged him to renew the tossing of his hands in every possible direction, with great vexation of manner and theatrical effect.

"You seem to have an invasion of the troublesome insects."

"Yes; some bee-hive has been upset," he angrily mut-

tered; "but I don't like their company,"—his hands being in active motion as he was further provoked by the
"buzz, buzz," when, finding himself overcome, and with
the perspiration on his brow, he attempted a hasty retreat,
when I coolly walked up to him and buzzed in his face, in
this manner announcing myself the king bee.

"Is it possible I have been so deceived?" he murmured,
with amazed looks.

"Yes, sir. You see you are not impervious to the false
conceptions you accuse others of."

"Most true, Signor. It is a moral for the future; I
shall never forget my battle with the bees, and always hold
you in remembrance for your skill and waggery, also your
happy illustration of man's infirmities."

This triumph over the principal administrator of justice
was auspicious and opportune. It gave not only a rebuke to
the parties who advocated my indictment for a wizard and
of being a dangerous person, but likewise silenced those
whose feeble imaginations were restless and discontented, as
they could no longer hope for the intervention of the law
to satisfy their fanatical and malevolent spirits, for I had
conquered the chief power—the only one able to molest or
injure me. The alcalde, when consulted in regard to my
legitimate course, did not hesitate to declare I was in every
way a rational being, without guile, and accomplished my
feats by the extraordinary perfection of my peculiar talents,
and that his own experience had convinced him that the
sinful acts imputed to me were without foundation; that I
was more a benefit than a harm, for I dissipated those theo-
ries that had prevailed, and given importance to the most
simple principles from the dark ages until the present.

All further endeavors to persecute me ceased, but
opinions as to my life continued varied and unabated. In
the meantime, so general was the attention I engrossed,

that numbers followed me continually through the streets, watching every step and pause I made. Numbers would urge me to fill their pockets with gold, and change old and tattered clothing to new, with many more preposterous requests which these poor deluded people honestly believed me capable of performing. Such exhibitions of feeble minds are melancholy illustrations of how deep and serious are the impressions produced by superstition. Is it not a deplorable dereliction from duty on the part of any government to wilfully neglect the education of the mind, and thus keep the unfortunate masses in the fetters of ignorance and degradation?

Every device was invented for the purpose of discovering the philosopher's stone, or the talisman which report gave me credit for possessing. There was no end to these speculations, but they were so conflicting that it was amusing to listen to them, while my success continued unabated, especially as I constantly introduced new attractions.

One morning I was waited upon by an elegantly-dressed lady, of middle age, who, in presenting herself, said that the object of her visit was to ascertain if I could give her information in regard to a property litigation in which she was interested, and whether she would gain her suit. It was impossible for me to satisfy her mind, as I was unacquainted with the circumstances; and even with the most favorable knowledge it was not in my power to anticipate events, as I was not gifted with the art of divination. She was evidently prepared for this reply, as she continued,—

"Have you not made a doubtful confession, Signor, for one whose touch is like Prospero's wand?"

"You are extravagant, Signora, in your appreciation of my genius."

"No, no; you are the king of miracles."

"I make no presumption to that title, Signora."

"Why," she continued, with a declamatory earnestness, "you give strength to the sick, provide happiness for the miserable, and wealth for the poor. What is there you are unable to accomplish? Surely you know my future, especially if you allow me to relate my history."

To this I consented, which I will give, as narrated by her, in the next chapter.

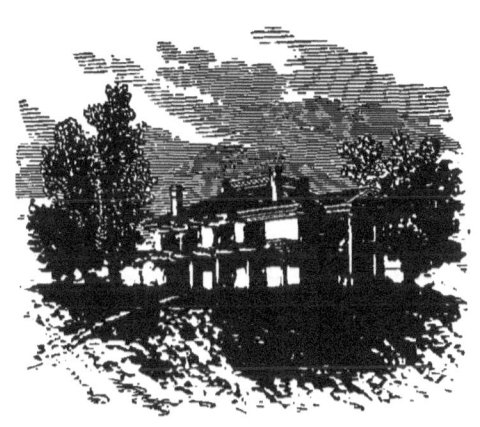

CHAPTER XXXIII.

"WHERE shall I commence," said she, "to tell my sad story, and the great injustice that I have experienced? My parents were natives of Cuba, dearly devoted to the interest and prosperity of the island, neither were their feelings and attachments less ardent toward the Spanish crown, for they fully believed and maintained that the rights and prerogatives of kings were necessary and absolute. My father, through, the influence of his family connections, obtained a commission in the army, a position he greatly desired. His strict and unwearied attention to his official duties, and the pride and interest which he manifested for its great improvement and tone of character, attracted the attention of his superiors, who advanced his promotion rapidly. Perhaps the service had no better disciplinarian, or one so admirably calculated to perfect its status among the grand armies.

"For a long period he was employed on the island, but when war was proclaimed between the adherents of Don Carlos, the usurper, and the rightful heir to the throne of Spain, he became a faithful partizan of the latter, defending his rights with not only distinguished valor, but with the contribution of his fortune, which was princely. Previous to embarking for the field of glory, he disposed of his property, all of which he patriotically presented to the government, reserving fifty thousand dollars as a contingency for my mother in case of his death. This sum he entrusted to the care of his most intimate friend, Don Felix, between whom and my father there existed an affection and confidence so pure and unsullied that they were called Damon and Pythias. Born and educated in the same locality, participants in all youthful enjoyments and pleasures, they advanced in life inseparable in feeling and action, with the one exception that Don Felix was engaged in commercial pursuits, while my father was devoted to a military life. They held each other's honor as sacred; therefore no receipts or papers were given or required.

" As the time approached for my father to leave his native island, Don Felix became moved with grief and melancholy. He could not meet what appeared to him to be the terrible dispensation of parting with the companion of his earlier and later years. It provoked a dark and gloomy aspect, an apprehension that they would never meet again. The effect upon my father was quite the opposite; his warm devotion to his friend, and the noble traits he was endowed with, had no parallel, and although the separation deeply agitated his mind, yet those emotions yielded to a higher sense of duty and consideration—a love of country, an abiding interest in defending the national will. These obligations imposed themselves so emphatically as to the line of action he should pursue, that he did not hesitate to sacrifice his social and private endearments for the public good. This was not, however, accomplished without his experiencing the most touching pangs. It was impossible to erase from memory the scenes of his boyish days, how he had wandered with Don Felix in the groves, and sheltered themselves from the burning sun beneath the luxuriant foliage of the palm and orange trees. He looked upon the past as the panorama of a pleasant life, for memory, ever active, would bring before him fresh and vivid recollections of bright and joyous days and happy hours he had spent beneath skies bright and cloudless.

"As time advanced, my father and Don Felix, ever inseparable, passed their leisure hours in solacing each other; it was mournful to hear and witness their conversation, how joy and sorrow mingled as they pictured the changes which destiny had decreed.

"When the morning arrived for the final separation, the whole city was alive with excitement. The bells of churches and convents tolled a farewell in language of their own metallic ring; the private dwellings and public offices were decorated with flags and other complimentary emblems.

"At noon, my father, at the head of his regiment, marched from the garrison, escorted by various troops and their bands. The streets and housetops were filled with masses of human beings, whose cheers and good words echoed on the air. The blessings that escaped the lips, and tears that moistened the eyes of the multitude, affected the sympathy of the most stern and resolute.

"The wild hurrahs, the waving of hats and handkerchiefs, mingled with the sweet strains of music, were unmistakable evidences that the hearts of the people were with the gallant men about to leave their homes and country. It was an ovation honorable and remarkable in the annals of the island. The farewell scene between my father and mother cannot be depicted. The embracing and tears would have moved the coldest observer, for past joys, future fears and hopes, were mingled in their minds and feelings. It was a struggle between love and honor. To the last moment they were insensible to surrounding objects and the passing observations of strangers. They knew of nothing worldly beyond the fond love for each other, which, however seemingly selfish, was natural to the occasion.

"My fond father devoured me with kisses, and bade my mother to live for my sake, that in due time I would become her companion and confidante,—a comfort and blessing, as he fondly trusted.

"The bugle sounded for all to be on board, yet my father made no movement to obey until the last signal was given to weigh anchor, when, with lightning velocity and considerable physical strength, he withdrew himself from my mother's arms, and, with unusual agility, succeeded in reaching the boat as it was making its final return, plying its course midst the thundering echoes of the guns of the forts, and acclamations of thousands of people.

"When my father reached the ship he was greeted by his friend, who was present, by mutual arrangement, to take a last adieu. Their manly characters yielded to the sorrows of the moment. It was a conflict of no ordinary power: not a fictitious sensibility, but a sterling appreciation of each other's virtues. With clasped hands and saddened features, they talked of the days when freedom to them had no boundary, or life a seeming mystery.

"Thus time was consumed until the ship and her consorts had long passed the Moro Castle. This fact was communicated to them by the captain, who also intimated the approach of a storm, and as my father's friend had but a small boat, he would suggest, as a matter of prudence, that he should return to the city without a moment's delay, for by so doing he might escape serious consequences. This information, so unexpected and alarming, effectually terminated the parting scene. Don Felix's head fell upon the neck of my father, whose hands were bound around his friend with an iron grasp. After this manifestation of feeling they went to the vessel's side, when Don Felix descended the ladder into the boat, which was speedily loosened, and directed toward the city, already many miles dis-

17*

tant.· The winds and waves were fast becoming angry, as the motion of the ship gave evidence. My father stood, watched, and turned a hundred times toward the boat, which was only occasionally visible, riding on the surging sea, and when last seen, was rolling and ploughing with desperate efforts, the raging deep.

" As night advanced, the clouds darkened and the storm increased terrifically ; for it seemed as if all the boisterous elements of heaven and sea had combined their forces to devastate and destroy. No one—not even the oldest seaman—remembered its equal. The position of the ship was critical and dangerous in the extreme ; yet nobly she battled with the tempest, trembling from bow to stern. Her sails were torn and spars broken, while amid all the wild tempest, crash after crash was heard. My father, unconscious, as well as indifferent, to all personal danger, turned his thoughts to his wife, child, and dear friend, respecting whose safety he was exceedingly anxious. He pictured the little boat, her frail structure struggling amidst the foaming surf. The more he reflected, the more his thoughts were troubled.

" Morning at length dawned, and the mighty winds and raging billows had quelled their strife, and, gradually, a gorgeous sun unveiled his grandeur. The sky betrayed a smiling softness—an omen that peace and harmony prevailed ; and now the ship was repaired as she pursued her course, arriving in Spain after an unusually rapid passage.

" Not so fortunate was Don Felix. His tender craft for a time, like the stormy petrel, pierced the maddened waters, and bounded over their white-peaked caps with a fairy grace, as if she held the enchanted wand. For miles she rode thus at the mercy of the gale, and was tossed by the angry waves, yet the occupants were inspired with hope. It was a miracle—how she maintained herself : it was not by skill or human wisdom, but by a perfect submission to the violence of the hurricane. The endurance of the sufferers was not less marvellous. They sustained themselves with a pertinacious fortitude, suitable for the occasion. But God did not intend their escape : a few hours brought them near the shore, when the boat was dashed to pieces by the treacherous sea. The skipper, who alone was saved by clinging to a rock, heard the piteous cries for help, but darkness and the necessity of saving his own life made it impossible to render the least assistance.

" This misfortune produced the greatest sorrow and mourning, for Don Felix was much beloved for his philanthropy and nobleness of character. It was a sad event—an irreparable loss to the community, and pecuniarily disastrous to my mother.

" When the death of Don Felix was communicated to my father, his grief and pain was great. His manly mien was depressed and dejected, operating on his sensitive mind so seriously as to affect its usual firmness of purpose ; but this feeling, though it never ceased to exist, soon became absorbed in his daily military duties. The sick and wounded were the constant recipients of his attention, and while the principles and associations of life, with all their endearments, were nevertheless sacred to his heart, they did not impair the interest in the conflict; for, day and night, his active spirit animated the indolent and inspired the brave, the necessity of which was indispensable.

" Man is an excitable being when interested, and ofttimes, blood alone will assuage or satisfy his passions. It is mournful for the mind to reflect on this failing. To account for this imperfection in nature has ever been a theme for the philosopher.

" War, unfortunately, continued, as usual, with all the horrors imaginable. The sight of the dying, the cries of the wounded, the suffering from hunger and thirst, can be but feebly portrayed.

"My father was not a sentimentalist. His conduct was ruled by an action of principle. He fought, as he conceived, for his lawful sovereign. The fatigue he endured gradually undermined his constitution, but he remained devoted to his post. The engagements were active and resolute, with an unrelenting determination. Though frequently defeated, they rallied and obtained reinforcements, in defiance of every obstacle. Their course was not popular with the inhabitants of the mountain and rural districts, for they loved the usurper Don Carlos, for his Jesuitical character interested their hearts. It was a civil war, with the most frightful results.

"My father's health, in defiance of every precaution, failed daily. His wounds, severe marches, and the fatigue of the camp, completely incapacitated him for exertion or duty. It was a misfortune to the army and the cause to which he was devoted. His medical advisers urged for him an immediate leave of absence, with the earnest hope that rest and change of scene might not fail to recuperate his strength.

"The announcement, though not unexpected, was received with universal regret and an unanimous prayer for his speedy restoration. My father at first peremptorily declined to separate himself from his comrades; he knew the important necessity of every officer's presence, and its moral effect upon the ardor of the troops. This resolution he was unable to sustain : his feebleness increased until utter prostration compelled submission.

"Accompanied by a faithful servant, he proceeded to the south of France to seek health, that golden treasure without which man is indeed poor. He wrote my mother constantly, with all the warmth of a lover. Every letter was a chronicle of events. Instantly upon his arrival in France, he informed my mother of the perilous state of his health, and that, if in a brief time he realized no advantage, it would be prudent and advisable for her to join him in Europe.

"My mother's fears increased hourly, which, together with an excitable brain, brought on a fever, and for many days she lingered unconscious of anything that took place, her friends and attendants despairing of her life. Favorable symptoms, however, appeared, and she rallied.

"My father, with every benefit that skill and a balmy atmosphere combined could give, and with the best possible attention, obtained no relief, but gradually his shattered life calmly declined as the setting sun. His heart, bright with expectation, wandered over the broad waters to my mother and myself, with an affection inseparable and undivided. Nobly he fought the battle of life, and now his gentle nature, content and grateful for the past, brightly visioned the future. The only affliction he felt was the absence of those he loved; but their presence was denied him. The destroying angel, true to his Master's law, was imperative; he came to obtain his own, not with vengeance, but a slow and patient forbearance. As night put on her sable mantle, and the busy scenes of life were at rest, his mortal spirit happily and serenely passed away into the kingdom of righteousness. His last words were for his wife and child.

"When my mother was notified of the event, she became delirious, and ultimately a confirmed maniac. The community of Havana were overwhelmed with gloom. No efforts were unheeded to console her broken heart, or alleviate her mental suffering; but reason had fled, and in a short time her spirit joined that of my father, in the realms of heaven. Her burial was one of mourning; not of pomp or affectation, but of sincerity and affection.

"Time, while it softens our trials, does not eradicate their reality. The loss of both of my parents was a distressing affliction. A friend of my mother's kindly—not from impulse, but feeling—received me as a member of his family for a long period ; but a true sensibility of what was just to him, and honorable to my own independence, dictated my removal.

"After the settlement of my father's estate, but little remained, with the exception of the fifty thousand dollars he gave in trust to Don Felix, in behalf of my mother and myself. His ample means, with this exception, had, as I before stated, been devoted to the war. My only reliance was, therefore, upon the payment to me of this sum. This was refused by the brother of Don Felix, Raymond Felix, and who was heir to his estate. His refusal was based upon the want of proof, on my part, that the money was ever intrusted by my father to the care of Don Ferdinand Felix. The result of this misfortune arose from the great confidence existing between the latter and my father being so abiding and mutual that they had no reference to death, or the necessity of an obligation in case of an emergency.

"The refusal to refund the sum to me has occasioned an appeal to the courts of law, where I had hoped to recover my legal rights, but the wealth and position of my opponent has enabled him to postpone the trial from term to term, till I am discouraged, and I now beseech you to employ your profession in my cause, and impress, either by art or reasoning, the justice of my suit. I know you can bring influences to bear upon the minds of others, that are irresistible."

"I have listened to your history with much interest," I replied ; "and nothing would add so much satisfaction to myself as to be instrumental in your obtaining the restitution of your rights ; but I fear I cannot."

"Oh! sir, do not express yourself so emphatically, for you have only to consult the oracles of *diablerie* to insure success."

"It is out of the question to presume for a moment that I can exercise any potent will upon a man whose principles are deficient of those attributes which contribute nobleness to character. A thought has, however, impressed me, which, if it is possible to execute, I may afford you important assistance. I will endeavor to obtain an interview with Señor Raymond Felix, and if I find my endeavors to induce him to acknowledge your rights a failure, I will apply a course which I think will be successful."

This announcement greatly animated my visitor's countenance, and excited her ardent hopes, so that she left me satisfied in the belief of the fulfilment of her ardent wish.

It was a serious and responsible undertaking on my part, for the person I had to encounter was a man of strong nerve and mind, abounding in strong prejudices; consequently it became the more requisite to be prepared for any opposition that might arise. I therefore made it a point to obtain an interview with him in the evening, concluding it to be more advantageous to discuss important matters at a time when the mind was released from business cares and responsibilities.

My introduction was of a character fraught with apprehension and difficulty; for in relating my mission and its object, he appeared cool and collected, questioned me as to my motive and interest in the affair. "It is," he said, "a delicate interposition on your part, an entire stranger to all parties concerned, and unless you came possessed of the most incontrovertible proof of the indebtedness of my brother's estate to the daughter of his friend, I must decline discussing the subject."

I remarked that I came as a friend, provided with the

most undoubted and unanswerable facts, so positive that
they left not a doubt of their correctness, and they explained themselves in connection with the intimacy, affection, and confidence which commenced in youth, and
continued through manhood.   It was almost conclusive testimony in respect to Don Felix being the repository of the
amount claimed.

He combated my argument, and finally closed by declaring the improbability of the money ever being received
without a written acknowledgment, or, at least, a memorandum of the transaction.

"That such a matter could have taken place, I am positive," he spoke with much spirit and assurance, "was
utterly impossible; and if that picture of my brother"—
pointing to a portrait suspended on the wall—"could speak,
it would declare the falsity of the claim."

"No, no," said a voice, coming from the likeness, "not
so.   I received the money, and desire its prompt payment,
for the sake of justice to, and happiness of, the child of my
friend, who is now in heaven with me."

These words produced the most thrilling effect upon
Señor Raymond Felix, who withdrew his chair from the
table, under great excitement, and, for full two minutes,
gazed wildly at the painting.   Recovering himself, he expressed his conviction of the marvellous intervention of
Providence, and the undeniable justice of Colonel Alonzo's
daughter's claim to the inheritance, of which, he assured
me, he should make immediate restitution.

"Will you accompany me to her residence, that in your
presence I may give a check for the full sum?"

"Honorable brother!   Justice at last!" exclaimed the
portrait.

Tears flowed copiously from the eyes of Señor Raymond, as he turned them toward the magic tone of his

brother's voice. Excusing his absence, he retired to an adjoining apartment much agitated, and overcome with mental agony. In a reasonable time he returned with a check for the principal sum and interest. We proceeded, without delay, to the residence of Señorita Alonzo, whom we fortunately found at home. Our appearance was unexpected, and our object even more so. She manifested great delight, and upon receiving the check, her feelings nearly overpowered her. She wept and smiled alternately: it was a struggle between doubt and certainty,—a romance in real life, and, withal, a triumph of her father's honor, and justification of her own rightful claim and course taken to obtain it.

The conclusion is not void of a moral that truth is greater than fiction, or that the most difficult point may be gained by the ingenious skill of a ventriloquist, whose special object in life has been both to amuse and do good, by rendering the service of his art to the sick, poor, needy, and oppressed.

From Señorita Alonzo I received every demonstration that could emanate from a grateful heart. Her thanks knew no limit, and she offered to place at my disposal any portion of the money I had been instrumental in securing for her. This, of course, I absolutely refused, satisfied with the reward of being the oracle that obtained for her the fortune. It may be gratifying to my readers to be informed that she was finally married to a wealthy planter, who appreciated her worth, and honored her love in the circle of a family of children. She was not less inspired with the graces of a sweet nature, than she was courted and admired by society at large, for her virtue, liberality, and great kindness to the poor and needy.

CHAPTER XXXIV.

INCIDENTS AND ADVENTURES ELSEWHERE.

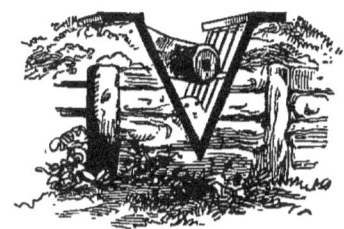 ERY soon after my return from my West India tour, I had occasion to travel in many States, and as a natural consequence, met with many comical events and droll adventures, some few of which I will here relate.

THE LANDLORD AND HIS GUEST.

A few years since, in the dusk of evening, while travelling through Virginia, in a sulky, leisurely pursuing my way, I overtook a negro going home from ploughing, who was singing the favorite Ethiopian melody—

> "Gwine down to Shin-bone Alley,
> Long time ago."

I hailed him: "Halloo, uncle!"

"Sah?" said Blackey, holding in his horses.

"Is that the Half-way House a-head yonder?"

"No, sah, dat Massa Billy Lemon's 'Otel."

"Hotel, eh? Billy Lemon?"

"Yes, sah. You know Massa Billy—he used to lib at de mouf o' Cedar Crick. He done move now—keeps mons'ous nice tavern now, I tell you!"

"Indeed!"

"Yes, sah. You stop dah dis ebenin', I suppose ? all 'spectable gentlemen put up dah. You chaw 'bacca, Massa ?"

"Yes, Sambo, here's real Cavendish for you."

"Tankee, Massa, tankee, sah ; Quash my name."

"Quash, eh ?"

"Yes, sah, at your service. O-oh !" grunted the delighted African, "dis is nice; he better 'an Green Riber; tankee, sah, tankee."

"Well, Quash, what kind of a gentleman is Mr. Lemon?"

"Oh! he nice man, sah, mons'ous nice man, sah—mons'ous nice man ; empetain genplemen in the fuss style, and he take care ob de horses. I 'longs to him, and do I say it, Massa Bill mighty clebby man; he funny, too,—tell heap o' stories about ghosses and spirits, notwithstandin' he 'fraid on 'em heself, my 'pinion."

"Afraid of ghosts, eh ?" said I, musing. "Well, go ahead, Mr. Quash; as it's getting late, I'll tarry with this Mr. Lemon to-night."

"Yes, sah. Gee up, hoa! go 'long, lively !" and setting off at a brisk trot, followed by myself, the musical Quash again broke out with,—

"Gwine down to Shin-bone Alley."

The burthen, "Long time ago," was taken up by some one apparently in an adjacent cornfield, which occasioned Quash again to prick up his ears with some surprise. He continued, however, with—

"Dah I meet ole Johnny Gladdin,"

and the same voice responded from the cornfield,—

"Long time ago."

"Who dat?" said the astonished negro, checking suddenly his horses, and looking around on every side for the cause of his surprise.

"Oh! never mind; drive a-head, Snowball. It's some of your master's spirits, I suppose."

Quash, in a very thoughtful mood, led the way to the tavern, without uttering another word. Halting before the door, I was very soon waited upon by the obliging Mr. Lemon, a bustling, talkative gentleman, who greeted me with,—

"'Light, sir, 'light—here, John! Quash!—never mind your umbrella, sir—here, Quash! take off that rug—give me your whip, sir—take off that trunk—walk in, sir—John, take out the chair-box—come, sir—and carry this horse to the stable—do you prefer him to stand on a chip-floor, sir?"

"If you please, sir; he's rather particular about his lodgings."

"Carry him to the lower stable, Quash, and tend to him well. I always like to see horses well tended, and this is a noble critter, too," continued the landlord, slapping him on the back.

"Take care, will you!" said the horse.

"What the d—l!" exclaimed the landlord, starting back.

"None of your familiarity!" said the horse, looking round at the astonished tavern-keeper.

"Silence, Beelzebub!" said I, caressing the animal; and, turning to the landlord, observed, "You must excuse him, sir. He's rather an aristocratic horse—the effect of education, sir."

"Woa, hoa, Beelzebub! Loose the traces, Quash. What are you staring at? He won't eat you."

"Come, landlord," said Beelzebub, "I want my oats."

Quash scattered; the landlord backed up into the porch,

and I was feign to jump into my vehicle and drive round in search of the stables myself. Succeeding to my satisfaction in disposing of the horse, with some assistance from Quash, who was careful to keep his distance, I returned to the tavern.

Anon supper came on. The eggs all had chickens in them. The landlord was in confusion at such a mortifying circumstance, and he promised me amends from a cold pig, which, as he inserted the carving-fork, uttered a most piercing squeal, which was responded to by a louder one from the landlady. Down went the knife and fork, and the cold perspiration began to grow in large beads upon the forehead of the poor landlord, as he stood looking fearfully at the grunter. His attention was soon taken, however, by voices from without, calling,—

"Halloa, landlord!"

"Aye, coming, gentlemen. More travellers. Do help yourself, sir."

"Landlord!"

"Coming, gentlemen. Here, John, a light—bring a light to the door. Sally, wait on the gentleman!" and out the landlord bounced, followed by John, with lights, but soon returned, with a look of disappointment. He declared that there was no living being without.

The voices called again; and the landlord, going out, returned a second time, declaring his belief that the whole plantation was haunted that night by evil spirits.

I presently arose from the table and drew my chair toward the fire, having made a pretty hearty supper from the eggs and young porker, their cries to the contrary notwithstanding.

That night, rumor saith, Mr. Billy Lemon slept with the Bible under his head, and kept a candle burning; and those who pass there to this day, may, upon close examination, discover the heels of old horseshoes peering above the door casement, as a bulwark against the witches, hobgoblins, and all other evil spirits.

In the morning I gave my name to mine host, who shortly afterward made out the following bill:

Signor Blitz and his Educated Horse,
　　　　　　　　　　To *William Lemon*,　　　　Dr.
　To Board for self and horse, -　　　　　　　　$5.00
　　　　　　　　　　　Wᴵᴸᴸᴵᴬᴹ Lᴇᴹᴼᴺ.

I paid the amount, and left with the good wishes of the landlord and his wife.

A Sᴜʀᴘʀɪꜱᴇ-Pᴀʀᴛʏ Sᴜʀᴘʀɪꜱᴇᴅ.

One pleasant evening, between eleven and twelve o'clock, a surprise-party from the southern section of the city of Philadelphia, entered a car at Fairmount, for the purpose of returning home. The party consisted of fourteen females and as many males. Of course, the car was crowded, and a more joyful number of friends never got together. I was seated in a corner, wearing a slouched felt hat, drawn partly over my face, and appeared as though asleep. Various pleasantries were indulged in between the happy ones, as the car moved homeward.

Presently the horses stumbled, and the wheels bounded over a turnout, when "O my! I'm killed!" came as a voice from beneath the car.

"There is somebody run over!" exclaimed several of the young ladies.

"It's Charlie," said another; "I know his voice."

"Oh! my legs! How can I walk?" was next heard.

The car was speedily partly emptied, and a search was made under and around the wheels and rear platform, but no crushed individual could be found, and no one could divine the reason of the outcry. All felt sure that somebody was injured; but on assuring themselves that nothing of the kind had occurred, returned, and the car passed on its way.

Among the party was a very pretty young lady, who seemed to be lost in thought. Presently she gave a loud snore.

"Wake up, Maggie, wake up!" said the one sitting next to her, as she gave her a nudge.

"I'm not asleep; I'm only tired," she replied.

Then came another snore; again another nudge. The subject was the cause of much merriment, at the expense of Maggie, who declared she was never more wide awake in her life.

A canary bird now chirped in different parts of the car, and the railroad time-keeper ticked much louder than usual. A sort of an awful pause came over the whole party, as though by enchantment. Everybody thought there was something queer in these strange noises, but nobody could tell the reason.

One young lady said, "Oh! quit that! Why don't you behave yourself?"

Another said, "Well, I didn't enjoy myself at all."

"O Jennie! how could you say so?" remarked a gentleman.

Thus the time passed away, until at last I attempted to leave the car; but as I was elbowing my way out, the light shone full in my face and revealed my features, when I soon found myself in a tight place, for the young ladies would not let me out before they reached the southern terminus of the route; but I experienced a delightful time, and was so well pleased that I invited the whole party to attend my entertainment in the Assembly Building.

OLD SCRATCH.

Contrary to my usual custom, I consented to stop at a small town on my route through the British Provinces, by the assurance of certain persons that it would pay me well, for the amusements were scarce and the "free list" small. I accordingly gave a short series of performances in a hall at the principal hotel in the place, which was a large, old-fashioned structure.

The hall was crowded to its fullest capacity on each of the three evenings, and everything worked to a charm until the last night, when a mischievous boarder conceived the idea of varying the programme slightly.

One of the most popular parts in my exhibition was the ventriloquism. I had an animated conversation with "Peter," in the chimney, which was situated on one side of the hall, near the middle. The aforesaid boarder was aware that the smoke-house, in which his daily slice of bacon was cured, was situated over the hall, and an aperture in the main chimney at that spot gave access to the place, which led from the fireplace of the ball-room. He captured a large cat, a few minutes before the ventriloquism commenced, and ensconced himself in the smoke-house just before I was to begin. When I called "Peter," he allowed me to converse with the imaginary interlocutor for a short time, without interruption; but when I requested "Peter" to come down near the fireplace for a little familiar chat, the boarder's voice replied that he would see me in a certain place of punishment first, and even then he wouldn't!

I was scarcely able to conceal my astonishment at this reply, but the audience thought I was outdoing myself, and cheered me tremendously.

"Peter, come down, will you?"

"See ye in my home first; but my name ain't Peter; he keeps the keys of t'other place."

"What is your name?"

"I am Old Scratch."

The audience thought I was getting rather profane. I knew I was a victim, but could think of nothing better than to continue the talk.

"Are you Old Scratch, the fire king?"

"Yes."

"I would be happy to see Old Scratch here."

"Well, are you ready!"

"Yes, all ready."

The words had scarcely entered the chimney, when the big tom-cat came tumbling and scratching down, filling my eyes with soot, and the audience with uncontrollable laughter.

The cat's eyes glared like a flash of two lucifer matches, and he disappeared with a bound. I was utterly discomfited, and compelled to close the performance without finishing the last scene.

A Prison Scene.

During one of my visits to Pittsburgh, Pennsylvania, I was induced very reluctantly to accompany some friends to the prison, and see Hugh Carrigan, then under sentence of death for murdering his wife. On arriving at the condemned man's cell, he was introduced, and expressed great pleasure at seeing me, as he said he had heard a great deal of my performances, but as he could not attend my place of entertainment at this time, owing to events beyond his control, he should be obliged if I would show him a trick or two to gratify his curiosity. To this I objected, and reminded him of his fearful position; that it would be improper for me to abstract his thoughts from more serious

18

reflections, consequently he must excuse my declining. He, however, importuned me so earnestly, that my companions entreated me to comply. I consented, although quite repugnant to my own feelings. I borrowed a twenty-five cent piece, which I gave him to mark, so that he could recognize it again. He procured a knife from one of the gentlemen, and retired to one corner of the cell, where he carefully made an incision on the piece of money. I then, after some time, wished him to return me the quarter. He replied he had not the money. I insisted he had. He searched his pockets, and found it, greatly to his surprise and amazement. Eyeing me very closely for a few moments, he requested me to repeat the feat, which I did, and again desired him to hand back the piece of silver. This time he protested quite violently, saying that I was mistaken, for he had watched me very closely, and he was positive I had the money myself. I finally prevailed upon him to feel in his pockets once more, which he did, and again found the quarter. He then scanned me more suspiciously than before, and moved away, remarking he would *" hate very much to meet me in the dark ! "*

I replied, *" That* was the place in which I should object to encounter him ! "

The wretched man murdered his wife on a Friday, burnt her remains in the vicinity of his house on Saturday, went to Pittsburg on Sunday, and Monday gave evidence before the District Court; returned home, and was arrested on Tuesday, tried and convicted Wednesday, and Thursday sentenced to be hung; but a few days before the time appointed for his execution, he took poison, and thus ended his career.

Carrigan was wealthy, and about sixty years of age. He resided on a farm in Westmoreland County, where he committed the dreadful deed. He had a respectable appearance, and from the little conversation I had with him, I should judge him to be well informed; but his habits of intemperance were of the most degraded and vicious character, and while in this state he perpetrated the crime for which he forfeited his life.

It is almost beyond belief that a being could be found so totally depraved and indifferent to his own wickedness and the punishment that awaited him by betraying so great an interest in the frivolities of the world. What I exhibited to him interested his mind far more earnestly than the great tribunal beyond, before whom he had so shortly to appear. The evil effects of drinking were probably never more sadly illustrated. Here was a person well off in pecuniary matters, and when not excited by the demon liquor, his deportment, I was informed, was such as entitled him to the respect of his fellow-men; but he could not withstand the temptation—thus his dreadful end.

A Merry Sleighing-Party.

Some years since, when the city and country were covered with snow, and our streets literally thronged with sleighs, those of our ladies whose better-halves could not afford to keep one of those convenient articles, usually availed themselves of a merry and cheap sleigh-ride in a public conveyance. On one of those days one of our public sleighs was proceeding up Chestnut street in fine style, crowded with men, women, and children, highly enjoying the ride, although their noses exhibited a little touch of Jack Frost. The horses were jogging along at a slow pace, when, coming to one of those spots in the street where it was very thickly thronged, the voice of a female cried out,—

"Driver, stop, I want to get out!"

The driver pulled up and turned around, but no person seemed ready to make their exit. The driver asked who told him to stop, but no one knew. He, however, came to the conclusion he was mistaken; so whack went the whip, and jingle went the sleigh-bells, and the horses into a slow trot. They had not gone more than a square, when the gruff voice of a man spoke,—

"Hold up, driver."

Accordingly, the driver stopped, and turning to receive his fare, the passengers looked at each other, but none of them seemed to know who it was that spoke.

"Who told me to hold up?" said the driver.

But no answer was made to his inquiry. The driver was evidently inclined to get angry. After receiving no answer, he turned and started his horses, but when about to turn into one of those streets through which the line passes, the voice of a child was heard,—

"Stop! stop! stop! I want to get out!"

The driver stopped his horses, but no one moved.

"Now, looker here, what do you folks mean? Why, if you keep me stopping all day this way, I will never be able to get to the end of my route," said the driver.

"Oh, drive on, do; I am cold and in a hurry to get home," said the husky voice of a man.

On went the sleigh again. When he had gone about a block, all of a sudden the voice of a woman screamed out,—

"Driver! driver! somebody is trying to pick my pocket!"

The driver turned quickly, and exclaimed,—

"Which one, madam, is it?"

No one answered.

"Who was the lady that said somebody was trying to pick her pocket?"

"That's the lady, dressed in black," said a man's voice.

"Oh! what a whopper! I said nothing of the kind," exclaimed the lady in black, to the man opposite her.

"My dear madam, I said no such thing," answered the man, endeavoring to exonerate himself.

"Well, did you ever!" exclaimed the lady, in surprise.

At this state of affairs, a gent in the sleigh, being in somewhat of a hurry to get home, and seeing that a quarrel was likely to ensue, said:

"Come, this is carrying the joke too far. Ladies and gentlemen, Signor Blitz, the ventriloquist, is sitting here in the corner."

This was enough; the driver was about to storm out, but it was of no use—a hearty laugh broke from all in the sleigh. The driver seized his reins, and off went the horses at a lively gait, and all hands seemed to enjoy the joke. All was soon forgotten in the joyful sound of the sleigh-bells, and the merry laughter of those flying over the crusty ice.

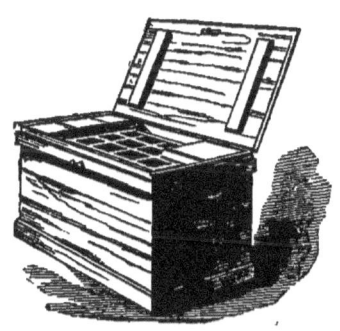

CHAPTER XXXV.

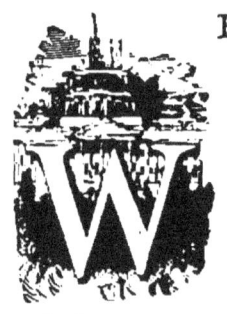HEN I had returned from Havana, I located myself permanently in Philadelphia, where I am now residing with my family, very comfortably situated in my own house, and with ample means for all the necessaries and comforts of life, surrounded also by a host of very near and dear friends, whose warm hearts and smiling faces always greet and cheer me.

The gigantic civil war of 1861–5, called into existence all the combined resources of the nation. Most liberal were the contributions; and the amount of good that was accomplished thereby, history has yet to record—previous to which party spirit and all the bitter sensitiveness of the present generation must pass away and be forgotten. How patiently a patriotic, charitable and feeling people can afford to submit to the necessity of time, to signalize their magnanimity and greatness of heart, must rest upon the conviction of having fulfilled the duties and obligations during a period of the most momentous trials and afflictions. When loss of life and destruction of property, accompanied by all the horrors of war, were hourly exciting the fears and sorrows of every age and class, how nobly were the people developing all the best qualities of their nature, without regard to pecuniary cost or labor! Surely, the like demonstration of pure generosity and touching evidences of millions of people united in Christian sympathy has no parallel in ancient or modern annals. Neither can we find any similar amount of devotion and loyalty—where the youth of every grade in society, separating themselves from their families and homes, by *voluntarily* enlisting in the ranks, shirking no responsibility or duty, however dangerous or fearful, and being animated by a love of country and its principles, immolated their lives with a heroism sacred to memory and virtue.

With what grace and humane tenderness did the masses return their gratitude How, in conjunction with the Sanitary and Christian Commissions, did every community and local district form Aid Societies, under the direction and influence of the ladies, and what wonderful results from their labor and coöperation! With what tenacity of purpose they toiled, night and day, in the making of garments to clothe and comfort the soldier in the perils of campaign—to soothe his wounds and relieve his sufferings! How like guardian angels they visited the battle-fields and hospitals, administering hope, consolation and religion, with every possible attention, to the living and dying sufferers! Great self-denial and patriotic efforts were exhibited, no class withholding their services, but cheerfully nursing the sick, and dispensing those delicacies that were soothing and welcome to the patient. In these duties were found the most refined minds, and those of great wealth; and equally zealous as Samaritans were their poorer sisters. There was no distinction or jealousy in regard to station or circumstances; a perfect concord prevailed, and all remembered the soldier in his perilous absence; even little children were animated by the warmest motives of love for "the army," united with a simplicity of affection. The schools and churches were constantly occupied in promoting the benefit of the invalid soldier. The fairs and subscriptions heavily taxed the people, but they gave, and that freely. If only a faithful exhibit could be made of the amount of money collected, and the noble labors and sacrifices of the American ladies during this period, the world would be amazed; and the period must necessarily arrive when full justice to the efforts and liberality of all will be better known and appreciated, and patriotism and virtue will shine bright as the evening star.

Philadelphia enjoyed the privilege and great honor of being the principal depot for the sick and wounded. It was literally a city of hospitals, for in almost every district, convenient and commodious establishments were provided. Those erected especially for this purpose were of a marvellous magnitude; the wards alone of the West Philadelphia and Chestnut Hill hospitals were each several miles in extent, and occupied a full morning to inspect medically. Frequently there were three thousand patients at one time in each of them. All, without distinction, were the recipients of the kindest treatment and most distinguished skill. The sanitary appliances were conducted in an admirable manner and with great care, and the amount of deaths averaged a far less percentage than in similar institutions of smaller capacities. The system and excellence of management greatly encouraged all interested. Everything that ingenuity of the mind could devise was provided for comfort and amusement. Committees of ladies were detailed daily at every hospital, to assist and protect the inmates from any neglect, whose smiles and feelings of sympathy gave hope and promise to many a weary heart. Nothing escaped their observation. They administered constantly, and, to cheer the desponding, amusements of every character were provided, and the most prominent singers, lecturers, and artists were invited. The vocal and instrumental concerts frequently combined the highest order of talent. Accomplished amateurs found delight in warbling their sweet notes to the unfortunates, and some gentleman or lady would preside the whole day at the piano, charming the invalid hearers. How much these entertainments were enjoyed, no one can better testify than myself.

My own exhibitions were remarkably popular with the soldiers. Constantly I was written to, and personally solicited by the surgeon and his assistants, or the ladies of the committees, for my services. Occasionally some convalescent patient would procure permission to call, and entreat me personally, in behalf of his comrades, to come and amuse them; a request I am thankful I never refused.

How the poor fellows loved to laugh, and drive away their pains and cares! It certainly appeared of more advantage to them than medical attendance. Whenever it was known that I was to appear, unusual excitement prevailed. Men whose limbs had been amputated but a few days, although forbidden by the physician, begged to be dressed, that they might attend; and the same was the case with the feeble and exhausted, who were confined to their beds; who, when reminded of the imprudence and danger, replied, "A good laugh will raise our spirits, and bring about a speedy recovery." "Is not laughing good for health?" said one unfortunate man, who had lost a leg, and was suffering from a gunshot in the arm; he reminded the surgeon that there was no medicine like laughing. One observed that if the doctors suffered as much as their patients, they would be as anxious for a laugh to remove their thoughts from the aches of body and *ennui* of mind. Generally these appeals triumphed, and they were carried down in chairs, and, after the recreation, were taken back in a happier state of mind, if not better health.

One good and active lady, who deeply interested herself

18*

in the spiritual welfare of the men in the hospital at Broad
and Cherry streets, addressed me one day by saying, "Oh,
Signor, if you would attend here on Sunday morning, and
exercise the same influence over the soldiers in prevailing
upon them to attend Divine Service, what an agreeable
effect you would produce! for when the drum beats at the
hour for prayer, few or none are present."

No doubt her heart was for the purpose she expressed,
and it would not have been less a victory for me to produce
the results she so earnestly desired; but my forte was in an
opposite direction—rather to remove solemnity and produce
mirth.

Perhaps no place afforded so much gratification for its
social as well as rational pleasures as the

SOLDIERS' READING-ROOM.

This room was located in Eighteenth street, and was
fitted up as a theatre and library, which contained many
hundred volumes. The institution was organized under
the auspices of a band of kind ladies, with the special object of attracting the men from bar-rooms and drinking
saloons, who, when health was improving, were permitted
daily recreation outside the hospital, from 8 A.M. until 6
P.M. The main floor of the "room" contained numerous
tables, at which the visitors could sit and instruct themselves with books, periodicals, and newspapers, not only
those published in that city, but from every other State.
They also found scattered around light games, and they
were further provided with refreshments. It was a charming and popular retreat, where minds could mingle and discuss their battles and sufferings.

Occasionally dinners were supplied, when hundreds
dined and enjoyed all the luxuries of the season, the appro-
priation for which was entirely contributed from the purses

of the ladies. The happy gatherings on these occasions were sights that rendered more than ordinary enjoyment to those favored with the privilege of being observers. I exhibited at the reading-room a number of times, and once before what was termed a *limbless audience.* Every man had either lost a leg or an arm; it was truly a pathetic sight to witness the mutilations of so fine a body of soldiers. I need only remark that it inspired me with extra exertion in my endeavors to entertain these afflicted ones, and was fully compensated by their light hearts reflected from their smiling faces. It was remarkable with what freedom they would volunteer to assist me on the platform, aided by their crutches, and, at times, those minus an arm, proving how completely they were interested. A little reflection cannot otherwise than teach a moral of contentment to those gifted with health, wealth, and all the blessings of life; and in the midst of their enjoyments, they should not forget that where misery and bodily deprivations exist, pleasure is to be found.

The reading-room established in Philadelphia was entirely under the supervision of the most respectable ladies of the city, moved by the loftiest motives of Christian principles, constantly present in person to superintend and provide for their wants. All honor to such generosity and womanly patriotism! Truly, these benefactresses cannot be without their reward.

The most affecting picture I remember, was the anxiety to witness my performance at Twenty-third Street Hospital, where two young men, each deprived of both legs, were present, seated in front of my platform, in easy chairs. Their faces were remarkably beautiful, of a feminine character, with a great delicacy of feature and complexion, scarcely ever seen on any manly form. Apparently in the full enjoyment of mirth, they had forgotten their helpless condition. Their countenances beamed with pleasure, and almost inclined me to wish that even *I* was not less discontented or aggrieved by misfortunes incidental to life.

That I faithfully performed my duty during these severe trials, it will only be necessary for me to state that I gave 132 entertainments before 63,000 soldiers, at the following hospitals in Philadelphia: West Philadelphia, Chestnut Hill, Hestonville, Broad and Cherry, St. Joseph's, Twenty-second and Wood, Christian Street, Sixth and Master, Fifth and Buttonwood, Sixteenth and Filbert, McClellan, Episcopal, and Soldiers' Reading-room. I also gave three weeks of untiring labor, every afternoon and evening, at the "Great Sanitary Fair" in Logan square.

It could not be otherwise than expected that, before so large a number of people, there would be some ebullition of superstition developed. Many declared I was the devil in disguise; others exclaimed, "That man is Satan's agent;" others affirmed I would be dangerous in a crowd, for they were assured I could empty every man's pocket at will; while others thought I was the person to go to the front, and extract the bullets from the enemy's guns. Not a few considered me anti-religious, because I performed, apparently, such wicked things. These, and hundreds of similar remarks, were all made in public, and did not fail to create immense glee.

My ventriloquial powers produced no less mystery. At the Chestnut Hill Hospital a soldier was positive I had fifty tongues in my head; another, that I must have devoured a regiment, to have so many voices within me. These expressions are not to be taken as the general character of the men's minds, for the mental superiority of so many thousands was their most remarkable feature; this is strongly corroborated in their style of reading. All the hospitals contained a library with more or less volumes, and fre-

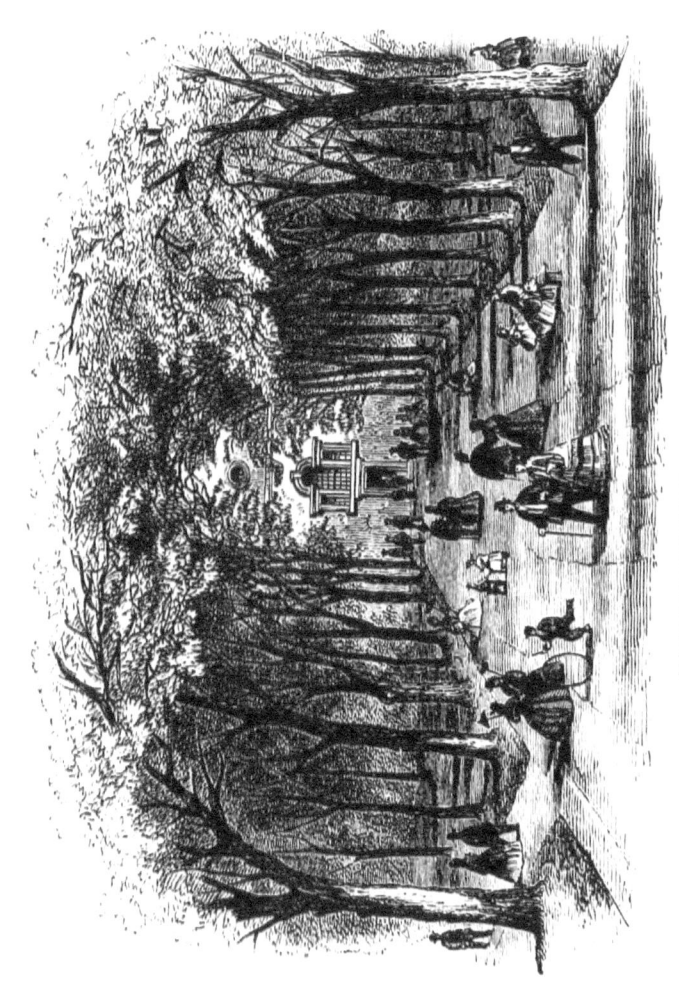

INDEPENDENCE SQUARE.

quently application would be made for books of a theological or scientific nature, that was surprising. The Rev. Mr. Speckman, chaplain of the Chestnut Hill Hospital, told me he was astonished beyond measure at the books the patients would request. Many applied for mathematical, chemical, or philosophical works of the most abstruse character, which he had to procure from the mercantile and various libraries in the city. This is certainly strong evidence of the superiority of the intelligence that composed the army. The armies of the world never exhibited a similar display of intellect and patriotism combined, as did these noble defenders of their country.

INDEPENDENCE HALL.

The great State of Pennsylvania, with its three millions of people, and its immense and varied interests, took active measures to crush and put down the rebellion, and gave pledges of her patriotism, fidelity, and love of the Union, by generous gifts, both of men and money, to the cause. Even before the secession conventions, there was an immense assemblage of citizens in Independence square, in Philadelphia, which was addressed by men of all parties, and all deprecated war, and expressed a willingness to make every possible concession consistent with honor, for the preservation of peace and union.

At the end of the avenue of trees stands the venerable State House, in which great hall the Declaration of Independence was discussed, adopted, and signed. It was commenced in 1729, and completed in 1734, at a cost of £5,-600—about $30,000. There is no spot so sacred to the American people, containing, as it does, the remembrances and portraits of the great and good who so wisely and nobly proclaimed universal liberty. One of the most conspicuous relics of that important period is the bell that first sounded the notes of freedom. As an evidence of the interest manifested by the citizens of every section of the country, no less than 1,500 persons daily visit it, and on public occasions, 15,000; and since the commencement of the present century, it is estimated that nearly five millions of people have visited the hall.

Some four years since, a bill passed the State Senate and House of Representatives, granting the privilege to the original thirteen States to erect, at their own expense, a statue of each of the Signers to the Declaration; but from untoward circumstances, and by reason of the war, the object has been neglected. When, however, the present incumbrances are removed, the busts of patriots will adorn and ornament the square, and thus give to Philadelphia an attraction for all time.

Many anecdotes are related in regard to visitors. Some have been known to expectorate profusely upon the floor, and when requested to desist, exclaimed, " Why, is this not Independence Hall—where our forefathers signed the Declaration, and cannot we do as we like ? "

Another instance is told of a man from one of the Western States, who, just at the closing of the doors at night, was observed to place his portmanteau upon the floor, and spread his coat upon it; and when questioned as to his motive, declared his intention to sleep there.

" Cannot do that, sir," replied the janitor ; " this is no place for sleeping people."

" Why, here's where freedom was declared! What's to stop me ? "

He had, however, to yield, notwithstanding his enlarged ideas of liberty.

CHAPTER XXXVI.

THE Merchants' Exchange is one of the prominent architectural beauties of the Quaker City—a rich pile of white marble—as chaste in design as it is imposing in appearance.

Strangers invariably visit the Exchange, and are as well pleased with its interior arrangements as its external grandeur. It is the Rialto of commercial men, and the daily resort of those who roam the sea; for the amiable and obliging superintendent gives a cordial welcome to all.

The newspaper files, in the well-arranged reading-room, are, as all business men know, placed on racks a little higher than a man's head, with papers on both sides of the rack, so that readers stand unseen face to face, though the space above and below the rack being open, there is nothing to obstruct the sound.

A BUZZ ON 'CHANGE.

It was here, in this quiet condition of things, that a short, square-built, ruddy-faced little gentleman, of some fifty-five years, was intently poring over one of the files, the interest of his subject rendering him oblivious to almost everything passing around him, when at length his ear was disturbed by the buzzing sound of a bee. At first it was

low and indistinct, but gradually descending from the high
dome, the sound grew louder, until a sudden dodge of the
head seemed necessary to keep the impudent intruder from
actual contact with his ear, but it passed him, while the
deeply engaged reader, without raising his head, continued
on reading. In less than a minute the buzzing was again
heard, as if it were steadily approaching the burly reader's
ear, and this time it came so near, that not only a dodge of
the head, but a quick and somewhat spiteful blow of the
hand seemed necessary to prevent its running directly into
that sensitive organ of sound. Again the buzzing passed
by, and was faintly heard some eight or ten yards up near
the dome. The reader, placing his finger upon the paper
to keep his place, cast his eyes above, but seeing nothing,
applied himself to his reading again. He had hardly run
through the first sentence, however, before the buzzing of
the bee returned, and so loud and direct was it, as fairly to
divide the reader's attention with his matter. From a slight
twitching of the lips and pursing of the brows, it was evident that patience and forbearance were fast wearing out,
and with an impulsive bracing up of the whole person, the
appearance of the vexatious intruder was anxiously awaited.
As if conscious of the rising wrath of his victim, the bee
seemed studiously to delay its approach, though the sound
told plainly that it was on its road back—and back eventually it came—and this time with that loud, peculiar whizzing tone, that the reader fancied it had fairly entered his
ear. The blow directed at the approaching sound missed
its aim, and, exasperated beyond endurance, a "damn the
bee," involuntarily slipped from between his firmly set teeth.
A long and intent gaze was now thrown after the receding
sound of the bee, until it was at last lost in the distance. He
had hardly, however, resumed his reading, before again the
buzzing was heard, each moment louder and more distinct,

the mental excitement of the reader rising faster than the disagreeable whizzing descended. Setting his hat firmly on his head, and gradually tightening his clenched fist, he, with that irascibility peculiar to the *English commandant*, awaited the enemy's approach, and when the sound indicated him sufficiently near, let drive vigorously, missing the bee, but knocking loose the file of papers and emptying its contents on the floor. The noise and confusion now called up the superintendent, yet the buzzing was still heard; but where was the bee? All eyes were directed upward. The old merchants wiped their specs, and the young clerks pulled out their eye-glasses, but all to no purpose—the buzzing continued, up and down and all around; but the bee was nowhere to be seen. All was confusion, and a perfect hornets' nest seemed to be aroused. The superintendent wondered, the captain swore, and all were surprised, excepting one, who seemed to be intently poring over the papers immediately facing the vexed gentleman, whom the bee had selected as its victim.

Just at this moment in popped a reporter of the press, who, with that foresight peculiar to his calling, saw through the whole case at a glance, and, to explain all, begged the captain to allow him to make him acquainted with Signor Blitz, the ventriloquist. Cards were exchanged, I dined with the captain, and in the evening he visited my hall, where the same *buzzing* of the bee greeted his ear.

THOUGHTS AND SAYINGS OF CHILDREN.

Early impressions are fanciful images. In after years they appear the reflection of sweet promise and hope— golden days without realization—a summer's prospect bereft of a single thought as to winter or its blighting effects upon the glittering sunshine of a brighter season.

Few live from childhood to the close of life and escape

passing through the vicissitudes and disappointments that mankind is heir to. What joys and brilliant pictures are visioned in boyhood, and how undimmed and clear is the perspective of the landscape of·the future to the inexperienced and ready mind, we *all* know from our own anticipations.

When we reflect on the happy days of childhood, with the thousand associations of their pure love, sweet prattle and welcome footsteps, we perceive the streams that supply the fountain from which are gradually developed truth and knowledge. But youthful imaginations are undoubtedly the offspring of those evidences which, in their natural sense, are dreams of innocence.

Who does not recollect full well the effect of circumstances on his early age? How he gazed with amazement at the conduct and movements of others; with what interest and pleasure he regarded trifles; how the mind wondered at beholding and the heart desired to possess and participate!

These views recall pleasantly to memory my own personal enjoyment in scenes as they then impressed me— when the moon and stars bewildered my struggling brain as to their majesty and beauty at night, and their whereabouts during the day. So with the sun—its marvellous absence of heat in dreary winter. How I started with fear at the thunder's loud peal—the snow, rain, green grass, rivers, flowers, and *all* were a mystery! Happy ignorance was this; yet how strangely are children gifted with an instinct that is remarkable—the most perfect judges of physiognomy and character, and in their appreciation of kindness, infinitely more grateful than those advanced in life.

Few have, perhaps, enjoyed the love and confidence of children more than myself. There are but few whose opportunities have been so numerous to excite and attract their curiosity, or to perceive the peculiar astonishment with which they regarded me, and all appertaining to my profession.

Their belief in the reality of what they witnessed, and their desire to imitate, invariably enhanced my pleasure, and stimulated me to introduce the feats and amusements which contributed to their happiness.

Fortunately, I never possessed the inclination to refuse their applications, and always in return found myself liberally compensated, either in their confidence, gratification, or imaginative expressions.

A bright boy of ten years was assisting me upon the platform, when I proposed to pass several pieces of silver into his pockets. He shook his head, resolutely declaring I "could not do that."

" Why not ? "

"Because I have only one, and that *has a large hole in it !* "

I need not state his ingenious reply produced great laughter and applause among the audience.

I remember once saying to a lovely child of six summers —who had the most perfect confidence in whatever I attempted—that I could turn her into a canary bird. She rejoicingly replied,—

"Oh! do! do! because I shall have wings, and can fly to heaven and see God."

This was so sweet, I promised her a bird, and the next day carried her the choicest warbler I could purchase.

An amusing remark was made by a boy who looked amazed at my apparently *compelling* a gentleman to speak in a ventriloquial scene. The lad came to me at the close of the exhibition, and with a supplicating face entreated me to "call at his grandpa's house and make Uncle George talk," who was deaf and dumb. I shook the little fellow's hand,

and explained to him the deception, expressing sorrow at his uncle's affliction. How much I admired his affectionate feeling!

At one of my exhibitions, a small girl inquired if I could turn her cat into a rabbit, for her kitty had scratched her brother's face, and hurt him very much; so badly, that he could not come with her to my exhibition.

I replied, "She is certainly a very bad cat, and if I had the power to change naughty puss, I certainly would."

"Well, you can, for this afternoon you made an orange into a guinea pig, and sugar-plums from canary seed."

"Yes; but *you* only thought so; it was not a reality."

"Why, I thought you *did it real*. Will you, Signor Blitz, show me how to play them?"

She left much disappointed, and thought I was not the great man she expected.

The Dead Canary.

On another occasion a delicate and beautiful child came to me previous to the commencement of the entertainment, with a countenance the picture of grief and melancholy, and placed in my hand a piece of white paper with something enclosed.

"What does it contain, my little angel?"

I opened it, when there appeared a dead canary. Her little tongue feelingly uttered,—

"He died last night; please make him alive again. He always used to talk and sing to me, poor Dickey, did you not?" smoothing his feathers with her little hand.

"Who told you to bring it to me?"

"No one, sir; only I loved him so much, and I have seen *you* put a bird to sleep, and look as if he were dead, and then when you spoke to him he would jump up and fly around and sing."

"Very true, my dear; but he was trained to do so."

"Well, why not do the same with Dickey?"

"I cannot."

Finding her wish could not be gratified, she commenced sobbing and kissing the bird with a tenderness so truthful in a child's affection. The more I endeavored to console her, the more she repeated, "Dear Dickey! dear Dickey!" Ultimately, I proposed to present her with one of my own; this checked her falling tears, and in a moment she smiled and looked happy. When she returned home she carried her new pet, expressing her intention of burying poor Dickey beneath some flowers in her pa's garden—for she also took the dead bird as tenderly as the living one. This was an interesting and earnest incident, which furnished me with much pleasure, and the wish that there existed a more general kindness and attachment toward animals.

Visiting the house of a friend, an active, intelligent boy ran to me, exclaiming,—

"Signor Blitz, ma told me you could take money out of other people's pockets! Can you?"

"Sometimes."

"Well, you could not do that to me."

"Why not?"

"Because I have none in my pockets."

We all laughed, and in consideration of his *great poverty*, I gave him a five-cent piece. There was silver then.

These are but a very few of the incidents which occurred in my exhibitions before the children, but they are sufficient to demonstrate the ample opportunities I have possessed of understanding and learning their character, love, and originality, and the invariable delight which surrounds those that can make them types of affection; yet there are many in life who never perceive a child or a flower, but traverse the world without beholding a single beauty in either.

A Servant of the Public.

The realities and vagaries of a public life are little understood or appreciated. The surroundings are only known to those subject to their vicissitudes, so that the pleasure of pleasing frequently becomes a labor. The varied and continual demands upon the physical and mental nature, and the time occupied to amuse and entertain, is no doubt flattering to those whose philosophy is without judgment, as it is strikingly wanting in discretion. These people form a large class of society, and are to be found in public and private. They assume to themselves peculiar privileges, which they advance with an assumption that is rude and offensive. To escape from their intrusions is impossible. Unless you gratify their curiosity to an unlimited extent, you are denounced as being ungenerous and selfish, so that you actually become a captive to their whims and ignorance. The obligations which professional duties impose are at times both humorous and perplexing; yet while a punctilious regard to every engagement is required, they are occasionally unnecessarily so. A dull and inanimate audience discourages and suppresses the spirits and injures the performance, while an enthusiastic one inspires confidence and action. Perhaps the most trying position is that of frequently appearing before a company comprised of so few that the lights exceed by far in number the people present, whose quiet and sombre countenances and gloomy expressions convey not a single mark to cheer. How numerous these instances are, and their effect upon the feelings, experience alone can relate.

I remember on one occasion, while exhibiting in Philadelphia, in the lecture-room of the Chinese Museum, that the wind blew a perfect hurricane, and the streets were so impassable that it was neither wise nor safe to leave the agreeable comforts of a good and pleasant home—at least it required a brave resolution and an extraordinary induce-ment to do so—when, to my utter surprise and astonish-ment, I found a lady and her son—a boy of ten years—present for the entertainment. After waiting considerably past the appointed hour, I delicately communicated to her the impossibility of my giving an exhibition under the circumstances.

"Oh, dear! we came *six* miles in the storm from the country expressly to see you. This is a sad disappointment to my son. He is obliged to leave to-morrow for his school in the interior of the State."

"Indeed, I regret it should be such an unfortunate time."

"Well, now, Signor, in a measure it is my fault, for I have been promising to bring him for the last two weeks. Observe the sorrow depicted on the poor little fellow's face; *do* exhibit, and we shall never forget your kindness."

Here the lad looked up at me most pitifully, and in quiet eloquence, petitioned himself. His appeal was triumphant, for on an instant's thought I consented to perform. At this announcement the mother and youth became trans-ported with delight. The former exclaimed, "Good, Sig-nor!" The boy clapped his hands and danced with joy.

The undertaking was a difficult one, but I had given my word; so, to increase the audience, I invited the professor of the piano and the ticket receiver to take seats, and, with-out further delay, commenced the entertainment, when I became so intensely interested, that I continued for two un-broken hours to gratify my *four* spectators, one of whom paid *twenty-five*, the other *twelve and a half cents!* The re-maining two, being employés, were free. This is the smallest audience, and the least pay, I ever received during my long professional career, but was one of those untoward events that performers are subject to, and which leave their impressions for life, enabling one to learn the singularities of mankind.

A thousand similar circumstances could be related to substantiate the remarkable predicaments that are connected with the life of a public man—the servant of *all*, but never the master of himself. No profession or calling can escape from the appeals of the people, and the more eminent the position, the greater the demands; so that a man's own enjoyments are sacrificed in contributing to the gratification of friends, and often strangers, many of whom are unable to comprehend or appreciate. Besides these annoyances, a public man is subject to pecuniary applications, at all times and for every purpose, consequently his liberality is severely tested, and his good nature tried upon every occasion. Those elements of character so generally admired secure to him a popularity at an expense which renders him poor in purse, and often he is unable in his declining years to furnish means for the necessities of life, when he must suffer or become under obligations to others.

Such are the vicissitudes of the life of a public performer!

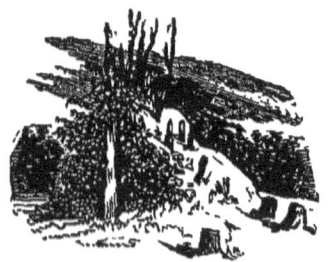